REVISION WORKBOOK

Public International Law

Third Edition

DR VICKNESWAREN KRISHNAN
LLB (Hons), LLM, MA, Barrister, ACI Arb, AIPFM, AFSALS, ACII, PhD

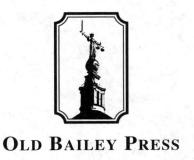

OLD BAILEY PRESS

OLD BAILEY PRESS
at Holborn College, Woolwich Road,
Charlton, London, SE7 8LN

First published 1997
Third edition 2004

ISBN 1 85836 559 7

British Library Cataloguing-in-Publication.

A CIP Catalogue record for this book is available from the British Library.

Printed and bound in Great Britain.

Contents

Acknowledgement

Some questions used are taken or adapted from past University of London LLB (External) Degree and the University of Glasgow examination papers and our thanks are extended to the University of London and the University of Glasgow for their kind permission to use and publish the questions.

Caveat

The answers given are not approved or sanctioned by the University of London or the University of Glasgow and are entirely our responsibility.

They are not intended as 'Model Answers', but rather as Suggested Solutions.

The answers have two fundamental purposes, namely:

a) to provide a detailed example of a suggested solution to an examination question; and

b) to assist students with their research into the subject and to further their understanding and appreciation of the subject.

Introduction

This Revision WorkBook has been designed specifically for those studying public international law to undergraduate level. Its coverage is not confined to any one syllabus, but embraces all the major public international law topics to be found in university examinations.

Each chapter contains a brief introduction explaining the scope and overall content of the topic covered in that chapter. There follows, in each case, a list of key points which will assist the student in studying and memorising essential material with which the student should be familiar in order to fully understand the topic.

Additionally in each chapter there is a key cases and statutes section which lists the most relevant cases and legislative provisions applicable to the topic in question. These are intended as an aid to revision, providing the student with a concise list of materials from which to begin revision.

Each chapter usually ends with several typical examination questions, together with general comments, skeleton solutions and suggested solutions. Wherever possible, the questions are drawn from the University of London external public international law papers, with recent questions being included where possible. However, it is inevitable that, in compiling a list of questions by topic order rather than chronologically, not only do the same questions crop up over and over again in different guises, but there are gaps where questions have never been set at all.

Undoubtedly, the main feature of this Revision WorkBook is the inclusion of as many past examination questions as possible. While the use of past questions as a revision aid is certainly not new, it is hoped that the combination of actual past questions from the University of London LLB external course and specially written questions, where there are gaps in examination coverage, will be of assistance to students in achieving a thorough and systematic revision of the subject.

Careful use of the Revision WorkBook should enhance the student's understanding of public international law and, hopefully, enable you to deal with as wide a range of subject matter as anyone might find in a public international law examination, while at the same time allowing you to practise examination techniques while working through the book.

Studying Public International Law

Public international law is a unique species of law and as such creates problems for students more familiar with the functioning of conventional forms of law. Although analogies in content do exist, international law is unlike the law of tort or the law of contract. In particular, international law lacks a coherent and comprehensive body of judicial doctrine and does not operate in terms of the doctrine of precedent. International statutes do not exist and therefore rules of international law, and in particular customary law, have to be determined by reference to state practice and international behaviour.

Its unconventional and problematic nature are elements which are inherent in the functioning of the legal system itself. Students studying international law have no alternative but to address these problems and acquire skills and techniques which vary considerably from those used in the study of other areas of law.

International law often cannot be explained without a basic knowledge of contemporary world politics. The development of this subject is fundamentally dependent upon surrounding extra-legal circumstances. There is no legislature and judicial precedent plays a nominal role in this field. The subject is integrally related to international politics and as a result non-judicial historical precedents are frequently cited as state practice which approximates to the role of precedent in national legal orders.

Many students confronted with the application of rules of international law have difficulty ascertaining the exact nature of applicable rules. The proper application of rules to factual situations in international relations is an acquired skill in itself. In this regard, the particular methodology used in approaching problems of international law becomes acutely important. Different skills must be developed to accommodate the fact that international law operates at the interface of law and politics.

In order to fully understand the subject of international law, it is important to acquire a comprehensive and overall framework of the subject and to understand how the different areas of the law relate to each other. International law is characterised by an extensive overlapping in topics. Points brought up in one topic, such as the sources of international law or the use of force by states, continuously recur throughout other areas of the subject. This is to be anticipated since international law is a dynamic and complex subject. An overall general knowledge of each individual subject matter will ultimately facilitate the acquisition of an extensive and detailed knowledge of each individual subject matter.

Once the basic skills and methodology have been acquired in approaching problems involving questions of international law, the task of identifying and applying law to facts is increasingly simplified. These skills may best be acquired through a study and appreciation of the techniques involved in answering examination questions. The object of this text is therefore not primarily to provide students with pro forma answers to questions, but to teach them the skills involved in approaching questions which have international legal implications.

Revision and Examination Technique

Revision Technique

Planning a revision timetable

In planning your revision timetable make sure you do not finish the syllabus too early. You should avoid leaving revision so late that you have to 'cram' – but constant revision of the same topic leads to stagnation.

Plan ahead, however, and try to make your plans increasingly detailed as you approach the examination date.

Allocate enough time for each topic to be studied. But note that it is better to devise a realistic timetable, to which you have a reasonable chance of keeping, rather than a wildly optimistic schedule which you will probably abandon at the first opportunity!

The syllabus and its topics

One of your first tasks when you began your course was to ensure that you thoroughly understood your syllabus. Check now to see if you can write down the topics it comprises from memory. You will see that the chapters of this WorkBook are each devoted to a syllabus topic. This will help you decide which are the key chapters relative to your revision programme, though you should allow some time for glancing through the other chapters.

The topic and its key points

Again working from memory, analyse what you consider to be the key points of any topic that you have selected for particular revision. Seeing what you can recall, unaided, will help you to understand and firmly memorise the concepts involved.

Using the WorkBook

Relevant questions are provided for each topic in this book. Naturally, as typical examples of examination questions, they do not normally relate to one topic only. But the questions in each chapter will relate to the subject matter of the chapter to a degree. You can choose your method of consulting the questions and solutions, but here are some suggestions (strategies 1–3). Each of them pre-supposes that you have read through the author's notes on key points and key cases and statutes, and any other preliminary matter, at the beginning of the chapter. Once again, you now need to practise working from memory, for that is the challenge you are preparing yourself for. As a rule of procedure constantly test yourself once revision starts, both orally and in writing.

Strategy 1

Strategy 1 is planned for the purpose of quick revision. First read your chosen question carefully and then jot down in abbreviated notes what you consider to be the main points at issue. Similarly, note the cases and statutes that occur to you as being relevant for citation purposes. Allow yourself sufficient time to cover what you feel to be relevant. Then study the author's skeleton solution and skim-read the suggested solution to see how they compare with your notes. When comparing consider carefully what the author has included (and concluded) and see whether that agrees with what you have written. Consider the points of variation also. Have you recognised the key issues? How relevant have you been? It is possible, of course, that you have referred to a recent case that is relevant, but which had not been reported when the WorkBook was prepared.

Strategy 2

Strategy 2 requires a nucleus of three hours in which to practise writing a set of examination answers in a limited time-span.

Select a number of questions (as many as are normally set in your subject in the examination you are studying for), each from a different chapter in the WorkBook, without consulting the solutions. Find a place to write where you will not be disturbed and try to arrange not to be interrupted for three hours. Write your solutions in the time allowed, noting any time needed to make up if you are interrupted.

After a rest, compare your answers with the suggested solutions in the WorkBook. There will be considerable variation in style, of course, but the bare facts should not be too dissimilar. Evaluate your answer critically. Be 'searching', but develop a positive approach to deciding how you would tackle each question on another occasion.

Strategy 3

You are unlikely to be able to do more than one three hour examination, but occasionally set yourself a single question. Vary the 'time allowed' by imagining it to be one of the questions that you must answer in three hours and allow yourself a limited preparation and writing time. Try one question that you feel to be difficult and an easier question on another occasion, for example.

Misuse of suggested solutions

Don't try to learn by rote. In particular, don't try to reproduce the suggested solutions by heart. Learn to express the basic concepts in your own words.

Keeping up-to-date

Keep up-to-date. While examiners do not require familiarity with changes in the law during the three months prior to the examination, it obviously creates a good impression if you can show you are acquainted with any recent changes. Make a habit of looking through one of the leading journals – *Modern Law Review*, *Law Quarterly Review* or the *New Law Journal*, for example – and cumulative indices to law reports, such as the *All England Law Reports* or *Weekly Law Reports*, or indeed the daily law reports in *The Times*. The *Law Society's Gazette* and the *Legal Executive Journal* are helpful sources, plus any specialist journal(s) for the subject you are studying.

Examination Skills

Examiners are human too!

The process of answering an examination question involves a communication between you and the person who set it. If you were speaking face to face with the person, you would choose your verbal points and arguments carefully in your reply. When writing, it is all too easy to forget the human being who is awaiting the reply and simply write out what one knows in the area of the subject! Bear in mind it is a person whose question you are responding to, throughout your essay. This will help you to avoid being irrelevant or long-winded.

The essay question

Candidates are sometimes tempted to choose to answer essay questions because they 'seem' easier. But the examiner is looking for thoughtful work and will not give good marks for superficial answers.

The essay-type of question may be either purely factual, in asking you to explain the meaning of a certain doctrine or principle, or it may ask you to discuss a certain proposition, usually derived from a quotation. In either case, the approach to the answer is the same. A clear programme must be devised to give the examiner the meaning or significance of the doctrine, principle or proposition and its origin in common law, equity or statute, and cases which illustrate its application to the branch of law concerned. Essay questions offer a good way to obtain marks if you have thought carefully about a topic, since it is up to you to impose the structure (unlike the problem questions where the problem imposes its own structure). You are then free to speculate and show imagination.

The problem question

The problem-type question requires a different approach. You may well be asked to advise a client or merely discuss the problems raised in the question. In either case, the most important factor is to take great care in reading the question. By its nature, the question will be longer than the essay-type question and you will have a number of facts to digest. Time spent in analysing the question may well save time later, when you are endeavouring to impress on the examiner the considerable extent of your basic legal knowledge. The quantity of knowledge is itself a trap and you must always keep within the boundaries of the question in hand. It is very tempting to show the examiner the extent of your knowledge of your subject, but if this is outside the question, it is time lost and no marks earned. It is inevitable that some areas which you have studied and revised will not be the subject of questions, but under no circumstances attempt to adapt a question to a stronger area of knowledge at the expense of relevance.

When you are satisfied that you have grasped the full significance of the problem-type question, set out the fundamental principles involved.

You will then go on to identify the fundamental problem (or problems) posed by the question. This should be followed by a consideration of the law which is relevant to the problem. The source of the law, together with the cases which will be of assistance in solving the problem, must then be considered in detail.

Very good problem questions are quite likely to have alternative answers, and in advising a party you should be aware that alternative arguments may be available. Each stage of your answer, in this case, will be based on the argument or arguments considered in the previous stage, forming a conditional sequence.

If, however, you only identify one fundamental problem, do not waste time worrying that you cannot think of an alternative – there may very well be only that one answer.

The examiner will then wish to see how you use your legal knowledge to formulate a case and how you apply that formula to the problem which is the subject of the question. It is this positive approach which can make answering a problem question a high mark earner for the student who has fully understood the question and clearly argued their case on the established law.

Examination checklist

a) Read the instructions at the head of the examination carefully. While last-minute changes are unlikely – such as the introduction of a compulsory question or an increase in the number of questions asked – it has been known to happen.

b) Read the questions carefully. Analyse problem questions – work out what the examiner wants.

c) Plan your answer before you start to write.

d) Check that you understand the rubric before you start to write. Do not 'discuss', for example, if you are specifically asked to 'compare and contrast'.

e) Answer the correct number of questions. If you fail to answer one out of four questions set you lose 25 per cent of your marks!

Style and structure

Try to be clear and concise. Fundamentally this amounts to using paragraphs to denote the sections of your essay, and writing simple, straightforward sentences as much as possible. The sentence you have just read has 22 words – when a sentence reaches 50 words it becomes difficult for a reader to follow.

Do not be inhibited by the word 'structure' (traditionally defined as giving an essay a beginning, a middle and an end). A good structure will be the natural consequence of setting out your arguments and the supporting evidence in a logical order. Set the scene briefly in your opening paragraph. Provide a clear conclusion in your final paragraph.

Table of Cases

Table of Statutes

Table of Treaties

Including Covenants, Treaties, Conventions, ICJ Statute and UN Charter

Table of Other Documents

Including Agreements, Declarations, Resolutions etc

Chapter 1

The Nature of International Law

1.1   **Introduction**

1.2   **Key points**

1.3   **Key cases and legislation**

1.4   **Questions and suggested solutions**

1.1 Introduction

The absence of an international legislature, courts with compulsory jurisdiction and a centrally organised enforcement mechanism have given rise to misgivings as to whether international law can really be law properly so-called. Given this widespread criticism of international law, it is hardly surprising that examiners frequently paraphrase the question 'is international law really law?'. Students should be familiar with the most common criticisms of the international legal system. In addition, they should be able to identify the mechanisms through which international law operates to induce legal behaviour, and ought to be able to describe the relationship between the structure of international society and the nature of contemporary international legal order. A knowledge of the historical evolution and development of the international legal system is also desirable.

1.2 Key points

a) The question 'is international law really law?' raises two separate, but related, issues.

   i) Does an international body of rules exist to which states refer in the processes of international decision-making and which exercises a normative influence on state behaviour?

   ii) Does the international legal system qualify as a legal order by reference to some objective model of legal order created on the basis of the institutions present within municipal legal systems?

   It is important to understand that failure by the international legal system to possess those attributes which characterise municipal law will not conclusively establish the non-existence of a body of rules and principles regulating the relationships of states inter se.

b) A number of extra-legal factors help to exaggerate the popular perception of international law as a legal system which cannot effectively regulate state conduct. The existence of an international dispute does not automatically imply a violation of the rules of international law. Other factors are often the direct cause of breakdowns of international relations.

   i) Frequently the facts surrounding a particular controversy are incapable of being impartially ascertained. As a result the opposing parties allege the existence of two distinct factual situations to which different interpretations of international law are applicable. Although this difference in opinions is equally plausible in domestic litigation, reference to an impartial body such as a court is the appropriate remedy in municipal law.

   ii) Even if the facts of the issue in question are settled, differing interpretations of the law may be offered by the parties involved in the dispute. International law is often not a settled body of law and divisions in content are often present which frequently correspond to the North-South and East-West divisions of the international community. This phenomenon is clearly manifested in issues such as compensation for expropriation, the new international economic order, human rights and many of the matters dealt with in the Law of the Sea Convention 1982.

   iii) The cause of an international confrontation might well be an unfriendly but nevertheless legal act. For example, the testing of nuclear weapons by France in South Pacific colonial possessions, whilst having manifest implications for the environmental stability of the region, is nevertheless a legitimate act of sovereignty. Similarly states may, in the absence of treaty commitments to the contrary, impose tariffs on the products of other states regardless of the economic impact of such actions.

   iv) An international dispute might be caused by a transgression against hortatory expressions of intent or alternatively principles which at present merely constitute lex feranda. For example, the human rights statements contained in the UN Universal Declaration of Human Rights 1948 or the Helsinki Declaration of 1975 do not constitute international law although statements are frequently made by governments alleging violations of these understandings by other nations.

c) The efficacy of the institutional organs of contemporary international law

   Municipal legal systems commonly possess features for changing rules of law, for adjudicating on disputes and for enforcing authoritative interpretations of the law. In accordance with the doctrine of the separation of powers, these commonly take the form of a legislature, a judiciary and an executive. Are these organs present at an effective level in the international legal order?

   i) Legislature

   Legislative enactment is the means adopted by most societies for responding to the changing legal needs of the community. Frequently this mechanism takes the form of a sovereign body or person issuing edicts in the form of commands. On the international plane, multilateral treaties most correspond to legislative promulgations. However, clearly treaty obligations remain consensual as opposed to imperative and cannot be imposed against the will of a state.

ii) Judiciary

A court hierarchy is another typical attribute of domestic legal order. The presence of such processes facilitates the proper identification and application of the relevant rule of law. However, within the international sphere, judicial adjudication remains a matter of mutual consent, and the International Court of Justice is not only devoid of compulsory jurisdiction, but in actual fact is rarely involved in the settlement of international disputes.

iii) Executive

In the past jurists such as Austin have asserted that the enactments of the sovereign authorities must regularly be met with the threat of force for the existence of legal order. See J Austin, *The Province of Jurisprudence Determined* (1832). On a daily basis this task is carried out by the national police authorities. In contrast, the enforcement of legal obligations in the international legal order remains decentralised and no impartial system of sanctions or compulsion exists to ensure compliance with the precepts of international law.

d) The relationship between international society and the nature of the international legal system

The structure of the present international legal order has been dictated largely by the nature of global society. It must be borne in mind that international society is:

i) composed of a multiplicity of sovereign states which for the better part of approximately 300 years have been virtually omnipotent within their territories;

ii) composed of only around 173 members which, in contrast to their human counterparts, are virtually perpetual;

iii) substantially more heterogeneous than any other previous society of individuals.

Since every society engenders a legal superstructure, international law must be seen as a reflection of the unique nature of global society which is characterised by decentralisation and horizontal division into a multiplicity of interdependent, yet sovereign, states.

International law has been built to accommodate the limitations of this structure which has been perpetuated throughout history because states have been unwilling to cede effective authority for anything but the most crude manifestation of law and order. International law per se is not responsible for its weak normative influence.

Responsibility for the lack of order in world society lies firmly with the community of nations.

e) Motives which induce states to comply with international law

A number of factors compel states to conform to the rules of international law. Note however that these remain decentralised and are not administered through an international body.

i) The existence of a 'law habit'. Those who make light of international commitments fail to observe that the vast majority of obligations are continuously and regularly observed even at considerable inconvenience and under adverse conditions.

ii) International law is a reflection of the collective wills of states desiring to co-operate and harmonise international relations and interactions. See the *SS Lotus Case* (1927) PCIJ Rep Ser A No 10. It is therefore most likely that conformity to the rules of international law will be, at the very least, in the strategic interests of most states.

iii) States will hesitate to violate covenants or commitments owing to the fact that they may well lose the reciprocal benefits which would be obtained from overall participation. Examples of such reciprocal interests are the obligations of diplomatic protection, the majority of rights established in bilateral treaty obligations and international trade commitments.

iv) International public opinion can be mobilised against a state which has violated international obligations. A state may face alienation and ostracism for violation of fundamental principles of law. The most obvious example of this process is the public and private restrictions placed on Zimbabwe as a consequence of its continued abuse of human rights.

v) Perhaps the ultimate deterrent against violations of international obligations is the possibility that the international community will sanction the use of self-help by a state which has had its international rights materially infringed, eg the Cuban missile crisis. However, this is subject to the obvious limitation that the infringing nation must be less powerful than the enforcing state.

vi) The possibility of collective sanctions through an international organisation, although extremely unlikely, cannot actually be ignored, eg sanctions against Rhodesia 1966; UN action in Korea 1950; UN Force in Cyprus (UNFICYP) 1964; Iraq 1990; Libya 1992; Serbia and Montenegro 1992. The sometimes 'politically sensitive' role of the Secretary General of the United Nations is exemplified through the high profile tasks undertaken by the Secretary General. Recent direct negotiations between the Secretary General and Iraq (February 2003) illustrate this point.

vii) The authority of a decision rendered by the International Court of Justice concentrates international political pressure to compel compliance with the terms of the judgment. However, this sanction is only available against those states which have submitted to the Optional Clause of the ICJ Statute. An illustration of the role of the International Criminal Tribunal for the Former Yugoslavia (ICTY) in policing international law can be seen in the Slobodan Milosevic prosecution in 2001.

1.3 Key cases and legislation

- *SS Lotus Case: France* v *Turkey* (1927) PCIJ Rep Ser A No 10
  Provides a definition of international law

- *Trendtex Trading Corporation* v *Central Bank of Nigeria* [1977] 1 All ER 881
  Provides a definition of international law in terms of its impact on English law

- United Nations Charter – designed to ensure that the signatory member states comply and respect international obligations deriving from the charter

1.4 Questions and suggested solutions

QUESTION ONE

To what extent would it be true to say that the character of international society has shaped that of international law, rather than vice versa?

University of London LLB Examination
(for External Students) Public International Law June 1984 Q1

General Comment

A broad question raising the general issue of the relationship between international law and international society. This requires a description of the structure of the international society and how this system has affected the development of the present international legal system.

Skeleton Solution

The nature of international law as rules regulating sovereign states – the relationship between law and society – the structure of global society: the system of sovereign states; decentralisation and horizontal power devolution.

Suggested Solution

International law constitutes that body of rules which governs the relationships between sovereign states. These rules of law emanate from the free wills of states as expressed in conventions or by usages which are generally accepted as expressing principles of law. The object of these rules is to regulate the relations between these co-existing independent communities as a means of achieving common aims deemed important in the collective opinion of the international community: see the *SS Lotus Case* (1927) PCIJ Rep Ser A No 10. Since international law is the product of forces within international society, in order to understand the nature of the international legal system, it is necessary to analyse the structure and processes which function within the global society.

Historically, although several systems of international law have existed since antiquity, contemporary international law has its origins in Medieval Europe. Arguably, the most notable historic development was the signing of the Peace Treaty of Westphalia 1648 which established an embryonic sovereign state system in Europe. Prior to this agreement, the creation of a sovereign state system had been retarded by the transnational authority of the Pope in spiritual matters and the control of the Holy Roman Emperor in political concerns. In the signature of the Treaty the Emperor acknowledged restrictions on his dominion in favour of the territorial autonomy of the various nation states which had previously composed the Empire, whilst simultaneously the treaty recognised the limits of the authority of the Pope.

International society since then has remained a pluralistic structure of sovereign states. Sovereignty in the relations between states is synonymous with independence. This independence allows states to regulate the internal constitution of their territories and to enter into international relations with other sovereign states. (See the statements of Umpire Huber in the *Island of Palmas Arbitration* (1928) 2 RIAA 829, and Judge Anzilotti in the *Austro-German Customs Union Case* (1931) PCIJ Rep Ser A/B No 41.) Sovereignty as a legal concept is only limited by international law and in particular the legal principle that states are not permitted to exercise their authority in the territory of another state.

It is a cardinal principle of political science that law may only exist within a social framework and further that every society engenders some sort of framework of law. The legal superstructure which emanates from a society reflects the nature of that society. If this contention is accepted, international law must be seen as a mirror of the unique nature of international society which is characterised by decentralisation and the division of authority on a horizontal basis. International law has no alternative but to accommodate those features and deficiencies and in fact is forced to function within the parameters and limitations set unconsciously by that society. Since states throughout history have been unwilling to cede anything other than fragments of authority, this scenario is to be expected.

The weaknesses of international law are not therefore the result of deficiencies within the legal system itself. The international legal order could be made to function effectively if states were willing to establish an effective legal order. The limits of international legal efficacy have been deliberately set by a society in which sovereignty is perceived as the most valuable political and legal principle. The society of sovereign states is content in the knowledge that international law will never erode the state-centric power structure of the international community in the absence of the requisite political will.

Both the complexities and efficacy of legal systems vary in relation to the maturity of the particular social group. International society, being essentially primitive in terms of both social structure and evolution, has produced an almost inchoate form of legal order despite the complex nature of its substantive content. The absence of legislative, judicial and executive organs at an effective level infers that international society has not yet attained the stage at which such institutions are technically feasible. International society is not sufficiently mature for the embodiment of the doctrine of the separation of powers.

Although in certain senses international society is becoming increasingly interdependent, particularly in economic matters, at the same time forces are at work which indicate that international society is increasingly tending towards regionalism. This may be attributed to a number of developments. As long as international society consisted of European states, their common Christian background and traditions conditioned their relationships and however precarious the observance of international law may have been during this period it did incorporate those values and ideals most respected in contemporary European society. With the enlargement of the international community this common ethical foundation has effectively dissipated. The advent of communism and the effect of decolonisation are now being manifested in the expression of changing attitudes and perceptions within the international society to contemporary problems in international relations and the rejection of many of the European ideals upon which much of the law of nations is founded. The deterioration of international law reflects the degree to which international society conditions international law as opposed to vice versa.

QUESTION TWO

'The study of international law in a historical and sociological perspective is essential for a thorough understanding of the operation of the contemporary international legal system.' Discuss.

University of London LLB Examination
(for External Students) Public International Law June 1986 Q1

General Comment

A variation on the general theme, but specifying the approach and methodology required to correctly answer the question.

Skeleton Solution

The nature of public international law: the lack of a proper legal system; the Austinian theory – international law in historical perspective: European origins; the concepts of sovereignty, equality and independence – international law in its sociological perspective: the functions of the law of nations; power, reciprocity, community.

Suggested Solution

Since the origins of the science of jurisprudence itself, sceptics have argued that there can be no international law since no international legislature creates edicts, no international executive organ enforces these rules, and no international judiciary develops these principles or resolves disputes on a mandatory basis. From Austin to present day commentators, this conclusion has been arrived at after an appraisal of the inability of the international legal system to possess effective legislative, judicial or executive organs. These attributes have traditionally been deemed essential for the operation of legal order. However, by exaggerating the role of such institutions, and by failing to comprehend the historical evolution and contemporary sociological processes at work in the operation of international law, it is clear that such critics have misconceived the nature and role of international law.

In historical terms, the evolution of international law was closely linked with the emergence of the European society of sovereign states. Sovereignty as a political concept was first conceived by the French political philosopher Bodin as a means of describing the historical and political events occurring in the sixteenth century. By evaluating historical events in the European political arena and hypothesising on contemporary political developments Bodin was able to describe sovereignty as the 'absolute and perpetual power' which was subordinate only to the law of nature. Such authority existed legally in vacuo, uninhibited by positive moral power.

This formulation was readily received within the European society of this period as it represented the optimum vehicle for the attainment of order within the borders of a nation as well as a means of consolidating power for the monarchs of Europe. Since this time, sovereignty has remained the paramount concept in international legal theory. As the rights and duties of sovereign states were being consolidated, the application of the principle was globalised, until today when it represents the cardinal precept in international law.

In legal terms, sovereignty has come to connote the existence of a certain bundle of rights and duties imposed by international law on these legal subjects. Not only does it place the supreme power within the state, but since all states are equally sovereign, it also conveys the idea of independence. Sovereignty is limited only by international law, a cardinal principle of which is that beyond the scope of a state's boundaries, where its writ does not run, the independence of each state imposes limits on the authority of others.

Since the patterns of international legal relations flow outwards from each sovereign state, it is axiomatic that no sovereign authority prevails over international society. The United Nations is incapable of exercising legislative, judicial or de facto executive authority over the community of nations because it was never conceived as a greater authority than the sovereign state. Given the nature of the societal structure of inter-state relations, it seems reasonably clear that the social processes which exist in international relations also explain the structure and lack of efficiency in the international legal order. The decentralised nature of international society explains the limitations of international law. International society is at present incapable of sustaining an omnipotent central law-giving organ, nor any form of law-enforcing authority. International law, in fact, is compelled to vacillate between two polar extremes, both decentralised in character for its very efficacy: identical or complementary interests and objectives among the various states; and the distribution of a semblance of an effective equality of power – a balance of power – among the international community.

Since international law is a function of the political community of nations, the alleged technical shortcomings of this order can be attributed to the relationship between law and the embryonic character of the community in which it operates. The characteristic feature of international society – the horizontal structure of authority – has devolved a decentralised system of law which has been perpetuated by the unwillingness of states to delegate sovereign power. Factors explaining this unwillingness to devolve authority have ranged from insecurity, ambition, power differentials, ideological differences, cultural heterogeneity, to pure human irrationality.

Notwithstanding these limitations, international law does possess a surprising degree of efficacy within the international community. In those areas of state intercourse in which mutual objectives may be achieved without the delegation of sovereign authority, international law is extremely effective: communications, transportation, trade, finance and the settlement of disputes not involving elements of a high policy content. In the absence of controversial political determinates influencing the decision-making processes of states, international disputes are most likely to be settled in international legal forums and according to law. However, it is when political factors are at work that international law breaks down which clearly reflects the divisions within the international society itself.

QUESTION THREE

Where does the greatest weakness of international law lie: in its lack of a legislature, in its lack of an effective system of courts or in its lack of sanctions?

University of London LLB Examination
(for External Students) Public International Law June 1987 Q1

General Comment

Although the theme remains the relationship between international law and society, this question is considerably more specific and requires additional detail.

Skeleton Solution

Decision: which is the greatest weakness of international law? – the absence of legislation, compulsory judicial settlement and sanctions in international law and its effect.

Suggested Solution

In the majority of states three organs of government can be identified: a legislature which enacts the law; a judiciary which tries violations of the law; and an executive which, among other things, enforces the decisions of the legislature and the judiciary. Although in the international legal system these institutions are present in an embryonic form, it is irrefutable that they are ineffective. States create international law for themselves under international conventions or by means of custom. These states cannot be compelled to accept a new rule of international law unless they agree to it nor need they appear before an international court or tribunal unless they consent to do so. In addition, there is also no central executive body with the task of enforcing the law. All three of these deficiencies are the cause of weakness in international law, but it is a matter of opinion as to where the greatest weakness lies.

The absence of a legislature in international law has led some jurists to deny that international law is 'law properly so-called', but this defect is not regarded as crucial nowadays. It is true that the absence of a legislature creates difficulties in accommodating the needs of a changing and evolving international society. However, at the same time, the absence of a legislature is a source of strength for international law as it allows states, to a large extent, to create law for themselves. Since it is most unlikely that they will create law which is not in their interests, this is a factor which will mitigate the temptation to violate the principles of law.

A greater weakness is the absence of an effective system of courts. It is a fundamental principle of international law that no state may be compelled to submit a dispute to international arbitration or judicial settlement without first obtaining its consent. The judicial organ of the United Nations, the International Court of Justice, is rendered virtually redundant because its jurisdiction in contentious proceedings is dependent upon the consent of the state parties. No compulsory jurisdiction exists on the part of the Court in the municipal sense, but acceptance of the compulsory jurisdiction of the Court may be signified by means of a prior declaration in accordance with art 36(2) of the Statute of the Court, known as the 'optional clause'. However it is apparent that attempts to found jurisdiction of the Court upon declarations made under the optional clause are often futile. Participating states have entered so many reservations that in effect they are accepting no obligation to litigate international disputes. All that may be said is that the International Court of Justice is an institution which provides machinery for the judicial settlement of disputes between states which are confident of winning. Indeed if a state is not prepared to lose it can proceed to exorbitant lengths to undermine the jurisdiction of the Court. Perhaps the best illustration of this is the case between Nicaragua and the United States of America concerning *Military and*

Paramilitary Activities in and against Nicaragua: Nicaragua v *United States (Jurisdiction)* (1984) ICJ Rep 392. A more recent example is the step taken by the USA against Iraq despite the United Nations lack of support for the USA.

However, the principal weakness seized on by most contemporary sceptics when debasing international law, is the absence of sanctions. In addition to the absence of obligatory judicial settlement, no centralised executive authority exists to enforce judgments. This criticism raises two questions: whether sanctions are essential for the existence of law; and if sanctions are necessary for this purpose, whether the international legal order possesses such a capacity.

It is clear that not all rules are enforced at all times within a legal order since this would be an intolerable burden on a police force. The existence of a legal rule merely implies that a certain standard of conduct is required for a society to be properly regulated. A sanction is not a cardinal element of all manifestations of law, eg laws of capacity and laws conferring rights. Sanctions are only a predominant element in penal statutes. Legal rules are not invariably predicated on sanctions and, as Goodhart points out, 'It is because a rule is regarded as obligatory that a measure of coercion may be attached to it; it is not obligatory because there is coercion': Goodhart, *Law and the Moral Law* (1953), p17.

However, if it is accepted that coercion or sanction is a necessary element of law, then there has always been a body of international lawyers that has considered that the international legal order possesses the element of enforceability, even if only in a rough and rudimentary form. Kelsen, for example, concludes that international law is true law because, broadly speaking, it provides sanctions, such as the adoption of reprisals, war, and the use of force generally, and makes the employment of these sanctions lawful as a countermeasure against a legal wrong, but unlawful in all other cases. Therefore, if a state commits an illegal act against another state, and refuses to make reparations or to appear before an international court or tribunal, there is only one sanction in the hands of the injured state – self-help. But this only works effectively if the victim state is more powerful than the delinquent state.

But today, the use of force has been prohibited by art 2(4) of the United Nations Charter which has given rise to the problem that, in so far as the use of force was a means, however crude, by which a state could assert or defend its legal rights, the position is now that international law is less effective today than it has ever been in the whole of its history, for no substitute has been put in place of force as a means of enforcing international obligations. There is, of course, within the Charter of the United Nations, a mechanism for the enforcement of international law through the imposition of sanctions and there has been a tendency for sanctions to be imposed by a large number of states working through the United Nations. But the enforcement powers of the United Nations are illusory when considered in the light of the veto.

However, too much relevance must not be attributed to the absence of sanctions. They are not the main reason why law is obeyed. Notwithstanding the absence of effectively organised sanctions, states obey international law far more often than most people believe. The great majority of the rules of international law are generally observed by all nations without actual compulsion, for it is generally in the interests of all nations concerned to honour their obligations under international law. As Brierly stated, 'it is not the existence of a police force that makes a system of law strong and respected, but the strength of the law that makes it possible for a police force to be effectively organised': J L Brierly, *The Law of Nations* (1963), sixth edition, pp68–76.

QUESTION FOUR

Identify and evaluate those factors that lead certain commentators to consider that international law is not law at all.

University of Glasgow LLB Examination 1988 Q1

General Comment

A question requiring a detailed knowledge of the criticisms most frequently levelled against international law as a true system of law.

Skeleton Solution

Identification of the individual criticisms of the efficacy of international law – reply to these criticisms.

Suggested Solution

In order to ascertain whether international law qualifies as law properly so-called, it is first necessary to define the nature of law itself. Although no objective definition of law has yet been enunciated, a number of features of municipal legal orders are frequently identified as embodying the essence of law. Most commonly, legislative, judicial and executive organs are picked out as being in some manner necessary to the operation of legal order. The absence of these institutions at the effective level in the international legal system is the source of speculation that international law does not qualify as law.

Speculation that international law did not qualify as law properly so-called may be directly attributed to the growth of the 'positivist' movement in jurisprudence. The founder of this school of thought was Bentham who undertook a rigorous investigation into the nature of law and concluded that legal order consisted in a number of fundamental attributes. International law failed to measure up to this standard because of the absence of judicial processes and means of enforcing judgments. Austin followed this line of reasoning, and interjected that an additional deficiency of international law was the absence of a sovereign or legislative body. As a result, international law did not qualify as 'law properly so-called' but was relegated to the vague subsidiary classification of 'positive morality'.

These three principal characteristics were portrayed as being somehow essential to the existence of law and although variations have been made on these, they remain the factors which lead commentators to suggest that international law is not law. The question which naturally arises is how relevant are such concepts to the identification of legal order?

If a legislative organ is an essential prerequisite for legal order, this would imply that the accepted legal conceptions of customary law, constitutional law and common law, as well as international law, would be automatically excluded from the definition of law. Further, such a rigorous description of the law would also exclude those so-called primitive forms of legal order based on class and lineage as well as the accepted ancient legal traditions based on religion such as Judaism and Islam: see T Nardin, *Law, Society and the Relations of States* (1983), p121. Although legislative bodies characterise Western legal systems, the diversity of mankind's legal experience tends to suggest that this institution is not a definitive feature of law. Equally, it cannot be stated with certainty that those systems of law with legislative organs have a monopoly on the use of the term 'law'. Within other legal systems, integration, innovation and uniformity are all achieved by means other than legislative co-ordination.

Similarly, the presence of judicial organs is not determinative of the existence of law. The settlement of disputes regarding the basis of common rules requires the selection of the applicable principles from among competing ones. However, it is self-evident that such rules or principles must exist prior to adjudication in order for such a selection to be made. Thus, adjudication merely serves to formally identify and determine the content and application of such rules. Since this is the case, the existence of such a structure is only contingently related to the efficacy of a particular legal order. Further, as a matter of historical evolution, since law, particularly in the form of customary law, preceded the existence of tribunals and courts, such institutions acquire a secondary significance in the identification of law.

Finally, it is a common proposition that the certainty of enforcement is an essential element of law which is lacking in the international sphere. Thus Austin believed that the commands of the sovereign should be regularly met with the threat of force for the existence of legal order. Equally, Kelsen expressed the opinion that a sanction should be provided as a matter of the content of a norm in order that a normative system be classified as law. However, it is because a law is regarded as mandatory that a sanction is provided for violation. A law is not obligatory because deviation will result in punishment, but rather because the law creation processes have established rules of conduct. Further, a law does not have to be enforced on a continuous and uninterrupted basis in order to remain a law.

Coercion alone does not explain the creation of valid rights and duties. Other motives induce compliance and physical force need rarely be applied in order to maintain legal order. Since the motives on which law has come to rely appear to be mainly coercive, the concepts of law and coercion have tended to be assimilated. Fear of punishment remains only one among many motives inclining a population towards obedience to the law.

At the same time it must be admitted that the forms, occasions and degree of enforcement are elements which contribute towards the efficacy of a legal system. Although there appears to be no logical objection to the existence of a decentralised legal order such as the international one, it must be conceded that this will be considerably less efficient than a centralised system. However, it is only when the vagaries of enforcement result in rules generally being ignored that it could be possible to state categorically that no law and order is present in the legal system.

Consequently, in reply to the criticism that international law is not law properly so-called, it is clear that law is not dependent on the existence of a legislative, judicial or executive organ and the absence of these institutions in the international system does not mean that international law is not law. All that can be said of theories which identify these mechanisms or aspects of legal order is that they are common in Western legal systems and that theories identifying these criteria are prevalent. Whether international law is law or not cannot depend on a subjective value judgment of legal order itself.

Chapter 2

Sources of International Law

2.2   Key points

2.3   Key cases and legislation

2.4   Questions and suggested solutions

2.1 Introduction

Collectively the 'sources' of international law constitute that reservoir of authoritative rules and principles to which the international lawyer must refer in order to ascertain the content of the law. An international lawyer must be able to deduce rules of international law in order to substantiate legal opinions supporting particular courses of action. The cogency and consistency of a legal argument will stand or fall depending on the familiarity of the lawyer with these sources of law. It is therefore of the utmost importance that each student understands the nature of these sources and their interaction with each other, and is accustomed to the methodology involved in citing these sources as authority for particular propositions.

2.2 Key points

Formal and material sources of law

A distinction is frequently made by commentators between formal and material sources of law.

a) Formal sources of law establish constitutional processes and methods which authorise the creation of binding legal rules which are generally applicable to the subjects of the legal system.

b) Material sources of law provide evidence of particular or specific rules of law which, when proven, are applicable to a particular dispute.

A formal source is that from which a rule of law derives its force and validity. A material source is that from which the content, not the validity of the law, is derived. The material source provides the substance of the rule to which the formal source gives force and authority.

Article 38(1) of the Statute of the International Court of Justice (ICJ), which is recognised as the authoritative statement of the sources of international law, declares that the Court shall apply the following sources of law to any disputes submitted for settlement:

a) international conventions, whether general or particular, establishing rules expressly recognised by the contesting states;

b) international custom, as evidence of a general practice accepted as law;

c) the general principles of law recognised by civilised nations; and

d) the judicial decisions and the teachings of the most highly qualified publicists of the various nations, as subsidiary means for the determination of the rules of law.

International conventions, custom and general principles of law are generally acknowledged as formal sources of law while judicial decisions and doctrinal writings are deemed material sources which, inter alia, may be advanced as evidence of a material source of law in one of the other three forms. For example, a rule will be legally binding if it meets the requirements of custom (which is a formal source of law) and its substance will be ascertained from state practice (which is the material source of custom).

The International Court is also authorised to decide a case ex aequo et bono, under art 38(2) of the Statute. This allows the Court to apply the principles agreed between the parties for the settlement of the dispute: see the *Frontier Dispute Case* (*Burkina Faso* v *Mali*) (1986) ICJ Rep 554.

Hierarchy of priority

This specific enumeration of sources does not constitute a definitive statement of the relative substantative authority of these sources. However, from the jurisprudence of the ICJ, it is clear that in practice this order represents the methodology which the Court will habitually adopt in the resolution of an international dispute. This is true because this arrangement of sources proceeds from the application of particular rules towards the application of general principles of law. Article 38(1) is therefore simply based on a hierarchy of convenience and not on the relative legal authority or weight of the sources.

The individual sources of international law

It is important that students should be familiar with the following basic details relating to the sources of international law.

Treaties

a) A treaty is an international agreement between two or more states in written form and is subject to regulation and interpretation in accordance with the principles of international law. As a general rule, treaties are classified as either:

   i) Multilateral treaties which are agreements between more than two states. When such agreements can be shown to represent the views of the international community, these may be termed 'law-making' treaties. Such treaties create general norms for future conduct which are identical for all parties subject only to specific reservations. Those parts of the United Nations Charter which do not concern constitutional questions relating to the competence of the organisation illustrate such treaties.

ii) Bilateral treaties which are international contracts between two states. The purpose of such restricted agreements is to create legal obligations in relation to specific matters on which universal consensus would prove unattainable or, alternatively, to establish rights and duties which the contracting states would be unwilling to assume on a multilateral basis.

b) Matters such as negotiation or accession, validity, amendment, modification, reservations, interpretation, suspension and termination of treaties are dealt with by the Vienna Convention on the Law of Treaties 1969. See Chapter 10 below.

c) Unilateral statements and declarations concerning legal rights and duties in relation to factual situations may create valid legal obligations. If a state manifests the intention to legally bind itself to a particular course of action by making a unilateral statement to that effect, that intention may confer the character of a legal undertaking on that declaration and a state may be obliged to follow a course of conduct consistent with that statement: see *Nuclear Test Cases* (1974) ICJ Rep 253, para 43.

d) Treaties may provide evidence of customary law in any one of the following three ways.

i) A series or recurrence of bilateral treaties laying down an identical or similar rule may result in a rule of general customary law to the same effect: see the *SS Lotus Case* (1927) PCIJ Rep Ser A No 10.

ii) A treaty concluded by a limited number of parties may become custom if the rules contained therein are generalised by international state practice and the existence of the requisite opinio juris can be shown: see the *North Sea Continental Shelf Cases* (1969) ICJ Rep 3.

iii) A treaty concluded among a limited number of parties may be shown to codify pre-existing rules of international custom and consequently bind third parties. See the preambles to the Geneva Convention on the High Seas 1958 and the Treaty on Principles Governing the Activities of States in the Exploration and Use of Outer Space 1967.

Custom

a) The necessary elements of custom are:

i) State practice: the sufficiency of state practice is contingent on the duration, uniformity (or consistency) and generality of the usage in question: see the *Fisheries Jurisdiction (Merits) Case* (1974) ICJ Rep 3 and the *North Sea Continental Shelf Cases* (1969) ICJ Rep 3.

ii) Opinio juris et necessitatis: this is the subjective intention or belief on the part of states to accept certain patterns of state practice as being obligated as a matter of law. In the *Lotus Case*, ibid, the International Court indicated that opinio juris could not be inferred from a particular pattern of practice unless the state involved was 'conscious of having a duty' in that regard. This view was reiterated in the *North Sea Continental Shelf Cases*, ibid, although a less rigorous approach has been adopted in other cases: see *Nicaragua* v *United States (Merits)* (1986) ICJ Rep 14.

b) Evidence to support the existence of custom includes the following: diplomatic correspondence, policy statements, press releases, the opinions of official legal advisers, executive decisions and practices, comments by governments on drafts produced by the ILC, national legislation, national judicial decisions, recitals in treaties and other international instruments, the practices of international organs and resolutions relating to legal questions in the UN General Assembly.

c) A state may contract out of the development of a customary rule of international law by persistently objecting to its formation. Evidence of objection must be clear and there is probably a rebuttable presumption in favour of acceptance. See *Anglo-Norwegian Fisheries Case* (1951) ICJ Rep 116. However, the subsequent objector which acquiesced during the processes of formation of the custom would not be able to escape being bound by emergent custom.

d) It is possible for a customary rule of law to exist at a local level, either between two states or on a regional basis. In such cases, the requirements for the creation of general custom must be replicated on a local basis: see the *Asylum Case* (1950) ICJ Rep 266 and the *Rights of Passage over Indian Territory Case* (1960) ICJ Rep 6.

General principles of law

a) This source of law was inserted into the text in order to furnish principles and rules where treaties and custom failed to provide guidance. Reference to such principles would prevent the occurrence of lacunae in the law and would substantiate the doctrine of non liquet. However, it has remained unresolved whether the text refers to general principles of international law or general principles of municipal law.

b) Doctrine in general supports the wider interpretation of this concept. The intention of the drafters of the Statute appears to have been to allow the Court to refer to general principles of municipal jurisprudence, and in particular of private law, in so far as these can be applied to the relations of states.

c) Examples of such principles adopted by the Court have included good faith, estoppel, res judicata, circumstantial evidence, equity, pacta sunt servanda and the finality of awards and settlements: see *Diversion of Water from the Meuse Case* (1937)

PCIJ Rep Ser A/B No 70; *Temple of Preah Vihear Case (Merits)* (1962) ICJ Rep 6; and the *Corfu Channel Case (Merits)* (1949) ICJ Rep 4.

d) The ICJ has rarely resorted to this particular source of law and in those cases in which such a reference is made, this has been restricted to issues of procedure as opposed to matters of substance. Further, such references normally appear without any formal reference or label, as an element of judicial reasoning.

Judicial decisions

a) International jurisprudence

The International Court of Justice follows the civil tradition of legal reasoning insofar as it is not bound by the doctrine of stare decisis. Article 59 of the Statute of the ICJ specifically states that 'the decision of the Court shall have no binding effect except between the parties and in respect of that particular case'. This has two implications.

   i) The Court does not acknowledge the concept of precedent and prior decisions technically are not binding. In the *Certain German Interests in Polish Upper Silesia Case* (1926) PCIJ Rep Ser A No 7, the Court stated:

   'The object of [art 59] is simply to prevent legal principles accepted by the Court in a particular case from being binding on other states or in other disputes.'

   ii) Judgments of the Court do not constitute a formal source of law. The role of the Court is to determine the existence of applicable rules of law and not to create legal principles.

Previous decisions of the International Court, as well as other international adjudicatory bodies, have only persuasive value. The degree of this influence varies in accordance with the origins of the dictum, the voting patterns of the judges and the reception of the international community to the judgment.

Notwithstanding the absence of the doctrine of precedent in the global legal order, judgments of the International Court have undoubtedly affected the development of international law. Dicta in the *Reparations Case* (1949) ICJ Rep 174, the *Reservations to the Convention on Genocide Case* (1951) ICJ Rep 15, and the *Fisheries Jurisdiction Case* (1974) ICJ Rep 3, have all established new rules of law which the Court would be forced to consider in cases dealing with similar facts.

b) National jurisprudence

Decisions of national courts may provide indirect evidence of state practice. Municipal decisions are most persuasive when dealing with matters of international concern such as extradition, diplomatic immunity and recognition.

c) In terms of international jurisprudence, references to the decisions of national tribunals have infrequently been made except in individual and dissenting opinions: see the individual opinion of Judge Hudson in the *Diversion of Water from the Meuse Case* (1937) PCIJ Rep Ser A/B No 70, at 76–77.

Doctrinal writings

a) The role of the jurist in international law has always been more pronounced than in municipal legal systems and this fact is recognised by the Statute acknowledging that the teachings of publicists constitute a subsidiary source of international law. Indeed, in the historical development of international law, the influence of writers such as Grotius, Vattel, Oppenheim and Lauterpacht has been so profound that these authors are acknowledged as institutional writers with a degree of authority which escapes classification as a subsidiary source of law.

b) In contemporary international law the function of writers is more restricted to the analysis of facts, the formulation of opinions and the making of conclusions in relation to trends within international law. Such processes are invariably subjective and frequently result in a biased statement of legal principles. As a result, the Court is reluctant to identify writers in its judgments and advisory opinions.

c) The opinions of law officers are not to be seen as doctrinal writings, but may be seen as evidence of state practice. Draft articles from the International Law Commission are analogous sources to the writings of publicists.

Resolutions of the General Assembly

a) General Assembly resolutions have a binding effect when made in relation to those issues in which this body is given an authoritative constitutional function within the United Nations. In general this relates to administrative and budgetary affairs. Article 10 of the Charter circumscribes the role of the Assembly in other areas to discussions and the making of recommendations.

b) Since the General Assembly has been given no constitutional mandate to create principles of international law, the sole means through which such norms may be created is through the procedures prescribed by customary international law. Where resolutions reflect the opinio juris of states on specific issues, and where state practice remains at a formulative stage, such as the case with outer space in the early 1960s, then resolutions may assist in the creation of customary law.

c) In order to ascertain the opinio juris behind a resolution, it is necessary to consider whether the voting reflects the intention of states to establish legal or political rules. Not all declarations by the General Assembly are intended to express legal rights and duties. For example, the Universal Declaration of Human Rights 1948 expressly states that it is proclaimed as 'a common standard of achievement' and was not intended as a statement of existing law.

2.3 Key cases and legislation

- *Asylum Case* (1950) ICJ Rep 266
  Supports the existence of local customary laws

- *Diversion of Water from the Meuse Case* (1937) PCIJ Rep Ser A/B No 70
  Considered equity as a general principle of international law

- *Fisheries Jurisdiction Case* (1974) ICJ Rep 3
  Illustrates an example of customary international law

- *North Sea Continental Shelf Cases* (1969) ICJ Rep 3
  Illustrates the requirements needed for the establishment of a custom

- *Nuclear Test Cases* (1974) ICJ Rep 253
  Addresses the issue of unilateral statements

- *SS Lotus Case: France v Turkey* (1927) PCIJ Rep Ser A No 10
  Provides a meaning of 'opinio juris et necessitatis'

- *Texaco v Libya* (1977) 53 ILR 389
  Other sources of international law were considered

- Statute of the International Court of Justice (ICJ) – address the issue of sources of international law, amongst others

2.4 Questions and suggested solutions

QUESTION ONE

George, the Chief Justice of Ruretania, has been invited to sit on the International Court of Justice as an ad hoc judge in a case now before the Court. After many years of dealing with domestic legal issues, he is experiencing some difficulty in assessing the materials submitted to the Court by the parties. These materials include:

a) an article in the 'American Journal of International Law' written by an eminent jurist;

b) draft articles prepared by the International Law Commission;

c) a decision of the Supreme Court of one of the parties to the dispute;

d) a United Nations General Assembly Resolution;

e) a treaty to which only one of the parties to the dispute is a party;

f) a statement by the foreign minister of one of the parties; and

g) a previous decision of the International Court of Justice.

Prepare a memorandum for George explaining the sources of modern international law, advising him in particular as to the weight that he should attach to the above materials as sources and evidence of international law.

University of London LLB Examination
(for External Students) Public International Law June 2000 Q1

General Comment

It is quite common for a paper in public international law to include a question on the nature of sources. This particular question involves applying knowledge to a number of specific areas. A candidate answering this question will not only need to know something about sources, but should also be able to comment sensibly on the interaction between the law of treaties and customary international law. A good student will also draw attention to the distinction between sources in the narrow sense and matters that may constitute evidence of international obligations. Any candidate answering this question needs to be able to say something about a number of issues, and say a little about the weight to be given to each item.

Skeleton Solution

Brief description of the role of an 'ad hoc' judge – jurisdiction of the International Court of Justice – individual analysis of items (a)–(g), applying principles of customary international law in reaching sensible conclusions.

Suggested Solution

We are asked in this problem to advise George, the Chief Justice of Ruretania who has been asked to sit as an ad hoc judge in the International Court of Justice in respect of a case before the Court. As a preliminary point it should be noted that an ad hoc judge is often a specialist in international law. In some cases the judge may be a highly regarded municipal lawyer who has no difficulty in dealing with the issues of international law arising (eg Barwick CJ in the *Nuclear Test Cases: Australia* v *France; New Zealand* v *France* (1974) ICJ Rep 253). There is little point in nominating an ad hoc judge unless that individual is of sufficient intellect and knowledge to play a full role in proceedings. For this reason, states that wish to nominate an ad hoc judge will normally seek a person of knowledge, experience and proven intellect.

As a further preliminary point we should advise George that the sources relied upon by the International Court of Justice are those set out in art 38 of the Statute of the International Court of Justice 1945, which repeats almost verbatim the provisions that appeared in the Statute to the Permanent Court of International Justice 1920. It is true that the actual word 'sources' is not used in the text, but the article is seen as the authoritative statement of the sources. It is sensible now to refer to each matter in turn.

a) *The article in the 'American Journal of International Law' written by an eminent jurist*

Founded in 1907, the 'American Journal', published by the American Society of International Law, is probably the most important journal in the field of public international law and the quality of its articles is a matter of record. Distinguished scholars from many countries contribute. Under the terms of art 38(1)(d) the 'teaching of the most highly qualified publicists' is regarded as a subsidiary source of international law. What is important is whether the subject of the article is relevant to the case before the court, and whether the impartiality of the jurist is accepted. That seems to be the case in the present instance. It is unlikely that the Court will openly refer to the matter in its judgment, but nevertheless the writings of scholars are often relied upon by the judges.

Another sense in which the article might be relevant is if the learned jurist has attempted to trace or state a rule of customary international law. The article might be influential in helping the Court form a conclusion as to the existence of a rule of customary international law, which is of course a distinct source under art 38(1)(b).

b) *Draft articles prepared by the International Law Commission*

George will have to be told that the draft articles are relevant and need to be considered. The draft articles may simply be declaratory of the state of customary international law, in which case they represent a source under art 38(1)(b). Alternatively, the draft articles may have contributed to the formation of customary international law if they have been followed by consistent state practice. The International Law Commission has not preserved a distinction between codification and progressive development of international law. It may be that the draft articles contain articles that declare customary international law as well as articles that seek to develop the subject. This is of course the case with the International Law Commission Draft Articles on State Responsibility in the years 1996 and 2001. George will have to consider each article in turn and ask whether it states, or simply seeks to develop, customary international law. It is not a case of considering the draft articles as a whole: it will be necessary to examine the status of each individual article.

Further, George will have to consider whether the draft articles are to form the basis of an international law-making conference. Draft articles of the International Law Commission are often followed either by an international law-making convention or by a General Assembly Resolution. If that is the case then these sources will need to be considered. George will have to be told that the draft articles may constitute evidence of the state of customary international law for the purpose of art 38(1)(b).

c) *A decision of the Supreme Court of one of the parties to the dispute*

In strict terms a decision of a municipal court comes within art 38(1)(d) and may be regarded a subsidiary source. However, one must enter a number of caveats. First, not all Supreme Courts are held in equal esteem; some (such as the Supreme Court of Canada or the Supreme Court of the United States) are highly regarded. Other courts may not be held in such high regard. Second, the value of the judgment and the weight to be attached to it will depend on its relevance and the manner in which it deals with the relevant issues of international law. For example, *The Schooner Exchange* v *McFadden* (1812) 7 Cranch 116 is a municipal judgment frequently cited today. The fact that the judgment here derives from the courts of one of the parties is only one factor; what matters is whether it represents a sensible impartial analysis of the relevant issues in international law. If the municipal court has not exhibited an awareness of the issues in international law, then the judgment will be valueless. If the judgment contains a detailed analysis of the issues in international law by distinguished judges, then it will be of value. We should advise George that he will need to read the judgment, but it is only a subsidiary source and the value to be given to it will depend on the quality of the judgment. In particular, much will depend on whether the municipal court has correctly identified the issues in international law.

d) *A United Nations General Assembly Resolution*

In strict terms a General Assembly Resolution is not a source of international law. But in recent years parties have sought to place General Assembly Resolutions within the terms of art 38(1). A General Assembly Resolution may be declaratory of customary international law if it is drafted in precise terms and the resolution is passed unanimously or by a large majority: see General Assembly Resolution 1803: Declaration on Permanent Sovereignty Over Natural Resources 1962. Second, if the General Assembly Resolution is passed unanimously or by a large majority, it may contribute to the formation of custom if it is followed by consistent state practice. Our advice to George is that the United Nations General Assembly Resolution must be considered in relation to its possible role in declaring or creating customary international law.

e) *A treaty to which only one of the parties to the dispute is a party*

A treaty is a source of international law and is listed as such in art 38(1)(a). However, the general rule of international law is that a treaty only binds a state that is a party to it. This principle arises from the consensual nature of treaties and the sovereignty of individual states (see art 34 of the Vienna Convention on the Law of Treaties 1969): however, the fact that a state is not a party does not mean that the treaty is devoid of legal effect.

As indicated in the *North Sea Continental Shelf Cases* (1969) ICJ Rep 3 the treaty might be declaratory of customary international law, in which case it could have binding effect as a rule of custom on a non-party. Alternatively the treaty might have stated a particular rule that has then been followed by such a consistency of state practice that the treaty can be seen to have contributed to the formation of a rule of customary international law. Such a degree of subsequent state practice has to be demonstrated by evidence; such conduct would have to be extensive, virtually uniform and of appreciable duration. It is certainly possible that, if this is a multilateral treaty, it may be either declaratory or constitutive of customary international law. We should therefore advise George that this is a document that may have to be considered in the context of art 38(1)(b).

It is also germane under this head to note that if the treaty is adjudged to be a 'dispositive treaty' then it will bind a non-party as an exception to the general principle. Further, although not directly mentioned, George will have to consider the text of the treaty to determine whether it stipulates benefits or imposes obligations on non parties (see arts 35 and 36 of the Vienna Convention on the Law of Treaties 1969).

f) *A statement by the foreign minister of one of the parties*

Clearly this is not a source within art 38(1); however, the statement may be one that attracts legal consequences. In broad terms it will be necessary to know the context in which the statement was made. Article 7(2) of the Vienna Convention on the Law of Treaties 1969 expressly states that a foreign minister shall be taken as capable of representing his state.

In this context it is important to know whether the statement was made unilaterally or was made in negotiations as part of a quid pro quo. In *Qatar v Bahrain (Jurisdiction and Admissibility)* (1994) ICJ Rep 112; (1995) ICJ Rep 5 a statement made in negotiations was sufficient to found jurisdiction. Further, in the *Legal Status of Eastern Greenland: Denmark v Norway* (1933) PCIJ Rep Ser A/B No 53 the statement of the Norwegian foreign minister in negotiations was held to have substantive effect. In the later *Nuclear Test Cases: Australia v France; New Zealand v France* (1974) ICJ Rep 253 the unilateral statement of the French foreign minister was held to have legal consequences. We should therefore advise George that the statement, while not a source, has to be examined in its context and it may be evidence of acceptance of jurisdiction or may have effect in determining the substantive rights of the parties. It is a matter that cannot be ignored, although its precise weight will depend upon the context.

g) *A previous decision of the International Court of Justice*

Any mature legal system has to strike a balance between stability and flexibility. Article 38(1)(d) indicates that, subject to art 59, judicial decisions are a subsidiary source of international law. Article 59 reads that 'the decision of the Court has no binding force except between the parties and in respect of that particular case'. Although the precise meaning of this provision is the subject of some debate, it is generally agreed that while the International Court of Justice does not operate a strict system of precedent, it does seek to develop international law in an orderly fashion by adhering to the broad thrust of past decisions. Past judgments and Advisory Opinions are often cited to the Court in written and oral argument; past case law is often cited in the judgments. Any mature legal system has to strike a balance between consistency and flexibility. The International Court of Justice would forfeit all respect if it engaged in extreme deviations from past decisions; thus the tendency has been to be guided by past decisions, particularly in the more technical areas of international law. Thus the *North Sea Continental Shelf Cases* (1969) ICJ Rep 3 refers to the *Anglo-Norwegian Fisheries Case: United Kingdom v Norway* (1951) ICJ Rep 116, while the *Legality of the Threat or Use of Nuclear Weapons (Request for Advisory Opinion by the General Assembly of the United Nations) Case* (1996) ICJ Rep 66 refers to the Advisory Opinion on the *Western Sahara Case: Advisory Opinion* (1975) ICJ Rep 12.

The other relevance of past judgments of the International Court of Justice is that they tend to be adopted by the standard textbooks on the subject and, as in municipal law, they are cited in argument before the Court. We should advise George that any ad hoc judge will need to be familiar with past case law and, like a municipal judge, may need to distinguish past authorities. In giving judgment the Court is often concerned to stress legal principles that emerge from past case law. It should not be forgotten that the duty of the Court under article 38(1) is 'to decide in accordance with international law such disputes as are submitted to it'.

Conclusion

Our conclusion in this matter can be briefly stated. George will be unable to ignore any of the matters listed if he is to discharge his judicial function.

QUESTION TWO

To what extent, and in what circumstances, can it be said that United Nations General Assembly Resolutions are sources of international law?

University of London LLB Examination
(for External Students) Public International Law June 1999 Q1

General Comment

It is not unusual for an examination in public international law to contain a general question on sources. In this particular instance the focus is on General Assembly Resolutions. The candidate is expected to be able to draw a clear distinction with resolutions of the Security Council and will be able to refer to the traditional statement of sources in the Statute of the International Court. At first blush art 38 of the Statute does not make mention of General Assembly Resolutions but the well prepared candidate will be able to indicate how General Assembly Resolutions have acquired an increasing prominence in the last two decades.

Skeleton Solution

The sources of public international law – the nature of the General Assembly – the role and duties of the General Assembly under the terms of the United Nations Charter 1945 – matters of interpretation – General Assembly Resolutions declaratory of international law – General Assembly Resolutions contributing to the formation of customary international law – examples drawn from recent case law – conclusions.

Suggested Solution

We are asked in this question to consider the status of General Assembly Resolutions and the extent to which they may be considered as a source of public international law. It is generally said that the sources of public international law are set out in art 38 of the Statute of the International Court of Justice which, insofar as it is material, lists:

'(a) international conventions, whether general or particular, establishing rules expressly recognised by the contesting States;
(b) international custom, as evidence of a general practice accepted as law;
(c) the general principles of law recognised by civilised nations;
(d) subject to the provisions of art 59, judicial decisions and the teachings of the most highly qualified publicists of the various nations, as subsidiary means for the determination of rules of law.'

It is relevant to note at the outset that General Assembly Resolutions do not appear within this express list: this in itself is hardly surprising, since the present art 38 is traceable back to the sources recognised by the Root-Phillimore Committee in 1920 which drew up the Statute of the Permanent Court. Further, it is important to observe the precise role of the General Assembly within the structure established under the United Nations Charter 1945. The status of the General Assembly is set out in arts 9–22 of the Charter and it is clear that the relevant provisions (a) do not establish the General Assembly as an international legislature, and (b) most of the provisions entitle the General Assembly to 'discuss' (art 10), to 'consider' (art 11) or 'to make recommendations': art 13. Moreover, given the nature of voting in the General Assembly it would clearly be absurd if a large number of sparsely populated states could make law for the majority of the world's population. In a forum in which the smallest state has the same voting power as the most populous this absurdity had to be avoided. Those who set up the United Nations had no intention of giving express legislative power to the General Assembly and a clear contrast exists with the regulatory power of the Security Council.

Turning to General Assembly Resolutions themselves, one should note as a matter of language that many are incapable of creating legal rights and duties. The Resolution may simply be calling for future action and may as a matter of language and interpretation be insufficient as a source of legal rights and duties. Secondly, in considering General Assembly Resolutions one must set aside those internal matters upon which a vote may have legal consequences: examples would be matters pertaining to the setting of the budget, the election of the Security Council and the appointment of judges.

However, the question is concerned with the possible external effect of General Assembly Resolutions. Not being specifically mentioned in art 38, an attempt has been made to fit them within the general framework of customary international law. Thus the general question in effect becomes one of asking: 'in what circumstances can a General Assembly Resolution be considered as contributing to the formation of custom?'. First one starts from the proposition that General Assembly Resolutions are normally viewed as recommendations. Second, although there is not complete agreement on the question, many writers hold that where a General Assembly Resolution has been passed unanimously or by a large majority and it purports to state an abstract principle of law, it may serve as a declaration of customary international law or as a convenient statement of custom already established. (See General Assembly Resolution 1803: Declaration on Permanent Sovereignty Over Natural Resources 1962.)

Third, it is arguable that General Assembly Resolutions may be instrumental in constituting custom if the Resolution is passed unanimously or by a large majority and is then followed by consistent state practice. (See General Assembly Resolution 1884: Declaration of Legal Principles Governing Activities of States in the Exploration and Use of Outer Space 1963.) This will certainly be the case if the substance of the Resolution is repeated in similar terms over a number of years. So while it is true that General Assembly Resolutions do not constitute an independent source, it has been held that such Resolutions are state practice and evidence of custom: they may thus elaborate existing custom or contribute to the formation of a new customary rule. Examples of General Assembly Resolutions falling within this category are: General Assembly Resolution 1514: Declaration on the Granting of Independence to Colonial Territories 1960; General Assembly Resolution 2625: Declaration on the Principles of International Law Concerning Friendly Relations and Co-operation among States in Accordance with the Charter of the United Nations 1970. It is noteworthy that in some areas where evidence of state practice is required, evidence of actual conduct may be lacking (eg space law in the early 1960s or the deep sea bed in the early 1970s). In these circumstances widespread agreement in respect of a General Assembly Resolution may constitute the best evidence available.

The actual treatment of General Assembly Resolutions is best determined by an examination of the jurisprudence of the International Court of Justice. In the Advisory Opinion on the *Western Sahara Case* (1975) ICJ Rep 12 the International Court of Justice made extensive reference to the principle of self-determination as instanced in a succession of General Assembly Resolutions. At a later date in *Nicaragua* v *United States (Merits)* (1986) ICJ Rep 14 the same tribunal outlined the development of the law in relation to the use of force by reference to a number of General Assembly Resolutions. More recently in the *Legality of the Threat or Use of Nuclear Weapons Case* (1996) 35 ILM 809 the Court relied on General Assembly Resolutions to chart the development of the law relating to the use and possession of nuclear weapons.

Thus, in reviewing the evidence, the rational conclusion is that the General Assembly was not established as a legislature and its Resolutions are not expressly stated to be sources of international law. However, in some instances a General Assembly Resolution may be declaratory of customary law, or may be instrumental in the formation of a new customary rule. Whether this is the case is a matter of context and depends on an historical survey of the particular subject area.

QUESTION THREE

Assess the importance of opinio juris in the creation of rules of international law.

University of London LLB Examination
(for External Students) Public International Law June 1996 Q1

General Comment

This is a rather narrow question. The candidate should be able to define what is meant by opinio juris and analyse how it works in practice. Two of the leading cases (see below) need to be examined as well as the attitude of the ICJ towards the Universal Declaration on Human Rights and GA Resolution 1514. The position of the post-1945 states needs to be considered as well as the wording of art 53 of the Vienna Convention on the Law of Treaties 1969.

Skeleton Solution

Introduction: the practice of states – psychological aspect and definition of opinio juris – *North Sea Continental Shelf Cases* – *SS Lotus Case* – Universal Declaration on Human Rights and GA Res 1514 – position of 'new states' – common consent of states – regional customary law and opinio juris – conclusion.

Suggested Solution

Customary law is in part to be found in the practice of states in relation to each other. In the Hellenistic international system, for example, the rules which applied to diplomatic immunity and the regulations governing the declaration of war and the signing of peace treaties arose from practices of the Greek city states. Once such a usage has taken on the form of, inter alia, predictability, certainty and uniformity it has gone part of the way into metamorphosing into a rule of customary international law. It is not enough on its own to classify a particular usage, however certain in its definition, as a customary rule. What is missing to complete the picture is the psychological aspect of the behaviour of states. The opinio juris direction of international law assumes that the usage is regarded by states as having an obligatory character. This may be compared to the traditional theory of conventions in British constitutional law. It is by the obligatory character of the states' practices that a customary rule will be formed, as opposed to a state practice which states will follow because they are minded so to do rather than being obliged as a matter of law. This distinction was discussed in the *North Sea Continental Shelf Cases* (1969) ICJ Rep 3, where the ICJ held:

> 'Not only must the acts concerned amount to a settled practice, but they must also be such, or be carried out in such a way, as to be evidence of a belief that this practice is rendered obligatory by the existence of a rule of law requiring it … the States concerned must therefore feel that they are conforming to what amounts to a legal obligation. The frequency, or even habitual character of the acts is not in itself enough.'

Whether a state wishes to avail itself of a customary rule of law is that state's privilege. The fact that the rule is only used in an intermittent manner does not invalidate its character. This was considered in the *SS Lotus Case: France v Turkey* (1927) PCIJ Rep Ser A No 10. A collision took place on the High Seas between a French ship, the *SS Lotus*, and a Turkish ship, the *Boz-Kourt*. A number of individuals on board the Turkish ship were drowned and Turkey alleged that the French officer of the watch had been negligent in his duties. When the *SS Lotus* entered Istanbul harbour and Turkish territorial waters the French officer of the watch was arrested and charged with manslaughter.

The issue for the Permanent Court was to ascertain whether Turkey had jurisdiction to try the French officer. In order to establish or refute this contention the Court had to determine whether there was a rule of law denying or supporting this jurisdiction. The Turkish argument was based on the premise of a permissive rule of international law. This meant that Turkey was permitted to try the individual but not compelled so to do. France argued the contrary, saying that Turkey was under an obligation not to try the officer.

The Court supported the argument of Turkey. It held that although there were only a limited number of cases in which states had acted in the way that Turkey had, nevertheless the other states involved in those cases had not protested. The question to be asked, the Court argued, was not whether states had refrained from prosecution, but whether they felt obliged to refrain. The answer is that they abstained from initiating judicial proceedings of their own free will.

The conclusion from the above is that a new rule of customary law may be formed by states carrying out certain actions and other states failing to protest. Thus it would appear that an objection, and indeed a single state's protest, could prevent a new practice of states taking on an obligatory character. Customary international law has therefore to receive either active or passive approval.

This may be illustrated by examining the nature of General Assembly Resolutions. General Assembly Resolutions have no constitutional authority to create norms of international law. The majority of GA Resolutions are not therefore legally binding. Some Resolutions may, however, reflect the opinio juris of states on a limited number of issues. How, then, is this determined? The voting pattern is crucial. If there are any votes against a GA Resolution then that Resolution is incapable of forming customary international law. If on the contrary there are no votes against and only a limited number of abstentions then the Resolution may evolve into a rule of customary international law. For instance, the Universal Declaration of Human Rights 1948 was initially supported as just that, a declaration. It did not attract any votes against it, and was passed by a vote of 48 to 0 with eight abstentions. This and its subsequent adoption in international documents and general approval might have changed its character.

In the *Namibia (South West Africa) Case* (*Legal Consequences for States of the Continued Presence of South Africa in Namibia (South West Africa) Case* (1971) ICJ Rep 16 at 55) Vice President Ammoun stated:

> 'Although the affirmations of the Declaration are not binding qua international convention ... they can bind States on the basis of custom ... whether because they are constituted a codification of customary law or because they have acquired the force of custom through a general practice accepted as law.'

Similarly with the Declaration on the Granting of Independence to Colonial Peoples

(Res 1514), the self-determination Resolution. The pattern of voting might indicate its transformation into a binding obligation: there were no votes against and nine abstentions.

All the above assumes that all states are present to object to a creation of a rule of customary international law, which is obviously not the case. The majority of states have come into existence following the collapse of the Western European empires and latterly with the collapse of the Soviet Union. These states are bound by already existing customary international law even though they were not in existence to object to any aspect of it.

Thus far it has been assumed that the acceptance of any obligation has to be unanimous. Not all the authorities agree on this, thereby opening the way for a more fertile development of customary law. As it has been seen, an abstention in the General Assembly does not signify as an objection. Moreover in *West Rand Central Gold Mining Co v R* [1905] 2 KB 391 the English court was prepared to talk about the 'common consent of civilised nations' as forming law which the municipal tribunals (of the United Kingdom) would apply. What amounts to a 'common consent' was not elaborated upon. This line of reasoning is also found in art 53 of the Vienna Convention on the Law of Treaties 1969, which states that a norm of jus cogens must be 'accepted and recognised by the international community of states as a whole'.

International customary law may also exist on a regional level and the same requirement of obligation is needed. If an obligation is asserted in respect of a local practice the state making the assertion is required to show that the practice flows from a legal requirement rather than a regional usage. Such was the situation in relation to Portugal's right of passage over Indian territory from its colony in Goa. This 'right of passage' was recognised by both Portugal and India as being obligatory: *Rights of Passage over Indian Territory Case: Portugal v India* (1960) ICJ Rep 6.

In order for a practice or usage to become customary international law the states of the world community must regard themselves as being bound by the custom. An objection to a practice will prevent it becoming part of customary international law. Acceptance may be active or passive (not objecting), but there must be this acceptance. Whether the acceptance has to be unanimous or by general consent is open to question.

QUESTION FOUR

What is opinio juris? Why and for what is it needed? How, if at all, can one ascertain what is the opinio juris of a state regarding an alleged rule of general international law? Does the necessity of proving the existence of a generally shared opinio juris in favour of the existence of a rule of general international law make it excessively difficult to prove the existence of such rules?

University of London LLB Examination
(for External Students) Public International Law June 1994 Q2

General Comment

A general question requiring analysis of the concept of 'opinio juris' and rules governing the recognition and acceptability of the concept.

Skeleton Solution

ICJ Statute art 38: opinio juris and definitions – function of opinio juris – opinio juris in case law: *North Sea Continental Shelf Cases*; *SS Lotus Case*; *Nicaragua* v *US* – proof of opinio juris: standard of proof – high or low?

Suggested Solution

Under art 38(1)(b) of the Statute of the International Court of Justice (ICJ), the Court is required to apply 'international custom, as evidence of a general practice accepted as law'. Customary international law thus comprises two elements: the material or objective element of 'general practice' and the subjective or psychological element that the practice is 'accepted as law'. This latter, the opinio juris sive necessitatis, requires not merely that states in their practice do, or abstain from doing, something, but that their acts or abstentions are based not on mere convenience, habit or usage, but rather on a sense of obligation. As the ICJ explained in the *North Sea Continental Shelf Cases* (1969) ICJ Rep 3, the practice must have occurred in such a way:

> '... as to be evidence of a belief that this practice is rendered obligatory by the existence of a rule of law requiring it. The need for such a belief, ie the existence of a subjective element, is implicit in the very notion of the opinio juris sive necessitatis. The States concerned must therefore feel that they are conforming to what amounts to a legal obligation.'

It is this recognition of a legal obligation that constitutes the opinio juris.

The function of opinio juris is to enable a distinction to be drawn between mere practice and obligatory behaviour; thus, as a matter of comity, ships on the high seas will normally salute the flag of another ship of a different nationality. States do so, however, because this is customary practice and not because they feel any sense of obligation to act in such a way; a failure to comply with the practice will not engage the responsibility of the state. Opinio juris thus enables a distinction to be drawn between state practice which is, and practice which is not, binding: custom is merely practice; customary international law, however, is practice coupled with legal obligation.

Even at the theoretical level, this explanation of opinio juris can give rise to difficulties since, as Akehurst explains, it seems to require that 'states must believe that something is already law before it can become law': M Akehurst, 'Custom as a Source of International Law' (1975) 47 BYIL 1, 32. In practical terms, it may well be difficult to establish opinio juris in any concrete case; how, for example, can one ascertain the subjective beliefs of a state? Since this is well-nigh impossible to do, the existence or not of this psychological, subjective 'state of mind' must be subjected to objective assessment. Opinio juris may have to be established as an inference from all the circumstances of the case and, therefore, one has to consider the question of proof of opinio juris.

Whether or not it is, as the question suggests, 'excessively difficult to prove the existence' of rules of customary international law depends ultimately upon the standard of proof: the higher the standard, the more difficult it is to establish a rule of customary international law; clearly, the converse applies. It is generally argued that in the *SS Lotus Case* (1927) PCIJ Rep Ser A No 10 the Permanent Court of International Justice (PCIJ) adopted a high standard of proof. In rejecting France's argument that since in their practice states abstained from instigating criminal prosecutions in respect of offences committed on board a foreign ship there was a rule of customary international law requiring abstention and, thus exclusive jurisdiction in such cases was conferred on the flag state, the PCIJ held that mere abstention was insufficient to give rise to customary international law unless it was 'based on [states] being conscious of a duty to abstain'. It was not posssible to infer opinio juris and, hence, customary international law merely from the practice of abstention.

This 'high standard' approach has been followed by the ICJ in both the *North Sea Continental Shelf Cases* and *Nicaragua* v *United States (Merits)* (1986) ICJ Rep 14. It is, however, important to appreciate the context in which this approach was adopted. In the *SS Lotus Case*, the Court proceeded from the assumption that 'Restrictions upon the independence of states cannot ... be presumed': to require a high standard of proof of opinio juris is entirely consistent with such a presumption. In the *North Sea Continental Shelf Cases*, the Court was asked to declare that a conventional rule had generated a rule of customary international law so that West Germany (as it then was) was bound by the latter, even though it was not party to the former; a high standard thus seems apposite. In *Nicaragua*, while the Court referred to its judgment on opinio juris in the *North Sea Continental Shelf Cases*, it did so in the context of an argument that recent state practice had created a 'general right for states to intervene ... in support of an internal opposition in another state'; it is hardly surprising that a high standard of proof would be required to justify such an assertion.

The alternative view, which also finds support in the jurisprudence of the ICJ and in the writings of publicists, argues that the opinio juris may in essence be inferred from a sufficiently general and consistent state practice. Thus, Lauterpacht (*The Development of International Law by the International Court* (1958), p380) argued in favour of a presumption of opinio juris, evidenced by the 'uniform conduct' of states, save where a contrary intention (ie that the practice was not recognised as obligatory) was expressed. In the *North Sea Continental Shelf Cases*, Judge Sørensen, dissenting, relied on Lauterpacht to argue that 'the practice of states ... may be taken as sufficient evidence of the existence of any necessary opinio juris'. Indeed, it is apparent that in both the *North Sea Continental Shelf Cases* and *Nicaragua* the standard of proof required by the Court to establish, respectively, the declaratory force as customary international law of arts 1–3 of the Continental Shelf Convention (Geneva Convention on the

Continental Shelf 1958) and the customary prohibition on the use of force was not especially high and might fairly be described as an inference from sufficiently consistent and general state practice.

In conclusion, most authorities require the presence of opinio juris to transform practice into a rule of customary international law. The practical difficulty of ascertaining opinio juris cannot detract from the requirement so to do. But it is true that, particularly in contemporary international society, with its recent influx of new members, to impose too high a standard of proof would be self-defeating in that it would make it 'excessively difficult to prove the existence' of customary international law; and it is submitted that the ICJ does not in fact always require a high standard. Rather, as Brownlie argues, the 'choice of approach appears to depend upon the nature of the issues … and the discretion of the Court': *Principles of Public International Law* (4th ed, 1990), p7.

QUESTION FIVE

'It is of course axiomatic that the material of international law is to be looked for primarily in the actual practice and opinio juris of Sates, even though multilateral conventions may have an important role to play in recording and defining rules deriving from custom or indeed in developing them.'

Discuss this statement, providing examples.

University of London LLB Examination
(for External Students) Public International Law June 1993 Q5

General Comment

An apparently very wide general question on the sources of international law is thankfully made narrower (and therefore much easier to answer) by focusing specifically on the relationship between treaties and custom, thereby avoiding any need for a verbose and discursive commentary on sources generally.

Skeleton Solution

Introduction: the traditional domination of custom and the rise of treaties – law-making treaties – treaty-contracts – the importance of custom today: the relationship between custom and treaties.

Suggested Solution

Traditionally, until relatively recently, the most important source of international law was always considered to be custom. But since 1945, with the advent of the United Nations and the subsequent proliferation of specialised agencies, international organisations and other public bodies operating around the world, along with the huge increase in the number of sovereign states, custom has ceased to be so all-important. Friedmann, writing as early as 1964, has described custom as 'too clumsy and slow-moving a criterion to accommodate the evolution of international law in our time': quoted in DJ Harris, *Cases and Materials on International Law* (4th ed, 1991) at p71. This has now come to be the received opinion among jurists.

The main perceived problems with custom today are that it is cumbersome and awkward – a long period of time can elapse before a practice comes to be considered a custom; it is often very vague and imprecise – most of the leading cases on sources are devoted to sorting out whether a particular custom is applicable or not to the case in hand … or, indeed, whether it can be said to be a custom stricto sensu at all; some of its requirements – most notably opinio juris et necessitatis – are notoriously difficult to prove; and, according to De Visscher:

> '… custom can neither establish itself, nor evolve and so remain a source of living law, when, owing to the rapidity with which they follow each other or to their equivocal or contradictory character, State activities cease to crystallise into "a general practice accepted as law".' (Harris, op cit, p45)

For these reasons, treaties have today supplanted custom as the primary source of international law. Their only real weaknesses are perhaps that they are too rigid and inflexible by comparison with custom, and each individual treaty is too narrow and limited in its scope; also, they only apply to the states that have expressly consented to be bound by them. But these criticisms notwithstanding, treaties are now almost universally recognised as providing the quickest, most efficient and most stable method of both making law and providing for its enforcement. One commentary on treaties which is worth noting is Fitzmaurice's view that treaties are a source of obligation, rather than an actual source of law. According to this approach, treaties are not a truly creative source of international law (that role being properly reserved for custom) – they merely provide evidence of what the parties to a given treaty believe the law to be, and lay down a mechanism for the specific enforcement of that law. They can then only formulate rights and obligations, and are thus only formal sources of international law, not material sources.

There are two types of treaty, and the precise relationship between each treaty and the custom related to it depends on which category the treaty falls into. 'Law-making treaties' are directly creative of international law and the closest thing there is to international legislation. They are used where a particular problem arises that urgently requires the creation of new law, because there is little or no custom relating to it and the matter is of such urgency that it would be impractical to wait for the emergence of a customary rule. Good examples would be the UN Convention on the Prevention and Punishment of the Crime of Genocide 1948, the International Convention for the Prevention of Pollution of the Sea by Oil 1954 and the Tokyo Convention on Offences and Certain Other Acts Committed on Board Aircraft 1963.

'Treaty-contracts' are the other type of treaty – the more common of the two – and it is here that the relationship between treaties and custom becomes prominent. This relationship can form in one of two ways: either the treaty crystallises certain long-established rules of customary international law into formal treaty form (thereby in effect codifying them) – this is the more common of the two – or a succession of treaties laying down similar rules on the same or similar subjects may eventually give rise to a binding customary rule; this happens extremely rarely and the International Court of Justice has been most reluctant to hold that such a process has taken place.

By far the most informative and comprehensive discussion of the nature of the relationship between custom and treaties is the decision of the ICJ in the *North Sea Continental Shelf Cases: West Germany v Denmark and the Netherlands* (1969) ICJ Rep 3. The ICJ indicated that the Federal Republic of Germany could not be bound by art 6(2) of the Geneva Convention on the Continental Shelf 1958 (enshrining the 'equidistance principle' for the delimitation of continental shelves) because the equidistance principle had not formed part of customary international law prior to 1958; certain other articles of the Convention whose application was disputed, however, were held to be applicable to the FRG because they had existed as custom before 1958 and the Convention had in effect merely codified them. The law of the sea had evolved over centuries, with a clear body of customary international law having been formed; thus the application and effect of the Convention was found to be very much dependent on the precise status in customary international law of the specific rules invoked.

The ICJ also flatly rejected the Danish and Dutch argument that even if art 6(2) did not crystallise a custom relating to the equidistance principle, and no such principle had existed in customary law before 1958, the effect of art 6(2) was to create a legally binding customary norm based partly on the impact of the Convention itself and partly on subsequent state practice. While the ICJ admitted that such a process was 'perfectly possible' and did 'from time to time' occur, it insisted that 'this result is not lightly to be regarded as having been attained'. In so holding, the ICJ stressed the traditional attitude to opinio juris et necessitatis as articulated by the Permanent Court of International Justice in the classic *SS Lotus Case: France v Turkey* (1927) PCIJ Rep Ser A No 10, namely that opinio juris (the opinion that a custom is in fact legally binding) must be strictly proved. The more helpful attitude of Judge ad hoc Sorensen in his Dissenting Opinion, to the effect that opinio juris may be presumed to exist if a uniform practice is proven, was ignored, and the majority on the Bench preferred the strict approach.

The opposite process, however – that treaties can and very often do codify pre-existing customary law – was clearly given judicial sanction in the *North Sea Continental Shelf Cases*. What is really important, though, is the fact that the applicability of certain provisions in a treaty was found by the ICJ to depend on the previous status of the rules in question as custom. This represents the continuing importance of custom as a material source of international law today, while the role of treaties as a formal source in codifying and clarifying customary rules cannot be doubted. In so doing, treaties became state practice and thus contribute to the development of international law rules derived from custom. The United Nations Conventions on the Law of the Sea I (1958) and III (1982) are excellent examples of the function of treaties in relation to custom, as they codify and clarify a set of previously confused and inconsistently applied customary norms.

QUESTION SIX

'The legal environment of international business in public international law is not based solely on law. An understanding and appreciation of the political forces and economic theories and assumptions that underpin the legal order of international business relations is necessary to understand how public international law has developed.'

Critically evaluate this statement.

Written by the Author

General Comment

Although this question appears to sound general, it requires a specific discussion of the sources of public international law, particularly in relation to the business environment.

Skeleton Solution

State the different sources of public international law – distinguish briefly between private and public elements of international law; customary sources; law of treaties; jus cogens; municipal law versus international law; conventions; judicial decisions of the International Court of Justice – evaluate these sources as against the development of international business.

Suggested Solution

Historically, there has always been the need to adopt a criterion for international law. During the eighteenth century, Jeremy Bentham proposed a need for international law by stating that a codification of law between states should exist. This was written in his text, *Principles of International Law* (1786–1789). He envisaged a scenario whereby states would come together in harmony and create 'everlasting peace'.

There was a further important advance in the promotion of international law when, on 22 September 1924, the Resolution of the Assembly of the League of Nations was born. Here, the Committee of Experts for the Progressive Codification of International Law was created, so as to represent 'the main forms of civilisation and the principle legal systems of the world' (see: www.un.org/law/ilc). Delegates from 47 governments participated in a Codification Conference which met at The Hague in March 1930. In 1947, the International Law Commission was established by the General Assembly. The committee was set up to 'promote the progressive development of international law and its codification'. From then on, many more committees were arranged to uphold the basis of international law, including the birth of the United Nations on 24 October 1945.

International law is defined as being 'the body of rules and norms that regulates activities carried on outside the legal boundaries of states'. It looks after three main relationships that occur internationally: those between states and states; between states and persons; and between persons and persons. There are essentially two types of international law: public and private international law. Public international law deals with the rights and duties of states and intergovernmental organisations, whereas private international law deals with individuals and non-governmental organisations in their international affairs. Strictly speaking, these two types of international law are increasingly becoming more blurred in terms of their context. Nowadays, both public and private international laws are dealt with under the same umbrella within a given context.

International law is considered law simply because states and individuals regard it as such. This contrasts with the explanation of international comity. Comity is 'the practice, or courtesy, between states of treating each other with goodwill and civility'. It is not considered law, as states do not actually have to oblige to it.

Within nations, law is made by legislatures, courts and other agencies of government. In the United Kingdom, for instance, the House of Commons decide and implement national rules and regulations. The House of Lords, on the other hand, 'considers legislation, debates issues of importance and provides a forum for government ministers to be questioned'. The House of Lords is the highest court in the UK. Comparatively, on an international level, there is no actual body to create international laws. This is therefore achieved by states coming together and forming agreements regarding certain issues or laws. These agreements can also be known as conventions or treaties. Such agreements only come into effect when states consent to them.

Statements or evidence of general consent can be found in the International Court of Justice (ICJ). The Court has a dual role: to settle in accordance with international law the legal disputes submitted to it by states, and to give advisory opinions on legal questions referred to it by duly authorised international agencies. Article 38(1) of the Statute of the International Court of Justice lists the sources that the court should use to settle international disputes.

The primary source of international law to be considered is treaties. A treaty is 'a legally binding agreement between two or more states'. It does not, however, constitute any municipal laws within the states. Most of the rules that govern treaties can be found in the Vienna Convention on the Law of Treaties 1969 (which came into force in 1980). Article 2(1)(a) of the Vienna Convention states that 'a Treaty means an international agreement concluded between states in written form and governed by international law'. A treaty does not conflict or affect the state's national sovereignty. When a treaty is formed, states have the option to opt out of certain criteria within the treaty if they do not agree with some of the terms. If they do accept the terms, though, then they have to sign the agreement in front of a 'third party'. This is to ensure validity. Another form of agreement is a convention, which is defined as being similar to a treaty but which is sponsored by international organisations, such as the United Nations. Both a treaty and a convention are binding upon member states because of a shared sense of commitment. Examples of treaties would be the Treaty of Rome and the Maastricht Treaty; while examples of conventions would be The Hague Conventions and, more relevantly, the Vienna Convention (see above).

Another source of international law to be considered is custom. It is a long established tradition or usage that becomes customary law if it is consistently and regularly observed and recognised by those states observing it as a practice that they must obligatorily follow. It is essentially rules that have been observed for such a long time that they become a given set of principles. There are three requirements to something becoming a custom: nec vi (without force), nec precario (without permission) and nec clam (without secrecy). It is noteworthy that even though states have a set of customary laws, they do change along with time. An example of this would be the rules of war. After almost every major war that has occurred, the rules have been constantly revised to reflect the circumstances. To prove that customary practice is in fact customary law, two elements must be established, namely behavioural and psychological. The first requires consistent and repeated action, whereby the second must reflect upon the states actually binding to it. The behavioural aspect is fairly self-explanatory; however, the psychological element needs some further clarification. States must recognise the custom as being something that they follow, instead of it just being out of courtesy, or comity. This is often referred to by the Latin phrase 'opinio juris sive necessitatis'.

The third source, and one which courts use to decide international disputes, is general principles. These are principles of law common to the world's legal system. Essentially, there are three main legal systems operating in the world: the Anglo-American common law, the Romano-Germanic civil law and Islamic law. The first two systems have many similarities between them, and this is what allows the courts to base the general principles upon. An example of a case which involved custom is the *Asylum Case: Columbia* v *Peru* (1950) ICJ Rep 266 undertaken by the ICJ. Essentially, it concerned how Columbia granted political asylum to a failed Peruvian politician in its embassy in Peru, then wanted the Peruvian government to hand him over safely to the border, though the Peruvian government did not want to. Columbia then sued Peru in the ICJ. The custom argued here was that diplomatic asylum was something of a custom amongst Latin-American states and should be respected.

The next source of international law is equity. It is literally translated from the Latin word æquitas, which means 'even' or 'fair'. Fundamentally, it is any justice which is applied in certain circumstances not covered by the rules of law. The involvement of equity came about through the extensive use of English common law, and originated from the King's Chaplain, or Chancellor, to provide parties with a remedy when none was available in the King's courts. It plays 'a subsidiary role in supplementing existing rules'. Other subsidiary elements which may be used when settling international disputes are judicial decisions and writings. Another way in which an international dispute may be solved is by observing some decisions made in the municipal courts.

Article 38 of the Statute of the ICJ states that if a municipal case is relevant to the dispute, it can be implemented.

Other possible sources of international law could be that of international and regional organisations, the International Law Commission and jus cogens. Examples of international and regional organisations would be the United Nations and the European Union. Jus cogens is the 'technical term given to those norms of general international law which are of a peremptory force and from which, as a consequence, no derogation may be made except by another norm of equal weight'.

States wishing to make ties with other states internationally do so for several reasons. Such ties may be for tourism, for health and safety reasons, for information and knowledge, but inevitably in most cases it is for the exchange of money. This is most commonly achieved through trade. Sometimes, however, certain states inevitably break some of the rules of trading. International law would still come into play here, but in realistic terms not all the time. In reality, it depends on the state in question.

With regards to international law, there are no sanctions per se if the state does violate some of the terms. In municipal law, breaking the rules results in punishment. Within an international scope, if a state were to break the rules, they would appear in front of a tribunal which would decide its fate. However, in my opinion, this is heavily dependant upon how politically strong the state is (ie how much power it has). For instance, the United States (known for having a lot, if not the most amount of political power compared with other states) has, in the past, gone 'around' some of the rules in order to achieve certain things. A recent example arguably is the war in Iraq. The US were essentially the leading force behind it (ignoring other states' pleas to avoid war), and now that it is virtually over, there are only American-based companies in Iraq taking charge of rebuilding. This example is not intended to be a critical assumption of the political ways of the US, but merely a case in point to illustrate how political power sometimes overrides international law.

When it comes to international law, it is most commonly believed that the United Nations have utmost authority regarding the issue. But on some occasions, even this organisation cannot take control over some international disputes. Another international organisation, the International Monetary Fund, controls a lot of international business. It does so by 'ensuring the stability of international monetary and financial systems'. With regards to the point about the importance of political power, it is to be noted here that the US is in fact the largest shareholder of the Fund (with 17.8 per cent of total votes).

International law exists with the incentive of bringing peace and harmony between states. As previously mentioned, there has always been a need for law to exist between states. One of the reasons for this is to allow business to develop internationally. However, it can be seen that law does not apply all the time internationally. Political forces come into play some of the time, and in many cases overrules any international courts or tribunals.

Because there is no world government as such, some have raised the question of whether or not international law is really law at all. In my opinion, because states and individuals regard it as such, it is in fact law. Whether or not it is a 'fool-proof' system that works all the time remains to be seen. It is arguable, however, that certain states with high political powers and influences in international law should use their authority to improve the system and not to just manipulate it at their own will. This would inevitably make international business prosper, and eventually create global harmony, as once anticipated by Jeremy Bentham.

Chapter 3

The Relationship between International and Municipal Law

3.1 Introduction

3.2 Key points

3.3 Key cases and legislation

3.4 Questions and suggested solutions

3.1 Introduction

In spite of the obvious practical importance of applying international law to disputes before municipal legal tribunals, students are often left unclear as to the precise relationship between these two apparently distinct forms of law. A number of competing theories have been formulated to either define or describe the interaction between international and municipal law. The product of this competition has been the creation of an uncertain and ill-defined area in the public international law syllabus. The United Kingdom passed the International Criminal Court Act 2001 which is an adoption of the Rome Statute of the International Criminal Court (the ICC Statute). The Act received Royal Assent on the 11 May 2001 and it broadly seeks: (1) to incorporate offences within the ICC Statute into domestic law; (2) to enable the UK to meet its obligations under the ICC Statute and so enable ratification to take place; and (3) to enable agreement to be reached with the ICC so that persons convicted can serve prison sentences in the UK. This illustrates the ever-growing significance of international law in the UK.

3.2 Key points

The expansion of contemporary international law into dimensions once considered the exclusive domain of states has created an extensive overlap of subjects over which both international law and municipal law purport to regulate. This has led to problems in the application of municipal law before international tribunals and, in turn, international law in domestic forums.

Competing theories defining the relationship between international law and municipal law

Three main theories attempt to describe this interaction.

a) Monism (or incorporation) – this theory asserts that international law and municipal law are both elements of one all-embracing and universal system of law, in which the overriding principle is the supremacy of international law.

b) Dualism (or transformation) – according to this formulation, international law and municipal law are two distinct and separate systems of law which do not exist in a relationship of superiority or inferiority to each other. As a result national law may be applied in a manner inconsistent with international law.

c) Harmonisation (or co-ordination) – this theory refutes the existence of common subject matters in which co-ordinate competence could arise and therefore no conflict between the two orders may arise. States may promulgate valid domestic laws at variance with international law but will, as a result, incur international responsibility for such actions.

In practice, the distinction between these theories is only relevant to the application of international law in domestic forums because, at the international level, all three theories allow for the exclusive application of international law within international tribunals.

The application of municipal law in international tribunals

The proposition that a provision of national law may prevail over the international obligations of a state has never been accepted by any international tribunal. If such a possibility was embraced, states would be able to circumvent their international obligations through the adoption of appropriate legislation. The application of this principle has a number of consequences.

a) A state may not invoke a provision of national law as a defence to a claim based on international law. In the *Free Zones of Upper Savoy and the District of Gex Case* (1932) PCIJ Rep Ser A/B No 46, at 167, the International Court stated: 'It is certain that (a state) cannot rely on her own legislation to limit the scope of her international obligations.' This principle applies to both treaties and customary principles of international law: see *United Nations Headquarters Agreement Case* (1988) ICJ Rep 3.

b) A state may not plead that an absence of statutory authority justifies failure to observe international obligations: see the *Alabama Claims Arbitration* (1872) 1 Moore Int Arb 485.

c) Municipal law may evidence international custom or general principles of law in accordance with art 38(1) of the Statute of the ICJ.

d) Since international law may leave questions to be decided in accordance with municipal law, international tribunals occasionally find themselves in a situation of having to apply the municipal law of a state: see the *Serbian Loans Case* (1929) PCIJ Rep Ser A No 20.

International law before the English courts

The application of international law before municipal courts has arisen in the past in relation to the rights and duties of diplomats, jurisdiction over foreign nationals, limits on the breadth of the territorial sea and expropriation.

In the jurisprudence of the English courts, a distinction is evident in the application of international obligations based on treaties on the one hand and customary law on the other.

Treaties

The English courts have adopted a strictly monist view of international obligations created on a treaty basis. In the leading case, *The Parlement Belge* (1879) 4 PD 129, Phillimore stated that treaties negotiated by the Crown in the exercise of the prerogative power to enter into treaties have no effect unless incorporated into English law by enabling statute. In a later case, *R v Chief Immigration Officer, ex parte Bibi* [1976] 1 WLR 979, Lord Denning unreservedly stated: 'Treaties and declarations do not become part of (English) law until they are made law by Parliament.'

However, unincorporated conventions and declarations may have two possible functions in English law.

a) They may be used as an aid to interpreting statutes: see *IRC v Collco Dealings* [1962] AC 1. This rule of construction does not, however, extend to the interpretation of subordinate legislation: see *R v Secretary of State for the Home Department, ex parte Brind* [1990] 2 WLR 787.

b) There is a rebuttable presumption that Parliament did not intend to violate an international conventional obligation. See *Salomon v Commissioners of Custom and Excise* [1967] 2 QB 116, where Diplock LJ stated:

> 'There is a prima facie presumption that Parliament did not intend to act in breach of international law; and if one of the meanings which can reasonably be ascribed to the legislation is consonant with the treaty obligations and another or others are not, the meaning with its consonant is to be preferred.'

Conversely, where a treaty has been incorporated into English law, it has equal authority to an Act of Parliament. The treaties constituting the European Community are directly applicable in British courts by virtue of s2(1) of the European Communities Act 1972. This also gives direct enforceability to judgments of the European Court of Justice. In contrast, no enabling Act has been passed to give effect to the European Convention on Human Rights 1950 and as a result its provisions form no part of English law. See the statement by Denning MR in *R v Chief Immigration Officer, ex parte Bibi*, op cit. In *Sidhu v British Airways plc* [1997] 2 WLR 26 the House of Lords considered the jurisdiction of the Warsaw Convention 1929. Similarly, in *Re H (Minors) (Abductions: Acquiescence)* [1997] 2 WLR 653 the House of Lords attempted to harmonise the interpretation of international conventions in different jurisdictions. Another interesting case which illustrates the application of international law before the United Kingdom courts is that of *R v Uxbridge Magistrates' Court, ex parte Adimi and Others* (1999) The Times 12 August.

United Nations Resolutions

With the greater degree of co-operation among the five Permanent Members of the Security Council, UN Security Council Resolutions have become a more important form of international law. However, within the UK, incorporation of the terms of these Resolutions requires implementing legislation.

Inside the UK, Resolutions are given effect by means of the United Nations Act 1946 which empowers the relevant minister to enact subordinate legislation. In the absence of such an instrument, the Resolution has no internal effect.

There have been four recent occasions when this power has been used.

a) Iraq and Kuwait (UN Sanctions) Order 1990 (SI 1651/1990) – imposed restrictions on the exportation and importation of goods into the UK from Iraq and Kuwait and prohibited certain specified related activities and dealings.

b) Libya (UN Sanctions) Order 1992 (SI 975/1992) – imposed restrictions on the export and supply of arms and related materials to Libya as well as on air flights.

c) Serbia and Montenegro (UN Sanctions) Order 1992 (SI 1302/1992) – placed restrictions on the export and import of goods to and from these two countries.

d) Haiti (UN Sanctions) Order 1993 (SI 1784/1993) – placed restrictions in relation to the supply of arms and petroleum products to Haiti and in relation to the transfer of funds.

The effect of these orders is to prohibit transactions relating to these activities which will not be given effect by the UK courts: see *Wahda Bank* v *Arab Bank* (1992) The Times 23 December.

Customary international law

The original rule of English law was that customary international law formed part of English law which is a clear reception of the doctrine of incorporation. In the early case of *Triquet v Bath* (1764) 3 Burr 1478, Lord Mansfield declared that 'the law of nations, in its full extent (is) part of the law of England'. However, in the case of *R v Keyn* (1876) 2 Ex D 63, the English courts reversed this position. Jurisdiction of the English courts under international law over the territorial sea could not be constituted under customary international law but only by Act of Parliament.

The position was further confused by the dictum of Alverstone LCJ in the case *West*

Rand Central Gold Mining Co v *R* [1905] 2 KB 391, in which he appeared to reaffirm the original position by pronouncing that 'whatever has received the common consent of civilised nations must have received the assent of our country, and that to which we have assented along with other nations in general may properly be called international law, and as such will be acknowledged and applied by our municipal tribunals when legitimate occasion arises for those tribunals to decide questions to which doctrines of international law may be relevant.'

Once again reversing the apparent direction of the law, in *Chung Chi Cheung* v *R* [1939] AC 160, Lord Atkin, delivering the opinion of the Privy Council, stated that 'so far, at any rate, as the courts of this country are concerned, international law has no validity save in so far as its principles are accepted and adopted by our own domestic law'. *R* v *Secretary of State for the Home Department, ex parte Thakrar* [1974] QB 684, affirmed the position that a rule was not automatically a part of English law merely by being a part of international law.

In the most recent case in point Lord Denning in *Trendtex Trading Corp* v *Central Bank of Nigeria* [1977] QB 529 reversed his earlier dualist opinion in *ex parte Thakrar* by declaring:

> 'Under the doctrine of incorporation, when the rules of international law change, our English law changes with them. But, under the doctrine of transformation, the English law does not change. It is bound by precedent ... As between these two schools of thought, I now believe that the doctrine of incorporation is correct. Otherwise I do not see that our courts could ever recognise a change in the rules of international law ... The rules of international law, as existing from time to time, do form part of our English law.'

In effect, this statement represents a return to the original position stated by Lord Mansfield.

If applied through the processes of judicial reasoning, international law may become binding on the courts as a matter of precedent. Lord Scarman, in the case *Thai-Europe Tapioca Service Ltd* v *Government of Pakistan* [1975] 1 WLR 1485, observed that 'a rule of international law, once incorporated into our law by decisions of a competent court, is not an inference of fact but a rule of law. It therefore becomes part of municipal law and the doctrine of stare decisis applies as much to that as to a rule of law with a strictly municipal provenance.'

However, the principles behind the reception of customary law before the English courts remains, at the least, incoherent and unsettled.

In recent years it has become a matter of common knowledge that in respect of treaty obligations the United Kingdom tends towards a dualist approach. In normal circumstances a treaty which affects the rights of British citizens or modifies the common law must be followed by parliamentary legislation if it is to be given effect to in the courts.

European Community law

European Community law is neither international law nor national law, but in fact is better described as supranational law. Nevertheless, the sources of Community law are the three Community Treaties, as amended, and the regulations and directives made under the authority of these constitutional agreements. Consequently, the foundations of Community law are based on international agreements entered into by the (now) 25 Member States.

The European Court has, for a long time, recognised the supremacy of Community law over national law: *Costa* v *ENEL* [1964] CMLR 425. However, the British courts have, until recently, resisted the adoption of this principle into our municipal law. This resistance has been based on the desire to maintain the principle of the sovereignty of Parliament and in particular the supremacy of Acts of Parliament.

The UK courts were initially reluctant to endorse the concept of the supremacy of Community law. But, in *R* v *Secretary of State for Transport, ex parte Factortame (No 2)* [1990] 3 WLR 818, the force of the principle became irresistible. This case involved the application of the EC Treaty to the Merchant Shipping Act 1988 which was incompatible with the terms of the Treaty. The issue of whether the terms of the EC Treaty or the UK Act prevailed eventually came before the House of Lords which upheld the terms of the EC Treaty.

In justifying the modification of the doctrine of parliamentary sovereignty in the case of Community Treaty provisions, Lord Bridge observed:

> '[W]hatever limitation of its sovereignty Parliament accepted when it enacted the European Communities Act 1972 was entirely voluntary. Under the terms of the Act of 1972 it has always been clear that it was the duty of a United Kingdom court, when delivering final judgment, to override any rule of national law found to be in conflict with any directly enforceable rule of Community law ...'

This dualist approach was recently illustrated in the case of *R* v *Evans and Others, ex parte Pinochet Ugarte* [1998] 3 WLR 1456 (HL). Similarly, in *Ex parte Amnesty International* (1998) The Times 11 December the court rejected a submission based on a duty arising under art 7 of the UN Convention against Torture and Other Cruel or Degrading Treatment or Punishment 1984, on the basis that the duty arose under international law and has not been incorporated into domestic law. This may now be interpreted differently in the light of the Human Rights Act 1998 which incorporated the European Convention on Human Rights into English law.

The reception of international law in other states

The approach adopted by states to the validity of international law before municipal tribunals varies in relation to the constitution of the state in question.

United States

In the United States Constitution, art VI provides that treaties between the United States and other countries, properly negotiated under the authority vested in the constitution, 'shall be the supreme law of the land'. In relation to customary international law, the US Supreme Court, in the *Paquete Habana* 175 US 677 (1900), stated 'international law is part of our law, and must be ascertained and administered by the courts of justice of appropriate jurisdiction, as often as questions of right depending upon it are duly presented for their determination'.

Germany

Article 25 of the German Constitution specifically provides that 'the general rules of public international law are an integral part of Federal law. They shall take precedence over the laws and shall directly create rights and duties for the inhabitants of the Federal territory.' German jurisprudence indicates that international law is superior to municipal law, but does not prevail over the constitution itself.

The Netherlands

Article 60 of the Netherlands Constitution provides that treaties have priority over domestic laws and that municipal law is invalid if it conflicts with international law. This is generally accepted to be the closest possible reception of the monist position.

France

The French Constitution of 1958 declares that treaties properly ratified and published shall have the force of law. The effect of this provision is mitigated by the fact that, in a number of situations, the same constitution stipulates that certain international agreements must be ratified by legislative processes.

3.3 Key cases and legislation

- *Ex parte Amnesty International* (1998) The Times 11 December
  Provides an example of the importance of incorporation

- *R v Evans and Others, ex parte Pinochet Ugarte* [1998] 3 WLR 1456 (HL)
  Illustrates the dualist approach of the United Kingdom in respect of international obligations

- *R v Secretary of State for the Home Department, ex parte Bhajan Singh* [1976] 1 QB 198
  Treaties are not part of English law unless incorporated

- *R v Secretary of State for Transport, ex parte Factortame (No 2)* [1990] 3 WLR 818
  Exemplifies the principle that community law prevails over national law

- *R* v *Uxbridge Magistrates' Court, ex parte Adimi and Others* (1999) The Times 12 August
  Provides an example of the relationship between international law and domestic law

- *Standard Chartered Bank* v *International Tin Council and Others* [1987] 3 All ER 257
  Addresses the implications of bankruptcy of an international organisation in English law

- *Trendtex Trading Corporation* v *Central Bank of Nigeria* [1977] QB 529
  Affirms the fact that English courts recognise the doctrine of incorporation

- *United Nations Headquarters Agreements Case* (1988) ICJ Rep 3
  International law prevails over national law, in the event of inconsistency at an international level

- *Wahda Bank* v *Arab Bank* (1992) The Times 23 December
  Illustrates the approach of the British courts towards the Security Council Resolutions

- European Communities Act 1972 – provides the basis for the application of Community law in the UK

- Human Rights Act 1998 – incorporates the European Convention on Human Rights into English law

- International Criminal Court Act 2001 – adopts the Rome Statute of the International Criminal Court

- United Nations Security Council Resolutions – provide an important form of international law in the signatory states

3.4 Questions and suggested solutions

QUESTION ONE

'The question of the relationship between international law and municipal law can give rise to many practical problems, especially if there is conflict between the two.' (Akehurst)

Critically analyse this statement.

University of London LLB Examination
(for External Students) Public International Law June 2000 Q4

General Comment

It is said by many writers that the most important question in public international law is its relationship with municipal law. Most examinations on public international law contain a question on this topic. The well prepared candidate will appreciate the difficulties that can arise when international law comes into contact with constitutional law. This quotation is drawn from the English writer Michael Akehurst, whose standard text on international law appeared in its first edition in 1970 and is now in its seventh edition under the authorship of Professor Malanczuk. Candidates should be able to illustrate their answer with reference to constitutional provisions and relevant case law.

Skeleton Solution

The relationship between international law and municipal law – possibility of conflicts between the two – resolution.

Suggested Solution

We are asked in this question to consider a quotation by the late Michael Akehurst who argues that the relationship between international law and municipal law may give rise to practical problems, if not conflict. With respect to the learned author this conclusion must be open to question.

First, the subject of international law has always included a debate between those who favoured a natural law view and those who adopted a positivist approach. Those who favoured the former approach tended towards the monist doctrine, while those inclined to positivism tended towards a dualist approach. That division has generated a great deal of debate in civil law countries, but has not proved a source of conflict in the United Kingdom. Second, while international law has grown in scope in the twentieth century, it is arguable that its relationship with municipal law is much clearer than it has ever been. There are now many more states in the world and most operate under some form of written constitution. It is quite normal for a written constitution to indicate in clear terms the extent to which international law is to be given effect in municipal courts. In such circumstances the relationship between the two could not be clearer. In this context there is much to be said for the observation of the distinguished jurist Professor Starke, who observed in his book on international law that written constitutional provisions 'appear to support the positivist thesis that before international law can be applicable by municipal courts some specific adoption by municipal law is required, since it is only in virtue of these provisions of municipal constitutional law that the rules of international law are valid and applicable within the municipal sphere'.

In considering the statement, it is important to pay regard to the nature of international law. In broad terms public international law comprises rules of customary international law and obligations arising under treaties. If one examines the written constitutions of many states, provision is made that such rules shall be given effect to in municipal courts, save where they conflict with express statutory enactment: see the Constitutions of Austria (1955) art 9; Germany (1949) art 25; Italy (1948) art 10; France (1946 and 1958) Preamble to Constitutions of both the Fourth and Fifth Republic. If we then compare the position with the United Kingdom, which has no written constitution, the position is much the same in that established rules of customary international law will be given effect to in English courts provided they do not conflict with express statutory enactments: see *West Rand Central Gold Mining Co v R* [1905] 2 KB 391; *Commercial and Estates Company of Egypt v Board of Trade* [1925] 1 KB 271; *R v Bow Street Metropolitan Stipendiary Magistrate, ex parte Pinochet Ugarte (No 1)* [2000] 1 AC 61. It is also clear that the doctrine of precedent will not be an obstacle to giving effect to rules of customary international law: see *Trendtex Trading Corp v Central Bank of Nigeria* [1977] QB 529.

If one then turns to treaty obligations most written constitutions deal with the topic; some constitutions may provide that certain treaties shall have the force of law immediately, while other provisions may stipulate that treaties shall not affect private rights until they have been followed by legislation: see art 53 of the French Constitution 1958. Clearly such express provision does not indicate any lack of clarity. In the common law world, particularly in Commonwealth countries, the normal requirement is for treaties affecting private rights to require legislation: see *Union of India v Jain and Others* (1954) 21 ILR 256. This of course reflects the dualist view that pertains in many common law jurisdictions.

So, in many states the relationship between municipal law and international law is clearly stated in the constitution of the state. It is important to consider why this should be so. Most political scientists since Montesquieu (1689–1755) accept that government functions can be divided into the legislative, judicial and executive. In broad terms it is accepted that treaty obligations are negotiated by the executive branch of government; indeed under the United Kingdom Constitution the making and ratifying of treaties is an executive act affected under the prerogative power. However, it is also clear that in a democracy changes in domestic law must be effected with the consent of elected representatives in the legislature. If this were not the case, the prerogative power could be used to change domestic law; this would have the effect of reversing the result of the Civil War in England (1642–1647): see *BBC v Johns* [1965] Ch 32. So, as the quotation from Michael Akehurst indicates, there is a possible conflict between the principle that in international law treaties should be honoured, and the equally important principle that changes in municipal law require the consent of the legislature.

Thus the relationship between international law and municipal law can normally be determined by examining the written constitution of a particular state. However, the quotation raises the question of a possible conflict between the two. In practice this does not happen very often. In the context of obligations arising under customary international law, it is normal for such obligations to be applied as part of municipal law unless they conflict with express statutory enactments. It is important also to consider the tribunal; if the forum is an international tribunal then international law will be applied as a matter of course, so that any problem can only arise before a municipal court where a judge will apply the law that his constitutional tradition dictates.

However, the claim that the two systems conflict presupposes that they operate within a common sphere of activity. As Gerald Fitzmaurice indicated in his Hague Academy lectures in 1957, this is not the case; international law operates on the international plane and national law operates within the municipal sphere. The standing of international law within a national system will be determined by the written constitution of the state. So there cannot be a conflict of the legal systems; what may occur is that national law, as interpreted in the municipal court, says one thing while international obligations provide for something else. In principle a state, having assumed international obligations, should change its domestic law to give effect to such obligations; but if it fails to do so there will not be any conflict of legal systems; there will merely be a conflict of obligations.

If one examines the evidence of the case law it is clear that the English judiciary consider the rules to be well established. Although the case of *R* v *Keyn* (1876) 2 Ex D 63 may not be a model of clarity, this cannot be said of *West Rand Central Gold Mining Co* v *R*. For over a century in England it has been accepted that the municipal court regards customary rules as part of the common law, save in so far as they are not contradicted by statute. In respect of treaty obligations, legislative action is required if they are to change domestic law. Although the United Kingdom does not possess a written constitution, the relationship between national law and international law is clear and has recently been confirmed by the House of Lords in the cases of *Maclaine Watson & Co Ltd* v *Department of Trade and Industry* [1990] 2 AC 418 and *R* v *Bow Street Metropolitan Stipendiary Magistrate, ex parte Pinochet Ugarte (No 1)*. It is not possible to point to a case in England where a judge has found difficulty in analysing the relationship between international law and municipal law. It may be that a case arises where a municipal court does not act in accordance with obligations accepted on the international plane, but the remedy lies in the sphere of diplomatic protest. All the evidence indicates that the approach set out by Gerald Fitzmaurice in 1957 accords with reality rather than the unduly pessimistic assessment of Michael Akehurst.

The conception that municipal law might be out of line with international obligations arose in England in the years prior to the Human Rights Act 1998, when citizens relying on rights under the European Convention on Human Rights and Fundamental Freedoms 1950 succeeded in actions before the European Court of Human Rights. In such cases domestic law in the United Kingdom would then be changed to give effect to the treaty obligations.

QUESTION TWO

'International courts and tribunals owe their existence to international agreements between states. But to exist is one thing; to have competence in respect of particular states in regard to particular claims is another.'

Discuss with relevant examples, explaining how that competence arises in each case.

University of London LLB Examination
(for External Students) Public International Law June 1999 Q4

General Comment

This question is directed to two aspects. First it raises the question of how international courts and tribunals come into existence. Second it requires the candidate to consider the jurisdiction of such bodies. As the quotation indicates these are distinct aspects and it is sensible to deal with each separately. While it is normally true that such bodies arise from agreements between states, it is arguable that bodies created by the Security Council come within a separate category.

Skeleton Solution

Introduction – how international tribunals and courts come into existence – the concept of jurisdiction – the limitations on the exercise of jurisdiction by international courts and tribunals.

Suggested Solution

We are asked in this question to examine a particular quotation. The quotation refers to two aspects, namely the existence of international courts and tribunals, and the competence or jurisdiction of such bodies. The quotation proceeds to assert that the two concepts are not the same. It is sensible to examine each aspect in turn.

As regards existence, it is sensible to start from the first principles. In the eighteenth and nineteenth century the basic unit in international society was the state; indeed the positivists believed that international law was no more than the minimum rules that states would accept. Thus the sovereign state was the centre of international law. In the nineteenth century statesmen began to consider how methods might be strengthened to facilitate the peaceful settlement of disputes. Arbitration as a method can be traced back to the Jay Treaty 1794 or the Treaty of Ghent 1814. Arbitration was consistent with the structure of international law because it involved sovereign states consenting to submit the dispute to a third party. The *Alabama Claims Arbitration* (1872) 1 Moore Int Arb 485 marked the beginning of the modern trend: however, in the nineteenth century arbitral tribunals were ad hoc bodies whose existence was attributable to a compromise (or agreement). The trend was taken further in the Hague Convention for the Pacific Settlement of International Disputes 1899. Since that date arbitration between states has been supplemented by private arbitration agreements which may be invoked by individual companies. In the years after 1913 states such as the United States began to insist that treaties should include provision for arbitration in the event of dispute. As the quotation indicates, for the last 100 years the existence of such arbitral tribunals was founded upon either a treaty provision or a compromise. In the period since 1945 there has been a growth in mixed arbitrations that are between states and non-state entities, as indicated by the International Centre for the Settlement of Investment Disputes (ICSID) or the Iran-US Claims Tribunal.

After 1919 the desire to regulate international affairs lead to the establishment of the Permanent Court of International Justice (in 1919); this body was later supplanted by the International Court of Justice. In respect of questions of existence, the International Court of Justice (established in 1946) derives from the provisions of the United Nations Charter (arts 92–94) which stipulates that all members of the United Nations are ipso facto parties to the Statute of the International Court of Justice. In more recent years bodies such as the Law of the Sea Tribunal have been established by treaty. To this extent the first part of the quotation is undoubtedly correct in pointing to the role of treaties and agreements in establishing international bodies. However, it should be noted that international bodies may arise under other methods. Thus the International Tribunal for the former Yugoslavia was created under Security Council Resolution 827 of 25 May 1993 while the Rwanda Tribunal was set up on 8 November 1994 under the terms of Security Council Resolution 955.

The second aspect of the question refers to the jurisdiction of such bodies. Jurisdiction itself involves three aspects; namely, jurisdiction in respect of parties, time and matter. Normally such questions of jurisdiction are to be determined by examining the constituent document of the tribunal or court in question. Thus an arbitral agreement may set out the matters that come within the scope of the arbitration, while the Statute of the International Criminal Court 1998 lists (in arts 5–21) the matters that fall within the jurisdiction of that body. This is no different to the position in municipal law where the relevant statute or court rules will set out the limits of jurisdiction.

However, the quotation is directed to a narrower matter; it specifies that the court or tribunal may lack competence 'in respect of particular states in regard to particular claims'. To look at the constituent document will often not be enough. In an arbitral tribunal it will be sufficient to look at the agreement or compromise, while in the case of a tribunal established by treaty the scope of jurisdiction will be determined by the treaty. However, that tribunal will have to determine whether, on the facts, jurisdiction arises. Jurisdiction to be exercised has to arise in its three aspects: ratione personae; ratione temporis; and ratione materiae. All three aspects will have to be satisfied before jurisdiction can be exercised.

In the case of the International Court of Justice contentious jurisdiction may arise under the terms of a treaty; thus in the *Hostages Case* (1980) ICJ Rep 3 jurisdiction arose under the terms of the Vienna Convention on Diplomatic Relations 1961. In some cases the International Court of Justice may acquire jurisdiction because the parties specifically refer a dispute to it in the form of a compromise: see *Minquiers and Ecrehos Islands Case: France v UK* (1953) ICJ Rep 47. Alternatively the parties may agree in advance to submit to the jurisdiction of the court under art 36(2) of the Statute of the International Court of Justice. The problem is that less than a third of states have valid declarations in force. Moreover, such declarations may be subject to conditions, time limits or reciprocity, so that actual jurisdiction is the lowest common denominator of the two declarations filed: see *Norwegian Loans Case: France v Norway* (1957) ICJ Rep 9. It is not unusual to include within the declaration reservations as to time or subject matter or objections ratione personae. As cases such as *Nicaragua v United States (Jurisdiction)* (1984) ICJ Rep 392 indicate, the first phase of international litigation is often concerned with whether jurisdiction arises. The reasons for this are twofold; first jurisdiction can only arise from the consent of the state. Second, states are sometimes reluctant to submit a highly charged dispute to an external judicial body. Thus some of the more intractable problems in the modern world, such as sovereignty over the Falkland Islands or the Iraq/Kuwait boundary, are unlikely ever to come before an international tribunal. A further difficulty is that some states filing declarations under art 36(2) seek to reserve the power to determine jurisdiction themselves; whether this practice is valid is open to question: see *Norwegian Loans Case: France* v *Norway*. In addition the International Court can only rule if there is an actual dispute in existence (*Northern Cameroons Case* (1963) ICJ Rep 15) and will not rule if the matter is no longer in issue: *Nuclear Test Cases: Australia* v *France; New Zealand* v *France* (1974) ICJ Rep 253.

In relation to the quotation we can note that since the state is sovereign its submission to the jurisdiction of an international tribunal is founded on its consent, even if, as with the doctrine of forum prorogatum, that consent arises after the initiation of proceedings. In the modern world states are often prepared to allow technical matters to be determined by an independent tribunal, but they tend to take the view that in the case of politically charged matters, or in those areas where the rules of international law are less certain, it is better to resolve the dispute by negotiation. As Professor Higgins has noted in her published writing, one of the most difficult problems in international law is the limited number of states who have signed the optional clause under art 36(2). Our conclusion must be that the assertion contained within the quotation is broadly correct.

QUESTION THREE

'The approach of municipal courts in dealing with questions of international law increasingly reflects the monist doctrine.'

Do you agree?

University of London LLB Examination
(for External Students) Public International Law June 1997 Q2

General Comment

It is very rare indeed for a paper in public international law not to contain a question on the relationship between international law and municipal law. Some teachers consider this to be the most important subject on the syllabus. To answer this question the student needs to be aware of: (1) the difference of opinion between monists and dualists as to the relationship between international law and municipal law; and (2) the importance of analysing the constitutional structure of any particular State. The United Kingdom's obligations as a result of the Human Rights Act 1998 need examination, particularly in relation to international law. This is a very fair question directed to a cardinal subject in international law.

Skeleton Solution

Introduction – the role of the municipal court – the relationship between the rules of customary international law and municipal law – the relationship between treaty provisions and municipal law – decided cases on the topic – conclusion.

Suggested Solution

This question is concerned with the relationship between public international law and municipal law. For the reasons that appear below the sensible conclusion must be that the quotation represents too broad a proposition.

The relationship between public international law and municipal law is contingent upon the question as to whether one takes a natural law or positivist approach to the basis of international law. The two schools of monism and dualism are reflections of this basic difference of approach. In broad terms, a monist holds that international law and municipal law are part of the same legal order and that international law is supreme. Advocates of a monist approach may be influenced by ethical considerations (eg, Hersch Lauterpacht), or by logical deductions from Kantian philosophy (eg, Hans Kelsen). However, the dualist, being influenced by Hegelian philosophy, holds that international law and municipal law are distinct legal systems, and that in the event of conflict municipal law prevails.

The quotation requires to be analysed by reference to its component parts. The first extract reads 'the approach of municipal courts'; this creates little difficulty. Manifestly a municipal court is concerned to hear the evidence, find the facts and apply the relevant law. In the United Kingdom this will involve consideration of statute law, case law and the relevant and paramount laws of the European Union.

The second element of the quotation reads 'in dealing with questions of international law'. This part requires careful analysis. A diplomat may deal with questions of international law but a municipal court applies legal rules to proven or established facts. The sources of public international law are set out in art 38(1) of the Statute of the International Court of Justice. For present purposes the two principal sources may be expressed as: (1) the rules of customary international law; and (2) treaty provisions.

It is certainly true that many States operate under written constitutions that include a provision that the rules of international law are to be given effect by the municipal court without implementing legislation; indeed, many such clauses may go further and provide that in certain circumstances rules of international law are to prevail over rules of municipal law: see on this art 25 German Constitution 1949; art 55 French Constitution 1958; The Netherlands Constitution 1983, arts 93 and 94. However, the presence of such provisions does not support the monist school; rather it is only by virtue of the provisions in the constitution that the rules of international law are applicable in the municipal sphere.

It is true that for over 200 years rules of customary international law are deemed automatically part of the law of the United Kingdom (*Buvot* v *Barbuit* (1737) Cases Talbot 281; *Triquet* v *Bath* (1764) 3 Burr 1478; *R* v *Keyn, 'The Franconia'* (1876) 2 Ex D 63), provided that such rules are capable of precise formulation (*R* v *Secretary of State for the Home Department, ex parte Thakrar* [1974] QB 684) and not merely the opinion of writers: *West Rand Central Gold Mining Co* v *R* [1905] 2 KB 391. However, such rules will not prevail in the event of a conflict with statutory provisions: *Chung Chi Cheung* v *R* [1939] AC 160; *R* v *Secretary of State for the Home Department, ex parte Thakrar*. The United Kingdom is thus in line with the view of the majority of States in providing for the application of rules of customary law provided there is no conflict with existing municipal law. Thus, it is the relevant precedents of municipal courts that determine the extent of the incorporation of customary international law. This is little support for the monist approach and is perfectly consistent with the dualist school of thought.

In respect of treaty provisions there is even less support for the monist position. The problem is that in the modern world treaties are normally negotiated by the executive branch of government, but if such treaties were capable of changing internal law then the role of the legislature as an organ of democratic government would be undermined. In the United Kingdom it has always been clearly understood that an unincorporated treaty cannot confer legal rights: *The Parlement Belge* (1880) 5 PD 197; *R* v *Secretary of State for the Home Department, ex parte Brind* [1991] 1 AC 696. In Germany and the United States legislation is necessary for all non self-executing treaties. In Belgium legislation is required in respect of all treaties. While there is no uniform practice in respect of treaties, and in each country it is necessary to examine the provisions of the constitution, the fact remains that it is very rare for a treaty per se to supersede municipal legislation. The weight of State practice in both common law and civil law systems is in line with the dualist position.

The quotation alludes to recent practice. In this context it is worth remembering that in recent years there have been three important House of Lords' judgments concerning international obligations arising under treaty. In all three cases the judgment was founded upon the dualist approach: see *R* v *Secretary of State for the Home Department, ex parte Brind; Maclaine Watson & Co Ltd* v *Department of Trade and Industry* [1990] 2 AC 418; *Arab Monetary Fund* v *Hashim (No 3)* [1991] 2 AC 114.

Some might argue that the presence of regional human rights treaties after 1945 is some support for the monist position. This argument is misconceived. It is certainly true that many States now allow a citizen to bring a case before an external human rights court. However, a municipal court will not normally enforce the provisions of a human rights treaty unless that treaty has been incorporated. The fact that many States have legislated to give effect to the European Convention on Human Rights and Fundamental Freedoms 1950 validates the dualist position. The United Kingdom, for example, is now bound by the articles of the European Convention on Human Rights as a result of the Human Rights Act 1998.

A careful analysis of the available evidence supports the dualist position. The dualist approach has been dominant since the eighteenth century when positivists endeavoured to assert the sovereignty of the European nation State. In the nineteenth century dualist arguments were used to justify the Realpolitik of Bismarck and Cavour. It is certainly true that in the twentieth century human rights treaties and efforts at environmental co-operation have attempted to modify the excesses of State sovereignty. However, the fact that public international law is now based on co-operation between States serves to sustain the dualist rather than the monist approach. For these reasons, the proposition stated in the quotation is not supported by an impartial review of the evidence of State practice.

QUESTION FOUR

What problems does a municipal court face in dealing with the legal capacity, constitution and powers of an international organisation?

University of London LLB Examination
(for External Students) Public International Law June 1996 Q2

General Comment

In order to answer this question in a satisfactory manner it is, the writer submits, necessary to consider how the courts of a particular jurisdiction deal with the problem. Analysis of the approach of the United Kingdom courts to this issue is required, with detailed examination of the relevant case law. The candidate will need an understanding of the *Tin Council Case, Arab Monetary Fund* v *Hashim* and *Westland Helicopters Ltd* v *Arab Organisation for Industrialisation*. The relationship between international law and municipal law needs to be understood.

Skeleton Solution

Introduction: status of international organisations – monism and dualism – *J H Rayner* v *Department of Trade and Industry* (*Tin Council Case*) – International Organisations Act 1968 – *AMF* v *Hashim* – *Westland Helicopters* v *AOI* – *Trendtex Trading Corp* v *Central Bank of Nigeria* – conclusion.

Suggested Solution

Whether or not an international organisation is a legal personality and therefore a subject of international law may be ascertained from the treaty setting it up or its personality may be ascertained by examining its functions. The leading authority on this matter is contained in an Advisory Opinion of the ICJ in the *Reparations for Injuries Suffered in the Service of the United Nations* (1949) ICJ Rep 174. The Court was of the opinion that the UN had an international legal personality so that it could achieve its international functions as laid out in the Charter. The Court opined that:

'... 50 States, representing the vast majority of the members of the international community, had the power, in conformity with international law, to bring into being an entity possessing objective international personality, and not merely personality recognised by them alone ...'

While the above provides a guideline for the international community it does not, however, provide a definitive answer for the municipal courts as to whether an international organisation has a legal capacity in the domestic setting. In order to find a starting point for this discussion it is necessary to consider whether the State concerned adheres to the monistic or dualistic view of international law. According to monism, international law and State law are concomitant aspects of the one system, that is law in general. Dualism, on the other hand, sees international law and municipal law as being separate systems of law operating in their own spheres. If a state adheres to the monistic system then international organisations will present the municipal courts with no problem as to their legal capacity. The courts can ascertain this from looking at the decisions of international tribunals and treaties. If, on the other hand, the municipal law adheres to the dualistic system, then the state's courts may not without domestic intervention utilise international legal decisions or treaties to ascertain the existence of a putative international personality.

This problem was highlighted in the United Kingdom when considering the existence or otherwise of three separate international organisations. In *J H Rayner (Mincing Lane)* v *Department of Trade and Industry* (known as the *Tin Council Case*) [1990] 2 AC 418 the House of Lords was presented with the problem of the status of the International Tin Council. This international organisation was set up by treaty and the United Kingdom courts had to ascertain whether it had a status in English law. In the matter of treaties the United Kingdom courts adhere to the 'transformation approach' whereby treaties do not form part of the law of the United Kingdom unless they are 'transformed' into United Kingdom law by an Act of Parliament. Treaties are signed and ratified by the Crown under its prerogative power so to do and the Crown cannot make laws, only an Act of Parliament can: *Case of Proclamations* (1611) 12 Co Rep 74. A treaty and its terms are not part of the law of the United Kingdom and treaties to which the United Kingdom is a party are not self-executing: they do not create rights and obligations.

Therefore, the United Kingdom Parliament had to pass the International Organisations Act 1968 by which Her Majesty's government by Order in Council had the power to 'confer on [an] organisation the legal capacities of a body corporate' if it is an organisation of which the United Kingdom government is a member or if it maintains or proposes to maintain an establishment in the United Kingdom.

Thus the *Tin Council Case* had to establish whether there was such an Order in Council which invested the Tin Council with a separate legal personality. The House of Lords answered in the affirmative. This did not mean, however, that the Council would be treated in the same manner as a United Kingdom organisation. It was a separate persona ficta created by the Order in Council. Without the Order in Council such an organisation is not a legal person and therefore has no legal capacity. With the Order in Council – which Lord Donaldson MR in *Arab Monetary Fund* v *Hashim (No 3)* [1991]

2 AC 114 described as a 'magic wand' – it becomes a person. Lord Donaldson went on to describe it as a person sui generis:

> '... which has all the capacities of a United Kingdom juridical person, but is not subject to the controls to which such a person is subject under United Kingdom law. It is not a native, but nor is it a visitor from abroad. It comes from the invisible depths of outer space.'

The above meant that although the Tin Council was a legal person this did not entail liability for the State-members of the organisation. Lord Oliver in the *Tin Council Case* said:

> '... the ITC though not formally incorporated, was invested with a legal personality distinct from its members, with the consequence that, when it entered into engagements it and not the membership was the contracting party.'

Further problems were raised before the United Kingdom courts when considering the legal status of the Arab Monetary Fund (AMF). In 1976 the Fund was established by international agreement among 20 Arab states and the Palestine Liberation Organisation. Article 2 of the agreement provided that the organisation was to have 'independent judicial personality and ... in particular the right to own, contract and litigate'. The headquarters of the organisation were established in Abu Dhabi. In 1977 the United Arab Emirates passed legislation giving the treaty force of law and thereby conferring legal personality on the AMF, the plaintiff.

Hashim, a former director general of the organisation, was alleged by the plaintiffs to have absconded with around $50 million in funds belonging to the Fund. The plaintiff subsequently found Hashim resident in London and began an action to recover the missing money. In *Arab Monetary Fund* v *Hashim (No 3)* the House of Lords had to consider the legal status of the Fund and whether it was entitled to bring an acton. The United Kingdom had not been a party to the treaty establishing the Fund, nor had the treaty been transformed into English law. Following the reasoning of earlier cases, and in particular the *Tin Council Case,* it would appear that the Fund would have no legal capacity to sue in the United Kingdom courts. However the present case was distinguished in that the Fund was incorporated under the laws of the United Arab Emirates, a State recognised by the United Kingdom, and the United Kingdom courts would recognise a corporate body created by the law of a foreign State so recognised. The AMF was not brought into existence by a treaty in the eyes of the United Kingdom courts, but rather by a decree of a recognised government. This issue is further discussed in *Westland Helicopters Ltd* v *Arab Organisation for Industrialisation* [1995] 2 WLR 126. The Divisional Court was again confronted with the issue of an unenacted treaty (ie, not transformed) which had created an international organisation (see below). Coleman J utilised the reasoning in *Arab Monetary Fund* v *Hashim (No 3)*, holding that the AOI had legal personality in United Kingdom law as a result of it being incorporated by the law of a recognised State: Egypt.

How then are the English courts to interpret the constitutions and powers of an international organisation which the courts have established exist? An answer to this problem was in part supplied by *Westland Helicopters Ltd* v *Arab Organisation for Industrialisation*. Four Arab states (Egypt, United Arab Emirates, Qatar and Saudi Arabia) established by treaty the Arab Organisation for Industrialisation (AOI). The treaty stated that the organisation was to have international personality and that it was not to be governed by the domestic law of any one State. Following a disagreement all the participating States, with the exception of Egypt, called for the Organisation to be disbanded. Egypt, on the other hand, passed a law which purported to take control of the Organisation. The Egyptian law stated that the Organisation was to become an Egyptian legal personality governed by Egyptian law.

Westland Helicopters, following this event, terminated its relationship with the AOI and sued for compensation from the liquidation tribunal of the AOI in Saudi Arabia. Westland failed in this attempt, but after a successful arbitration proceeding in Geneva they sought a garnishee order against British banks which held the AOI funds.

Coleman J in the Divisional Court had to tackle the problem of which law to apply; the Egyptian municipal law or public international law. Egypt claimed that the Egyptian AOI was the successor organisation and that it was therefore the owner of the funds held in the United Kingdom.

Coleman J held that any dispute as to the meaning of the treaty was to be determined by reference to the treaty and to the principles of international law rather than a particular municipal law. If one State's laws were to have priority in the interpretation of the workings of an international organisation this would affront all the other Member States whose laws were to be ignored. It was irrelevant that the Organisation's Headquarters were in Cairo. Inter-State issues are not amenable to resolution by the application of the domestic law of a particular State.

In looking at the constitution and powers of an international organisation the English courts will apply public international law and 'give effect to clearly established rules of international law': *Oppenheimer* v *Cattermole* [1976] AC 249 quoted in *Westland Helicopters* v *AOI*. Customary international public law rules will be 'incorporated' into English law by the courts, provided that they are not at variance with the common law or an Act of Parliament. The common law is, however, presumed to be consistent with the principles of international law and the courts will not apply a precedent which is at variance with a new development of international law: *Trendtex Trading Corp* v *Central Bank of Nigeria* [1977] QB 529. Shaw LJ stated in *Trendtex* that 'the English courts must at any given time discover what the prevailing international rule is and apply that rule'.

When dealing with an international organisation, an English court must determine its existence in the eyes of the United Kingdom and then apply the relevant public international law. If an organisation and its parent treaty have not been transformed into domestic law then the court may adopt a creative approach, as demonstrated with the *Arab Monetary Fund* and *Westland Helicopters* cases. Having established its existence and capacity, the English court must, in the words of Shaw LJ, 'discover' the international rule before interpreting the constitution and powers of the international organisation.

QUESTION FIVE

Caledonia is to gain its independence from Angleterre next year. A conference has been called to draft and to adopt a constitution for Caledonia. You have been entrusted with the task of preparing a draft of that part of the constitution which is to deal with the relationship between Caledonian law and international law.

Draft a provision or provisions to deal with this issue.

Write a brief commentary upon each of your proposed provisions outlining the reasons why the provisions which you are proposing should be preferred to other possible ways of dealing with the relationship between Caledonian law and international law.

University of London LLB Examination
(for External Students) Public International Law June 1993 Q3

General Comment

A reasonably simple question in three parts on the relationship between international law and municipal law. The drafting part depends on the personal opinion of whoever is answering the question, but – whatever that opinion may be – it must be carefully explained and justified in the commentary part, which forms an analysis of the second section of the answer.

Skeleton Solution

Introduction: the importance of securing a satisfactory relationship between international and municipal law – jurisprudence: the two main theories of monism and dualism – judicial approaches in case law – draft constitutional provisions (not a literal attempt at legal drafting!) – commentary: justification of the proposed provisions.

Suggested Solution

It is far from uncommon for cases to arise in which a conflict between international and municipal law occurs; such cases can and do arise at both the national and the international arbitral level. Because these cases often cause surprising acrimony and confusion and can be extremely complicated in their ramifications and effects in constitutional law, it is obviously very important clearly to define the relationship between the two types of law, especially in the municipal sphere. A good example of an ongoing conflict between the two types of law is the *Lockerbie Case: Libya* v *UK and USA* (1992) ICJ Rep 3 and 114, in which case Libya is claiming that it cannot extradite the two Libyan secret service officers suspected of perpetrating the 1989 bombing of a PanAm airliner over Lockerbie in Scotland, because the Libyan constitution prohibits the extradition of any Libyan nationals – but the act of terrorism of which they are suspected is an international crime which is subject to the principle aut dedere, aut punire and is governed by the Montreal Convention for the Suppression of Unlawful Acts against the Safety of Civil Aviation 1971 (to which Libya is a party), as well as general international criminal law relating to jurisdiction and extradition. Libya is thus invoking provisions of its municipal law in order to evade compliance with its international obligations.

There are two main jurisprudential theories concerned with this problematic relationship: monism and dualism. They revolve around the controversy over whether the two types of law are separate or intertwined. Monism holds that both systems are part of the same legal order and therefore one or other of them must be supreme over the other within that order; dualism regards them as two separate legal orders, existing quite independently of one another, so that now one of them is supreme, now the other. Sir Gerald Fitzmaurice – agreeing with the Italian jurist Anzilotti – dismisses the entire controversy as 'unreal, artificial and strictly beside the point', because the two systems are applicable in entirely different fields of activity (quoted in DJ Harris, *Cases and Materials on International Law* (4th ed, 1991) at p69). Fitzmaurice argues that whenever either of them can be said to be in any way superior to the other, that superiority arises not from the content, but from the field of operation – in other words, international law is supreme in the international sphere because that is where it operates. Fitzmaurice's conclusion is:

> '… international law and domestic law as systems can never come into conflict. What may occur is something strictly different, namely a conflict of obligations, or an inability for the State on the domestic plane to act in the manner required by international law.' (Harris, op cit, p71)

This line of argument suggests that when such conflicts do occur they properly form part of the body of rules relating to the conflict of laws, also known as private international law.

The main problem in the UK has always been the doctrine of parliamentary sovereignty which, in the terms of this controversy, has traditionally been interpreted to mean that international law – specifically, treaties – cannot apply in the UK until Parliament has passed legislation to enact them in domestic law. There have of course always been maverick judges, the most prominent of whom has arguably been (the late) Lord Denning, MR (as he was then), who repeatedly in such cases held that customary international law was automatically applicable in the UK without any need for parliamentary enactment – a good example of such a judgment from Lord Denning was his decision in *Trendtex Trading Corporation* v *Central Bank of Nigeria* [1977] QB 529 in relation to the UK's position on state immunity, which was then still at odds with that of the rest of the world. Lord Denning in the *Trendtex* case insisted that whenever international law changed, English law on the relevant point automatically changed with it, whether Parliament liked it or not, and the English courts can and should apply such changes without waiting for statutory enactment.

It must be remembered that Lord Denning's view, eminently sensible though it is, is the view of a maverick, and some much older judicial decisions must be borne in mind. In *Buvot* v *Barbuit* (1737) 25 ER 777 Lord Talbot declared that 'the law of nations, in its full extent, [is] part of the law of England'; in *Triquet* v *Bath* (1764) 3 Burr 1478 Lord Mansfield insistently repeated the same view. In *R* v *Keyn* (1876) 2 Ex D 63, however, Cockburn LCJ in the Court for Crown Cases Reserved indicated that an English court could never apply a previously untested rule of international law in the absence of parliamentary enactment because '[in] so doing we should be unjustifiably usurping the province of the legislature' and categorically stated that even 'the clearest proof of unanimous assent on the part of other nations' was insufficient to justify the application by an English court of a rule of international law not expressly consented to by Parliament. As Hersch Lauterpacht has pointed out, Lord Cockburn's opinion in *R* v *Keyn* does not amount to an outright rejection of the presumption that international law is part of English law, but it is a distinctly cautious and unenthusiastic approach to the problem. Similarly Alverstone LCJ, in *West Rand Central Gold Mining Co* v *R* [1905] 2 KB 391, insisted that any doctrine of international law invoked in an English court must be strictly proved as having been accepted to be binding on nations – in other words, the doctrine of opinio juris et necessitatis. An even more conservatively and dogmatically phrased approach was adopted by Lord Atkin in *Chung Chi Cheung* v *R* [1939] AC 160, when he categorically stated that in the English courts:

'... international law has no validity save in so far as its principles are accepted and adopted by our own domestic law. There is no external power that imposes its rule upon our own code of substantive law or procedure.'

With regard to the validity in English law of treaties, Sir Robert Phillimore in *The Parlement Belge* (1879) 4 PD 129 accepted that the power to make treaties is a prerogative power of the Crown, but added the proviso that any treaty affecting 'the private rights of the subject ... required the sanction of the legislature'. Subsequent judgments have confirmed this attitude, perhaps the most notable one being that of Lord Denning in *R* v *Chief Immigration Officer, ex parte Bibi* [1976] 1 WLR 979, in which he said:

'... I would dispute altogether that [the European Convention on Human Rights] is part of our law. Treaties and declarations do not become part of our law until they are made law by Parliament.'

This contention has now been displaced in the light of the Human Rights Act 1998 which incorporated the European Convention on Human Rights into English law. The case of *R* v *Uxbridge Magistrates' Court, ex parte Adimi and Others* (1999) The Times 12 August provides a useful illustration of the application of international law before the United Kingdom courts.

It follows from all this that whatever provisions are drafted for the Caledonian constitution should make it clear that international customary law will be directly and automatically applicable in the Caledonian courts, but that treaties shall require legislative enactment if – and only if – they affect the private rights of individual citizens; enactment of all other (public) treaties shall be deemed to have automatically occurred on ratification of those treaties by the Caledonian legislature.

The commentary should make it plain that this is the most sensible approach, in line with Lord Denning's pronouncement in the *Trendtex* case and those of Sir Robert Phillimore in *The Parlement Belge*. The other more dogmatic and inflexible attitudes discussed above (especially those of Lord Atkin, Lord Alverstone and Lord Cockburn) should be discarded as too likely to give rise to precisely the kind of problems that the constitutional provisions would be designed to circumvent.

Chapter 4

International Personality

4.1   Introduction

4.2   Key points

4.3   Key cases and legislation

4.4   Questions and suggested solutions

4.1 Introduction

The subject of international personality in international law is a relatively straightforward one which students in general have little difficulty in grasping. States have traditionally been accepted as the sole subjects of international law, but this position has been undermined to a certain extent by recognition of international organisations and individuals as subjects possessing limited capacity. This is the recurring theme of questions in this area of the law.

4.2 Key points

States are the primary subjects of international law

The legal criteria of statehood are generally accepted as being a permanent population, a defined territory, an effective government and capacity to enter into relations with other states. Particular emphasis is placed on the elements of effective government and the capacity to enter into external relations which together signify the independence of a state. However, in the past, entities which have not possessed all these attributes have been received as states by the international community.

Rights and duties of states as subjects of international law

Where states fulfil the criteria for statehood and exercise international personality, a number of rights and consequences flow.

a)   International law is essentially law between states and created by states and international personality permits a state to participate in this process.

b)   Decisions and judgments of the ICJ cannot bind states without their consent to participation in the hearing of the case. For example, in *Case Concerning Land, Island and Maritime Frontier Dispute (El Salvador v Honduras, Nicaragua intervening)* (1992) ICJ

Rep 351 where El Salvador and Honduras submitted their dispute to the Court for resolution and Nicaragua intervened in the proceedings, the decision was binding on Nicaragua only to the extent to which it participated in the proceedings.

c) Only states may institute proceedings before the International Court of Justice: see art 34(1) Statute of the ICJ.

d) In general, only states may seek a remedy for an international wrong, in which case the state is imputed to have suffered the harm: see the *Mavrommatis Palestine Concessions Case* (1924) PCIJ Rep Ser A No 2.

e) In pursuing a claim, a state does not act as an agent of the individual aggrieved, but in its own interest. Compensation obtained belongs to the state and the individual has no legal right to such sums: see *Civilian War Claimants Association v The King* [1932] AC 14.

Non-state entities

A number of international entities are denied status as international persons because they fail to meet the criteria deemed necessary for statehood.

a) Colonies: these are not states because of their lack of capacity to conduct external relations with other states.

b) Mandates and trusteeship territories: these are territories formerly governed by the Axis states prior to the First World War and subsequently placed under the administration of the League of Nations which was replaced by the trusteeship system under the auspices of the United Nations. Such territories have no legal personality while they remain dependent on the supervising state.

Controversial candidates for international personality

a) Liechtenstein was refused membership of the League of Nations because, while the principality possessed fixed frontiers, a permanent population and a stable government, it delegated responsibility for the conduct of foreign policy to other states. However, Liechtenstein is a party to the statute of the International Court.

b) The Holy See was established as a sovereign state by the Lateran Treaty of 1929 despite its minuscule territory and population. It has subsequently acquired membership of the International Labour Organisation and the World Health Organisation.

c) Cyprus attained independence in 1960 by agreement between the United Kingdom, Greece and Turkey and has been admitted to the United Nations. This membership was conferred despite limitations on its sovereignty imposed by art 4 of the 1959 Treaty of Guarantee which gives each guarantor the right to intervene in the internal affairs of the state to maintain the status quo established between the Greek Cypriot and Turkish Cypriot communities.

The personality of international organisations

In the *Reparations for Injuries Suffered in the Service of the United Nations Case* (1949) ICJ Rep 174, the Court upheld the claim of the United Nations to exercise limited international personality. International personality was essential to give effect to the purposes and principles of the organisation and could clearly be presumed from the intentions of the draftsmen of the Charter. The Organisation was a subject of international law and was capable of possessing international rights and duties and had the capacity to maintain its rights by initiating international claims.

Any claim incurred by the organisation must have been incurred in exercise of the legitimate functions of the organisation. As a result, the grant of personality is co-extensive with the powers of the organisation. These powers may be:

a) express: this would include a treaty-making power in relation to matters within the Charter, ie in relation to privileges and immunities under art 105 which resulted in the General Convention on Privileges and Immunities of the United Nations 1946;

b) implied: a power may be implied by necessary implication from the constitutional document of the organisation. For example, the UN possesses an implied treaty-making authority, eg Headquarters Agreement between the United Nations and the United States 1947.

In addition, regional international organisations may also be capable of exercising limited international capacity. Under art 133(3) of the EC Treaty the European Community is empowered to negotiate tariff and trade agreements with third countries to implement the Community's commercial policy.

The personality of international organisations in municipal law

Although the international personality of organisations has been recognised by the ICJ at the international level, it was not until recently that a national court had to consider the implications of this personality in national law. This occurred in *Arab Monetary Fund* v *Hashim and Others (No 3)* [1991] 2 WLR 729. In this case, the English courts held that an international organisation has no personality in English law in the absence of an order-in-council giving such effect, but in the circumstances of this particular case, the locus standi of this organisation could be upheld on the basis of the rule of private international law that confers standing in the English courts to foreign corporate bodies incorporated in other states.

In *Westland Helicopters Ltd* v *Arab Organisation for Industrialisation* [1995] 2 WLR 126 the United Kingdom courts had to interpret the constitutional documents of international organisations in private litigation.

On 9 December 1996 the United Kingdom passed the United Nations Personnel Act 1997 to ratify the Convention on the Safety of the United Nations and Associated Personnel adopted by the General Assembly of the United Nations in 1996. Royal Assent was given on 27 February 1997 and the legislations became effective on 27 April

1997. It provides that any person who attacks UN workers outside the UK shall be guilty of the same offence as if the attack took place in the UK.

Individuals

Individuals per se are deemed objects of international law and do not exercise international rights unless conferred expressly by treaty. In the case *Jurisdiction of the Courts of Danzig (Danzig Railway Officials) Case* (1928) PCIJ Rep Ser B No 15, the International Court held that where an agreement was specifically intended to establish 'definite rules creating individual rights and obligations and enforceable in national courts', international rights could be conferred on individuals. This interpretation of the law has permitted the creation of a number of mechanisms for the exercise of rights by individuals through due processes of international law. In particular, the following instruments are most relevant.

a) The European Convention on Human Rights 1950; the International Covenant on Civil and Political Rights 1966; and the International Covenant on Economic, Social and Cultural Rights 1966.

b) The provisions of the Treaty of Rome which permit individuals to institute proceedings before the Court of Justice of the European Communities.

At the same time, international law imposes duties directly on individuals. Of these the most important include:

a) the duty to refrain from acts of piracy which is defined as a crime humani generis;

b) the duty to refrain from committing crimes against peace, crimes against humanity, war crimes and genocide;

c) hijacking and associated acts are now considered to be crimes of quasi-universal jurisdiction as created by convention: see Tokyo Convention on Offences and Certain Other Acts Committed on Board Aircraft 1963; Hague Convention for the Suppression of Unlawful Seizure of Aircraft 1970; and the Montreal Convention for the Suppression of Unlawful Acts against the Safety of Civil Aviation 1971.

4.3 Key cases and legislation

*   *Case Concerning Land, Island and Maritime Frontier Dispute (El Salvador v Honduras, Nicaragua intervening)* (1992) ICJ Rep 351
    Illustrates the extent to which ICJ judgments are binding on signatory states

*   *East Timor Case: Portugal v Australia* (1995) ICJ Rep 90
    The right of peoples to self-determination is one of the essential principles of contemporary international law

*   *Namibia Case* (1971) ICJ Rep 16
    Deals with the legal status of mandates and trusteeship territories

- *Officer van Justitie* v *Kramer* [1976] ECR 1279
  Illustrates the implications of Community law in international law

- *Reparations for Injuries Suffered in the Service of the United Nations Case* (1949) ICJ Rep 174
  Addresses the issue of international personality of a state

- *Westland Helicopers Ltd* v *Arab Organisation for Industrialisation* [1995] 2 WLR 126
  The issue of the personality of international organisations was addressed

- Montevideo Convention on Rights and Duties of States 1933 – defines the criteria required for statehood

- Vienna Convention on the Law of Treaties 1969 – recognises the concept of 'ius cogens' in international personality

- United Nations Charter 1945 – states, inter alia, that a fixed territory is a basic requirement for statehood

4.4 Questions and suggested solutions

QUESTION ONE

'International law is primarily concerned with rules which govern relations between states, but states are not the only subjects of international law and entities other than states are of growing importance to the international legal system.'

Discuss.

University of London LLB Examination
(for External Students) Public International Law June 2000 Q5

General Comment

International law is concerned with matters that affect international society. In the years since 1945 there has been a significant increase not only in the number of states, but also other international legal persons have begun to emerge. It is not unusual for an examination in public international law to pay some regard to the concept of legal personality. Public international law remains principally concerned with the relations between states, but the well prepared student should also know something about international organisations, and the problems posed by multinational companies whose resources may be greater than that of the individual state. A well-argued answer should also pay some regard to the changing role of the individual within international law.

Skeleton Solution

Describe the role of the state – examine the development of international law – distinguish international organisations, NGOs, individuals and multinational companies – evaluate how legal personality is assessed in respect of insurgents, ethnic minorities and indigenous peoples.

Suggested Solution

The Law of Nations as it developed in the seventeenth and eighteenth century was principally concerned with relations between nation states. From the time of Reformation, Europe the state was the basic legal and political unit and the principal purpose of the Law of Nations was to regulate relations between states. At that time the scope of the subject was restricted to Western Europe, but the basic tenets of the Law of Nations were taken up by the United States after 1789. Just as the American colonists had drawn on John Locke and Thomas Paine in drafting the Constitution, so early Secretaries of State such as Jefferson and Madison had been students of Vattel. Thus the Law of Nations, with its emphasis upon the individual state, ceased to be restricted to Western Europe and was adopted in the New World. The role of the Law of Nations in regulating relations between sovereign rulers was noted by the United States Supreme Court in 1812 in *The Schooner Exchange* v *McFaddon* (1812) 7 Cranch 116.

So one of the roles of the doctrine of recognition was to determine which entities were entitled to acknowledgment as states or governments. It is not surprising, therefore, that some writers have pointed to the Law of Nations as constituting the basic 'rules of the club' in Europe and North America. This emphasis on the state continues today; states remain the central concern of international law, and if one reviews the principal subject areas of the discipline (eg the law of the sea, jurisdiction, the use of force) many are concerned with the rights and obligations of states. Indeed, the role of the state is more important than ever because, with the process of decolonisation, the number of states has risen from 50 in 1945 to over 192.

It is important to note the precise words of the quotation. The quotation begins by noting that 'international law is primarily concerned with rules which govern relations between states'. A sensible judgment is that this proposition is unobjectionable. However, the quotation then proceeds to observe 'states are not the only subjects of international law'. This second aspect, which is directed at the existence of other international legal persons, is certainly correct. One then turns to the third aspect, which reads 'entities other than states are of growing importance to the international legal system'. This is a reference to those entities that may or may not be international legal persons. Taking the three aspects of the quotation together, it is quite clear that one of the most important changes in international law since 1945 has been in the expansion of its scope – part of this is associated with the rise of international legal regulation.

In considering the role of other international legal persons, the author of the quotation has in mind the rise of the international organisation. Although international organisations have been in existence since 1815, they have risen to prominence in the period since 1945. Undeniably one reason for this has been an increase in the regulatory role of international law. Difficult questions can arise as to the powers of an international organisation; normally the organisation will have been established by a treaty made between states, and problems can arise as to matters of interpretation. It was established prior to 1945 that an international organisation, while a subject of international law, did not have a general competence but only enjoyed those powers endowed by its constituent statute: see *Jurisdiction of the European Commission of the Danube* (1929) PCIJ Ser B No 14. The legal personality of an international institution was settled beyond doubt in the *Reparation for Injuries Suffered in the Service of the United Nations Case* (1949) ICJ Rep 174. Thus, in the *Legality of the Threat or Use of Nuclear Weapons (Request for Advisory Opinion by the General Assembly of the United Nations)* (1996) ICJ Rep 66 the International Court of Justice could accept as trite law the fact that an international organisation was an international legal person, but only with a competence deriving from its internal constitution.

The quotation proceeds to note the importance of entities that, while not international legal persons, are of importance to the international legal system. One might first note the role of the Non Governmental Organisation (NGO). Although not strictly a subject of international law, it would be wrong not to pay proper regard to the role of the NGO. In some instances the NGO may have consultative status, as is the case with relations with the United Nations Economic and Social Council (ECOSOC) or the United Nations Commission on Sustainable Development. The history of post war politics testifies to the rise of single issue pressure groups, and international law is no exception. It is rare for an event in international society to pass without some involvement by an NGO. In recent years one only has to consider the role of Amnesty International in *R v Bow Street Metropolitan Stipendiary Magistrate, ex parte Pinochet Ugarte (No 3)* [2000] 1 AC 147 or the role of Greenpeace in the *Rainbow Warrior Case* (1987) 26 ILM 1346. One reason for this development is undoubtedly the technical nature of the material in areas such as environmental law and human rights law: a role clearly exists for the NGO that seeks to gather and analyse relevant information.

It was often said that the individual was the object, not a subject, of international law. Certainly this was so in the nineteenth century, when many European states did not even allow all their citizens the right to vote. However, since 1945 it is clear that this opinion requires to be modified; the individual may acquire rights and be subject to duties under international law. An individual may bring a case under international or regional human rights law against the government of a state, while at the other end of the spectrum individuals are increasingly answerable for breaches of international humanitarian law. This general trend will come to fruition when the Rome Statute on the International Criminal Court 1998 comes into force. In the case of human rights law, if the individual is treated as a legal person, such personality can only be derivative because it is the making of the treaty by the state that creates the legal right.

As the quotation indicates other entities are of importance within the international legal system. Of particular relevance is the Transnational Company (TNC) whose economic power may exceed that of many states. The decisions of such companies may have important effects on investment, employment and prosperity within particular states.

Indeed, multinational or Transnational Companies are often in a strong bargaining position when negotiating with individual states. In some instances companies may enter into agreements with states, and such agreements may include a choice of law clause indicating that any dispute is to be determined by international law. But, however powerful such entities, they will be subject to the municipal corporate law of their place of domicile, and while economically influential they are not international legal persons in the accepted sense. Thus an agreement between a state and a multinational enterprise is not a treaty: see *Anglo-Iranian Oil Co Case* (1952) ICJ Rep (Pleadings) 93. Nevertheless the increasing role of the corporate entity is illustrated by the changing rules on access to international and regional tribunals. While art 34 of the Statute of the International Court of Justice provides only for jurisdiction over states, the Iran-United States Claims Tribunal allows claims to be made by companies subject to certain conditions.

A review of international society indicates that there are other entities that may be regarded as distinct legal subjects. Particularly important is the status of insurgents. Such groups have been recognised as distinct subjects in international law, and arts 14 and 15 of the First Draft of the International Law Commission Draft Articles recognise the existence of such groups by providing that their activities shall not normally entail state responsibility. Various national liberation movements have been given observer status at the United Nations: see *Applicability of the Obligation to Arbitrate under s21 of the United Nations Headquarters Agreement* (1988) ICJ Rep 12.

In the years since 1945 the international community has been more concerned than in the past to promote the peaceful settlement of disputes. One of the major causes of tension in the modern world has been the rise of ethno nationalism. To combat this problem the United Nations has been anxious to accord respect to the rights of minorities, and this trend has been given effect to in the United Nations Declaration on the Rights Belonging to National, Ethnic, Religious and Linguistic Minorities 1992. Such a document indicates, however, that nothing is to be done to undermine the territorial integrity of existing states. It is not the case that such minorities are international legal persons, simply that international law recognises their rights; normally such rights are to be accommodated within the human rights framework of a particular state. Such an approach avoids the growth of potentially dangerous claims for self-determination.

One of the most significant academic trends in the last 50 years has been the steady development of interest in social and economic history. This development has lead to a steady rise in interest in the welfare of indigenous peoples, such as the Aborigines in Australia and the Indians (Native Americans) in the United States. The term 'indigenous people' has tended to focus on those groups that can show a historical continuity with pre-colonial society; in many cases such groups were badly treated in the past. The rights of such people were acknowledged in Principle 22 of the Rio Declaration on Environment and Development 1992 and later in the United Nations Draft Declaration on the Rights of Indigenous Peoples 1994.

In summary, therefore, we can say that the assertion made in the quotation is correct. International law is principally concerned with the relations between states, but as with any legal subject it has to accommodate to economic and social changes. The economic power of the Transnational Company is such that it cannot be ignored. Similarly, the potential for conflict arising from ethnic tension is such that it is sensible to pay regard to the interests of minorities and indigenous peoples. Most importantly, the abuses of state power in the twentieth century have lead to the development of an international and regional human rights law which makes the individual a central concern of international law. The quotation is therefore correct in observing that particular entities are now of growing importance, notwithstanding the fact that they may not all be full legal persons.

QUESTION TWO

Critically analyse the factors which determine whether an entity fulfils the criteria for statehood under international law.

University of London LLB Examination
(for External Students) Public International Law June 1999 Q3

General Comment

As the original role of international law was to regulate the relations between states, it is perhaps not surprising that examination papers often contain questions that centre upon legal personality and the criteria for statehood. This is understandable given that in the period since 1945 the number of states has increased almost fourfold to 180. The present question is directed to the criteria for statehood.

Skeleton Solution

The role of the state – the criteria for statehood in international law – territory – population – government – ability to conduct external relations – recognition – problems of secession – self-determination – acquisition of territory by force.

Suggested Solution

International law is concerned principally with relations between states. Although other international legal persons now exist, states remain the cardinal legal persons. The original role of international law was to regulate the relations between states. As a legal concept the state is subject to certain criteria. In the nineteenth century customary international law began to stipulate certain criteria: these were evidence of a defined territory, a permanent population and a government. A fourth requirement, namely the capacity to enter into relations with other states, has been added in the twentieth century.

In respect of the first requirement, while there must be territory existing between boundaries, the precise limits of these boundaries need not be permanently settled. The uncertainty of many such boundaries was recognised by the International Court of Justice in the *North Sea Continental Shelf Cases* (1969) ICJ Rep 3. The concept of territory includes air space above the land and the earth down into the centre of the globe. In accordance with the terms of the Law of the Sea Convention 1982, territory will include the 12 miles of the territorial sea. A state may be recognised notwithstanding that its precise boundaries are unsettled, as was the case with Israel in 1948. One of the principal objects of international law is to stipulate how a state may acquire territory, as is indicated below.

The second requirement of international law is that there should be a permanent population; the nature of the permanent population is defined by reference to the internal law of citizenship. In principle, a state is allowed considerable latitude as to who it considers to be its nationals, although much depends on the precise context: see *Nationality Decrees in Tunis and Morocco Case* (1923) PCIJ Rep Ser B No 4 and the *Nottebohm Case: Liechtenstein v Guatemala* (1955) ICJ Rep 4. The absence of a permanent population precludes statehood; however, the population may include nomads (as in the case of Somalia); the population may be small (as in the case of Belgium) or large (as in the case of China). In the modern world the economic power and influence of a state bears little relationship to the size of its population.

The third requirement is that there should be effective control by a government. This is a question of degree and temporary ineffectiveness is no barrier. However, if there is no control over the territory, the criterion has not been met; thus the 'State of Palestine' declared by Palestinian organisations in 1988 was not a state, because of a lack of effective control over the territory. However, the existence of a civil war may deprive the government of control, but it does not prejudice the existence of the state: so in *Republic of Somalia v Woodhouse Drake and Carey (Suisse) SA* [1992] 3 WLR 744 Hobhouse J regarded Somalia as a state, even though the evidence indicated that for a time it did not have an effective government. In like terms Lebanon continued to be regarded as a state even though, after 1975, civil war was endemic. Occupation as such does not lead to the extinction of the state, as was instanced by the experience of Germany and Japan after 1945. A state may continue to exist even where the effectiveness of its government depends on the power of others, as was the case with Afghanistan after the invasion of Soviet forces in 1979.

The requirement of effective control extends to both internal and external matters. The Montevideo Convention on the Rights and Duties of States 1933 reflects Latin American practice and adds the fourth criterion that the state should have the capacity to enter into relations with other states. Thus a state which agrees to act under the direction of another in the conduct of its external relations would not meet this test.

The criteria for the acknowledgment of the existence of a state are reasonably well established in international law. As with so many areas of law, the difficulty lies not in stating the general principles but in the application of those principles to concrete situations. In the context of actual recognition it is often the case that recognition in the modern world is collective. Clearly, recognition is an area influenced by political considerations and, regardless of whether its effect is constitutive or declaratory, it is obvious that practical problems can arise. It will be for historians to determine whether the decision of Germany to press for recognition of Croatia and Slovenia contributed to the spread of the conflict in Yugoslavia. As the civil war in Yugoslavia indicates, a new state may be refused recognition unless it is prepared to enter into certain guarantees about human rights. A second aspect of statehood is that most municipal legal systems provide for immunity from jurisdiction: this immunity will only operate if the fact of statehood can be established or some degree of recognition has been accorded: see *The Christina* [1938] AC 485.

A third aspect of statehood concerns the stability of the unit itself. In general, international law favours respect for the boundaries of existing states: see Declaration on the Principles of International Law Concerning Friendly Relations and Co-operation among States in Accordance with the Charter of the United Nations 1970. It therefore follows that international society does not support secession, and this reluctance has only been increased by the experience of the dismemberment of Yugoslavia. Thus in 1968 Biafra only received a limited number of recognitions, and the example of Bangladesh stands out as a limited exception.

Closely related to questions of secession is the principle of self-determination. This principle, which derives from the Versailles Conference in 1919, was easy to apply when it was simply a matter of ending colonial rule. The problem arises as to how it should be applied when there are a number of ethnic minorities within a particular state. The experience of the dismemberment of Yugoslavia indicates the turmoil that can arise when ethnic groups seek to carve out distinct territorial units. It has been clear from 1919 that there must be limits to how far the principle of self-determination can be pushed otherwise, as Robert Lansing noted, there would be a danger of having economically unviable states. A further point concerns the constitutional nature of the state itself. In the Anglo American tradition, a state may contain a number of ethnic or religious groups who share a common citizenship and are united by allegiance to certain political institutions. This view contrasts with that held in Europe which stresses the Volk or the ethnic nature of a state. The compromise after 1945 has increasingly been to stress the importance of maintaining existing territorial boundaries, but also to demand that the majority within that state pay proper regard to the civil liberties of the minority.

As well as respect for existing boundaries, international law is today founded upon a view that a state shall not seek to acquire property by force; this principle arose during the time of the League of Nations and is now set out art 2 of the United Nations Charter. There has thus been clear condemnation when any state sought to acquire territory by force; examples are afforded by the seizure of Manchuria in 1932 and the attempts to assert sovereignty in respect of the Falkland Islands (1982), Kuwait (1990) and Northern Cyprus (1983).

It is often said that the subject of the recognition of states is one of the areas of international law most influenced by politics. Sometimes the criteria have been met, but recognition is withheld for political reasons; the experience of East Germany after 1949 is often raised as an example. Today, because of the increasing importance of international organisations, a new state will be more concerned with meeting certain common standards. Collective recognition and admission to international organisations is of increasing importance. As the experience of the EU Commission on Yugoslavia indicates, any entity seeking recognition as a new state in Europe will have to offer constitutional guarantees of human rights. In the last 100 years the criteria for statehood have changed little: what has changed is the increasing insistence that governments within such states meet certain minimum standards of conduct.

QUESTION THREE

'The basis for international environmental law is the rule enshrined in Principle 21 of the 1972 Stockholm Declaration on the Human Environment which requires States to ensure that activities within their jurisdiction or control do not cause damage to the environment of other States or of areas beyond the limits of national jurisdiction. The major international environmental treaties, including those relating to ozone, climate change, biodiversity, hazardous waste, and the law of the sea, are simply footnotes on this fundamental principle of customary international law.'

Discuss.

University of London LLB Examination
(for External Students) Public International Law June 1997 Q8

General Comment

This is not a particularly easy question. The quotation itself is very broad and probably capable of more than one interpretation. The candidate is asked simply to 'discuss' the quotation. It is common today for a paper on public international law to contain a question on environmental law. The less well-prepared student may revise for such a question on the basis that it is self contained. This quotation covers a wide area and may be interpreted as giving rise to three questions: (a) did Principle 21 state the position in customary international law in 1972?; (b) if not, has it acquired the status of a rule of customary international law by virtue of conduct since that date?; and (c) has Principle 21 been adopted in any multilateral treaties? The examiner is not seeking a general discussion about the importance of environmental law but is asking the student to explain how the vague and uncertain provisions of customary international law have been set aside to such an extent that environmental law is now the fastest growing area of public international law.

Skeleton Solution

Introduction – customary international law in relation to the environment prior to

1972 – the context of the Stockholm Declaration 1972 and Principle 21 – developments since 1972 – the precise meaning of the quotation – conclusion.

Suggested Solution

There is no doubt that in the last quarter of a century environmental law has developed faster than any other area of public international law. The reasons for this change are probably threefold, namely: the realisation that environmental damage and pollution will affect more than one state; the knowledge that effective remedial action cannot be taken by a single state acting alone; and the realisation that many of the problems of environmental law involve a delicate balance between the demand for economic growth and the need for environmental protection. All these factors have contributed to the need for international co-operation within this sphere.

The quotation itself raises three aspects which may be expressed as follows: (a) the fundamental principles of customary international law as applied to the environment; (b) the precise meaning of Principle 21 of the Stockholm Declaration of 1972; and (c) the principles underlying the development of the treaty regime since 1972. It is sensible to take each of these matters in turn.

The fundamental principles of customary international law as applied to the environment

In customary international law there were few restrictions on the conduct of a state operating within its own territory. Most writers accept that prior to 1972 customary international law was in an early stage of development when dealing with environmental problems. In the *Trail Smelter Arbitration* (1941) 9 ILR 315 it was asserted that a state may not knowingly allow its territory to be used in a manner that would cause serious injury to the physical environment of another state. However, the arbitrators candidly acknowledged that they would be obliged to draw upon the content of municipal law, and they stated that even as late as the 1930s they were unable to locate any cases on air or water pollution decided by international tribunals.

Although there were later arbitrations (*Lac Lenoux Arbitration* (1957) 24 ILR 101; *Gut Dam Arbitration* (1968) 8 ILM 118) it cannot be claimed that they greatly extended the scope of customary international law in this field. Thus, in customary international law, particularly in cases of transboundary damage, the emphasis was upon general principles rather than the formulation of detailed rules. Examples would be the principle of sic utere tuo ut alienum non laedas (use your own so as not to damage another), or the principle of 'good neighbourliness' (ie, bon voisinage). Thus, the foundation of customary law was built on the concept of state responsibility and analogies drawn from unreasonable user of land in the municipal law of nuisance. The difficulty with asserting that there was a corpus of customary international law in this area was: (a) there were only limited precedents; (b) the cases concentrated upon remedies for damage after the event; (c) it was unclear whether a state was liable in the absence of negligence; and (d) it was far from certain whether the state would be liable if it had no knowledge of the offending act.

Therefore, insofar as the quotation implies that there was a coherent system of international environmental law prior to 1972, the evidence points in the opposite direction.

The effect of Principle 21 of the Stockholm Declaration 1972

It is generally accepted that international environmental law has developed following the United States Conference on the Human Environment held in 1972. In considering Principle 21 it is very important to note that the quotation omits the important preliminary words that read 'states have, in accordance with the Charter of the United Nations and the principles of international law, the sovereign right to exploit their own resources pursuant to their own environmental policies and the responsibility'. It was clear from the outset that the principle represented a difficult balancing act between 'rights' and 'responsibilities'.

The second important point to remember is that Principle 21 was to be read with Principle 22 and Principle 24. Principle 22 required states to co-operate in order to develop further international law on the environment, while Principle 24 required states to co-operate on matters pertaining to the protection of the environment. Manifestly the three principles have to be read together and since 1972 they have been interpreted as placing a duty upon a state not only to exercise due diligence to prevent environmental harm but also to co-operate with others in so acting. Moreover, this duty extended to common areas or, as Principle 21 expressed it, to 'areas beyond the limits of national jurisdiction'. It is beyond doubt that this was an advance on the position in customary international law where the emphasis was simply upon making recompense for damage done. The clear intention was that international environmental law should develop a framework of bilateral and multilateral treaties. There is little doubt that those drawing up the Stockholm Declaration intended to establish principles for the future; these principles were based not on specific rules of customary international law but on general ethical principles. Indeed, if one reads the preamble to the Stockholm Declaration it is clear that human rights thinking contributed much to the formulation of the principles. It must therefore be very doubtful whether the quotation is correct in implying that Principle 21 merely re-stated rules of customary international law.

Conduct since 1972

As the question indicates it is important to pay regard to the precise terms of the multilateral conventions drawn up since 1972. Many of these contain provisions that define obligations in terms of the exercise of due diligence. An example would be art 194(1) of the Law of the Sea Convention 1982 which reads in part 'states shall take, individually or jointly as appropriate, all measures consistent with this Convention that are necessary to prevent, reduce and control pollution of the marine environment from any source ... and they shall endeavour to harmonise their policies in this connection'. Examples of like provisions are to be found in the Vienna Convention for the Protection of the Ozone Layer 1985, art 2(1); Framework Convention on Climate Change 1992, art

3; UN Convention on Biological Diversity 1992, art 3; Basel Convention on the Control of Transboundary Movement of Hazardous Waste 1989, art 4. To the extent that the quotation implies that these treaties build upon the Stockholm Declaration 1972 then there can be no dispute. However, the detailed terms of these multilateral conventions go far beyond anything envisaged under customary international law.

The quotation itself

It is possible that the quotation should be interpreted as asserting that even if Principle 21 did not state a rule of customary international law in 1972 then developments since that date enable one to claim that it now represents the state of customary law. There is certainly some evidence for this viewpoint. First, the principle has been accepted in subsequent multilateral conventions, either in the text itself (art 3 UN Convention on Biological Diversity 1992) or in the preamble (Framework Convention on Climate Change 1992). Second, the principle in modified form has been inserted in subsequent 'soft law' sources such as art 2 of the Rio Declaration of the UN Conference on Environment and Development 1992. Third, it is important to note how the matter has been viewed by the International Court of Justice. Some writers argue that the *Corfu Channel (Merits) Case* (1949) ICJ Rep 4 propounded the principle that a state should not knowingly allow its territory to be used for acts contrary to the rights of other states. A generation later in the *Nuclear Test Cases* (*Australia* v *France*) (1974) ICJ Rep 253 counsel for Australia relied upon Principle 21, and the dissenting opinion of Judge de Castro appeared to proceed on the basis that Principle 21 had the status of a rule of customary international law. Having recognised the global nature of this problem, the Kyoto Treaty was signed in 2002. In very basic terms, this Treaty commits industrialised nations to reducing emissions of greenhouse gases, principally carbon dioxide, by around 5.2 per cent below their 1990 levels over the next decade. However, the Kyoto Treaty does not actually come into operation until 2008.

This theme was taken up again in the *Request for an Examination of the Situation in Accordance with Paragraph 63 of the Nuclear Test Cases 1974* (1995) ICJ Rep 288 where the Court made reference to 'the obligations of states to respect and protect the environment'. Indeed, the subject was taken further in the scholarly dissenting opinion of Judge Weeramantry. Shortly afterwards, in the *Advisory Opinion on the Threat or Use of Nuclear Weapons* (1996) 35 ILM 809, the Court observed:

> 'The existence of the general obligation of States to ensure that activities within their jurisdiction and control respect the environment of other States or of areas beyond national control is now part of the corpus of international law relating to the environment.'

Conclusion

The sensible conclusion must be that it is going too far to claim that Principle 21 codified customary international law in 1972. However, the acceptance of Principle 21 by the International Court of Justice, and its adoption in multilateral law-making conventions, means that it is strongly arguable that the principle has now acquired the force of a rule of customary international law. Subject to the reservations stated above the quotation is broadly correct.

QUESTION FOUR

'The subjects of law in any legal system are not necessarily identical in their nature or in the extent of their rights, and their nature depends upon the needs of the community.' (Opinion of the International Court of Justice in *Reparation for Injuries Suffered in the Service of the United Nations.*)

Discuss, with references to the subjects of the international legal system.

University of London LLB Examination
(for External Students) Public International Law June 1991 Q2

General Comment

An essay-type question concerning the relationship between the subjects of international law and international society.

Skeleton Solution

Traditional position – states as international persons – the decision of the ICJ in the *Reparations Case* – examples of organisations with personality.

Suggested Solution

Traditionally, states were believed to be the sole subjects of rights and duties, but since the Second World War, international organisations have increasingly been recognised as possessing such attributes. In contrast, individuals are rarely considered to be capable of exercising international rights and duties. Despite the existence of human rights instruments such as the 1950 European Convention on Human Rights and the 1966 International Covenant on Civil and Political Rights, in the absence of treaties establishing petition mechanisms, individuals generally continue to remain excluded from the international domain.

The two main subjects of the international legal system are therefore states and international organisations.

Statehood is generally defined by art 1 of the Montevideo Convention on the Rights and Duties of States 1933. This defines a state as follows:

'The State as a person of international law should possess the following qualifications:
(a) a permanent population;
(b) a defined territory;
(c) a government in control;
(d) the capacity to enter into relations with other states.'

Whether or not a state possesses a permanent population and a defined territory is largely a matter of fact. Further, it is generally acknowledged that there are no lower limits on these criteria. For example, the state of Nauru has less than 10,000 inhabitants and is only eight square miles in territory. Similarly, the Holy See, Lichtenstein, and Monaco are all recognised as states despite their small size in terms of both population and territory.

The requirement of a government gives rise to greater problems. This brings into play the issue of recognition by other states of governments that have come to power through extra-constitutional means. Recognition of governments is a political process that has little to do with factual circumstances. Thus, the United Kingdom and the United States declined to recognise the government of the Soviet Union after the 1917 revolution for a considerable number of years. Equally, the United States refused to recognise the Communist government of China and prevented it taking its seat in the United Nations until the 1970s by means of the veto.

The capacity to enter into foreign relations with other states is a question of the degree of independence maintained by an entity. To qualify as a state, the entity must be subject to no other sovereign power or the will of another state; it must be able to act independently subject only to the obligations established by international law.

There are numerous subsets of statehood, although these have acquired less and less significance as colonial domination has been reversed. In the past, colonies, mandate territories, and protectorates all existed. After the decolonisations of the 1960s, only protectorates remain a relevant classification. But, nowadays, since the termination of the trusteeship of the United Nations, protectorates are no longer a significant category, although the case of Namibia remains unsettled despite four references to the ICJ.

There is no international treaty defining the rights of international organisations to participate in the international legal system. To a large extent, the applicable principles have been established by the International Court, particularly in the *Reparations Case* (1949) ICJ Rep 174 which concerned the issue whether the United Nations could validly make a claim against Israel for the loss of one of its officials. The Court had to answer two main questions: (a) whether the United Nations possessed international personality; and (b) if the answer to the first question was affirmative, whether the organisation had capacity to bring an international claim.

The Court answered the first question in the affirmative. The members of the United Nations had given the organisation functions and tasks. These functions could 'only be explained on the basis of the possession of a large measure of international personality and the capacity to operate upon an international plane'. Therefore the members had endowed the organisation with the competence to carry out these functions effectively.

The Court also acknowledged that the United Nations possessed capacity to bring the claim. The competence of the organisation was derived from its purposes and functions 'as specified or implied in its constituent documents and developed in practice'. Competence to bring such a claim was, in the circumstances, an implied power derived from the principle of reparation in the event of the commission of a wrong against an international person.

Numerous international organisations have been created with express international personality. Thus, the three European Communities Treaties, and in particular the EC Treaty, expressly provide that 'the Community shall have legal personality'. This extends not only to the Community's position within the legal systems of the Member States, but also to its international activities. Although the European Community has never initiated an international claim before the International Court, it participates in numerous international organisations, including the GATT, it maintains diplomatic personnel in many countries, and has entered into numerous bilateral and multilateral agreements with other states.

QUESTION FIVE

a) 'Only the sovereign states enjoy international legal personality.' Discuss.

b) Under the constitution of the Federation of Amelia, the province of Barabia is guaranteed full autonomy in respect of certain 'provincial' matters and the right to enter into agreements with other states on matters within the competence of the provincial legislature. The constitution of the state further provides that federal troops are not to be deployed in the province without the consent of the provincial government. Recently, the federal government of Amelia has threatened to station troops in Barabia, irrespective of whether the Barabian provincial government consents or not. It has also threatened to terminate certain agreements concluded by the Barabian provincial government with the neighbouring state of Candida.

To what extent, if at all, does international law prevent the federal government of Amelia from carrying out its threats?

University of London LLB Examination
(for External Students) Public International Law June 1988 Q4

General Comment

A question relating to international personality but with an added complication.

Skeleton Solution

A defence of the view that only states have international legal personality – criticisms of that view: international organisations – further criticisms of that view: individuals also, in certain circumstances have international legal personality.

Suggested Solution

a) The view that only states enjoy legal personality is supported in part by the definition set out in the Montevideo Convention on the Rights and Duties of States

1933, which elaborates a number of criteria for statehood that were generally recognised in customary law. Article 1 of the Convention stipulates:

'The state as a person of international law should possess the following qualifications:
(a) a permanent population;
(b) a defined territory;
(c) a government in control;
(d) the capacity to enter into relations with other states.'

This statement has substantial ramifications. A state requires a non-nomadic population, and therefore permanency would exclude the population of the Holy See from being a state. The fact that Israel did not possess a defined territory did not prevent that state from becoming a state in 1948. Further, effective government is a criteria which is subject to evaluation in the light of political decision-making.

A state does not cease to exist, however, when it is temporarily deprived of an effective government as a result of civil war or similar upheavals. The requirement of effective government is strictly applied when part of a population attempts to break away from a pre-existing state. Overt foreign intervention in these situations is often the decisive factor in determining statehood since such intervention raises the possibility that the local authorities may not in fact be a government but merely agents of the intervening power. Independence from foreign control is thus essential for independence and sovereignty. This brings us to the final criterion of statehood: independence and capacity for foreign relations.

If a state fails to have the capacity to conduct foreign relations with other states, it cannot be considered in terms of international law to be a complete international entity. However, throughout history there have been exceptions to this rule.

i) Liechtenstein

    The League of Nations determined that since Liechtenstein 'had chosen to depute to others some of the attributes of sovereignty' (such as customs, postal administration, diplomatic representation and the maintenance of armed forces) it would be unable to 'discharge all the international obligations which membership of the League entailed'. Liechtenstein, however, is a party to the Statute of the ICJ which is limited to states: arts 34 and 35.

ii) Mini or micro states

    Monaco, Nauru, the Vatican City and the Holy See all fail to meet the criteria of statehood, as listed in the Montevideo Convention, but are considered states by the international community.

iii) Protected states

    As a product of nineteenth century imperialism, a number of de facto states were subject to foreign control of their external policy, leaving internal authority to the indigenous population. For example, Bhutan agreed in the 1949 Treaty of

Friendship between India and Bhutan 'to be guided by the advice of the Government of India with regard to its external relations'. However, Bhutan was admitted to the United Nations in 1971 and has expanded its relations with China and Nepal since 1980.

Other than such state entities, international organisations and individuals may be subjects of international law.

In the *Reparations Case* (1949) ICJ Rep 174, the International Court determined that the United Nations Organisation had limited international personality. The Court decided that there could be legal persons with rights different from those of states. The UN Charter had established the organisation for particular purposes and according to specific principles. International personality was essential to give effect to those purposes and principles and could therefore be presumed to have been intended by the drafters of the Charter. The UN Charter had conferred 'objective international personality' on the organisation erga omnes. Many other international organisations have also been granted a limited form of legal personality (eg the European Community).

Traditionally, individuals were considered to be merely objects of the law and not subjects. In the *Mavrommatis Palestine Concessions Case* (1924) PCIJ Rep Ser A No 2, the Court stated:

> 'By taking up the case of one of its subjects ... a state is in reality asserting its own rights – its rights to ensure, in the person of its subjects, respect for the rules of international law.'

However, the Court reviewed this position in the subsequent case *Jurisdiction of the Courts of Danzig* (1928) PCIJ Rep Ser B No 15. The Court held that the agreement between the free city of Danzig and Poland was specifically intended to establish 'definite rules creating individual rights and obligations and enforceable in national courts'. Thus, it was recognised that states could by treaty, give individuals the status of direct subjects of international law.

Similarly, the Fourth Geneva Convention 1949 protects individuals who fall into the hands of enemy forces during an armed conflict or military occupation. Both the European Convention on Human Rights 1950, in art 25, and the Inter-American Convention on Human Rights 1969, art 44, allow individuals to petition internationally constituted commissions and cases may proceed to a Court of Human Rights.

Thus, the individual is increasingly endowed with international legal rights and the capacity to pursue these. Such rights are derived from agreements between states, but can also be exercised against states. The statement that 'only sovereign states enjoy international personality' reflects a traditional theory that no longer holds good today. C Hillgruber in his article, 'The Admission of New States in the International Community' (1998) 9 EJIL 491, argues that if a 'new state' passes the requirements imposed by the international community then it will be recognised as a new a sovereign state.

b) Amelia is a federation, that is a union of states. The basic feature of federal states is that authority over internal affairs is divided by a constitution between the federal authorities and the member states of the federation, while foreign affairs are normally handled exclusively by the federal authorities.

Barabia is thus unusual for a province in that it has been granted the right to enter into agreements with other states. This is reminiscent of the 1944 Constitution of the USSR which allowed the Ukraine and Byelo-Russia (two member states of the USSR) to become members of the United Nations along with the USSR itself. More recently, the Province of Quebec has signed treaties relating to cultural matters with France and other French-speaking countries under powers delegated by the federal government of Canada.

International law is concerned with states capable of carrying on international relations – consequently the federal state is regarded as a state for the purposes of international law, but the member states of the federation are not. However, Barabia has concluded agreements with the neighbouring independent state of Candida and Candida must have been satisfied that Barabia was able to enter into such agreements. Amelia would have to prove that Barabia did not have the legal authority to carry out those agreements and at any rate as the federal authority she would be ultimately responsible for the acts of the provincial government. Candida could well argue that she only entered the agreement because she understood that Amelia would ultimately be responsible. Therefore, Amelia cannot terminate the agreements entered into by Barabia.

Among the most cardinal principles of international law are the sovereign equality of states and the related rights of domestic jurisdiction and non-interference. Amelia has every right to station troops in Barabia if she so pleases. No other state might intervene on behalf of Barabia unless it can be shown that Barabia has a right to self-determination (on the grounds that it has full autonomy in certain matters and the limited capacity to enter into international relations). Even then, this claim would not succeed since Resolution 1514 (XV) passed by the General Assembly in 1960 declares inter alia:

> 'Any attempt aimed at the partial or total disruption of the national unity and the territorial integrity of a country is incompatible with the purposes and principles of the Charter of the United Nations.'

Chapter 5

Recognition of States and Governments

5.1   Introduction

5.2   Key points

5.3   Key cases and legislation

5.4   Questions and suggested solutions

5.1 Introduction

The concept of recognition functions at the interface between law and politics in international relations. Recognition of states and governments is essentially a political act which involves international and municipal legal implications. Between these two dimensions, the legal effects and consequences of recognition vary considerably. However, both doctrine and state practice have remained incoherent and indecisive in relation to the role of recognition in contemporary international affairs. Students should be aware of the growing dichotomy in theory and in practice relating to the operation of recognition and should also be familiar with both the international and municipal legal connotations associated with recognition and non-recognition.

5.2 Key points

Recognition of states and governments

The doctrine of recognition applies equally to states and governments but only operates where changes in the political landscape have been brought about through extra-constitutional means such as civil war, wars of independence or self-determination or through the intervention of foreign powers in the internal affairs of a state. Recognition may be employed as a political device and used to express approbation or denunciation of the political nature of the state or government in question. Expressions of political approval or disapproval are more often reserved for the recognition or non-recognition of revolutionary governments and not newly emergent states.

Express and implied recognition

Recognition may be express, through a formal acknowledgement of the existence of a state or government or in the negotiation of a bilateral treaty formally regulating the relations between the states or governments in question. Alternatively, recognition may be implied by an unequivocal act intended to indicate that recognition is being conferred. Implied recognition is commonly achieved through the exchange of ambassadors or diplomatic missions.

Constitutive and declaratory theories of recognition

In international legal doctrine a profound difference of opinion has emerged as to the effects of recognition in international law. This difference has resulted in the formulation of two separate theories of recognition.

a) The constitutive theory provides that states and governments do not legally exist until recognised by the international community. Unless and until recognition is afforded, no international personality is established.

b) The declaratory theory asserts that the coming into existence of a state or government is a matter of fact and recognition is merely an acknowledgment of an existing factual situation. According to this view, states and governments are conferred with international personality at the moment at which they come into existence.

Criteria for the recognition of states

To recognise a state is to acknowledge that an entity fulfils the conditions of statehood as required by international law. The Montevideo Convention on Rights and Duties of States 1933, art 1, provides:

'The state as a person of international law should possess the following qualifications:
(a) a permanent population;
(b) a defined territory;
(c) a government in control;
(d) the capacity to enter into relations with other states.'

These criteria are generally acknowledged to express principles of customary international law.

In reality, the recognition of states is not as controversial as the recognition of governments and practice suggests that recognition of states fulfilling these requirements will be infrequently withheld.

Recognition of governments

State practice suggests that there is no legal duty incumbent on individual members of the international community to recognise a new government. It remains a matter of policy for individual states to decide whether recognition will be extended to a new government.

British practice

Since April 1980, the policy of the British government is no longer to accord express recognition to governments. The British Foreign Secretary, Lord Carrington, stated:

'[The British government] shall … decide the nature of our dealings with regimes that come to power unconstitutionally in the light of our assessment of whether they are able of themselves to exercise effective control of the territory of the state concerned and seem likely to continue to do so.'

This statement has been generally interpreted as an adoption of the Estrada doctrine which avoids express recognition of governments for danger that such an expression might be construed as a manifestation of approval.

In *Sierra Leone Telecommunications Co Ltd* v *Barclays Bank* [1998] 2 All ER 821 the High Court considered the relevant criteria to be satisfied for the recognition of a government.

United States practice

The United States government maintains a constitutive orientation towards the practice of recognising governments and as a result recognition may be used as a diplomatic weapon. However, in 1977 the US State Department acknowledged a slight change of approach by stating:

'In recent years, US practice has been to de-emphasise and avoid the use of recognition in cases of change of governments and to concern ourselves with the question of whether we wish to have diplomatic relations with the new governments.'

However, in recent years the US has been cautious in recognising the advent of new governments, particularly since the events of 11 September 2001.

Effects of non-recognition in international law

If the constitutive theory is embraced, then unrecognised states would, in effect, be subject to no duties and would possess no rights under international law. Early in this century such an approach was recognised as absurd. In the *Tinoco Arbitration* (1923) 1 RIAA 369, Arbitrator Taft stated:

'Non-recognition … cannot outweigh … the de facto character of Tinoco's government, according to the standards set by international law.

To hold that a government which establishes itself and maintains a peaceful administration, with the acquiescence of the people for a substantial period of time, does not become a de facto government unless it conforms to a previous constitution would be to hold that within the rules of international law a revolution contrary to the fundamental law of the existing government cannot establish a new government. This cannot be, and is not, true.'

This opinion clearly applied the declaratory theory of recognition to the rights of unrecognised de facto governments in international law. As a result, such governments continue to be subject to the duties set by international law and are entitled to exercise their international rights to the fullest extent practically possible. Thus, for example, a treaty entered into by a de facto government would have validity in international law if it otherwise conformed to the law of treaties.

In the case *Deutsche Continental Gas-Gesellschaft* v *Polish State* (1929) 5 AD 11, the declaratory approach was similarly applied to the recognition of an emergent state.

Recognition in UK law and the role of the courts

Since the policy of refraining from recognising governments was adopted by the UK government, the courts have been required to formulate principles to decide the question of the status of a foreign government as plaintiff/defendant in civil proceedings.

The leading case on this issue is *Republic of Somalia* v *Woodhouse Drake and Carey (Suisse) SA* [1993] QB 54 which concerned the recognition of the provisional government of Somalia in legal proceedings for enforcement of a commercial contract.

The judge, Hobhouse J, examined four criteria in order to decide whether the plaintiffs existed as the government of the state of Somalia:

a) whether the plaintiffs were the constitutional government of the state;

b) the degree, nature and stability of administrative control, if any, that the plaintiffs maintained over the territory of the state;

c) whether Her Majesty's Government had any dealings with the provisional government and, if so, what were the nature and extent of those dealings; and

d) the extent of the international recognition afforded by the world community as the government of the state.

Each of these considerations was, however, given different weight. The most significant factors were effective control over the population and territory as well as the nature of the dealings between the UK government and the foreign entity.

Effects of non-recognition in municipal law

Non-recognition of a state or government has a number of implications in English law. In particular:

a) Only a recognised government can raise an action in a British court: *City of Berne* v *Bank of England* (1804) 32 ER 636.

b) A recognised government is entitled to sovereign immunity in British law: *Luther* v *Sagor* [1921] 3 KB 532; *Gur Corporation* v *Trust Bank of Africa Ltd* [1986] 3 All ER 449.

c) The legislative, judicial and administrative acts of an unrecognised state are not applicable to problems involving conflict of laws: see *Carl Zeiss Stiftung* v *Rayner and Keeler Ltd (No 2)* [1967] 1 AC 853.

d) A de jure government may recover public debt and state assets: *Haile Selassie* v *Cable and Wireless (No 2)* [1939] Ch 182.

e) The act of de jure recognition has retroactive effect: *Civil Air Transport Inc* v *Central Air Transport Corp* [1953] AC 70.

5.3 Key cases and legislation

- *Austro-German Customs Union Case* (1931) PCIJ Rep Ser A/B No 41
  Separate Opinion of Judge Anzilotti deals with the requirement of independence for statehood

- *Case Concerning the Application of the Convention on the Prevention and Punishment of the Crime of Genocide (First Request for the Indication of Provisional Measures)* (1993) ICJ Rep 3
  Judgment relating to the right of a state to bring an international application against another state which does not recognise its existence

- *Deutsche Continental Gas-Gesellschaft* v *Polish State* (1929) 5 AD 11
  Dicta referring to the requirement of territory for the purposes of recognition

- *Duff Development Co* v *Government of Kelantan* [1924] AC 797
  Supports the proposition that a recognised state is entitled to sovereign immunity

- *Gdynia Ameryka Linie* v *Boguslawski* [1953] AC 11
  Contrasts the legal implications of de facto and de jure recognition of governments

- *Republic of Somalia* v *Woodhouse Drake and Carey (Suisse) SA* [1993] QB 54
  The principles to be applied by the UK courts in determining the status of foreign governments which have not yet been recognised by the international community

- *Sierra Leone Telecommunications Co Ltd* v *Barclays Bank* [1998] 2 All ER 821
  Addresses the issue of relevant criteria required for statehood

- *Tinoco Arbitration* (1923) 1 RIAA 369
  The acts of a de facto government have international legal implications regardless of non-recognition by certain states

- *Western Sahara Case* (1975) ICJ Rep 12
  Refers to the requirement of a defined population for statehood

- Montevideo Convention on Rights and Duties of States 1933 – sets out the qualifications for the recognition of a state as an international person

5.4 Questions and suggested solutions

QUESTION ONE

a) 'The policies followed until very recently by the United Kingdom and the United States on recognition of foreign governments were blunt instruments which frequently worked injustice for no good reason. The new approach is therefore to be warmly welcomed.'

Discuss.

b) The Blue government of state A, recognised de jure by the United Kingdom since 1949, was overthrown by unconstitutional means in 1997 and replaced by the Red government which has established GRAINCO, a state-owned corporation, to purchase grain from other countries. You have been asked to advise GRAINCO in relation to breach of contract proceedings which it is considering instituting in the English courts. Responding to your inquiry as to whether or not the United Kingdom government has recognised the Red government, the legal adviser to the Foreign and Commonwealth Office informs you that it is no longer the policy of Her Majesty's Government to grant recognition to governments. It is added, however, that the UK government has welcomed the development of trade relations between GRAINCO and British companies.

Advise GRAINCO whether the courts would recognise it as having locus standi in these circumstances.

Written by the Author

General Comment

This question requires an examination of the rules and principles used in order to recognise states and governments as legal personalities.

Skeleton Solution

a) Recognition in international law – express – implied – collective – the effects of recognition in international law.

b) The legal effects of recognition or non-recognition – *Luther* v *Sagor* – distinguish de facto and de jure recognition – principles applied by the court in determining status or locus standi.

Suggested Solution

a) Recognition is the willingness to deal with the new government as the representative of the state. It is a matter of intention and may be express or implied. There is a profound doctrinal controversy regarding the legal effects of recognition. On the one hand proponents of the constitutive theory argue that a government does not exist for the purposes of international law until it is recognised by the international community. On the other hand proponents of the declaratory theory advocate that the existence of a government is a question of fact and recognition therefore serves no legal effect being merely an acknowledgement of that fact.

Generally, prior to 1980 the United Kingdom practice on recognition of governments accorded broadly with the declaratory theory. The United Kingdom accepted the duty to recognise entities which fulfilled the factual requirements of government. The normal criteria employed by the United Kingdom government for the recognition of a new regime were that the new government enjoy, with a reasonable prospect of permanency, the obedience of the mass of the population; and have effective control over much the greater part of the territory of the state concerned. However, not withstanding this purported 'face the facts' approach there have been exceptions where the United Kingdom has refused to recognise certain Governments even though there is little doubt of the de facto status. In 1979, for example, de facto recognition of the Heng Samrin government of Cambodia was refused despite it being in control of the greater part of the territory of Cambodia. It was, however, placed in power by a foreign government, that of Vietnam.

Britain's attitude towards the Heng Samrin government would seem to be more in line with the constitutive theory of recognition formerly practised by the United States. The United States regarded recognition as a political decision and openly used recognition or the withholding of recognition as a diplomatic weapon in the conduct of international relations. However, the United States government was prepared to engage in quasi-diplomatic relations with unrecognised governments when it was in the United States' interest to do so, as can be seen from their relationship with the Peoples Republic of China before 1979.

Because the recognition or non-recognition of governments in international law also has effects in municipal law, any delay or refusal in granting recognition may lead to uncertainty and in some cases injustice. Generally the UK courts would not recognise a government unless the Foreign Office certified that it has been recognised by the British government. If a government was not recognised it was not entitled to sovereign immunity. It could not sue in a UK court. Its laws were not applied in the UK courts and it was not entitled to the property of the state which it claimed to govern.

But if non-recognition can be an expression of disapproval of a new government then it can be argued that recognition may be interpreted as implying approval of the new government, even in cases such as the Kadar government established in Hungary after the uprising, where no such approval was intended. To avoid such misunderstandings some states adopt the policy of never recognising governments, but instead grant or withhold recognition only in respect of other states. This doctrine, developed from the Estrada doctrine which originated in Mexico, has now been adopted by several other states including the United Kingdom and the United States.

The United Kingdom has since 1980 abandoned the practice of expressly recognising revolutionary governments. In future recognition is to be inferred from the dealings of the United Kingdom with the government concerned thus removing those problems inherent in the previous practice of express recognition.

b) In the past the English courts applied the same reasoning to the recognition of governments as they did to the recognition of states. They would not recognise a foreign government unless the Foreign Office certified that it has been recognised by the British government. For example in the case of *Luther* v *Sagor* [1921] 3 KB 532 it was stated that 'if a foreign government, or its sovereignty, is not recognised by the government of this country, the courts of this country either cannot or at least need not or ought not, to take notice of, or recognise such foreign government or its sovereignty'.

However, in April 1980 the British government decided to abandon the practice of expressly recognising new revolutionary governments which come to power in existing states. The Foreign Secretary stated that in future cases where a new regime comes to power unconstitutionally the question whether it qualifies to be treated as a government will be left to be inferred from the nature of the dealings, if any, which we may have with it, and in particular on whether we are dealing with it on a normal government-to-government basis.

It has long been decided that if a government has not been recognised de facto or de jure, it is not entitled to initiate proceedings in the British courts: see *Haile Selassie* v *Cable and Wireless Co Ltd (No 2)* [1939] Ch 182. Therefore, unless the Red government can establish that it is either the de facto or de jure government of state A, it will not be in a position to institute proceedings for breach of contract.

In the past, this issue was settled by executive certificates or statements extending or denying recognition to governments which came to power through extra-constitutional means. However, since the 1980 Statement, the British government has refrained from such statements. Thus, the status of a regime cannot be determined by reference to such statements.

The legal effect of the 1980 Declaration has been to pass the responsibility for determining the status of regime from the government to the courts. Whereas in the past this was a matter for the government to decide, now this must be settled by the courts. This development has had the effect of making such decisions less political and more legal.

The courts have only recently had an opportunity to consider the nature of the principles applicable to determining the status of foreign regimes. In *Republic of Somalia* v *Woodhouse Drake and Carey (Suisse) SA* [1993] QB 54 the Queen's Bench Division was asked to determine the status of the provisional government of Somalia which had raised an action for recovery of the price of undelivered goods in the English courts. The provisional government had come to power after overthrowing the former incumbent de jure government.

In deciding whether the plaintiffs were the legitimate government of Somalia, Hobhouse J applied four criteria: (i) whether or not the plaintiffs were the constitutional government of the state; (ii) the degree, nature and stability of administrative control, if any, exercised by the plaintiffs over the territory of the state; (iii) whether Her Majesty's government had any dealings with the provisional government and, if so, the nature and extent of those dealings; and (iv) the extent of the international recognition afforded by the world community as the government of the state.

For GRAINCO to establish standing, it would have to prove to the court that the Red government satisfies each of these criteria, to a sufficient degree, to allow it to be recognised as the legitimate government of state A. Only then would GRAINCO, as a state-owned corporation, be able to institute proceedings.

Not all of these criteria carry equal weight. While the courts place great emphasis on the need to establish the degree and nature of administrative control and the relationship between the provisional government and the British government, the extent of recognition by other states is only of marginal importance.

The statement by the British government that it welcomes the development of trade relations between GRAINCO and British companies, while not conclusive, is significant in this process. The same is true for any evidence of stability and control over the territory of state A that may be adduced by the Red government.

QUESTION TWO

What legal issues, if any, depend upon the recognition of a state or of a government?

University of London LLB Examination
(for External Students) Public International Law June 1993 Q1

General Comment

A straightforward, general essay question on the legal aspects of recognition. Although the question is essentially very simple and easy to answer, care must be taken to focus the answer on the legal consequences (not the legal criteria) of the act of recognition. The background of the law on recognition therefore needs to be referred to only briefly, in the form of a few general remarks.

Skeleton Solution

Preliminary remarks: the political nature of recognition – general remarks: the recognition of states – general remarks: the recognition of governments – the consequences of recognition in international law – the consequences of recognition in domestic law.

Suggested Solution

Recognition, put simply, is the expression of willingness to deal with a new state or government as a full member of the international community (in the case of states) or as a representative of the state (in the case of governments). Recognition occupies a crucial position in the fabric of international relations because of the continual political changes in the world – revolutions, coups d'état, changes in the type or style of government, dissolution of old states and formation of new ones – and the need for the international community to signal its reaction to those changes for the purpose of international affairs.

Sadly, an inevitable corollary of the ever-changing face of international society and the fast pace of international relations is that state practice on recognition is highly erratic and inconsistent; the result of that is that recognition is almost invariably a political decision. States are recognised (or not) as a matter of policy, and the legal doctrine of recognition is thus reduced to providing a vague legal framework for a political decision. Some countries – the United States providing perhaps the most shameful example – quite blatantly use recognition as an instrument of foreign policy to express approval or disapproval of a new situation. The political nature of recognition was expressly asserted in 1948 by W R Austin, the United States representative in the United Nations Security Council, when he referred to it as a 'high political act'. Further evidence of this sad state of affairs is provided by such contrasting episodes as the American recognition of the State of Israel within only a few hours of its declaration of independence in 1948, and its failure to recognise the German Democratic Republic until 1973 and the People's Republic of China until 1979, as well as its continued non-recognition of the People's Democratic Republic of Korea. More recently in May 2004 the European Union extended membership to ten other countries, bringing the total number of Member States to 25.

There are two types of recognition: recognition of states and recognition of governments. Of the two, the former is the more straightforward, both in theory and in practice. Once a territorial entity has satisfied the four legal criteria for statehood as set out in art 1 of the Montevideo Convention on the Rights and Duties of States 1933 (a stable population, a defined territory, an effective government and a capacity to enter into international relations), it is ready to be recognised as a state. The Anglo-German jurist Hersch Lauterpacht propagated the view that once the Montevideo criteria have been met there is a legal duty on the part of other states to extend recognition. However, the consistent approach of the international community as a whole has been that there is no such duty, and certain states that ostensibly satisfy the Montevideo criteria remain unrecognised – for instance, the entire Arab world (bar Egypt), along with most other Islamic states, refuses to recognise the State of Israel; similarly, the PDRK (North Korea) is still not recognised by the USA or the United Kingdom. These states, and others, are denied recognition for purely political reasons.

Recognition of governments is a very different matter. The traditional British criteria for recognising a new government were stated by Herbert Morrison, the then Foreign Secretary, in 1951 as follows:

'The conditions ... for the recognition of a new regime as the de facto government of a state are that the new regime has in fact effective control over most of the state's territory and that this control seems likely to continue. The conditions for the recognition of a new regime as the de jure government of a state are that the new regime should not merely have effective control over most of the state's territory, but that it should, in fact, be firmly established.'

However, in 1980 the British government adopted the Estrada Doctrine, under which formal recognition is not granted to any government. Instead, recognition has to be inferred from the nature of the dealings which the British government has with the government in question. The net result has been to render the law on recognition so vague and ill-defined as to be virtually meaningless. At least everyone is agreed, however, that there is no legal duty to recognise new governments.

Recognition can have effects – at least nominally – in both international and domestic law. There is, however, a profound doctrinal controversy regarding the legal effects of recognition in international law. The constitutive theory holds that a state or government does not technically exist in international law unless it is recognised; this theory makes legal nonsense in the case of states that are recognised by some nations but not by others (they are simultaneously 'international persons' and 'international non-persons', as Brierly has put it, and some of the consequences arising from such a situation would be contradictory to a ridiculous degree). Nevertheless, the constitutive theory's influence is evident in the attitudes some states have adopted towards the PDRK, the GDR (East Germany) and Israel, amongst others.

The declaratory theory, championed by Lauterpacht, is far more sensible: it holds that the existence of a state or government is a question of fact, and recognition (as a mere legal acknowledgement of that fact) therefore serves no legal purpose whatsoever. This theory was applied by the arbitrator in the *Tinoco Arbitration: UK* v *Costa Rica* (1923) 1 RIAA 369, who ruled that the Tinoco regime, which seized power in Costa Rica in a coup d'état in 1917 and was itself ousted by force in 1919, had as a matter of fact existed as a sovereign government, and that the general non-recognition of the regime abroad was therefore irrelevant in terms of international law. In *Deutsche Continental Gas-Gesellschaft* v *Polish State* (1929) 5 AD 11, the arbitrators said: 'The state exists by itself and the recognition is nothing else than a declaration of this existence.' In international law, therefore, the legal effects of recognition are virtually nil.

If there is one sphere in which the legal doctrine of recognition is of some genuine use, it is that of consequences in domestic law, in terms of enforcement of other states' laws, enactment of their administrative acts and so on. Recognition has a whole litany of effects in English law, many of which are related to the doctrine of state immunity: a recognised state has state immunity under the State Immunity Act 1978; an unrecognised state can neither sue nor be sued in the UK; the laws and administrative acts of an unrecognised government cannot be enforced or applied in the courts of the UK (*Luther* v *Sagor* [1921] 3 KB 532); a government which loses recognition is no longer entitled to property (situated in the UK) of the state which it claims to govern (*Haile*

Selassie v *Cable and Wireless Co Ltd (No 2)* [1939] Ch 182); a de facto regime can plead immunity even against the de jure sovereign of the same country (*The Arantzazu Mendi* [1939] AC 256); and the retroactive effect of recognition cannot affect the validity of the previous sovereign's acts outside the country in question: *Gdynia Ameryka Linie* v *Boguslawski* [1953] AC 11.

The most interesting cases are the ones which reveal the view that an unrecognised state does not exist legally as the nonsense that it is: *Carl Zeiss Stiftung* v *Rayner and Keeler Ltd (No 2)* [1967] 1 AC 853 and *Hesperides Hotels* v *Aegean Holidays Ltd* [1978] QB 205. In the former, the House of Lords evaded a strict application of the rule that 'non-recognition = non-existence at law' by the ingenious but artificial argument that the GDR was a subordinate authority of the Soviet Union, which – as the de jure sovereign of the Eastern Zone of Germany after 1945 – was perfectly entitled to delegate such authority to the GDR, whose acts then had to be accepted in courts in the UK, even though the GDR was not at the time recognised by the UK. In the latter case, Lord Denning MR ruled that the existence of a Turkish administration in effective control of Northern Cyprus was a matter of fact, and therefore its acts had to be recognised in the English courts, irrespective of the fact that the UK had refused to recognise that administration.

It should finally be noted that the application of all these principles since 1980 is uncertain because the UK no longer grants any formal recognition at all to new governments. This has the sad effect of rendering the actual law on recognition practically meaningless, although the theory of it is eminently sensible and indeed necessary to the functioning of international affairs.

QUESTION THREE

In 1981, elections were held in the State of Rhon. A political party called the United Popular Front (UPF) gained a majority in Parliament and consequently formed the government. In 1985, the UPF cancelled the elections due in that year, banned all other political parties and continued to govern Rhon. The People's Voice (PV), a political party which had held 20 per cent of the seats in Parliament, organised a rebellion to overthrow the 'illegitimate' UPF government. By late 1986, the PV controlled the major part of the territory of Rhon and had expelled the UPF authorities from the capital; but the UPF still had control of Rhon's second city, Zat. At this time, the UPF, purporting to act on behalf of Rhon, exchanged ratifications of the Treaty of Zat with the state of Shalbet. Shalbet at this time recognised the UPF as the government of Rhon. In the spring of 1987, the PV succeeded in gaining control of most of the remaining part of Rhon held by the UPF. Shalbet thereupon recognised the PV as the government of Rhon. The PV government seeks your advice on whether the Treaty of Zat, concluded by the UPF authorities, is binding on the State of Rhon.

Advise the PV government.

University of London LLB Examination
(for External Students) Public International Law June 1987 Q5

General Comment

A problem involving a complicated factual situation in which discussion of recognition remains the principal matter despite added legal complications.

Skeleton Solution

Introduction: the changing nature of the international community; the nature of recognition – the effects of recognition in international law and municipal law – the United Kingdom practice: the distinction between de jure and de facto recognition – the restrospective effects of granting de jure recognition – application to the problem; conclusions.

Suggested Solution

The international community is in a process of continuous change and new situations are constantly arising which affect the legal relations between states. Territorial changes may take place. New states are established. Revolutions occur which sweep aside existing governments and replace them with new regimes. Questions arise in relation to the legal consequences flowing from these factual situations. For example, if there is a change in government within a state, is there a duty on the part of other states to recognise the new government? If recognition is granted or withheld, what effect does this have in international and municipal law?

Recognition is a matter of intent and may be manifested expressly or impliedly. However, state practice shows that there is no legal duty incumbent upon the international community in general to extend recognition to new governments. Examples include the non-recognition by the United States and the allied Powers of the Tinoco regime which ruled Costa Rica between 1917 and 1919. The Soviet government which came to power in Russia in 1919 was not recognised by Great Britain until 1921 or by the United States until 1933.

For practical purposes, some governments, including the British government, distinguish between the de jure and de facto recognition of governments. For example, the United Kingdom considered that the conditions under international law for the recognition of a new regime as the de facto government of a state were that the regime had effective control over most of the territory of the state and that this control seemed likely to continue. The conditions deemed necessary for the grant of de jure recognition were that the new regime should not merely have effective control over most of the territory, but should in fact be firmly established. It may be argued that the distinction between de facto and de jure recognition is of little practical or legal consequence. The distinction may be simply political, the recognising state feeling that while circumstances require recognition to be accorded, its disapproval of the new regime can be expressed by the use of de facto rather than de jure recognition.

However, municipal courts have recognised one important principle relating to the transfer of de jure recognition to a previous de facto regime. The withdrawal of de jure recognition and the retrospective effect of the granting of de jure recognition to the successor does not affect the validity of transactions already completed by the previous sovereign authority. For example, consider the facts in the case *Gdynia Ameryka Linie* v *Boguslawski* [1953] AC 11. On 28 June 1945, the Government of National Unity in Lublin became de facto government of Poland and at midnight 5–6 July 1945, the British government extended de jure recognition to this government. Before this, the Polish government-in-exile in London had been recognised de jure by Great Britain. The question at issue was whether the de jure recognition of the Government of National Unity of 5–6 July had retroactive effect in relation to acts done by the government-in-exile in London, particularly as regards the Polish merchant marine and the personnel under its control.

The Foreign Office certificate stated that the question of the retroactive effect of recognition of a government was a question of law to be decided by the courts. Their Lordships were unanimous in upholding the validity of the actions of the government-in-exile. Although the recognition of the Government of National Unity might be retroactive in its effect as far as Poland was concerned, where the government has effective control, it could not apply retroactively to events over which it had no control, such as the actions taken in London prior to midnight 5–6 July by the government-in-exile.

Similarly, in the case *Civil Air Transport Inc* v *Central Air Transport Corp* [1953] AC 70, Viscount Simon stated that primarily, retroactivity of recognition operates to validate acts of a de facto government which has subsequently become the new de jure government and not to invalidate acts of the previous de jure government.

Regarding the facts of the particular problem under consideration: the United Popular Front (UPF) is the de jure government of Rhon. By late 1986, the People's Voice (PV) control part of the territory of Rhon, including the capital. However the UPF still control the second city, Zat. Therefore, while the UPF remains the de jure government of Rhon, the PV may be considered the de facto government. The UPF remained the de jure government while it concluded the treaty of Zat with the state of Shalbet. The UPF was therefore competent to conclude such an agreement at this time, especially as it concerns Zat which remains under its control. In the spring of 1987, the PV gain control of the remaining part of Rhon from the UPF. Shalbet then recognises the PV as the de jure government of Rhon. If the principle enunciated in the *Civil Air Transport* case is applied, this subsequent de jure recognition of the PV will operate to validate acts of the PV done when they were the de facto government of Rhon, but will not invalidate acts of the previous UPF government undertaken when recognised as the de jure government of Rhon.

On this basis, and always assuming that the agreement was entered into in accordance with the municipal law of Rhon for the purposes of art 46 of the Vienna Convention on the Law of Treaties 1969, the Treaty of Zat will be binding on the State of Rhon.

QUESTION FOUR

Outline the criteria previously and presently used, and the procedure followed, by the government of the United Kingdom in recognising new states and new governments.

University of Glasgow LLB Examination 1987 Q3

General Comment

A general essay question requiring knowledge of British foreign policy and recent changes.

Skeleton Solution

Pre-1980 practice of the United Kingdom government – contemporary practice of the British government – declining role of the United Kingdom government in the process and increased role of the European Community – example of Yugoslavia.

Suggested Solution

Prior to 1980, the British government adopted a policy which was closely assimilated to the declaratory theory. In relation to new governments, the British Foreign Secretary Morrison, in 1951, declared 'it is international law which defines the conditions under which a government should be recognised de jure or de facto ... A new regime (recognised) as the de facto government ... (must have) in fact effective control over most of the state's territory and this control (must seem) likely to continue ... Recognition as the de jure government (requires) that the new regime should not merely have effective control ... but should in fact be firmly established.' In cases involving litigation before the English courts, prior to 1980, the courts regarded as conclusive evidence a certificate of recognition from the Foreign Office.

However, such an approach created a number of problems. Recognition in circumstances where this was inevitable could appear to represent an endorsement of new regimes, their political objectives, or the means by which they acquired power. This predicament necessitated a change in British policy. In April 1980, the British Foreign Secretary announced that the United Kingdom would no longer accord express recognition to governments. Further, he continued, the United Kingdom would 'decide the nature of (its) dealings with regimes that come to power unconstitutionally in the light of (an) assessment of whether they are able of themselves to exercise effective control of the territory of the state concerned, and seem likely to continue to do so.'

This policy is an adaptation of the Estrada doctrine according to which diplomatic relations would be conducted in the absence of an expression of approval or disapproval of the new regime. All that is necessary is that the new regime has in fact established itself as the effective government of the state.

The new British policy on recognition makes two significant changes from the former policy. Firstly, the distinction between de jure and de facto recognition of governments and states has been abandoned. Secondly, the term 'of themselves' appears to imply that the British government will examine closely those situations in which governments relied on external support for their continued existence.

For the purposes of legal determination, the status of a new government is to be 'inferred from the nature of the dealings, if any, which (the British government) may have with it'. The responsibility for determining the legitimacy of a foreign government has therefore passed from the executive branch of government to the judiciary. Thus the English courts will now have to scrutinise the dealings between the British government and the emergent government in order to ascertain the status of that entity.

In practice, it appears that the Foreign Office remains willing to detail the dealings of the British government with the foreign entity in order that an appropriate evaluation of status may be made. In the case *Gur Corporation* v *Trust Bank of Africa Ltd* [1986] 3 All ER 449, the Foreign Office submitted an executive certificate detailing dealings between the United Kingdom and Ciskei, a South African dependent territory. However, this new policy is at best uncertain and has exposed the British courts to the turmoil involved in interpreting international law.

The United Kingdom government's policy towards the recognition of new governments and states has been significantly eroded by the participation of the United Kingdom in the European Community. Increasingly, the European Community has assumed responsibility for all Member States, not just the United Kingdom. The future policy of the United Kingdom must therefore be assessed in light of this development.

The most obvious example of the assumption of this responsibility was in connection with the former state of Yugoslavia. Originally, that state consisted of six republics – Slovenia, Croatia, Serbia, Bosnia-Hercegovina, Montenegro and Macedonia – and two autonomous regions – Kosovo and Vojvodina. After declarations of independence from Slovenia and Croatia on 25 June 1991, civil conflict broke out between the forces of the central government and those of the provisional Slovenian and Croatian governments.

The problem was perceived as a mainly European issue and the European Community took the lead in trying to resolve the conflict through diplomacy and other peaceful means. By December 1991 it had become clear that a peaceful settlement was unlikely as the rival republics persistently failed to agree the terms of a constitutional settlement.

On 16 December 1991 the European Community announced that it would extend recognition as sovereign states to those former republics which gave assurances that five conditions would be respected. These conditions were:

a) continued respect for the UN Charter and the Helsinki Final Act, particularly with respect to the rule of law, democracy and respect for human rights;

b) guarantees for the rights of ethnic and national groups and minorities in accordance with the commitments given within the framework of the CSCE system;

c) respect for the inviolability of all frontiers which were only to be altered by peaceful means and with mutual agreement;

d) acceptance of all international obligations concerning non-discrimination and nuclear non-proliferation as well as security and regional stability; and

e) undertakings to settle peaceably all questions concerning state succession and regional disputes.

The Community also affirmed that it would not recognise an entity as a state that came into existence as a result of aggression.

Recognition was extended by the Community to Slovenia and Croatia on 15 January 1992, and to Bosnia-Hercegovina on 6 April 1992, after receiving the appropriate undertakings from these republics.

Quite clearly the European Community used the device of recognition as a political tool to extract these commitments from the former republics of Yugoslavia which confirms the political nature of recognition. The policy adopted was one of conditional recognition whereby the Community withheld recognition pending political undertakings relating to security in the region.

It is unclear whether the European Community will retain this doctrine of conditional recognition or whether the circumstances of this particular case were unique.

But, by acting in unison at the Community level, the Community Member States, including the United Kingdom, significantly altered their own national policies towards the recognition of states.

QUESTION FIVE

Provincia, a colony of Metropolia, has proclaimed its independence. In a manifesto issued by the new government of the United Kingdom of Provincia it is made clear that it is the government's policy to disfranchise the minority Countie Tribe and resettle them in barren lands far from the centres of civilisation. As a result of the publication of the manifesto, very few states have recognised either the new state or its government. The Foreign Minister has stated in the Legislative Council that 'recognition is irrelevant in the modern world and Provincia can quite easily survive without it'.

Assess the legal accuracy of the Foreign Minister's statement, referring in your answer to recent changes in the British attitude to recognition.

University of London LLB Examination
(for External Students) Public International Law June 1985 Q2

General Comment

A problem-oriented question which combines the issue of recognition with other problems of interpretation of international duties.

Skeleton Solution

Permeating theme: recognition of state and government; the constitutive theory and the declaratory theory – United Kingdom practice with regard to recognition; abandonment of policy of expressly recognising revolutionary governments – the accuracy of the Foreign Minister's statement; effects of recognition in international law and municipal law.

Suggested Solution

Provincia is a colony which has exercised its right of self-determination and proclaimed its independence from Metropolia, the colonial power. Following the UN General Assembly Declaration on the Granting of Independence to Colonial Territories and Peoples, many international commentators believe that self-determination is an inherent legal right, at least when exercised in a colonial dimension. Therefore, in other circumstances, it might be expected that many states would recognise Provincia as a state and the government as the de facto, if not the de jure, government of Provincia. However, the treatment of the minority Countie tribe by the new regime has attracted international criticism and, as a result, very few states have recognised either the new state or its government.

British policy prior to 1980 accorded broadly with the declaratory theory of recognition. The British government applied the normal objective criteria of statehood for the purposes of recognising new states, viz: a permanent population, a defined territory and an effective government. So far as emergent governments were concerned the British government merely looked for the habitual obedience of the majority of the population to the edicts of the governing authorities and the exercise of effective control over the greater part of the territory of the state concerned. However, this policy has not been consistently applied, particularly where the pursuit of such a practice would interfere with the objectives of British foreign policy. Thus, for political motives, the British government refused to recognise the German Democratic Republic until February 1973, and withheld recognition of the Heng Samrin government of Cambodia in 1979, despite the fact that the regime controlled the greater part of Cambodia.

However, since 1980 the United Kingdom has abandoned the practice of expressly recognising revolutionary governments (statement by the Foreign Secretary, *Hansard* HL, Vol 408, Cols 1121–1122, April 28, 1980). In future, when a new regime comes to power unconstitutionally, whether it qualifies as a recognised government will be determined by the nature of the dealings it has with the British government. This, it is hoped, will remove the problems inherent in the previous practice of express recognition.

The accuracy of the statement that recognition has become irrelevant in the modern world is therefore contentious. It clearly is a statement supporting the declaratory theory that recognition is a mere formality serving no legal purpose. In accordance with this theory, states and governments exist as a matter of fact and recognition is merely acknowledgment of that fact. This theory has substantial judicial support. For instance, as regards the recognition of states, the declaratory theory was received by the mixed arbitral tribunal deciding the case *Deutsche Continental Gas-Gesellschaft* v *Polish State* (1929) 5 AD 11 and, as regards the recognition of governments, in the *Tinoco Arbitration* (1923) 1 RIAA 369, between Great Britain and Costa Rica. Further, it is axiomatic that today a number of states have survived despite the prima facie 'non recognition' by certain other states.

On the other hand, if the constitutive theory is applied to Provincia, despite possessing all the attributes and qualifications of international personality, the entity may be denied recognition as a state. So far as other states are concerned, Provincia will therefore remain without rights and duties under international law. However, recognition of Provincia may have more than theoretical implications since the granting of recognition has ramifications in municipal law. For example, so far as the British courts are concerned, a foreign state will not be recognised unless the Foreign Office certifies that it has been recognised by the British government. An unrecognised state cannot claim sovereign immunity and can therefore be sued in the courts whether it consents or not: *Duff Development Company* v *Government of Kelantan* [1924] AC 797. An unrecognised state, however, cannot sue in an English court and is not recognised for the purposes of conflict of laws: *Carl Zeiss Stiftung* v *Rayner & Keeler (No 2)* [1967] 1 AC 853. Similarly, an unrecognised government is not entitled to sovereign immunity (*The Arantazu Mendi* [1939] AC 256) and cannot sue in an English court: *City of Berne* v *Bank of England* (1804) 38 Ch D 357. That government's domestic laws will not be applied in English courts faced will questions of conflict of law (*Luther* v *Sagor* [1921] 3 KB 532) and it will not be entitled to any property of the state which it claims to govern: *Haile Selassie* v *Cable & Wireless (No 2)* [1939] Ch 182.

It may well be the case, therefore, that notwithstanding general acceptance of the declaratory theory, states may withhold recognition of the new state in protest at its manifesto and likewise recognition may be denied to its government as an expression of disapproval of its actions. While Provincia and its government may, in common with others denied recognition, survive the absence of recognition, this will not be without a denial of rights on both the international and municipal planes.

Chapter 6

Territorial Sovereignty

6.1   Introduction

6.2   Key points

6.3   Key cases and legislation

6.4   Questions and suggested solutions

6.1 Introduction

An essential criterion of sovereignty is the possession of an identifiable geographical area within which exclusive governmental and legal functions are exercised. The means through which states acquire such territorial sovereignty remain the most popular subject within this particular topic, although increasingly other matters in this field are becoming equally significant. The legal regimes established to regulate airspace and outer space and the legal claims of states in Antarctica are issues of growing legal interest. In addition, the development of self-determination as a legal principle relevant to the settlement of territorial claims is an issue which must be addressed.

6.2 Key points

The traditional modes of acquiring title to territory

Occupation

Occupation is a means of acquiring original title to territory which has never belonged to any state, or which was abandoned by the former sovereign. Virtually all of the globe has already been apportioned among nations, but this method of acquiring title has more than a historical significance since a number of territorial claims still remain disputed by states – for example the Falkland Islands and Gibraltar. Resolution of these claims and determination of title will ultimately require reference to the legal principles behind the concept of occupation.

To acquire title through occupation, a number of conditions must be satisfied.

a) The territory must be terra nullius, that is, 'land belonging to no one'. In colonial periods, when claims to territory were frequently based on this ground, the rights of the indigenous population were ignored where such peoples were insufficiently organised to constitute a recognisable government: see *Cooper v Stuart* (1889) 14 AC 286.

b) The possession which constitutes occupation must be carried out by a state and not private individuals.

c) The territory must be placed under 'open, continuous, effective and peaceful' control: *Island of Palmas Arbitration* (1928) 2 RIAA 829. The degree of control necessary will vary in accordance with the circumstances. Minimal overt action may be sufficient to establish effective occupation over small, uninhabited areas of territory. The exercise of a greater degree of authority will be necessary in other cases to establish effective control. However, possession must be actual and not nominal: see the *Clipperton Island Case* (1931) 2 RIAA 1105 and the *Minquiers and Ecrehos Islands Case* (1953) ICJ Rep 47.

d) The acquiring state must demonstrate an animus occupandi or will to act as a sovereign. This is generally evidenced by the creation of legal apparatus for the administration of the territory. In the *Legal Status of Eastern Greenland Case* (1933) PCIJ Rep Ser A/B No 53 the International Court ruled 'a claim to sovereignty based ... upon a continued display of authority, involves two elements each of which must be shown to exist: the intention and will to act as a sovereign; and some actual exercise or display of such authority'.

In order to effectively claim abandoned territory on the basis of occupation, it must be shown that the previous sovereign manifested an animus relinquendi which is the intention to relinquish sovereignty over the area: see the *Clipperton Island Case* (above).

Prescription

Prescription is a derivative means of acquiring territory which may originally have belonged to another sovereign whose rights have been extinguished for some reason by the passage of time. Acquisition of title by prescription may be achieved through two forms of possession:

a) immemorial possession, where the state acquiring the territory has maintained possession for such a period that possible competing claims of an earlier sovereign have been forgotten; or

b) adverse possession, where the previous sovereign is known, but the acquiring state has exercised control over the territory for such a period that the original or previous sovereign is deemed to have lost his title. This control must be accompanied by acquiescence on the part of the state relinquishing sovereignty and protests, particularly if vigorous and repeated, prevent acquisition of title by prescription: see the *Chamizal Arbitration* (1911) 9 RIAA 316.

In practice, the distinction between occupation and prescription is obscure and tribunals settling issues of title to territory have tended to render judgment only after due consideration of both means of acquiring title.

Accretion and avulsion

Accretion is caused by the gradual physical movement of land from one territory to another, such as occurs in the silting of river banks. Avulsion is the process of violent change, such as a dramatic change in the course of a river or the creation of volcanic formations within a state's territory.

If accretion occurs on a boundary river between two or more states, then the international boundary changes accordingly. But in cases of avulsion, despite changes in the physical landscape, the boundary remains the same. Detailed rules have been established to deal with the problems created by such natural occurrences: see *Louisiana v Mississippi* 282 US 458 (1940).

Cession

Cession is the transfer of territory from one state to another, usually in the form of a treaty, and requires that one party manifests an intention to assume sovereignty and the other an intention to relinquish it.

Cession is an example of derivative title and should defects exist in the ceding state's title, the purported cession from the previous sovereign will not cure the defect. Further, where third states have rights over the territory, such as rights of passage, these must be respected by the new sovereign.

Frequently cession occurs as an element of a peace settlement such as the Treaty of Versailles 1919 or the Treaty of Peace with Japan 1951. On occasion, cession has occurred in the form of sales and purchase. Examples in the past have included the purchase of Louisiana from France and Alaska from Russia.

Conquest

Prior to the creation of rules restraining the use of force, territorial changes brought about by such means were acknowledged as legitimate. Acquisition of territory by conquest could come about in two ways:

a) subjugation or debellation, where the armed forces of the state in question were absolutely destroyed, leaving the territory open to the victors to possess; or

b) implied abandonment, which involved the withdrawal of the armed forces of a state from its territory following military defeat leaving the territory open to conquest by the victor.

Through the creation of limitations on the use of force in 1945, modern international law does not recognise the possibility of acquisition by conquest. See, in particular, Security Council Resolution 242 (XXII) which emphasised the inadmissibility of acquisition of territory by force and the 1970 Declaration on the Principles of International Law which specifically states:

'The territory of a state shall not be the object of acquisition by another state resulting from the threat or use of force. No territorial acquisition resulting from the threat or use of force shall be recognised as legal.'

The issue of acquisition of territory was examined by the International Court of Justice in the *Case Concerning Maritime Delimitation and Territorial Questions between Qatar and Bahrain (Qatar v Bahrain)* (2001) The Times 16 March.

Doctrine of intertemporal law

In the *Island of Palmas Arbitration* (1928) 2 RIAA 829 Umpire Huber stated that 'a juridical fact must be appreciated in the light of the law contemporary with it'. This has become known as the 'doctrine of intertemporal law' according to which, in relation to the acquisition of territory, claims by rivals must be determined in accordance with the law in force at the time of the discovery of the territory.

Modern relevant principles for determining territory

Self-determination

The principle of self-determination has been considered significant in at least two cases involving questions of territorial sovereignty. The principle, elaborated in General Assembly Resolution 2625, provides that peoples have the right to select their own form of government and social organisation.

In the *Status of South-West Africa Case* (1950) ICJ Rep 6, the ICJ acknowledged that the principle of self-determination was a significant factor in deciding whether Namibia should become an independent state on the territory which was formerly South-West Africa. South Africa was therefore held to be under an obligation to fulfil the requirements of the mandate from the United Nations through which it had been given responsibility for the territory.

In addition, in the *Western Sahara Case* (1975) ICJ Rep 12, the Court applied the principle of self-determination to decide the claims of a number of states to the territory in the Western Sahara. The Court found, inter alia, that the claims of the indigenous populations of the area to self-determination did not prevail over the claims to territorial sovereignty espoused by the claiming states. However, Judges Boni and Dillard rendered strong dissenting decisions in support of the application of the principle. In particular, Judge Dillard asserted that:

'It is for the people to determine the destiny of the territory and not the territory the destiny of the people.'

Uti possidetis

The principle of uti possidetis was first developed by the former Spanish colonies of Latin American in order to settle frontier disputes. According to the principle, the former colonial administrative boundaries are to be adopted as the new frontiers between the independent states which have succeeded to the territories of the former colonies.

The principle was first employed by the International Court in the *Frontier Dispute Case (Burkina Faso v Mali)* (1986) ICJ Rep 554 in order to determine the frontiers between these two African states. The function of the principle is to preserve continuity in the demarcation of international boundaries between former colonial states.

The principle was again followed in the *Case Concerning Land, Island and Maritime Frontier Dispute (El Salvador v Honduras, Nicaragua Intervening)* (1992) ICJ Rep 351, which involved a dispute between El Salvador and Honduras concerning the land frontiers between their respective territories. Both parties agreed that the matter should be resolved according to the principle of uti possidetis and the Court delimited the disputed boundaries accordingly. The original colonial boundaries were therefore transformed into international frontiers.

Boundary treaties

Treaties defining borders have a special status in international law. Borders established by such agreements have a permanence that exists independently from the fate of the treaties which set them out. This principle was acknowledged by the ICJ in *Case Concerning the Territorial Dispute between Libya and Chad* (1994) ICJ Rep 6 where, commenting on a treaty of limited duration but which established a boundary between the two countries, the Court stated:

> 'The establishment of this boundary is a fact which, from the outset, has had a legal life
> of its own, independently of the fate of the 1955 Treaty. Once agreed, the boundary
> stands, for any other approach would vitiate the principle of the stability of boundaries,
> the importance of which has been repeatedly emphasised by the Court.'

Other cases concerning territorial boundaries have also been resolved by granting special status to this type of agreement. For example, in *Case Concerning Land, Island and Maritime Frontier Dispute (El Salvador v Honduras, Nicaragua Intervening)* (1992) ICJ Rep 351, the International Court resolved a long-standing territorial dispute between these two countries by reference to the terms of a treaty setting out the principles for the delimitation of the boundary between them.

The case *Case Concerning Kasikili/Sedudu Island (Botswana v Namibia)* (1999) ICJ Rep 5 provides a useful illustration of defined territory and sovereignty.

Airspace and outer space and celestial bodies

Article 1 of the Chicago Convention on International Civil Aviation 1944 which is generally accepted as declaring customary law proclaims that 'every state has complete and exclusive sovereignty over the air space above its territory'. As exceptions to the general principle of sovereignty, two freedoms of air transportation were created under another convention, the Chicago International Air Services Transit Agreement 1944. As stated in art 1, these are:

a) freedom of passage without landing; and

b) freedom of landing for non-traffic purposes.

In terms of height, sovereignty terminates where outer space begins, although it remains unclear at what exact height airspace becomes outer space. Problems arise because different legal principles regulate the different areas.

The legal principles applicable in outer space originate in customary law, created by the combined effect of:

a) General Assembly Resolution 1721 (XVI) of 1961 which declared that outer space could not be appropriated on a national basis; and

b) General Assembly Resolution 1884 (XVIII) of 1963 which constituted a declaration of legal principles applicable to outer space.

These customary principles were codified in the Treaty on Principles Governing the Activities of States in the Exploration and Use of Outer Space 1967. The main principles include:

a) The moon, celestial bodies and outer space are res communis and not res nullius. Consequently they are the province of all mankind and therefore incapable of appropriation.

b) International law, including the principles of the United Nations Charter, is applicable to the Moon and other celestial bodies on the same basis as to terrestrial activities.

c) The Moon and other celestial bodies shall be used by state parties exclusively for peaceful purposes. State parties to the treaty undertake not to place nuclear weapons or any other weapons of mass destruction in orbit around Earth.

d) State parties bear international responsibility for national activities conducted in outer space.

e) An international body is established for the registration of space vehicles in accordance with their nationality.

These obligations have been expanded upon in a number of international conventions including the Rescue and Return Treaty 1968, the Liability Convention 1971, the Registration Treaty 1975 and the Moon Treaty 1979.

Antarctica

A number of states claim some form of title to this territory based on different principles and concepts. As a result, a number of different views have emerged in relation to the legal status of the area:

a) The United States adopts the view that the acquisition of a large uninhabitable territory by discovery alone, in the absence of effective occupation, is legally impossible.

b) The United Kingdom asserts that title may be consolidated by discovery and the exercise of effective governmental and administrative authority.

c) A number of states including Chile claim that sovereignty of the region may be claimed by the application of the sector theory.

As well as the United Kingdom, Australia, Argentina, Chile, France, New Zealand and Norway claim areas of the region. The Argentinian, Chilean and British claims overlap.

In order to avoid a confrontation between the different states claiming part of Antarctica, the Antarctica Treaty 1959 was negotiated which imposed a moratorium on territorial claims in the region. Under art 4(1) no claims are recognised or renounced as a consequence of the principles embodied in the treaty and similarly no activities occurring during the life of the treaty will affect pre-existing claims. This international agreement has been supplemented by the Convention on the Regulation of Antarctic Mineral Resource Activities 1988 to which all 39 Antarctic Treaty nations are parties. The purpose of the agreement is to facilitate the commercial development of the minerals of Antarctica, and to that end the agreement contains a number of provisions allowing prospecting, exploration and exploitation of the mineral resources of the territory.

The exploration and exploitation system envisaged by the agreement has not yet come into operation because the convention expressly provides that no mineral resource activities are to take place until it is agreed that the technology and procedures are available to allow safe mining operations. To date, two meetings have taken place among the participating states to decide when these conditions will be satisfied. The first conference was held in Chile in November 1990 and the second in Madrid in April 1991. Both the United States and the United Kingdom are seeking a moratorium on development of an unspecified nature which would effectively prohibit mineral resource activities indefinitely.

6.3 Key cases and legislation

- *Burkina Faso* v *Mali* (1986) ICJ Rep 554
  Dictum of the ICJ relating to the application of the principle of uti possidetis

- *Case Concerning Kasikili/Sedudu Island (Botswana* v *Namibia)* (1999) ICJ Rep 5
  Illustrated the requirement of a defined territory and boundary in the context of territorial sovereignty

- *Case Concerning Land, Island and Maritime Frontier Dispute (El Salvador v Honduras, Nicaragua Intervening)* (1992) ICJ Rep 351
  Application of the principle of uti possidetis to South American countries

- *Case Concerning the Territorial Dispute between Libya and Chad* (1994) ICJ Rep 6
  Treaties establishing borders have a special status in international law and establish frontiers which continue to exist even after their expiry

- *Clipperton Island Case* (1931) 2 RIAA 1105
  Relates to obtaining title to res nullius by occupation

- *Colombia-Venezuela Boundary Arbitration* (1922) 1 RIAA 223
  Case involving the principles behind the concept of accretio

- *Island of Palmas Arbitration* (1928) 2 RIAA 829
  The leading case on the issues of occupation and prescription

- *Minquiers and Ecrehos Islands Case* (1953) ICJ Rep 47
  The degree of governmental authority necessary for proper occupation

- *Western Sahara Case* (1975) ICJ Rep 12
  Discussion of the concept of self-determination to the issue of title to territory

- Chicago Convention on International Civil Aviation 1944 – declares the customary law relating to territorial sovereignty

- Treaty of Peace with Japan 1951 – deals with the question of cessation

- Treaty of Versailles 1919 – deals with the question of cessation

- Treaty on Principles Governing the Activities of States in the Exploration and Use of Outer Space 1967 – sets out customary principles relating to exploration and other uses by states

6.4 Questions and suggested solutions

QUESTION ONE

To what extent, if at all, is the principle of uti possidetis compatible with the right of self-determination for purposes of determining State title to territory?

University of London LLB Examination
(for External Students) Public International Law June 1994 Q3

General Comment

A question requiring the candidate to examine the compatibility of the uti possidetis principle and self-determination.

Skeleton Solution

Introduction – definitions of uti possidetis and self-determination – relevant materials: GA Res 1514 (XV); GA Res 2625 (XXV); International Covenants – cases: *Frontier Dispute Case*; *Western Sahara Case*; *Land, Island and Maritime Frontier Dispute Case* – recent events: collapse of USSR; Bosnia – areas of incompatibility between the two – conclusions.

Suggested Solution

It is certainly arguable that the principle of uti possidetis juris, in its application to questions of state title to territory, is wholly incompatible with the right of self-determination. That is not the view of the International Court of Justice (ICJ) but, it is submitted, first, that the ICJ rather glossed over this issue in the *Frontier Dispute Case* (1986) ICJ Rep 554, and, second, that recent events have given new meaning and content to the right of self-determination. In order to establish this incompatibility, it is necessary to consider, first, the definition and significance of both uti possidetis and self-determination; this will be followed by an analysis of the relevant case law, a discussion of the impact of recent developments, and, finally, in the conclusion it will be submitted that the principle of uti possidetis is not at all compatible with the right of self-determination.

The principle of uti possidetis juris, roughly translated as 'as you possess, so shall you continue to possess' is, in essence, a principle of stability. Its applicability in international law dates from the independence of the South American colonies from Spain in the early nineteenth century; on achieving independence, much territory within those new states remained uninhabited or unexplored. Concerned both to prevent territorial disputes between the new states themselves and to avoid the dangers of intervention by acquisitive European colonial powers, it was decided that the former administrative boundaries created by Spain would simply be transformed into international boundaries. As the ICJ said in the *Frontier Dispute Case*: 'The essence of the principle lies in its primary aim of securing respect for the territorial boundaries at the moment when independence is achieved'.

Self-determination is not, by contrast, a principle of stability: quite the reverse. The right of self-determination, in its modern manifestation, is recognised in a number of General Assembly Resolutions and international conventions, particularly General Assembly Resolution (GA Res) 1514 (XV) (Declaration on the Granting of Independence to Colonial Territories and Peoples 1960) and Common art 1 of the International Covenants (International Covenant on Civil and Political Rights 1966; International Covenant on Economic, Social and Cultural Rights 1966). This latter provides that 'All peoples have the right of self-determination. By virtue of that right they freely determine their political status and freely pursue their economic, social and cultural development.' In GA Res 2625 (XXV) (Declaration on the Principles of International Law Concerning Friendly Relations and Co-operation among States 1970), the 'establishment of a sovereign and independent State, the free association or integration with an independent State or the emergence into any other political status freely determined by a people' were laid down as modes of implementing self-determination.

Self-determination was used as the key legal tool with which to effect and justify the process of decolonisation. Already by the late 1960s, however, states were concerned that its application outwith that context could lead to instability. Hence, in GA Res 2625, it was emphasised that exercise of the right did not authorise dismembering territorial integrity in existing states. That this was a real danger was illustrated by the rather contrasting experiences of Biafra and East Pakistan between 1967 and 1971.

In the *Western Sahara Case* (1975) ICJ Rep 12, however, the ICJ seemed clear that self-determination enjoyed the status of a right in customary international law. In the *Frontier Dispute Case*, the ICJ was equally clear that uti possidetis enjoyed status as a general rule of international law, requiring respect for territorial frontiers. Similarly, in the *Case Concerning the Land, Island and Maritime Frontier Dispute* (1992) ICJ Rep 351, the ICJ accepted the application of uti possidetis in a territorial dispute between El Salvador and Honduras. In the *Frontier Dispute Case*, the Court recognised the possibility of conflict between the two principles but concluded, rather lamely, that the 'maintenance of the territorial status quo in Africa is often seen as the wisest course ... to avoid a disruption'.

So, while uti possidetis mandates respect for territorial boundaries, self-determination potentially allows a 'people' to secede from a state, at least when that latter fails to conduct itself in accordance with the dictates of self-determination. Recent events (see, generally, M Koskenniemi, 'National Self-Determination Today: Problems of Legal Theory and Practice' (1994) 43 ICLQ 241), particularly the collapse of the USSR, suggest, however, that self-determination has considerable potential outwith the decolonisation process: the independence of the Baltic states could be explained by reference to self-determination; a variety of other self-determination claims are brewing in the former Soviet Empire (eg Georgia, Armenia, Moldava). In Africa, Eritrea, having seceded from Ethiopia after years of civil war, has been accepted as a UN Member State; Northern Somaliland, too, is attempting to secede from Somalia, although it still awaits recognition. But it is perhaps in the former Yugoslavia, where the doctrinal conflict between self-determination and uti possidetis has been transformed into armed conflict, that the incompatibility between the two principles is most apparent.

Ultimately, it is control of territory that is in practice the most important element of statehood. The respect for territorial integrity and the maintenance of frontiers in cases of independence or succession that is inherent in uti possidetis is thus attractive to states as a principle legitimising their title to territory. By contrast, the idea that rights might be conceded to 'peoples' – perhaps minorities within a state – and that, in exercise of its right to self-determination a people might secede to form its own state, carries with it the threat to existing states that their title to their territory is transient. To that extent, the answer to the question 'is the principle of uti possidetis compatible with the right of self-determination for purposes of determining State title to territory' must be 'no'.

QUESTION TWO

An application of the legal principles relating to the acquisition of territory requiring detailed knowledge of recent world events.

On 25 December 1970 the intelligence services of State K learned that State L's armed forces were planning to launch an attack on State K on 1 January 1971. On 30 December 1970 State K's armed forces launched an attack across the border between State K and State L. They quickly defeated State L's armed forces. On 4 January 1971 the commanders of State K's and State L's armed forces agreed to a ceasefire. State K's armed forces withdrew from most of that part of State L's territory which they had captured. However, they retained control of the Sierra Linda, a strategically important area of State L's territory which is located close to its border with State K. State K's armed forces have remained in control of that area to this day.

State M, a State which neighbours State K and State L, seeks your advice as to whether State K has any right under international law to retain control of the Sierra Linda.

University of London LLB Examination
(for External Students) Public International Law June 1993 Q7

General Comment

A direct and simple question on the law of armed conflict and the use of force, which focuses clearly and specifically on the occupation, annexation and retention of foreign territory as a result of military action in pre-emptive self-defence. Perfectly straightforward and easy to deal with.

Skeleton Solution

General comments on the use of force – the legality of pre-emptive strikes – the occupation and annexation of territory generally in modern international law – occupation as a result of anticipatory self-defence – buffer zones in strategic areas.

Suggested Solution

The issues raised in this problem relate to the acquisition of territory as a result of the use of force, so the first point to be considered is the permissibility of the use of force generally. The law on the use of force today is governed by art 2 of the United Nations Charter; in particular, art 2(4) outlaws the use of force completely except in certain very limited types of situation. The only exceptions when the use of force is to some extent permitted are basically in individual or collective self-defence (art 51, UN Charter) and in execution of collective measures authorised by the UN Security Council: art 4(2). Although there are one or two additional 'grey areas' where it is very occasionally and theoretically possible to justify military action – namely humanitarian intervention and the right of 'hot pursuit' under the law of the sea – self-defence and UN enforcement action remain the only viable possibilities for the justifiable use of force.

The particular use of force at issue in this problem is what is known as 'anticipatory self-defence': a pre-emptive strike. In customary international law, under the principles established in the *Caroline Case: USA v UK* (1837) 29 BFSP 1137, a pre-emptive strike was a perfectly lawful means of anticipatory self-defence in the face of a threat of force; indeed, it was the only possible means of defence against such threats as they could only be countered by an attack to pre-empt the harm that they would otherwise cause. Today there is an acrimonious dispute as to whether art 51 of the UN Charter (which permits the use of force in individual or collective self-defence 'if an armed attack occurs') was intended to be construed as restricting the rights in customary law to self-defence against a threat of force; in view of art 51's reference to not impairing 'the inherent right' to self-defence, a majority of international legal experts now assume this to mean that pre-emptive strikes are acceptable today, provided that the (already fairly narrow) doctrine of self-defence that emerged from the *Caroline Case* is observed – namely, that there must be an imminent threat or violation of the rights of the defending state giving rise to an instant and overwhelming need for self-defence, leaving no choice of means and no time for deliberation, and that the act of anticipatory self-defence must be strictly confined to preventing the violation and must be proportionate to the degree of force reasonably required to achieve this object. Since 1945 there is the additional requirement that a state intending to launch a pre-emptive strike must exhaust all possible means of settling the dispute peacefully first; in practice this usually involves notifying the Security Council of the pending action; which of course makes a nonsense of the whole notion of anticipatory self-defence as its essence is a sudden, swift, surprise attack.

The classic textbook example of a pre-emptive strike in modern times is the Israeli air strike against the Egyptian and Syrian air forces at the start of the Six Day War in 1967. In the weeks and months immediately preceding the Israeli strike, Egypt and Syria (which had already formally combined in a loose confederation entitled the United Arab Republic) had unified their military commands into a single centralised high command in Cairo, had issued numerous dark warnings about the Jewish State being wiped off the map, and had begun massing armoured formations near the Israeli frontier; in addition, Jordan (which was not part of the UAR) had begun blockading the sole Israeli outlet on the Red Sea, the port of Eilat. The Israeli cabinet met at the end of May 1967 to debate the urgency of the situation and, genuinely believing a massive armed attack from the UAR and Jordan to be imminent, voted for war. On 1 June Israel launched a pre-emptive air strike and destroyed the UAR air forces on the ground; six days later the Arab armies had been crushed and substantial tracts of Arab territory (the Sinai and Gaza Strip from Egypt, the West Bank of the River Jordan and East Jerusalem from Jordan, and the Golan Heights from Syria) were in Israeli hands. East Jerusalem was annexed outright by Israel in the aftermath of the war – the Israeli courts have recognised the 'united Jerusalem' as an 'inseparable part of Israel', as in *Hanzalis v Greek Orthodox Patriarchate Religious Court* (1969) 48 ILR 93 – but the other areas were never formally incorporated into Israel; instead, they remain officially Arab territories under temporary Israel military administration. However, a large-scale programme of building Jewish settlements in the Occupied Territories has produced a general belief that Israel is annexing the West Bank, especially, in all but name. In 1967 the consensus around the world (except among Arab League states and those sympathetic to them) was that the Israeli action was perfectly justified in view of the situation facing the Jewish State and constituted an absolutely legal use of force in anticipatory self-defence. This remains to this day the received opinion with regard to the pre-emptive strike itself.

The Arab-Israeli War of 1967 and its continued ramifications today are directly analogous to the scenario presented in this problem, with State K standing in for Israel, State L for the Arab states and the Sierra Linda for the Occupied Territories. The position on the acquisition of territory by force today is that, as a result of art 2(4) of the UN Charter, territory cannot legally be acquired by conquest, and any treaty of cession imposed by a victorious nation on a vanquished one is automatically null and void. Thus there could be no legal dispute, for instance, that the Iraqi annexation of Kuwait in 1990 was a flagrant violation of art 2(4) and completely illegal. The same was true of the Indian annexation of the Portuguese colonies of Goa, Danao and Diu in 1961, although general hostility towards colonialism and imperialism at the time allowed India to get away with it.

However, the situation here is slightly different, for the Sierra Linda was acquired by State K in the course of a legitimate pre-emptive strike – that is, a lawful use of force – and not by an unlawful act of aggression. We must therefore return to the status of the Occupied Territories of Israel to determine the legality of the Israeli occupation. The problem since 1967 in the eyes of the world community has been not Israel's original use of force but its continued occupation of Gaza, the West Bank and Golan (the Sinai was returned to Egypt under the Camp David Peace Treaty in 1979); also many states – including the UK – refuse to recognise the annexation of East Jerusalem. The generally accepted view is that the continued Israeli occupation of these territories is illegal, especially since the overriding right to self-determination of peoples has been accepted by the UN as a basic human right. The original point of Israel's occupation of the Territories, particularly the West Bank and Golan, was identical to that of State K's occupation of the Sierra Linda: to preserve a buffer zone for security reasons in a strategically important area. The consensus about this type of situation has become that temporary occupation strictly for pressing reasons of security is acceptable, but long-term (in the case of Israel, indefinite) occupation is not, and settlement with a view to annexation is out of the question. The UN Security Council, in Resolution 242 (XXII) (1967) has demanded Israel's withdrawal from the Occupied Territories and, in Resolution 465 (XXXV) (1980), declared the settlement programme to be illegal and demanded the suspension of all Jewish settlements on Arab territory. (Israel's occupation, since 1982, of a self-proclaimed Security Zone in South Lebanon as a buffer against Syrian forces and Iranian-backed terrorists has also attracted widespread condemnation.)

State K has been in occupation of the Sierra Linda since 1970, almost as long as Israel's occupation of the Territories. The final answer to State M's request must be that while State K's initial occupation of the Sierra Linda to form a buffer zone was permissible, its continued retention of the territory is illegal. The best solution to the problem would doubtless be to negotiate a peace treaty between State K and State L, whereby the Sierra Linda would be returned to its rightful sovereign, in exchange for guarantees of non-aggression, reinforced perhaps by the presence of an international peacekeeping force under UN auspices.

QUESTION THREE

'In the law relating to the acquisition of title to territory, recognition, acquiescence and estoppel often play a decisive role.'

'(T)he continuous and peaceful display of territorial sovereignty (peaceful in relation to other States) is as good as title.' (Huber)

Explain these two statements. How far, if at all, can they be reconciled to each other?

University of London LLB Examination
(for External Students) Public International Law June 1991 Q5

General Comment

A question requiring the student to contrast two apparently contradictory statements.

Skeleton Solution

Occupation, prescription, cession and accretion – occupation; continuous, effective and peaceful possession – prescription and the role of protest, recognition and estoppel – the relationship between these two principles in practice.

Suggested Solution

In modern international law, there are four recognised methods of acquiring title to territory – occupation, prescription, cession and accretion. The validity of title obtained by means of conquest or annexation is no longer permitted: see the Declaration on the Principles of International Law 1970. In both occupation and prescription, not only is the conduct of the state in possession important, but the validity of title also depends to a considerable extent on the behaviour of the international community towards the possession.

To obtain title by way of occupation, the territory in question must be terra nullius, that is, land belonging to no one. Further, the occupation must also be carried out by state functionaries, and not private individuals. But most importantly, as Umpire Huber pointed out in the *Islands of Palmas Arbitration* (1928) 2 RIAA 829, the acquisition of territory by means of occupation must be 'open, continuous, effective and peaceful'. The degree of control required will vary in accordance with the circumstances of the case. Minimum overt action is sufficient to acquire title to uninhabited areas by occupation but a greater degree of control is required where there are forces opposing the control of the governing authorities. In addition, the possession must be actual and not nominal: see *Minquiers and Ecrehos Islands Case* (1953) ICJ Rep 47.

The acquisition of territory by occupation, therefore, requires the continuous display of territorial sovereignty which is as good as title, although the acquiring state must also demonstrate an animus occupandi, or the intention of acting as a sovereign. This is generally evidenced by the creation of a legal structure to govern the territory.

The second quotation refers to territory claimed by way of prescription. Prescription is a means of claiming territory that previously belonged to another state. Since this usually involves competing claims, then the elements of recognition, acquiescence and estoppel become relevant. These factors are critical in determining which state has the better title to the territory.

Acquisition of title by prescription may be achieved in two ways. First, a state may claim that it has maintained possession for such a period that competing claims are extinguished through immemorial possession. Alternatively, where the previous sovereign is known, but the acquiring state has exercised control for such a duration that the original or previous sovereign is considered to have lost his title, prescription may also apply. Such control requires acquiescence on the part of the previous sovereign and protests, particularly if vigorously repeated, impede acquisition of title by prescription.

If a state has recognised the possession of territory that it once had, title passes to the state in possession from the relinquishing state. Recognition must be actual acknowledgement by one party of another's right in the territory. However, there are few illustrations of recognition of the passage of territory in this manner between states. The most common example is when two states settle territorial disputes through bilateral agreements. For example, the 1973 Treaty of Friendship between West Germany and Poland established the present border between the two states, implicitly recognising that title to the territory possessed by Germany prior to the Second World War had passed to Poland. The terms of this agreement were later confirmed in the Treaty on the Final Settlement with Respect to Germany 1990, agreed among the four wartime allied powers and East Germany and West Germany.

The principle of estoppel operates to prevent one party denying a state of affairs that it has consented to in the past. It is essentially a principle of equity. Although the principle is primarily evidential and cannot by itself found title, it has been applied in a number of cases to establish title to territory. For example, in the *Legal Status of Eastern Greenland Case* (1933) PCIJ Rep Ser A/B No 53, the Permanent Court considered that Norwegian acceptance of treaties with Denmark that incorporated Danish claims to areas of Greenland prevented Norway from challenging the title of Denmark to the territory. Similarly, in the *Temple of Preah Vihear Case* (1962) ICJ Rep 6, the International Court considered that Thai claims against Cambodia to a disputed area were barred because

Thailand had accepted the validity of maps drafted by the French colonial administration of Cambodia prior to the independence of that country. In other words, Thailand was estopped by its conduct from claiming the contested area on its frontier.

Therefore these statements may be reconciled by acknowledging that one applies to occupation and the other to prescription. Yet it is true that, in the cases that have been decided by international courts and tribunals, both principles have tended to become merged or confused with each other. Thus, the cases that have been decided have been rendered in the light of balancing these principles against each other.

QUESTION FOUR

'The modern jurisprudence of the International Court of Justice suggests that territorial disputes should now be settled primarily by reference to the principle of self-determination.' Discuss.

University of London LLB Examination
(for External Students) Public International Law June 1988 Q7

General Comment

A complex question which involves consideration and analysis of legal principles other than those relating to the acquisition of territory.

Skeleton Solution

The traditional modes of settling territorial disputes – the *Namibia Case* and the *Western Sahara Case* and their reference to self-determination – conclusion: the status of these decisions as advisory opinions; further the decision of the Court might vary in cases concerning specific rights with regard to title to territory.

Suggested Solution

The traditional means of settling territorial disputes are occupation, prescription, conquest and subjugation, cession and accretion. In the past, conquest and subjugation was the most popular way of settling territorial disputes, and indeed modern state boundaries are often the result of the conquests of the past. However, the Declaration on Principles of International Law Concerning Friendly Relations and Co-operation among States in accordance with the Charter of the United Nations of the General Assembly in 1970 declares that: 'The territory of a state shall not be the object of acquisition by another state resulting from the threat or use of force.' Further, the General Assembly Resolution of 1974 on the definition of aggression, in art 3(a), classifies as an act of aggression (use of force in violation of the Charter), 'any annexation by the use of force of the territory of another state or part thereof'. Article 5(3) emphasised that 'no territorial acquisition or special advantage resulting from aggression is or shall be recognised as lawful'.

Cession is the transfer of territory usually by treaty from one state to another. The terms of the transfer will usually be stipulated in the treaty itself. Accretion is a means of acquiring territory through the operations of nature. This occurs, for example, when a river silts or where volcanic islands emerge in a state's internal waters or territorial sea.

Occupation and prescription are the two main modes which the statement suggests have been displaced by self-determination. Occupation is the acquisition of terra nullius, that is territory which has never been inhabited or has been abandoned. Abandonment requires not only failure to occupy and exercise authority over the territory but also an intention to abandon: see *Clipperton Island Case* (1931) 2 RIAA 1105.

The main precedent on occupation is the *Island of Palmas Arbitration* (1928) 2 RIAA 829, where Umpire Huber laid down the main features of title by occupation. However, the case was an arbitration and the question is restricted to examination of the jurisprudence of the ICJ. For this purpose, the *Western Sahara Case* (1975) ICJ Rep 12 contains the pertinent statements relating to the nature of terra nulius. In this case the Court had to consider, amongst other issues, whether, at the time Spain acquired the Western Sahara in 1884, the territory had been terra nullius and, if not, whether 'legal ties' had existed between it and the neighbouring state of Morocco or the 'Mauritanian entity' (the forerunner of the present state of Mauritania). The Court held that the Western Sahara had not been a terra nullius in 1884 because 'the state practice of the relevant period indicates that territories inhabited by tribes or peoples having a social and political organisation were not regarded as terra nullius'. Such territories came under colonial control by 'cession' through agreements with the local rulers rather than by 'occupation'. This contrasts with the *Island of Palmas Arbitration* where the indigenous population were not considered as having any rights in the dispute between the United States and the Netherlands over the island.

Prescription in contrast to occupation was a means to acquire territory which might originally have belonged to another sovereign whose rights had been abolished through time. Two types of prescription have been identified:

a) immemorial possession: possible competing claims of some earlier sovereign have been 'forgotten';

b) adverse possession: here the sovereign is known but the 'usurper' retains possession. This raises issues of estoppel protest and acquiescence.

It is contended by some that there often is very little difference between prescription and occupation when the courts are trying to settle a territorial dispute. Huber in the *Island of Palmas Arbitration* referred to both modes, as did the PCIJ in the *Eastern Greenland Case* (1933) PCIJ Rep Ser A/B No 53. Peaceful uninterrupted possession is the key to prescription.

However, in two cases the International Court made reference to the principle of self-determination as the decisive principle in settling territorial disputes. Before drawing a conclusion as to the 'change' in the Court's methodology of settling disputes, it must be noted that both the *Namibia Case* (1971) ICJ Rep 16 and the *Western Sahara Case* are advisory opinions and therefore not primarily concerned with the specific rights with regard to title to territory since the cases were not brought by the disputants themselves but by the United Nations General Assembly.

a) *The Namibia Case*

Article 22 of the Convention of the League of Nations implied that the peoples inhabiting mandate territories would be allowed to exercise a right of self-determination at some time in the future, but it did not fix a date for the exercise of that right. South Africa refused to place South-West Africa into the trusteeship system of the United Nations, as all former mandatories of the League of Nations had done. The status of South-West Africa has thus given rise to a prolonged dispute between South Africa and the United Nations and to two advisory opinions and two judgments from the International Court.

In 1950 the ICJ held that South Africa was not obliged to place South-West Africa under the trusteeship system: *Status of South-West Africa Case* (1950) ICJ Rep 6. But unless it did so, South Africa remained bound by the obligations contained in the mandate and the General Assembly was the successor to the supervisory powers of the League under the mandate.

In 1960 Liberia and Ethiopia, two former League members, asked the Court to declare that South Africa had violated the mandate by introducing apartheid in South-West Africa. The Court in 1966 decided that Liberia and Ethiopia were not entitled to enforce rights which did not belong to them: *South-West Africa Cases (Second Phase)* (1966) ICJ Rep 6.

In 1971 the Court had to pronounce on the legality on the General Assembly's Resolution terminating South Africa's mandate over South-West Africa and the consequences for other states of South Africa's continued presence in South-West Africa (or Namibia).

b) *Western Sahara Case*

In the *Western Sahara Case* the ICJ addressed itself for the first time to the issue of decolonisation and to the status in law of the concept of self-determination, in particular the definition of the 'self'. The colonial era meant the freezing of territorial entities and a disregard for historical and ethnic ties across former colonial borders. Thus, in the post colonial period would the principles of self-determination, territorial integrity and national unity all fight for supremacy?

In 1965 the United Nations had asked Spain to enter into negotiations over the sovereignty of the Western Sahara. Morocco and Mauritania, neighbouring states of Western Sahara, had territorial aspirations to the area on historic, ethnic and other ties. The International Court had to address itself to the various strands of these claims. In order to decide the question of sovereignty, the two modes of acquiring title – occupation and prescription – were examined.

In order for territory to be acquired through occupation it was essential for that territory to be terra nullius. Jennings notes that occupation was accepted as the appropriation by a state of territory which is not at the time subject to the sovereignty of any state: see R Y Jennings *The Acquisition of Territory in International Law* (1962). The indigenous populations of the area were not considered states for this purpose. This would seem to suggest that in the process of colonisation, territories could be acquired totally disregarding the wishes of the inhabitants. The Court however ignored any reference to the process of colonisation and asserted that 'the state practice of the relevant period indicates that territories inhabited by tribes or peoples having a social and political organisation were not regarded as terra nullius'. Thus the Western Sahara was not terra nullius because the inhabitants, although nomadic, were socially and politically organised with chiefs appointed who were competent to represent them.

Morocco argued that it had possessed sovereignty over the territory by virtue of immemorial possession founded on the 'public display of sovereignty, uninterrupted and uncontested for centuries as evidenced by the general acquiescence of the international community which it was accorded for several hundred years'. The evidence was based on religious links with Morocco, which Morocco claimed amounted to political allegiance and military decisions taken by Morocco to expel foreigners from the territory. Morocco further laid emphasis on the geographical, ethnological and cultural ties that linked it with Western Sahara 'because international law attaches decisive importance to these factors'. Contiguity, it was claimed, was important when exercised by an immemorial possessor. 'Contiguity could be valid as the basis and support of real social relationships sustaining immemorial possession.'

Mauritania wished to reunify its people in order to reinforce its nationhood. Mauritania underlined the social, political, legal, cultural and economic ties it had with the nomadic tribes inhabiting the Western Sahara. The Court declared that while legal ties did exist between Morocco, Mauritania and the Western Sahara, they were not ties of sovereignty and could not affect the application of the principle of self-determination to the territory.

The questions posed by UN Resolution 3292 were firmly placed within the context of decolonisation. The Resolution affirmed the right of the people of the territory to self-determination as embodied in Resolution 1514. The Court regarded Resolution 1514 as the basis for the process of decolonisation. This resolution called for immediate steps to be taken in non-independent territories for the transfer of power in the light of the principle that all peoples have the right to self-determination. Resolution 1514 noted that self-determination could take the form of independence, free association with an independent state or integration with an independent state. In each case the essential feature was the free choice of the people.

Resolution 2625 also provided that each state was under a duty to promote the realisation of the principle of self-determination in accordance with the Charter. Further all the Resolutions adopted by the General Assembly with regard to Western Sahara had stressed the right of the population to self-determination. The Court affirmed that 'the right of that (the Western Saharan) population to self-determination constitutes a basic assumption of the questions put to the Court'. The conclusion of the Court was that no ties of territorial sovereignty could be established and thus no such ties could affect 'the application of Resolution 1514 in the decolonisation of the Western Sahara and in particular the principle of self-determination'.

The implication is that only ties of territorial sovereignty could affect the application of the relevant decolonisation principles. Shaw points out that the Court's attitude towards the possibility of past ties of sovereignty overruling the application of self-determination was ambiguous, based as it was on the Court's reasoning on either a view that the people entitled to self-determination were not a people or a view that due to special circumstances a consultation of the people was not necessary: M Shaw, *Title to Territory in Africa* (1985) pp1–11. Judge Boni thought that even if ties of sovereignty were found, there would be an obligation to consult the population, thus reaffirming the role of self-determination. Judge Dillard summed up the role of self-determination in the eyes of the Court when he stated: 'It is for the people to determine the destiny of the territory and not the territory the destiny of the people'. Judge De Castrio made the point that legal and factual changes could not be ignored. Colonisation had created ties and rights, just as General Assembly resolutions calling for decolonisation had created new facts. The continuation or re-emergence of historic rights had therefore to be judged in the light of the right of self-determination.

In conclusion, it can be said that the verdicts reached in the *Western Sahara Case* and the *Namibia Case* apply to non self-governing territories. Territorial disputes involving self-governing entities would still have to refer to the traditional modes of acquiring territory and the principle of self-determination would not have a primary role to play.

Chapter 7

State Jurisdiction

7.1 Introduction

Jurisdiction is the power of a state under international law to prescribe rules (prescriptive jurisdiction) and the authority to enforce judgments made in accordance with these rules (enforcement jurisdiction). Jurisdiction may be exercised in both the civil and criminal dimensions of municipal law, although, in terms of international law, emphasis is usually placed on the criminal jurisdiction of a state. In this context, the Geneva Conventions (Amendment) Act 1997 was passed to enable criminal proceedings to be taken in the United Kingdom for breach of the common art 3 of the Geneva Conventions 1949. The basic principles behind this concept are relatively simple and students should be thoroughly acquainted with their operation. The issue of jurisdiction is closely tied to the matter of immunity from jurisdiction dealt with in the next chapter.

7.2 Key points

The grounds of state jurisdiction in international law

Territorial jurisdiction

Territorial jurisdiction is the ground on which the vast majority of offences are prosecuted. All crimes alleged to have been committed within the geographical territory of a state may be heard before the municipal courts of the state in question. In the case *Compania Naviera Vascongado* v *Cristina SS* [1938] AC 485, Lord Macmillan stated:

> 'It is an essential attribute of the sovereignty of this realm, as of all sovereign independent states, that it should possess jurisdiction over all persons and things within its territorial limits and in all causes civil and criminal arising within these limits.'

This principle is applicable notwithstanding that the defendants are foreign nationals.

Territorial jurisdiction extends not only to crimes committed wholly within the territory of the state, but also to cases in which only part of the offence occurred in the state. Where a crime is a continuing one insofar as the perpetration of the criminal act extends to two or more states, all states involved may claim jurisdiction. This is because the territorial principle may be divided into two constituent parts.

a) States in which acts taken to initiate or perpetuate the offence may claim jurisdiction on the 'subjective territorial principle'. This is the normal meaning of the term 'territorial jurisdiction'. In *Treacy* v *DPP* [1971] AC 537, Lord Diplock declared that there is 'no rule of comity to prevent Parliament from prohibiting under pain of punishment persons who are present in the United Kingdom ... from doing physical acts in England, notwithstanding that the consequences of those acts take effect outside the United Kingdom'.

b) States in which injury takes place may claim jurisdiction in accordance with the 'objective territorial principle'. The objective territorial principle has been applied in a number of cases at the international, national and supranational levels.

i) The Permanent Court, in the *SS Lotus Case* (1923) PCIJ Rep Ser A No 10, recognised the objective territorial principle when it stated:

> '... it is certain that the courts of many countries ... interpret criminal law in the sense that offences, the authors of which at the moment of commission are in the territory of another state, are nevertheless to be regarded as having committed in the national territory, if one of the constituent elements of the offence, and more especially its effects, have taken place there.'

ii) In *DPP* v *Doot* [1973] AC 807 the House of Lords held that the English courts had jurisdiction over persons conspiring to import cannabis resin into the United Kingdom, despite the fact that the conspiracy to commit the offence had been carried out abroad. In considering the issue of jurisdiction, Lord Wilberforce stated:

> 'The present case involves "international elements" – the accused are aliens and the conspiracy was initiated abroad – but there can be no question here of any breach of any rules of international law if they are prosecuted in this country. Under the objective territorial principle ... the courts have a clear right, if not a duty, to prosecute in accordance with our municipal law.'

iii) The United States courts have adopted this principle in order to extend the scope of American anti-trust laws to cover alien individuals and companies whose activities, although perfectly legitimate in the foreign state in which they occur, have a certain effect on the economy of the United States: see *Timberlane Lumber Co* v *Bank of America* 549 F 2nd 597 (1976).

iv) The European Court of Justice has adopted an extra-territorial approach to the application of Community competition law: see the *Woodpulp Cartel Case* [1988] 4 CMLR 901.

Active nationality principle

The nexus established between a state and its citizens by the concept of nationality is another basis for the exercise of jurisdiction, even when the nationals in question are outwith the territory of the state itself. In such circumstances, jurisdiction is said to be founded on the nationality principle.

Civil law countries make extensive use of jurisdiction on this basis. Common law systems only claim jurisdiction on this basis for a limited number of serious crimes. It is a recognised principle of English law that British nationals are liable to be punished for treason, murder, bigamy and perjury, even in those cases in which their crimes were committed abroad. In *Joyce* v *Director of Public Prosecutions* [1946] AC 347, the House of Lords held:

'No principle of comity demands that a state should ignore the crime of treason committed against it outside its territory. On the contrary a proper regard for its own security requires that all those who commit that crime, whether they commit it within or without the realm, should be amenable to its laws.'

The principal problem which arises in the exercise of jurisdiction according to this principle involves the means selected by individual states for the granting of nationality to individuals. As a general rule, a state has discretion in the rules which it adopts for conferring nationality. However, this is circumscribed by international law which prohibits a state from infringing a state's obligations towards other states: see the *Nottebohm Case* (1955) ICJ Rep 4.

Passive personality principle

This principle grants jurisdiction to a state to punish alleged offences committed abroad against nationals of that state. An illustration of an exercise of jurisdiction on this basis was the request by the United States to Italy for the extradition of Palestinian nationals responsible for the murder of an American national aboard the Italian cruise ship the Achille Lauro in 1985. In this context it is worth noting that the international community has described the legal position of the 600 detainees held at the US-run Guantanamo Bay prison as a 'monstrous failure of justice' (*The Independent* 26 November 2003). The prisoners were apprehended by the US and its allies as a result of the 2001 war against the Taliban regime in Afghanistan in the wake of the 11 September 2001 attacks.

Another illustration of the application of this principle is *United States* v *Yunis* (1989) 83 AJIL 94, in which the United States courts founded jurisdiction over a Lebanese citizen accused of hijacking on the passive personality principle, even though none of the American passengers on board the plane were taken captive.

International law recognises jurisdiction on the passive principle basis but only subject to certain qualifications. It appears from the *Cutting Case* (1887) 2 Moore's Digest 228, that a state which does not acknowledge jurisdiction according to the passive personality principle is not bound to acquiesce to proceedings brought against one of its nationals on this basis. The United Kingdom has tended to reject the possibility of jurisdiction on this basis. At present the US Supreme Court has two cases pending concerning the issue of whether the US courts lack jurisdiction to consider challenges to the legality of detention of foreign nationals captured abroad. The cases are *Shafiq Rasul et al v George W Bush, President of the United States et al* and *Fazi Khalid Abdullah Fahad Al Odah et al v United States* (both cases are discussed in the May 2003 issue of the *American Journal of International Law*). It is anticipated that these cases will be heard in the summer of 2004.

Protective (or security) jurisdiction

This extensive principle of jurisdiction would permit jurisdiction to be exercised over foreign nationals whose conduct threatens the security of a state. This allows states to punish acts threatening to undermine national security such as plotting to overthrow the government, spying, forging currency and conspiracy to violate immigration regulations.

Two rationales for the exercise of jurisdiction on this basis are frequently asserted:

a) offences prosecuted on the protective principle involve consequences of the utmost gravity which actually threaten the stability of the state prosecuting; and

b) unless jurisdiction was exercised in accordance with the protective principle, many offences would escape punishment because they did not contravene the law of the place in which they were alleged to have been committed or because extradition would be refused because of the political nature of the offence.

In the case *Attorney-General for Israel v Eichmann* (1962) 36 ILR 5, the Israeli court applied the doctrine of protective jurisdiction in order to exercise jurisdiction over a Nazi war criminal. The linking point between the defendant and the state of Israel was crimes committed against the Jewish people which Israel had the right to pursue since the connection between the state of Israel and the Jewish people needed no explanation.

The Privy Council, on an appeal from the Hong Kong courts, has also applied the protective principle to found jurisdiction in that territory. In *Liangsiriprasert* v *Government of the United States* [1990] 3 WLR 606, the court held that a drug smuggler persuaded to go to Hong Kong by an American agent could be extradited to the United States by the Hong Kong courts and that jurisdiction over the plaintiff could be derived from the protective principle. In rendering its decision, the Court asked:

> 'If the inchoate crime is aimed at England with the consequent injury to English society, why should the English courts not accept jurisdiction to try it if the authorities can lay hands on the offenders, either because they come within the jurisdiction or through extradition procedures?'

The main objection to this principle is that 'security' is more often than not defined in an extensive manner in order to acquire jurisdiction. Such a process would permit the exercise of jurisdiction in an unlimited and unrestrained fashion.

Universality principle

The basis for jurisdiction in accordance with the universality principle is that the state exercising jurisdiction has custody of a person accused of perpetrating an offence recognised by international law as an international crime. In principle, three main forms of international crime exist.

a) Piracy jure gentium: this activity was recognised as an international crime under customary international law and was codified in arts 14–17 of the Geneva Convention on the High Seas 1958 and arts 101–107 of the Convention on the Law of the Sea 1982. A state which has apprehended an alleged pirate may try that person for that offence regardless of nationality and even if the activities of the pirate have had no adverse effect on the shipping of the state in question.

b) War crimes: although strictly violations of the laws of war, international custom has made war crimes offences of universal jurisdiction. See the judgment of the Nuremberg Tribunal.

In fact UK legislation does not rely on this principle as a basis for prosecution of war crimes against individuals present within the United Kingdom. The War Crimes Act 1991 instead relies on both the nationality principle and the territorial principle to supply the basis for jurisdiction.

c) War-related crimes: these are:

i) crimes against peace which include the planning or waging of aggressive war in violation of international law; and

ii) crimes against humanity which include extermination, enslavement, deportation and other inhumane acts.

Again see the judgment of the Nuremberg War Tribunal.

Limitations of the traditional principles

The traditional grounds for establishing jurisdiction have struggled to accommodate increased international crime – terrorism, hijacking, drug-smuggling and international fraud.

More and more frequently, courts in which persons accused of such offences appear are unwilling to relinquish jurisdiction simply because the traditional principles are so rigorous.

The United States courts especially have been willing to abandon the rigorous application of these principles in favour of asserting jurisdiction where possible over persons accused of committing offences against the national security of that country or against its nationals.

For example, in *United States* v *Alvarez-Machain* 112 S Ct 2188 (1992), the accused was a Mexican national charged with kidnapping, torturing and murdering an American drug enforcement officer in Mexico. The accused had himself been kidnapped and taken to the United States against his will.

The US Supreme Court held that the US courts had jurisdiction to try an accused charged with harming an American national as long as the manner in which the accused was brought before the court did not violate the terms of any treaty between the states involved.

This is undoubtedly a dangerous precedent for the US Supreme Court to have set but it is no doubt an expression of the frustration that is felt when the traditional grounds for jurisdiction allow perpetrators of transnational crimes to escape justice. However, if the traditional grounds of jurisdiction are no longer of any relevance, what rules should replace them? Echert AE provides a thought-provoking response to the issue of transnational crimes in his article '"Unlawful Combatants" or "Prisoners of Wars": the Law and Politics of Labels' (2003) 36 Cornell International Law Journal 59.

Jurisdiction in special circumstances and in accordance with international agreements

Offences committed against aircraft

Problems arise in hijacking because the offence is not necessarily committed in any particular territory but in transitu. A number of conventions have been established in an attempt to regulate the issue of jurisdiction over hijacking. These include:

a) Tokyo Convention on Offences and Certain other Acts Committed on Board Aircraft 1963. Article 4 grants jurisdiction over hijackers on the basis of the objective territorial principle, the passive personality principle, the protective principle and in order to enforce national flight regulations or international obligations.

b) Hague Conventions for the Suppression of Unlawful Seizure of Aircraft 1970. Article 4(2) establishes state jurisdiction on the universality principle to signatories of the convention regardless of any connection with the offence.

c) Montreal Convention for the Suppression of Unlawful Acts against the Safety of Civil Aviation 1971. This agreement enlarges the categories of aerial crimes to include sabotage of aircraft and related acts, on the same basis of jurisdiction as established under the Hague Convention.

    The defects in establishing jurisdiction over persons accused of crimes specified in multilateral treaties such as these were recently highlighted in the *Case Concerning Questions of Interpretation and Application of the 1971 Montreal Convention Arising from the Aerial Incident at Lockerbie* (1992) ICJ Rep 114. See also *Case Concerning Questions of Interpretation and Application of the 1971 Montreal Convention Arising from the Aerial Incident at Lockerbie (Preliminary Objections) (Libya v USA; Libya v UK)* (1998) 37 ILM 587.

Slavery

Slavery is prohibited by art 4 of the Universal Declaration of Human Rights 1948 and art 8 of the International Covenant on Civil and Political Rights 1966. This is now enforceable in English law through the Human Rights Act 1998 which incorporates into English law the European Convention on Human Rights.

Further, the International Law Commission draft on state responsibility declared slavery to be an international crime. However, it is unclear whether universal jurisdiction accompanies this particular international crime.

Extradition

The concept of extradition is based on treaty and no general right of customary international law exists. Extradition is usually regulated by a framework of bilateral treaties which generally have a number of features in common.

a) A statement of extraditable offences which is usually confined to serious offences. Alternatively, extraditable offences may be determined by reference to the principle of double criminality which requires that the offence be recognised by both states involved.

b) A definition of extraditable persons. This may be all persons accused of extradictable crimes or may exclude nationals of the extraditing state. The exclusion of nationals from extradition processes is common in the continental civilian countries.

c) An exception in cases of political, military or religious offences. Of these the most important is the defence of so-called 'political offence'. These are offences motivated by political objectives such as the overthrow of the government. Problems have arisen on this ground in relation to the extradition of terrorists. As a result, the tendency has been to restrict the category of political offence: see the European Convention on the Suppression of Terrorism 1976, art 1.

d) The inclusion of a specialty principle which means that the extradited person cannot be tried for a crime other than that for which extradition was obtained.

e) Provision for the prima facie proof of guilt. This is a common law phenomenon, unknown in extradition treaties between civil law states.

In the United Kingdom, the Extradition Act 1989 contains the relevant principles and procedures for extradition to and from the United Kingdom. This statute governs the procedure for extraditing a person accused of the commission of an extradition crime in the requesting state, or who is allegedly at large after conviction of an extradition crime by a court in such a state.

An extradition crime is defined as conduct which, if it occurred in the United Kingdom, would constitute an offence punishable by a term of imprisonment of 12 months or longer and which is also punishable in the law of the foreign state.

The procedures of the Extradition Act 1989 apply not only when the United Kingdom has entered into a bilateral extradition agreement with another state, but also when the United Kingdom is a party to a multilateral agreement which creates offences of an international character.

Special provisions have been drafted into the statute to deal with the problem of terrorism. In particular, under this legislation, no offence similar to that created by s1 of the Suppression of Terrorism Act 1978 shall be deemed a political offence.

The courts have recently had cause to interpret the Extradition Act 1989 in *R v Governor of Brixton Prison, ex parte Osman (No 3)* [1992] 1 WLR 36.

Status of forces agreements

Where troops of one state are present within the jurisdiction of another state with the consent of that state, jurisdiction over such forces is generally regulated by bilateral agreement: see *Wilson v Girard* 354 US 524 (1957).

In the case of American forces in Europe, jurisdiction is regulated by the NATO Status of Forces Agreement 1951, art 1 of which provides that the 'sending' military authorities shall exercise 'all criminal and disciplinary jurisdiction' conferred by military law over personnel, but the 'receiving' state shall exercise jurisdiction over such forces with respect to 'offences committed within the territory of the receiving state and punishable' by its law.

Article 3 regulates the issue of concurrent jurisdiction. The sending state has primary right over offences against military law while the receiving state has primary right over all other offences.

7.3 Key cases and legislation

*   *Attorney-General for Israel v Eichmann* (1962) 36 ILR 5
    Application of jurisdiction on the protective principle

*   *Gencor Ltd v EC Commission* Case T–102/96 [1999] 1 All ER (EC) 289
    Addresses the question of extraterritorial application of EC competition law

*   *Joyce v Director of Public Prosecutions* [1946] AC 347
    An example of the application of jurisdiction according to the nationality principle

*   *Liangsiriprasert v Government of the United States* [1990] 3 WLR 606
    UK courts' interpretation of the protective principle of jurisdiction

*   *Lockerbie Case (Libya v UK; Libya v US)* (1992) ICJ Rep 3 and 114
    Consideration of the problems of exercising jurisdiction on multiple grounds

*   *Lockerbie Case (Libya v USA; Libya v UK)* (1998) 37 ILM 587
    Considers the problems of exercising jurisdiction which is based on multilateral treaties

- *R* v *Governor of Brixton Prison, ex parte Osman (No 3)* [1992] 1 WLR 36
  judicial consideration of the terms of the Extradition Act 1989

- *SS Lotus Case: France* v *Turkey* (1927) PCIJ Rep Ser A No 10
  Support for the exercise of jurisdiction on an objective and subjective territorial basis

- *United States* v *Alvarez-Machain* 112 S Ct 2188 (1992) (US Supreme Ct)
  US Supreme Court ruling eliminating the need for US courts to rely on the traditional basis of jurisdiction

- *Woodpulp Cartel Case, Re, Ahlstrom and Others* v *EC Commission* [1988] 4 CMLR 901
  The extraterritorial application of EC competition law

- Geneva Convention on the Law of the Sea 1982 – recognises piracy as an international crime

- Hague Convention for the Suppression of Unlawful Seizure of Aircraft 1970 – illustrates the universality principle to signatories

- Human Rights Act 1998 – incorporates the ECHR into English law

- Montreal Convention for the Suppression of Unlawful Acts against the Safety of Civil Aviation 1971 – enlarges categories of aerial crimes

- Tokyo Convention on Offences and Certain Other Acts Committed on Board Aircraft 1963 – deals with jurisdiction in air space

- War Crimes Act 1991 – supplies the basis for jurisdiction

7.4 Questions and suggested solutions

QUESTION ONE

a) Explain the 'effects' doctrine and why it could be a controversial basis for the exercise of criminal jurisdiction in international law.

b) Advise States A, B and C on the bases for their respective claims to assert criminal jurisdiction.

   i) David, a national of State B, raped and then murdered Julia, a national of State A in the High Seas as they were both on holiday in a yacht registered in State C.

   ii) John, a national of State A, is wanted on terrorism charges in State C. He had conspired with Edward, a national of State B, to place a bomb in a plane with nationals of States C and A on board.

   iii) Dan, a national of State A, who operated a small laboratory in State A where he forged counterfeit banknotes of State C.

   David, John, Edward and Dan are all in the custody of State C which has announced its intention to prosecute. States A and B are also considering seeking extradition and prosecuting each of them.

University of London LLB Examination
(for External Students) Public International Law June 2000 Q3

General Comment

It is common for a paper on public international law to contain a question on the topic of jurisdiction. This question being split into parts (a) and (b) requires the candidate both to discuss the general principles and to then apply them. To answer this question, the candidate also needs to have some general awareness of the principles of extradition law and the circumstances in which the policy of dedere aut punire may be said to apply.

Skeleton Solution

a) Legal principles applicable to exercising criminal jurisdiction – the 'effects' doctrine – its ramifications.

b) Application of legal principles – in each situation to determine the existence of criminal jurisdiction.

Suggested Solution

a) We are asked in this question to consider the nature of the 'effects' doctrine and whether it might be considered a controversial basis for the exercise of criminal jurisdiction in international law.

Before turning to that specific point a number of preliminary remarks can usefully be made. First, states are traditionally more sensitive about matters of criminal jurisdiction than civil jurisdiction. In the nineteenth century the territorial principle was regarded as the central principle of jurisdiction. Since then, and following the *SS Lotus Case: France* v *Turkey* (1927) PCIJ Rep Ser A No 10, there are a number of principles upon which jurisdiction may be founded.

These are broadly: the nationality principle, the passive personality principle, the protective principle and the universal principle. In general it is accepted today that if a state wishes to exercise criminal jurisdiction, then it should do so in a manner that is consistent with the basic principles of international law that pertain to jurisdiction. Second, not all the principles of international law are accepted by all states. The most obvious example being the passive personality principle, which was subject to criticism in the *SS Lotus Case* and is today not accepted by all states, notwithstanding the fact that it formed part of the extradition request by Spain in *R* v *Bow Street Metropolitan Stipendiary Magistrate, ex parte Pinochet Ugarte (No 3)* [2000] 1 AC 147. Contrary to the ruling in the *SS Lotus Case* it is for a state to demonstrate that its claim to jurisdiction is consistent with international law. However, the scope of the relevant principles is the subject of some dispute.

So when one comes to consider the 'effects' doctrine it is in the context of differences of opinion about other relevant principles of jurisdiction. In reviewing the principle it is sensible first to consider the territorial principle. The objective territorial principle holds that a state can claim jurisdiction over offences which are completed within its territory, even though some elements constituting the offence have taken place abroad. Likewise the subjective territorial principle holds that a state has jurisdiction over all offences and matters commencing in its territory, even if some element or the completion of the offence takes place in another state. Related to this is the protective principle, which holds that a state may assert its jurisdiction over acts which produce an effect on the 'state' regardless of where the acts take place: see *Director of Public Prosecutions* v *Joyce* [1946] AC 347 per Lord Jowitt LC, approved in *Attorney-General for Israel* v *Eichmann* (1962) 36 ILR 5. In general the protective principle is invoked to protect the vital interests of a state, such as matters of defence and security.

It is against this background that the 'effects' doctrine must be considered. First, the 'effects' doctrine holds that State A may claim jurisdiction if conduct initiated in State B is having an effect within State A. This jurisdiction is claimed even though all the conduct objected to may have taken place outside State A. The principle is wider than the objective territorial principle, because in the latter case some elements of the offence have taken place in the state claiming jurisdiction. This was so in the *SS Lotus Case* where the death of the seamen took place on what was deemed to be Turkish territory. Second, the 'effects' doctrine is wider than the protective principle, because the latter is restricted to matters central to the security and defence of the state, while the former doctrine extends to commercial operations.

The 'effects' doctrine has been growing in prominence in recent years, particularly in the enforcement of competition law, or anti-trust law as it is sometimes described in the United States. One of the problems in this area of law is that states have different traditions in the enforcement of competition law. The United States has a long history of vigorous enforcement commencing with the Sherman Act 1890 and the Clayton Act 1914. After 1945 one can detect the emphasis on strong competition laws in Germany, which later influenced the content of arts 81 and 82 of the European Community Treaty.

In conformity with this tradition, the United States courts have claimed jurisdiction in anti-trust matters in respect of conduct entered into outside its borders, which has consequences within its borders: see *United States* v *Aluminum Co of America* 148 F 2nd 416 (1945). However, from the 1960s extra territorial claims by law enforcement agencies in the United States lead to blocking legislation in other countries: see the Shipping Contracts and Commercial Documents Act 1964. This response has lead to a modification in the approach by the courts in the United States. It now seems that for jurisdiction to be claimed: (i) the effect must be substantial, (ii) that the exercise of the jurisdiction should be reasonable, and (iii) that the claims of other states should be considered as well as the relationship of the parties with the United States: see *Timberlane Lumber Co* v *Bank of America* 549 F 2nd 597 (1976); *Mannington Mills Case* (1979) 66 ILR 487. The attitude of courts in the United States in respect of jurisdiction has lead to an increase in blocking legislation: see the Protection of Trading Interests Act 1980.

The quotation raises the question as to why such claims to jurisdiction are controversial. First, the conduct may often be lawful in the state where it is undertaken. This distinguishes it from cases under the protective principle, where injurious acts committed in State A and directed against the organs of State B are normally unlawful both at the place of inception and under the general rules of customary international law. Second, as indicated above, application of the principle brings the courts of one state into conflict with foreign governments and foreign nationals. Third, attempts by courts in states such as the United States to apply the doctrine have lead to blocking legislation being passed by other states, so leading to discord within the wider international community. Fourth, conflict is to some extent inevitable because the 'effects' doctrine has largely been applied in the area of commercial law where different states take different views as to the nature of commercial conduct. What is lawful in State A may be unlawful in State B, whereas other offences giving rise to jurisdictional disputes tend to be unlawful in both states (eg hi-jacking, drug trafficking, terrorist offences). Fifth, it has to be admitted that some trading blocs (such as the EC) while complaining about the 'effects' doctrine are not averse to invoking it in their own courts: see *ICI* v *Commission (Dyestuffs Case)* [1972] ECR 619; *Ahlstrom and Others* v *EC Commission (the Woodpulp Cartel Case)* [1988] 4 CMLR 901. Sixth, it has to be noted that some cases of the so called 'effects' doctrine concern attempts to disregard the separate legal personality of the wholly owned subsidiary company. This is as much a question of whether one is prepared to respect the separate legal personality of the company or acknowledge some form of enterprise entity doctrine.

Perhaps these are in the end superficial reasons. International law tends to favour the territorial principle; it may be extended where there is a link (eg nationality) or where the conduct is manifestly criminal, as is the case in instances of universal jurisdiction. But where claims are made beyond these limits then the sensitivities of states are engaged, particularly where the conduct may be lawful in one country and unlawful in another.

b) We are asked in this question to consider the possible claims for jurisdiction that might be made against David, John, Edward and Dan, who are all in the custody of State C and which has announced its intention to prosecute. We are also asked to consider any possible grounds for extradition that might be advanced by States A and B. It is sensible to take each individual in turn.

David

In this instance the charges are likely to be of murder and rape. It is arguable that as the offence took place on the High Seas, then prima facie jurisdiction should be exercised exclusively by the flag state of the vessel: see the *SS Lotus Case*; High Seas Convention 1958 (art 6); Law of the Sea Convention 1982 (art 92). That state will be the state of registration of the vessel, namely State C.

The only argument that might be advanced by State B is grounded on the nationality principle. However, for offences committed on the High Seas it is normally accepted that the jurisdiction of the flag state is exclusive. Second, State B would normally need to seek extradition and it is generally accepted in extradition treaties that where a crime has been committed on a vessel, then it is regarded as being committed in the territory of the flag state: see *R v Governor of Brixton Prison, ex parte Minervini* [1959] 1 QB 155. So there would be no locus standi to claim extradition. The only claim that be made by State A would be grounded on the passive personality principal, but that yields to the exclusive jurisdiction of the flag state. In any event not all states accept the validity of the passive personality principle.

On a practical point it seems that the vessel and David have been taken to State C; this State has therefore the jurisdiction and the evidence to mount a prosecution.

John and Edward

It is open to argument that John might be tried by State A in line with the nationality principle; however, that would require extradition from State C, who are also seeking to prosecute him. We are not told the state of registration of the aircraft, but it does seem that a court in State C might claim jurisdiction either: (i) because under the territorial principle the offence of placing the bomb took place there, or (ii) it was directed against an aircraft registered in State C (see art 3 Tokyo Convention on Offences and Certain Other Acts Committed on Board Aircraft 1963), or (iii) possibly under the protective principle that the offence was directed at the state airline of State C, or (iv) even if the agreement that formed the basis of the conspiracy took place abroad, then it was implemented in State C and jurisdiction arises under the objective territorial principle, or (v) that the offence was directed against nationals of State C and jurisdiction arises under the passive personality principle. It would seem that a court in State C has jurisdiction to try John either for conspiracy or for the actual placing of the bomb.

In respect of Edward it is arguable that he might be tried by State B on the nationality principle; however, as he is situated in State C the relevant question pertains to the jurisdiction of State C's courts. It would seem that State C's courts are entitled to claim jurisdiction: (i) on the basis that the conspiracy, although concluded outside State C, was implemented there (this might arise either under the objective territorial principle or by application of the 'effects' doctrine), or (ii) under the protective principle, or (iii) under legislation in State C if the aircraft was registered there, or (iv) under the passive personality principle in the sense that it was directed against nationals of State C.

The important point here is that the courts of State C only need to establish one basis of jurisdiction against John and Edward. It is relevant to observe that the evidence also appears to be located in State C. The general principle with a matter as serious as placing a bomb on an aircraft is that of prosecute or extradite. If there is no sensible request to extradite, then the prosecuting authorities in State C are duty bound under the Tokyo Convention 1963 and Montreal Convention 1971 to prosecute. It should be noted here that some writers take the view that the placing a bomb on an aircraft is such a grave act that it should be subject to universal jurisdiction.

Dan

In the case of Dan there is a possibility that State A might claim jurisdiction under the nationality principle or indeed the subjective territorial principle. However, State A is unlikely to wish to become involved, and Dan is now in State C and the damage was directed at the economy of State C. Thus the relevant question is whether the courts of State C have jurisdiction; it would seem that they could assert jurisdiction: (i) under the protective principle as an attempt was made to undermine the economy of State C, or (ii) under the objective territorial principle as the notes were put into circulation in State C and some element of the prohibited acts took place in State C, or (iii) under the 'effects' doctrine.

Our conclusion must be that the criminal courts of State C have jurisdiction in respect of all four individuals. It should be noted that even if there is a difference of opinion on a particular head of jurisdiction, only one head needs to be established to found jurisdiction.

QUESTION TWO

Between 1992 and 1994, Albert, a national of Utopia, was ambassador of the Kingdom of Utopia in Zenobia. In 1995, after his return to Utopia, he led a military coup which overthrew the monarchy and established a military government with himself as 'Supreme Leader'. During and after the coup, many monarchist supporters were tortured and killed. In 1998, Albert retired from the military government and took up residence in Zenobia. Albert now faces criminal proceedings in Zenobia in respect of the following charges:

a) crimes against humanity committed in Utopia during the period 1995–1998;

b) the killing, apparently on the orders of the King, of Carlos, an anti-monarchist exile, during Albert's tenure as ambassador in Zenobia; and

c) the rape of Marie, a Zenobian film star, in his embassy residence in 1993.

Advise Albert on the international law aspects of his position.

University of London LLB Examination
(for External Students) Public International Law June 1999 Q2

General Comment

It has often been noted that since 1945 there has been a tension in international law between the expansion of human rights law and the traditional doctrine of sovereign immunity. This question, set in 1999, owes something to the lengthy Pinochet saga, although somewhat surprisingly it was not answered well. This may be partly due to the fact that the question does not make clear whether the criminal charges in Zenobia represent (a) an actual prosecution, or (b) part of extradition proceedings to Utopia. This distinction is of some importance because, if there are criminal proceedings in Zenobia, then problems arise as to the jurisdiction of the criminal courts. It is probably sensible to interpret the question as meaning a straightforward criminal prosecution.

Skeleton Solution

Three main issues: crimes against humanity; the killing of Carlos; the rape of Marie – apply principles relevant in establishing state jurisdiction in international law – state the relevance of customary international law and the value of conventions within context.

Suggested Solution

We are asked in this problem question to consider the criminal liability of Albert who, while holding the citizenship of Utopia, has been resident since 1998 in Zenobia after relinquishing his previous political posts.

One preliminary point should be noted. The question refers to 'facing criminal proceedings in Zenobia'. This is a rather misleading expression because it could mean either a criminal prosecution or an application to extradite. It will be remembered that the Pinochet saga concerned an application to extradite, not an actual criminal trial. With this caveat in mind it is sensible to examine the various aspects of the problem.

The relevance of his period as ambassador in Zenobia (1992–1994)

Manifestly a distinction has to be drawn between the period when Albert acted as an ambassador in Zenobia and his subsequent political activities in Utopia. Further, it is clear that a distinction has to be drawn between official acts and acts of a private nature. Moreover it is clear that, until 1994, Albert was subject to the legal regime arising under the Vienna Convention on Diplomatic Relations 1961. In principle the Convention would have no bearing on acts taking place after he returned to Utopia: see art 39 of the Vienna Convention.

Crimes against humanity committed in Utopia (1995–1998)

As the Pinochet litigation indicated, the proper forum for such a trial is in Utopia. However, it seems that the courts in Zenobia wish to try the matter. A question would arise as to how the courts of Zenobia might have jurisdiction. It might be argued that such jurisdiction arose either because crimes against humanity constitute a universal crime, or that Zenobian citizens have been killed in the coup, or that Zenobia had introduced legislation of an extra territorial nature to give effect to the Torture Convention 1984. Be that as it may, there is first a question as to whether on the facts the courts of Zenobia have jurisdiction to try the matter at all.

The second question that Albert will wish to raise is the assertion that, even if the courts in Zenobia have jurisdiction, he can claim immunity. A first point to dispose of is that the State Immunity Act 1978 is of no relevance, because it cannot be assumed that Zenobia has identical municipal legislation. A second point is that *R v Bow Street Metropolitan Stipendiary Magistrate, ex parte Pinochet Ugarte (Nos 1 and 3)* [2000] 1 AC 61; [2000] 1 AC 147 is only of general interest because it cannot be assumed that the decision of a municipal court in England would be followed by a court in Zenobia. A third point to note is that it is important to reach a conclusion as to the precise date on which Albert became 'Supreme Leader' or Head of State. A fourth point is that the Zenobian court might well take the view that a claim to immunity can be made only for official acts and that, as a matter of customary international law, torture and murder cannot be the official acts of a Head of State. It will be remembered that reasoning of this sort appealed to the majority of the House of Lords in *Pinochet Ugarte (No 1)*. A fifth point under this heading is whether the proper claimant for immunity of a Head of State should not be Albert but the state of Utopia. It will be necessary to ascertain whether Utopia intend to make such a claim. Certainly Utopia will have locus standi before the Zenobian court. However, even if Utopia made a claim for immunity, or indicated their unwillingness to waive immunity, the court in Zenobia might rule that if Utopia has signed and ratified the Torture Convention 1984 then no claim for immunity should be allowed to stand. Alternatively the court might rule that immunity of a former Head of State arises under customary international law and cannot be invoked in respect of acts contrary to customary law; reasoning to this effect was accepted in *Pinochet Ugarte (No 1)*. The simple conclusion on this matter is that Albert should claim immunity as a former Head of State before the courts of Zenobia, even if such a claim may be rejected.

If Albert fails in his application for immunity, he might raise another argument. He might argue that the courts of Zenobia should decline to sit in judgment on the events during a coup in Utopia, as the matter is essentially non justiciable. The doctrine of non justiciability, or act of a foreign state, is a doctrine of private international law, but it did appeal to a minority of the judges in *R v Bow Street Metropolitan Stipendiary Magistrate, ex parte Pinochet Ugarte (No 1)* even though it was not raised in the later hearing. Whether such a doctrine will prevail depends on the rules of private international law operating in Zenobia. Finally, Albert might be minded to persuade Utopia to make an extradition request to Zenobia, thus enabling him to stand trial in his homeland. This would mean that the Zenobian courts would have the difficult task of determining whether to give priority to extradition or prosecution. In any event our advice to Albert must be to contest the matter.

The killing of Carlos during Albert's tenure in Zenobia

In principle the courts of Zenobia have jurisdiction over this matter, since the criminal act took place in the territory of Zenobia. The question that arises is as to whether Albert may, in 1999, make a claim for immunity from criminal prosecution. A first point to note is that the act took place during the period of his ambassadorship. It is said that the matter was ordered by the King of Utopia; the difficulty with this is that the King of Utopia has no jurisdiction in the sovereign state of Zenobia, so this cannot be regarded as a valid act of the Head of State. Moreover, since the intention is to bring a criminal prosecution against a named individual, conceptions of state immunity do not appear to be directly relevant.

The sensible view to take is that the matter was undertaken when Albert was in Zenobia and subject to the terms of the Vienna Convention on Diplomatic Relations 1961. At the time of the murder, Albert would have been entitled to immunity from criminal prosecution: see art 31(1) Vienna Convention 1961. However, after he has left his post he would only be entitled to immunity if the act was one 'performed by such a person in the exercise of his functions as a member of the mission': see art 39(2). Although there is some uncertainty as to what constitutes an official act, it is now accepted that the murder of a political opponent is not an official act, and in any event violates arts 3 and 41 of the Vienna Convention 1961, as well as the entire corpus of human rights law. Under this approach an act can only be official if it is lawful and constitutional under the law of Utopia and consistent with the spirit of customary international law; it is not official simply because it is undertaken by a person in power.

It is quite clear that the murder of a political opponent is an act outside the lawful functions of a diplomatic mission as stipulated in art 3 of the Vienna Convention. It is therefore strongly arguable that a court in Zenobia might follow the approach of Lord Steyn in *R v Bow Street Metropolitan Stipendiary Magistrate, ex parte Pinochet Ugarte (No 1)* and hold that the murder of a national is not an official act, and that no immunity can be claimed. The rational conclusion must be that a claim for immunity should be rejected, because the act violates the traditional duties of a Head of State and the express terms of the Vienna Convention on Diplomatic Relations 1961.

The rape of Marie, a Zenobian film star, in his embassy residence in 1993

In principle the courts of Zenobia have jurisdiction, because the alleged rape took place within Zenobia. At the time of the original attack in 1993 Albert, as ambassador, would have had immunity from any criminal proceedings: Vienna Convention on Diplomatic Relations 1961, art 31, para 1. Indeed the police would have been obliged then to treat the premises of the embassy as inviolable: Vienna Convention 1961, art 22. In respect of classification it is clear that rape is a private act and cannot be regarded as an official act. In these circumstances, Albert would lose his immunity at the expiration of his posting in 1994: see art 39(2) Vienna Convention 1961. It would seem therefore that a prosecution could be brought in 1999 in the courts of Zenobia.

However, it would seem that the prospects of a conviction are limited. If Marie had complained at the time of the rape in 1993, then Zenobia should have declared the ambassador persona non gratia under art 9 of the Vienna Convention; this was not done and he was allowed to serve out his posting. When he returned to Utopia no attempt was made to seek extradition. This is perhaps understandable because, after 1995, he was de facto Head of State and thus entitled to immunity in customary international law. After 1998 no attempt was made to charge him when he returned to Zenobia. It is also relevant to add that any prosecution would not be able to call upon embassy staff, because diplomatic agents are not compellable witnesses: art 31(2) Vienna Convention. Thus the rational conclusion is that Albert does not have immunity, but the evidentiary difficulties and the passage of time makes the prospects of a conviction limited.

In most systems of municipal law an act of rape is not only a criminal offence but also a tortious act. It would seem that Albert had immunity from civil proceedings in 1993 (see art 31(1) Vienna Convention 1961) but that such immunity was lost on the termination of his post in 1994: see art 39(2) Vienna Convention 1961. Although Albert had immunity from civil proceedings in the period 1995–1998, under customary international law as 'Supreme Leader' he was not immune after he resigned office and returned to Zenobia in 1998.

The resignation as Supreme Leader

Sometimes, when a military ruler leaves office, he persuades the legislature to grant him a declaration of immunity in respect of any future proceedings. The question does not say whether Utopia did in fact do this in 1998. If they did so, no Zenobian court should recognise it because (a) it is contrary to customary international law to make such a declaration in respect of crimes against humanity, and (b) such a declaration could not have extra territorial effect so as to extend to Zenobia.

QUESTION THREE

States K and L have made unconditional declarations accepting the jurisdiction of the International Court of Justice (ICJ) under art 36(2) of the Statute of the Court. State M has made a declaration accepting the jurisdiction of the ICJ but excluding 'matters falling within the scope of the criminal jurisdiction of State M'. Fernandez, a national of State M, currently residing in State L, conspired with six nationals of K to overthrow the government of State K. Before the plan is executed, however, the seven are arrested by the police of State L and charged with criminal conspiracy, to be tried in the courts of State L. The government of State K seeks to have all seven of the accused extradited to State K where mandatory death sentences are imposed on conviction for criminal conspiracy against the government. The government of State M fears that Fernandez will receive harsh treatment in the courts of State L and seeks to have him extradited for trial in State M. Recently, the courts of State L refused extradition applications from both States K and M, on the grounds that only State L had jurisdiction in respect of the alleged offences. Both States K and M claim concurrent jurisdiction and are separately considering reference of the issue to the ICJ.

Advise States K and M on:

a) the jurisdiction of the ICJ over their representative claims; and

b) the merits of their claims to jurisdiction over Fernandez.

University of London LLB Examination
(for External Students) Public International Law June 1996 Q3

General Comment

Part (a) of this question involves a consideration of the jurisdiction of the ICJ. Candidates should be able to discuss the issue of any Preliminary Objections which may be raised to State K's application. With regard to State M, an understanding of the workings of an automatic reservation and the principle of reciprocity is necessary. A discussion of the circumstances under which an extradition may proceed is also required.

Part (b) invites an analysis of the various ways in which a State may claim jurisdiction over an individual. The merits of the claims of States K and M raise different issues and should be dealt with separately. As the question contains a number of different hypotheses no one conclusion is necessary or possible.

Skeleton Solution

a) Jurisdiction of ICJ over the claim of State K – *South West Africa Cases* – political issue – State K and extradition – State M and automatic reservation – State M and reciprocity.

b) State K and protective principle – State K and effects doctrine – State K and passive personality principle – State M and nationality of Fernandez: *Nottebohm* – concurrent jurisdiction and enforcement.

Suggested Solution

a) The jurisdiction of the ICJ over the claim of State K will depend upon whether the claim is of an international character admissible before the Court. As both States K and L have made unconditional declarations accepting the jurisdiction of the Court, State L is likely to submit that although the claim is covered by the principle of reciprocity (see the discussion below) State K's claim is still inadmissible because State K has failed to establish any legal right or interest on its part. Before the ICJ can consider the merits of a particular case it has to consider preliminary objections to its jurisdiction. These objections are usually dealt with in a separate preliminary judgment. State L is likely to submit that the case of State K is not admissible because although it is of an international character State K has not suffered. The plan was not executed before the seven were arrested and State K has no legal right or interest in the enforcement of State L's laws. State L is likely to rely upon the *South West Africa Cases: Ethiopia v South Africa; Liberia v South Africa* (*Preliminary Objections* (1962) ICJ Rep 319; *Second Phase* (1966) ICJ Rep 6. Ethiopia and Liberia, two former members of the League of Nations, in 1960 instituted proceedings against South Africa before the ICJ claiming that South Africa had failed to carry out the obligations imposed upon it by the Mandate, by which it had agreed with the League of Nations to administer the territory. The Court held that South Africa's obligations under the Mandate were owed to the League and not to the individual members of the League. Ethiopia and Liberia had therefore failed to establish any legal right or interest in the matter.

State K will of course seek to distinguish itself from this case as the government of State K was a potential target of the criminal conspiracy. The citizens of State K were also presumably potential targets, as opposed to the position of Ethiopia and Liberia whose citizens were not affected by South Africa's actions in South West Africa.

State L may also argue that the matter is not within the competence of the Court because the issue is a political one rather than a legal one. In such cases some of the members of the Court have argued (for example in the *Nuclear Test Cases: Australia v France; New Zealand v France* (1974) ICJ Rep 253 and 457) that the political nature of the dispute will render a matter non-justiciable. This is unlikely to succeed, however, as State L wishes to try the accused for a criminal offence, rather than a political one.

State K would, in any event, having difficulty in establishing that the ICJ should be looking at the matter as there is no duty under customary international law to extradite. A duty to extradite would arise from a treaty and there is no evidence of such a treaty between State L and State K. Moreover, while State L sees the conspiracy as a simple criminal conspiracy, this is not the case with State K, which places a criminal conspiracy against the government in a separate category with a mandatory death sentence, raising the issue that it is a political offence. There is no general duty to extradite for an offence of a political character and State L will argue this.

The position of State M is somewhat different. State M has made a declaration excluding 'matters falling within the scope of the criminal jurisdiction of State M'. This is known as an automatic reservation as it leaves the scope of what is a matter of criminal jurisdiction to State M. The validity and application of such reservations was considered by the ICJ in the *Norwegian Loans Case: France v Norway* (1957) ICJ Rep 9. France brought a claim against Norway under the 'optional clause' on behalf of French holders of Norwegian bonds. The French Declaration which accepted the compulsory jurisdiction of the Court stated:

'This Declaration does not apply to differences relating to matters which are essentially within the national jurisdiction as understood by the Government of the French Republic.'

Norway relied upon the French reservation on the principle of reciprocity. A State accepting the jurisdiction of the Court under the optional clause does so, according to art 36(2), only 'in relation to any other State accepting the same obligation'.

The Court accepted Norway's argument and so Norway was able to invoke the reservation contained in the French Declaration.

In this case State L could rely upon State M's reservation, and while it might be problematical that the conspiracy to overthrow the government of State M is a crime under State L's laws, this is a matter for State L. State L may decide what falls within its criminal jurisdiction as State M has reserved that right so to do.

This, of course, undermines the function of the ICJ to determine its jurisdiction. Judge Lauterpacht argued in the *Norwegian Loans Case* that:

> '... the French reservation is ... contrary to one of the most fundamental principles of international – and national – jurisprudence according to which it is within the inherent power of a Tribunal to interpret the text establishing its jurisdiction.'

The party making the reservation is entitled to determine the extent and the very existence of its obligation and therefore State L, relying upon the principle of reciprocity, could argue that the trial of the conspiracy is within its criminal jurisdiction and outside that of the ICJ. State M is unlikely to succeed.

b) State K could claim jurisdiction over Fernandez on the basis of the protective principle. This allows a State to punish acts prejudicial to its security even when they are committed outside the jurisdiction by aliens. In this case Fernandez, a national of State M and therefore an alien in the eyes of State K, entered in to a conspiracy to overthrow the government of State K, clearly a prejudicial act.

State K may also claim jurisdiction on the effects doctrine, ie the effects of the act are harmful to the State. In *R v Sansom* [1991] 2 QB 130 jurisdiction was argued on the basis that the effects of the conspiracy, hatched outside the jurisdiction, would be harmful to the United Kingdom, and similarly with the case of *Liangsiriprasert v United States Government* [1991] 1 AC 225. It should also be noted in this problem that the conspiracy, while initiated outside the jurisdiction, would have to be effected in State K, ie the overthrow of the government.

The effects doctrine and the protective principle are often treated as one and the same, and it is often difficult to determine which category a situation falls into. Some decided cases fit uneasily into either of the two categories. In *Attorney-General of the Government of Israel v Eichmann* (1961) 36 ILR 5 the State of Israel argued, inter alia, that it had jurisdiction to try the accused on the basis that his actions were prejudicial to the State of Israel, although the State was not in existence at the time of his crimes.

State K might also invoke the passive personality principle, in that the potential victims of the crime (presuming that K citizens would have been killed or injured in the overthrow) were nationals of State K even though the crime was in the main part committed abroad. The nationality of Fernandez is, of course, irrelevant to the above claims of jurisdiction. The passive personality claim of jurisdiction is not accepted by all States and it would depend upon the attitude of courts of State K. In *United States* v *Yunis* 681 F Supp 896 (1988); (1989) 83 AJIL 94 the court, contrary to previous practice, accepted this principle, although as the case involved air piracy and the taking of hostages it had a universal application.

State K would, of course, be in a much stronger position if the planned crime had been executed. The State could then rely upon the territorial principle giving it jurisdiction over crimes committed within its territory. In this instance, where the conspiracy was plotted abroad, State K would be able to claim jurisdiction under the objective territorial principle if the crime was completed within its jurisdiction.

State M will seek to claim jurisdiction over Fernandez on the basis of nationality. A State may prosecute its nationals for crimes committed anywhere in the world. It will, however, depend on the law of State M as to which crimes have extra-territorial effect. In the United Kingdom, for instance, reserves the right to prosecute its nationals for murder, bigamy, treason, crimes against humanity and war crimes. If the laws of State M make it an extra-territorial crime to engage in a conspiracy to overthrow a foreign government then State M may claim jurisdiction on this basis.

One is told that Fernandez is a national of State M currently residing in State L. For a State to offer diplomatic protection to one of its nationals, that is to intervene internationally on their behalf, there must be 'a genuine connection'. This was discussed in the *Nottebohm Case: Liechtenstein* v *Guatemala* (1955) ICJ Rep 4 in which the ICJ stated that there must be 'a legal bond having as its basis a social fact of attachment, a genuine connection of existence'.

For State M to challenge the workings of the courts of State L and to seek the extradition of Fernandez to State M his nationality must be established. It is submitted that although he lives in State L Fernandez has not in any way abrogated his State M nationality and therefore State M may pursue his extradition. It is, however, unlikely to succeed because State M's argument as to the harsh treatment Fernandez will receive is unlikely to find favour in the courts of State L, unless there is a bilateral treaty designed to safeguard the treatment and rights of those being held. In issues of concurrent jurisdiction where more than one State has jurisdiction priority to exercise enforcement jurisdiction depends upon custody.

QUESTION FOUR

Amanda is a citizen of State A. In 1992 she hijacked an aircraft while it was over the Mediterranean Sea on a flight from State B to State C. The aircraft was owned and operated by an airline incorporated in State D. Amanda threatened the pilot of the aircraft and ordered him to fly the aircraft to State E. When the aircraft landed there, she announced that she would not release the passengers from the aircraft unless State F first set free a number of convicted terrorists. State F met her demands. Amanda then set free the passengers. As part of the deal, State E granted Amanda safe passage out of State E.

Certain of the passengers on the aircraft which Amanda hijacked were from State G. Stage G has now arrested Amanda and charged her with the crimes of hijacking, kidnapping, blackmail and assault.

Advise Amanda on what arguments, if any, she may draw from international law in order to prevent her conviction by State G's courts.

State C, State F and State G are parties both to the Hague Convention for the Suppression of the Unlawful Seizure of Aircraft 1970 and the International Convention Against the Taking of Hostages 1979. State A, State B and State D are party to neither of these conventions.

University of London LLB Examination
(for External Students) Public International Law June 1993 Q6

General Comment

A complicated, verbose problem on hijacking, terrorism and jurisdiction in international criminal law. Some care must be taken not to digress on the general principles of international penal jurisdiction but to concentrate on the point of the question, which is somewhat obscured by all the detail. Some minor aspects of the law of treaties are also involved, so this question should be approached with considerable caution.

Skeleton Solution

Jurisdictional problems in terrorism cases – the status of terrorism as an international crime – the passive personality and universality principles of jurisdiction – other states' rights and the option of extradition – the importance of custody in international penal cases.

Suggested Solution

It usually happens in prosecutions of terrorists involving more than one nation that there are concurrent claims to penal jurisdiction, giving rise often to complicated jurisdictional disputes, as the scenario will more often than not be similar to complexity to the one in this problem. The worst aspect of this is that very often the competing claims will all be equally valid, resulting in the application of the artificial and arbitrary rule that the state having custody of the suspect(s) has priority enforcement jurisdiction. An illustration of this type of conflict is provided by the *Lockerbie Case (Libya v UK; Libya v USA)* (1992) ICJ Rep 3 and 114 and recently in (1998) 37 ILM 587, wherein there are four competing jurisdictions, each claiming that they have 'locus' to try the two suspected Libyan terrorist in their own respective jurisdictions, although it must be said that Libya's obdurate behaviour has deprived it of the moral high ground, and its arguments are legally dubious though technically justifiable.

The scenario of this problem is far from uncommon in that every now and then the world hears of, for example, Palestinian terrorists hijacking a German airliner in Greece with American passengers on board and demanding the release of Lebanese or Iranian terrorists imprisoned in Italy or France. In fact, the Dawson's Field hijacking in Jordan in 1970 was remarkably similar to this scenario in its complexity and the number of nations involved. The first issue to be dealt with in this problem is the status of terrorism in international law. Terrorism (which includes hijacking and hostage-taking in its definition) is one of a group of so-called 'international crimes', along with piracy, war crimes, crimes against humanity, drug-trafficking, slave-trading and others. The prevention, suppression and punishment of these crimes are considered a priority by the international community at large, to the extent that any state, whether directly affected by the commission of such crimes or not, may punish the perpetrators if they should be apprehended by that state. The doctrine governing such cases is known as aut dedere, aut punire, which means that the state having custody of the accused should either punish them itself or extradite them to another country for punishment. This principle is decreed in both the international treaties applicable to the case of Amanda; the Hague Convention for the Suppression of the Unlawful Seizure of Aircraft 1970 and the International Convention against the Taking of Hostages 1979, of which both require the state apprehending the suspect either to prosecute him or to extradite him: aut dedere, aut punire. State G is a party to both these Conventions, and therefore no problem of application arises. The fact that three of the other states involved are not parties is ultimately destructive of any attempts they may make to obtain custody of Amanda, although theoretically they would be entitled to do so under general principles of international criminal law. Otherwise it is of no consequence.

The strength of State G's case against Amanda rests on the passive personality and universality principles of jurisdiction. According to the passive personality principle, a state may assert jurisdiction over an offender if the victims of the offence were nationals of that state. The passive personality principle was one of the bases of Turkey's assumption of jurisdiction in the *SS Lotus Case: France* v *Turkey* (1927) PCIJ Rep Ser A No 10, although it was expressly rejected by all six of the dissenting judges in that case; the Harvard Research Draft Convention with Respect to Crime 1935 commented that application of the principle was 'vigorously opposed' by the UK and the USA, both of which regarded it as contrary to international law, and added that of the five principles of jurisdiction, the passive personality one was 'the most difficult to justify in theory'. In spite of this reluctance to accept the principle it was used – no doubt unintentionally – by the USA against the Palestinian terrorists who hijacked the Italian cruise ship *Achille Lauro* in the Mediterranean in 1985 and murdered an American passenger. Amanda would no doubt be able in the court proceedings to point out the general hostility towards the principle in international law and – assuming that State G is not one of the few states to espouse it – might well be able to defeat this particular part of State G's case against her.

Unfortunately Amanda would find it extremely difficult to defeat State G's case on the universality principle. This applies only to international crimes like terrorism and allows any state to punish offenders accused of such crimes, even if the state in question was not directly involved at all in the commission of the offence. There can be no doubt that Amanda's crimes constitute terrorism and violate the Hague Convention for the Suppression of the Unlawful Seizure of Aircraft 1970 and the International Convention against the Taking of Hostages 1979, which subject Amanda to the principle of aut dedere, aut punire, as well as obviously coming within the ambit of the universality principle. It is difficult to find any arguments at all (except delaying tactics) which Amanda could use to prevent her conviction by the courts of State G.

The main – indeed, apparently the only – argument Amanda could attempt to use amounts to precisely such a delaying tactic: she could request extradition to another state, presumably State A as that is her native state, in order to be tried by the courts there. The courts of State A would then be applying jurisdiction over Amanda on the basis of the nationality principle: she being a citizen of State A, that state claims the right to punish her, even for crimes committed abroad (as in this case) which had no direct effect at all on State A. Application of the nationality principle is generally restricted to 'serious offences', which in the UK means treason, murder or bigamy – an example of its application, though incorrect on the facts of the case, was *Joyce v Director of Public Prosecutions* [1946] AC 347. Terrorism, as an international crime, would doubtless be included in the definition of a 'serious offence', but the problem here is that State A is a party to neither of the cited Conventions, which means that it cannot invoke them as grounds for extradition; its only possible claim to jurisdiction over Amanda rests exclusively on her nationality, and it is very unlikely that a court in State G would give the nationality principle precedence over the universality principle, especially since the espousal of the latter by the United Nations General Assembly in Resolution 2645 (XXV) (1970) as a basis for punishing hijackers. Moreover, the only legitimate way in which jurisdiction could be transferred from State G to State A is by extradition proceedings, and whether a demand for extradition would be feasible or not in this case depends on the existence and content of an extradition treaty between State A and State G. As the question does not supply any information relating to this, any comment can only remain speculative. In connection with this it should be noted that there is no obligation to extradite in customary international law, and the majority of states will not permit extradition in the absence of an extradition treaty in respect of the states and offences concerned.

The final important point to consider in this case is the fact that State G actually has custody of Amanda. It is clear in international law that priority to exercise enforcement jurisdiction depends solely on custody – this was acknowledged by the Harvard Research Draft Convention in 1935. State G therefore has the sole power to decide what to do with Amanda, and her fate is in its hands; this being the case, any arguments raised by Amanda to prevent her conviction are likely to cut very little ice with the courts of State G as they have the absolute power to dispose of her case as they wish. In that practical sense, Amanda's conviction in State G is probably inevitable.

QUESTION FIVE

What problems has international drug-trafficking posed for the law relating to jurisdiction? How has the law responded to cope with those problems? Has its response been satisfactory?

University of London LLB Examination
(for External Students) Public International Law June 1992 Q4

General Comment

This is a fairly common question requiring consideration of the traditional rules governing jurisdiction and the problems presented by international crimes.

Skeleton Solution

The five traditional grounds for jurisdiction – exotic problems caused by drug-trafficking: non-nationals; international conspiracies; non-acceptance of the offence as an international crime – approach of the English court in *Liangsiriprasert* case – review of the need to change the existing approach.

Suggested Solution

International law has traditionally recognised the right of states to exercise jurisdiction on a number of grounds. The common feature of these bases of jurisdiction is a nexus between the individual over whom jurisdiction is sought and the state seeking to exercise jurisdiction. Such a nexus may be territory, nationality, injury to the state or the commission of an international crime.

The most common ground for the exercise of jurisdiction is the territorial principle. This principle operates in two separate dimensions. First, there is the 'subjective territorial principle' which authorises states to exercise jurisdiction over persons committing offences within their national territories. The other aspect of this ground for jurisdiction is the 'objective territorial principle' which allows a state to found jurisdiction when certain activities have been initiated in another country but which produce effects in the territory of that state.

Jurisdiction based on the active nationality principle is based on the relationship established between a state and its citizens by virtue of the concept of nationality. Even when nationals are outside the territory of a state, their state may exercise jurisdiction if its nationals were the perpetrators of the offence. The common law legal systems of the developed world tend to reserve this ground of jurisdiction to crimes of a serious nature, such as treason, murder, etc, whereas those legal systems based on the civilian system make extensive use of this principle for lesser offences.

States are also entitled to exercise jurisdiction under the passive nationality principle which permits the punishment of alleged offences committed abroad against nationals of the state. The United States has been one of the most vigorous proponents of this principle and its courts have frequently recognised the possibility of exercising jurisdiction on this basis. For example, in *United States* v *Yunis* (1989) 83 AJIL 94, the American courts held that a Lebanese citizen lured aboard a fishing boat moored on international waters by American intelligence agents could be tried in the United States for hijacking even although the aircraft on which the offence occurred belonged to the Royal Jordanian Airline and none of the three American passengers aboard was taken captive.

A more controversial basis for exercising jurisdiction is the protective (or security) principle which permits jurisdiction over foreign nationals whose conduct threatens the security of the state. This allows states to punish persons committing acts intended to undermine national security such as plotting to overthrow the government, espionage, forging currency and conspiracy to violate immigration regulations. Until recently, the leading case in this area was *Attorney-General for Israel* v *Eichmann* (1962) 36 ILR 5 in which the Israeli secret service kidnapped a Nazi war criminal from Argentina to stand trial in Israel for offences against humanity. The prosecution in this case based the jurisdiction of the Israeli court on the protective principle and this argument was accepted by the court.

While at the time the *Eichmann* case attracted much attention and criticism, the courts of the West have gradually come to embrace this principle. Thus, the United States courts have recently asserted jurisdiction to try General Noriega, the former head of the State of Panama, on the grounds that his actions threatened the security of the United States. Trafficking in narcotics was in fact cited as one of the offences which allowed the United States judiciary to exercise jurisdiction.

The final generally-accepted traditional ground of jurisdiction is the principle of universality according to which a state has jurisdiction to try and punish private individuals for certain offences recognised by the international community as being of universal concern. Although the exact scope of this principle is as yet undefined, offences which fall within its scope include hijacking, piracy, genocide and war crimes.

Trafficking in narcotics has not yet been defined as an international crime. Unlike hijacking, where a series of multilateral treaties allow a number of states to try individuals for that offence, drug smuggling has been the subject mainly of bilateral agreements relating to police cooperation and enforcement. At the same time, there is little doubt that there does not exist sufficient state practice to declare drug smuggling an international crime in customary law.

The traditional grounds for founding jurisdiction evolved to regulate so-called common law offences such as murder, treason, assault, etc. Crimes such as terrorism, hijacking, trafficking in narcotics and international fraud, were relatively rare. Private individuals travelled far less and international communications were primitive. The opportunities for international crime, other than war crimes, were relatively restricted.

This is no longer the case. In the last 35 or so years, international travel has exploded and world-wide communication has become commonplace. The result is that crimes can now be planned on an international basis and coordinated in such a manner that at least some of the perpetrators are far from the scene of the crime while others are able quickly to leave the scene undetected until subsequent investigation at which time the perpetrators are resident in another country.

Drug trafficking is just such an offence. It involves separate operations for the growing, refining, transport, distribution and sale of narcotics. More often than not, each individual involved in this chain is situated in a different state. They are of different nationalities and are involved at different levels in the perpetration of the offence.

Given this cocktail of factual elements, the traditional bases of jurisdiction are, at least conceptually, ill designed for tackling the problem of jurisdiction over drug traffickers. However, in practice the courts of the Western countries have adopted a flexible approach to this problem. They have not allowed the rigidity of these rules to prevent the proper exercise of jurisdiction over individuals engaged in such practices.

Both the United States and the United Kingdom courts have demonstrated an aggressive approach in this context. In *DPP* v *Doot* [1973] AC 807, the House of Lords heard an appeal involving an accused charged with conspiracy to import cannabis resin into the United Kingdom. The accused was not a British national and the offences in question had been initiated outside the territory of the UK. However, Lord Wilberforce rejected the contention that the courts must deny jurisdiction in the following terms:

'... the present case involves "international elements" – the accused are aliens and the conspiracy was initiated abroad – but there can be no question here of any breach of any rules of international law if they are prosecuted in this country. Under the objective territorial principle ... the courts have a clear right, if not a duty, to prosecute in accordance with our municipal law.'

In a subsequent case another English court, this time the Privy Council, was prepared to go much further. In *DPP* v *Doot* there was a connection due to the fact that the drugs were to be imported into the United Kingdom. But in *Liangsiriprasert* v *Government of the United States* [1990] 3 WLR 606 the connection was far more tenuous. This case involved a Thai smuggler who was persuaded to go to Hong Kong by an American drug enforcement agent. Once present in Hong Kong, the smuggler was arrested by the authorities and a subsequent request for extradition was made by the American authorities. At first instance the lower court held that jurisdiction was competently based on the protective principle.

The Privy Council upheld the decision of the lower court and found that the offence was justiciable in Hong Kong even though no overt act in the conspiracy had been committed there simply because states must be allowed to protect their interests. In an unusually frank comment on the policy of the courts towards international crime, the court declared:

'Crime is now established on an international scale and the common law must face this reality. Their Lordships can find nothing in precedent, comity or good sense that should inhibit the common law from regarding as justiciable in England inchoate crimes committed abroad which are intended to result in the commission of criminal offences in England.'

Quite simply, and in other words, the English courts are not prepared to allow criminals to evade the law on the technical grounds that jurisdiction cannot be founded on one of the traditional bases of jurisdiction. These grounds will be expanded by the courts, if necessary, to take into account the developments in the field of international crime.

The United States courts have adopted a similar policy. In March 1992 the American courts held that a Mexican doctor who assisted in the interrogation of an American drugs enforcement officer by drug smugglers could lawfully be tried in the United States. It was considered no bar to the proceedings that the individual was a Mexican national and that the offence occurred in a foreign country. The offence related to an assault on an American official and therefore the individual could be tried on the basis of the passive nationality principle.

Chapter 8

Immunity from Jurisdiction

8.1   Introduction

8.2   Key points

8.3   Key cases and legislation

8.4   Questions and suggested solutions

8.1 Introduction

Immunity from municipal jurisdiction, which most frequently extends to states and their diplomatic representatives, is a complex counterpart of the subject of jurisdiction itself. Exceptions to the general principles permitting jurisdiction also arise in relation to the acts of international organisations and their representatives which, in certain circumstances, may be entitled to claim immunity from suit and, in addition, from the application of the act of state doctrine. It is important that students are familiar with the various conventions which regulate immunity at the international level, as well as the body of case law from both the United Kingdom and the United States which has evolved from this very practical aspect of international law. The recent Pinochet 'saga' provides a useful insight into the English judicial practice regarding state immunity.

8.2 Key points

Sovereign immunity

A state cannot exercise its sovereign dominium over other sovereign states, a principle which is embodied in the maxim par in parem non habet imperium – one equal cannot exercise authority over another equal. Since exercising jurisdiction over the actions of other states would be a manifestation of such authority, national courts and tribunals have consistently declined to permit citation of foreign heads of state or members of government.

The classic exposition of the principle of sovereign immunity was made by the US Supreme Court of *The Schooner Exchange* v *McFaddon* (1812) 7 Cranch 116, where Marshall CJ observed:

> 'One sovereign being in no respect amenable to another, and being bound by obligations of the highest character not to degrade the dignity of his nation ... can be supposed to enter a foreign territory only under an express license, or in the confidence that the immunities

belonging to his independent sovereign station, though not expressly stipulated, are reserved by implication, and will be extended to him.'

This principle was adopted into British law in a series of cases which included the following:

a) *De Haber* v *Queen of Portugal* (1851) 17 QB 196, in which Lord Campbell LJ concluded that:

> '... to cite a foreign potentate in a municipal court ... is contrary to the law of nations and an insult which he is entitled to resent ...'

b) *The Parlement Belge* (1880) 5 PD 197, where the Court of Appeal observed that every state:

> '... declines to exercise by means of its courts any of its territorial jurisdiction over the person of any sovereign or ambassador of any other state, or over the public property of any state which is destined to public use ... though such sovereign, ambassador or property be within its jurisdiction.'

c) *Krajina* v *Tass Agency* [1949] 2 All ER 274, in which the principle of sovereign immunity was extended to an organ of the Soviet government which was therefore entitled to immunity from jurisdiction.

d) *Baccus SRL* v *Servicio Nacional del Trigo* [1957] 1 QB 438, where the defendants, although a separate legal person under Spanish law, were in fact found to be an organ of the Spanish government and consequently entitled to sovereign immunity.

The English courts have adopted the practice of accepting an executive certificate from the Foreign Office as absolute proof of the status of a foreign entity as a sovereign state, and, as such, entitled to claim sovereign immunity: see *Duff Development Company* v *Kelantan* [1924] AC 797.

This traditional view of sovereign immunity as being in some way absolute has been eroded, particularly as a result of the growing involvement of states in international commerce. By judicial interpretation, absolute immunity gave way to the doctrine of restrictive immunity in a course of decisions which modified the original common law position. This approach was endorsed by subsequent legislation which embraced the restrictive approach to sovereign immunity.

The State Immunity Act 1978

The State Immunity Act 1978 was enabling legislation for the European Convention on State Immunity 1972 which was intended to harmonise and co-ordinate national policies towards the issue of sovereign immunity. The Act reaffirms the principle of sovereign immunity, but subject to a large number of exceptions.

According to s1(1), a state is not liable to the jurisdiction of the courts of the United Kingdom unless the actions of the state permit the exercise of jurisdiction. For the purposes of the statute, the term 'state' refers to the sovereign or other head of a state in their public capacity, the government of that state, or any department of the government: s14(1). This term does not, however, extend to any entity which is distinct from the executive organs of the government of a state and which is capable of suing or being sued. According to s21, a certificate from the Secretary of State shall be conclusive evidence as to whether an entity is a state for the purposes of the Act.

There are also numerous legal entities which are related to states or conduct quasi-state activities; the question is whether these entities are entitled to the protections of the statute. These bodies are referred to in the Act as 'separate entities'. These are bodies or organisations which are distinct from the executive organs of the government of a state and which are capable of suing or being sued in the courts of the United Kingdom. The test for whether such entity can benefit from the immunities of the Act is set out in s14(2) which provides that a separate entity is immune from jurisdiction if, and only if:

a)   the proceedings relate to anything done by the entity in the exercise of sovereign authority; and

b)   the circumstances are such that a state would have been immune had it performed the act in question.

This test was applied recently in *Kuwait Airways Corporation* v *Iraqi Airways Co and Another* (1998) The Times 12 May, where the Court of Appeal held that aircraft seized by the Iraqi airline from Kuwait could not be returned since the airline was acting on instructions from the Iraqi government in the exercise of the sovereign authority of Iraq. In these circumstances, the airline was entitled to shield behind the protection of the Act. This case also illustrated the relationship between state immunity and the principle of non-justicability.

Exceptions to the general principle of sovereign immunity are numerous under the statute. Under the statute a state shall not be immune to the jurisdiction of the British courts in relation to:

a)   Either commercial transactions entered into by a state or, alternatively, contractual obligations incurred by a state which are to be performed wholly or partly within the United Kingdom: s3(1).

This provision is inapplicable to those cases in which both parties in dispute are states or, in contractual obligations, where the contract (unless a commercial transaction) was negotiated in the territory of the state concerned and the obligation in question is governed by its administrative law.

A 'commercial transaction' includes: (a) any contract for the supply of goods or services; (b) any loan or other transaction for the provision of finance and any guarantee or indemnity in respect of any such transaction or of any other financial obligation; and (c) any other transaction or activity (whether of a commercial, industrial, financial, professional or other similar character) into which a state enters or in which it engages otherwise than in the exercise of sovereign authority.

The leading case dealing with the application of the 1978 Act to commercial transactions is *A Company Limited* v *Republic of X* [1990] 2 Lloyd's Rep 520. This involved an attempt to obtain an injunction to prevent the disposal of assets held by the government of State X in the United Kingdom in both bank accounts and property in order to enforce any decree obtained from an action for payment for the price of a consignment of rice ordered by the government of State X.

The court held that the intention and purpose of the clause in the contract was to place State X in the same position as a private individual for the purposes of legal proceedings.

Similarly, the fact that a state or embassy has lodged sums in accounts with normal banks does not protect these accounts from exposure to normal commercial risks. Thus, in *Re Rafidain Bank* [1993] BCC 376, the courts refused to extend the protection of the statute to protect sums lodged by Iraq with a private bank which had been the subject of a petition for liquidation.

b) Proceedings in which it has submitted to the jurisdiction of the British courts. This is known as waiver of immunity: s2(1).

c) Legal proceedings in respect of death or personal injury or damage to or loss of tangible property, in both cases caused by an act or omission in the United Kingdom: s5.

d) Proceedings relating to any interest of the state in, or its possession or use of, immovable property in the United Kingdom or any obligation of the state arising out of its interest in, or its possession or use of, any such property: s6.

e) Proceedings relating to:

   i) any patent or design rights belonging to the state and registered or protected in the United Kingdom or for which the state has made an application in the United Kingdom;

   ii) an alleged infringement by the state in the United Kingdom of any patent, trademark, design, or copyright; or

   iii) the right to use a trade or business name in the United Kingdom: s7.

f) Proceedings relating to membership of a body corporate, an unincorporated body or a partnership which has members other than states and is incorporated in accordance with British company law or has its principal place of business in the United Kingdom. The proceedings must concern issues or matters arising between the state and the body or its other members: s8.

g) Where a state has agreed in writing to submit a dispute which has arisen, or may arise, to arbitration, the state is not immune as regards proceedings brought in the United Kingdom which relate to the arbitration: s9.

In accordance with s13(2) of the Act, no relief may be given against a state by way of injunction, or order of specific performance, recovery of land or recovery of property, without the written consent of the state. Therefore, a freezing injunction cannot be obtained in an attempt to ensure that assets remain within the United Kingdom pending judgment: see *Trendtex Trading Corporation* v *Central Bank of Nigeria* [1977] QB 529.

Similarly, s13(2)(b) of the Act provides that 'the property of a state shall not be subject to any process for the enforcement of a judgment or arbitration award or, in an action in rem, for its arrest, detention or sale'. Such immunity may be expressly waived, but not by merely submitting to the jurisdiction of the court. However, in *Alcom Ltd* v *Republic of Colombia* [1984] 2 All ER 6, it was held by the House of Lords that a bank account would not fall within s13 where it could be established that 'the bank account was earmarked by the foreign state solely ... for being drawn on to settle liabilities incurred in commercial transactions'. The onus of proof lies on the applicant to establish that this is in fact the case.

In *Al-Adsani* v *Government of Kuwait* [1996] 1 Lloyd's Rep 104 the Court of Appeal considered the question of the entitlement of a state to plead immunity. See also the case of *Holland* v *Lampen-Wolfe* [2001] 1 WLR 1573 (HL) on the point of state immunity in respect of acts to promote education. In *P* v *P (Diplomatic Immunity: Jurisdiction)* (1998) The Times 2 March the Court of Appeal addressed the relationship between diplomatic immunity and state immunity. The customary approach of the English courts in determining issues of state and diplomatic immunity was recently put to test in the Pinochet 'saga': see *R* v *Bow Street Metropolitan Stipendiary Magistrate, ex parte Pinochet Ugarte (No 1)* [1998] 3 WLR 1456; *(No 2)* [1999] 2 WLR 272 (HL); and *(No 3)* [1999] 2 WLR 827 (HL).

Immunity of diplomats

The law relating to diplomatic immunity has been declared by the International Court, in the US *Diplomatic and Consular Staff in Tehran Case* (1980) ICJ Rep 3, 40, to:

> '... constitute a self-contained regime, which on the one hand, lays down the receiving state's obligations regarding the facilities, privileges and immunities to be accorded to diplomatic missions and, on the other, foresees their possible abuse by members of the mission and specifies the means at the disposal of the receiving state to counter any such abuse.'

See also the case of *Re Breard: Paraguay* v *United States* (1998) ICJ Rep 248 on the approach employed by the ICJ in addressing the issue of immunity.

The modern law of diplomatic immunity was both codified and developed in the Vienna Convention on Diplomatic Relations 1961. This was ratified by the United Kingdom through the Diplomatic Privileges Act 1964. A number of important rights and duties were consolidated by this conventional regime, including:

a) Immunity of the diplomatic premises. Article 22 of the Convention provides:

> 'The premises of the mission shall be inviolable. The agents of the receiving state may not enter them, except with the consent of the head of the mission.'

In addition, the receiving state is under a positive obligation to protect the mission against intrusion or damage.

Three principal theories have been advanced to define the basis for this special status:

i) the 'extraterritorial theory' which claims that the diplomatic premises constitute an extension of the sovereign territory of the sending state;

ii) the 'representative character theory' according to which diplomats are considered to personify the foreign sovereign which they were dispatched to represent; and

iii) the 'functional necessity theory' in which diplomatic privileges and immunities are justified as necessary to enable the proper functioning of the diplomatic mission.

Among these theories, it is the functional necessity theory which is least open to criticism. In *Radwan* v *Radwan* [1973] Fam 24 the court rejected the proposition that the Egyptian consulate in London was Egyptian territory.

Diplomatic premises are also protected against the enforcement of an judgment, decree or arbitral award made against the government of the state maintaining the premises: *A Company Ltd* v *Republic of X* [1990] 2 Lloyd's Rep 520.

b) Inviolability of diplomatic correspondence. Article 27 of the Convention stipulates three important rules.

i) The receiving state must permit and protect free communication between the mission and its government.

ii) Official correspondence of the mission shall be inviolable.

iii) The diplomatic bag shall not be opened or detained.

c) Inviolability of the diplomatic person and his freedom from arrest and detention. This right is clearly endorsed by art 29 of the Convention which provides:

> 'The person of a diplomatic agent shall be inviolable. He shall not be liable to any form of arrest or detention. The receiving state shall treat him with due respect and shall take all appropriate steps to prevent any attack on his person, freedom or dignity.'

This is the most fundamental right of diplomatic protection, and is fortified by the Convention on the Prevention and Punishment of Crimes against Internationally Protected Persons, Including Diplomatic Agents 1973.

d) Immunity of the diplomatic personnel from criminal jurisdiction and civil litigation. Article 31 of the 1961 Convention provides simply that:

> 'A diplomatic agent shall enjoy immunity from the criminal jurisdiction of the receiving state. He shall also enjoy immunity from its civil and administrative jurisdiction (subject to exceptions).'

Clearly, absolute immunity from criminal jurisdiction is granted whilst conditional immunity is conferred in relation to the civil jurisdiction of the receiving state. The exceptions to civil jurisdiction relate to private real property, succession and commercial activity carried on by the diplomat outwith official functions: see *Intpro Properties (UK) Ltd v Sauvel* [1983] 2 All ER 495 and *Shaw v Shaw* [1979] 3 All ER 1.

Further, a diplomat cannot be compelled to give evidence in a court of law: art 31(2). On the issue of diplomatic and consular immunity, the case of *In the Matter of La Grand: Germany v USA* (2001) The Times 27 June provides an interesting and useful illustration of the applicable principles.

Limits on the principle of the immunity of diplomats

Foreign diplomats and their families are not entitled to diplomatic immunity, nor the right to residence or to expedited immigration procedure, after the expiry of their secondment to their mission.

Once a person's appointment at a mission has ceased he or she is no longer a member of the mission and if the official or his family remain in the United Kingdom after the termination of an appointment, it is without the leave of the immigration authorities: *R v Secretary of State for the Home Department, ex parte Bagga and Others* [1990] 3 WLR 1013.

In *R v Evans and Others, ex parte Pinochet Ugarte* [1998] 3 WLR 1546, the House of Lords dealt with the immunity of a former head of state. This marked the beginning of the Pinochet 'saga' in which the court dealt with the issue of extradition under the Extradition Act 1989, amongst others.

Immunities of consuls

Consuls perform less political, and greater administrative, functions than diplomats and are therefore accorded a lesser degree of immunity from jurisdiction. Again the rights and duties of consuls are regulated by treaty, in this case the Vienna Convention on Consular Relations 1963. The following are the more important provisions of this agreement:

a) consular premises are inviolable and may not be entered without the consent of the authorities of the receiving state (art 31);

b) consular premises must be protected against damage and intrusion (art 33);

c) consular officers may not be arrested or detained except in the case of a grave crime and following a decision by a competent judicial authority (art 41); and

d) immunity from jurisdiction in the case of consuls is restricted in both criminal and civil matters to acts done in the official exercise of consular functions.

The immunities of international organisations

No customary rights of immunity from jurisdiction appear to be endowed upon international organisations and their representatives. However, a number of treaties regulate the rights and duties of such entities within the territory of the receiving state. Although the Vienna Convention on the Representation of States in Their Relations with International Organisations of a Universal Character 1975 would regulate this subject matter on a multilateral basis, it has not yet entered force.

Immunities of international organisations are therefore established on an ad hoc basis. Note in particular, the General Convention on the Privileges and Immunities of the United Nations 1946, 1 UNTS 15, which sets out the immunities of the personnel of the United Nations, whilst the US-UN Headquarters Agreement 1947 reiterates the rights and duties of the United Nations and its personnel in the United States.

The act of state doctrine

An important procedural distinction exists between sovereign immunity and immunity under the act of state doctrine. The first is a plea relating to the jurisdiction of the case, whilst the latter is an issue decided in the course of the merits of the case.

According to the act of state doctrine, as generally received in municipal jurisprudence, the courts of one country are unable to adjudicate upon the actions taken by a state in the exercise of that state's sovereign public acts. In *Underhill* v *Hernandez* 168 US 250 (1897), Fuller CJ of the US Supreme Court declared:

'Every sovereign state is bound to respect the independence of every other sovereign state, and the courts of one country will not sit in judgment on the acts of the government of another, done within its own territory.'

The exact status of the doctrine in British law is unclear, although in the English case, *Buttes Gas & Oil Co* v *Hammer* [1981] 3 All ER 616, Lord Wilberforce, in the House of Lords, stated that the British courts could not adjudicate on 'the validity, meaning and effect of transactions of sovereign states'. He continued to observe that an English court could not 'examine the validity, under international law ... of ... acts in the area of transactions between states'.

The basis of the doctrine in English law appears to be that judicial review of issues of foreign sovereign authority would be inappropriate and could result in serious international repercussions. Such questions belong more in the sphere of diplomacy than law. See *R* v *Secretary of State for Foreign and Commonwealth Affairs, ex parte Pirbai* (1985) The Times 17 October.

The Court of Appeal has established an exception to the general rule of immunity for acts of state. Where a state is engaged in commercial or private activities to which the defence is raised, the doctrine is inapplicable. See *Empresa Exportadora de Azucar* v *Industria Azucarera Nacional SA* [1983] 2 Lloyd's Rep 171. *A Ltd* v *B Bank* (1996) The Times 15 August is a recent illustration of this exception: the doctrine of sovereign immunity did not apply to a foreign State's commercial banking transactions, so it was not immune from the court's jurisdiction in this case, where infringement of the plaintiff's patent was alleged.

8.3 Key cases and legislation

* *A Ltd* v *B Bank* (1996) The Times 15 August
  An illustration of the commercial activities exception to the doctrine of sovereign immunity

* *Al-Adsani* v *Government of Kuwait* [1996] 1 Lloyd's Rep 104
  State Immunity Act 1978 is not subject to overriding principles of international law

* *Alcom Ltd* v *Republic of Colombia* [1984] 2 All ER 6
  Affirmation of the restrictive theory of sovereign immunity in English law

* *Attorney-General for the United Kingdom* v *Heinemann Publishers Pty Ltd* (1988) 62 ALJR 344
  Contains relevant statements on the act of state doctrine

* *Breard, Re: Paraquay* v *United States* (1998) ICJ Rep 248
  Illustrates the approach taken by the ICJ in deciding immunity

* *Company, A, Ltd* v *Republic of X* [1990] 2 Lloyd's Rep 520
  Illustrates the approach of the courts towards the interpretation of the State Immunity Act 1978

* *Holland* v *Lampen-Wolfe* [2000] 1 WLR 1573 (HL)
  Addressed the issue of the extent of state immunity

* *In the Matter of La Grand: Germany* v *USA* (2001) The Times 27 June
  Considered the issue of diplomatic and consular immunity

* *Kuwait Airways Corporation* v *Iraqi Airways Company* (1998) The Times 12 May
  Dealt with the relationship between state immunity and the principle of non-justicability

* *P* v *P (Diplomatic Immunity: Jurisdiction)* (1998) The Times 2 March
  Addressed the relationship between diplomatic and state immunity

* *R* v *Bow Street Metropolitan Stipendiary Magistrate, ex parte Pinochet Ugarte (No 1)* [1998] 3 WLR 1456; *(No 2)* [1999] 2 WLR 272 (HL); and *(No 3)* [1999] 2 WLR 827 (HL)
  Addressed the issue of state immunity in extradition proceedings

- *R v IRC, ex parte Camacq Corp* [1990] 1 All ER 173
  Limitations imposed on the principle of sovereign immunity for taxation purposes

- *R v Secretary of State for the Home Department, ex parte Bagga and Others* [1990] 3 WLR 1013
  Some limitations on the principle of diplomatic immunity after the period of duty has expired

- Diplomatic Privileges Act 1964

- European Convention on State Immunity 1972

- International Organisations Act 1968

- State Immunity Act 1978

- US Foreign Sovereign Immunities Act 1976

- Vienna Convention on Diplomatic Relations 1961

Note: the statutes and conventions deal with various aspects of state and diplomatic immunity.

8.4 Questions and suggested solutions

QUESTION ONE

Alphonso is employed as an administrative assistant and Bertram as a cook in the embassy of Ruretania in Swabia. The Swabian authorities, suspecting that Alphonso has been using Ruretania's diplomatic bag to import into Swabia drugs which are prohibited substances under Swabian law and that Bertram has been selling the drugs locally, arrest Alphonso and Bertram (who is himself a Swabian national) and charge them with drug offences. On hearing of this, the Ruretanian ambassador announces that he intends to dismiss Alphonso and Bertram from their employment with the embassy.

Advise Alphonso and Bertram:

a) as to the circumstances, if any, in which a plea of diplomatic immunity will be available in respect of the criminal charges against them; and

b) as to whether the Swabian courts will have jurisdiction under international law in respect of an action by Alphonso and Bertram for wrongful dismissal if their embassy employment is terminated.

University of London LLB Examination
(for External Students) Public International Law June 1997 Q3

General Comment

It is usual for examinations in public international law to contain a question on the subject of immunity from jurisdiction. In this question the examiner requires the candidate to give specific advice to two individuals in respect of possible criminal and civil proceedings before the courts of Swabia. The question requires the student to be aware of the general scheme of the Vienna Convention on Diplomatic Relations 1961 and the broad principles relating to sovereign immunity. The perceptive student will note that while the law on diplomatic immunity is subject to much common agreement, there are differences from State to State as regards the subject of sovereign immunity. In the United Kingdom such a matter would be regulated under the State Immunity Act 1978; in Swabia, however, the relevant legislation may display differences of detail. The examiner will, of course, award the highest marks to the candidate who advises Aphonso and Bertram as distinct from the candidate who simply writes a dissertation on immunity from jurisdiction.

Skeleton Solution

The possible criminal charges in Swabia: the position of Alphonso; the position of Bertram – civil action for wrongful dismissal and the likely plea of sovereign immunity.

Suggested Solution

We are asked in this matter to advise Alphonso (a Ruretanian national) and Bertram (a Swabian national) in respect of two distinct matters. It is sensible to take each in turn.

The possible criminal charges in Swabia

It seems probable that the prosecuting authorities in Swabia contemplate charges against Alphonso in respect of the importation of unlawful substances, and against Bertram in respect of the distribution of such substances. In essence the question arises as to whether either person will be able to rely on a plea of diplomatic immunity in respect for the charges against them. As the Vienna Convention on Diplomatic Relations 1961 has been signed and ratified by more than 150 States it is more than likely that Ruretania and Swabia are both parties. In any event it is generally accepted that the Convention today represents in broad form the content of customary law. Prima facie Alphonso as an administrative assistant is within art 1(f), while Bertram as a cook is within art 1(g) of the Vienna Convention.

In respect of Alphonso he is a member of the administrative staff and thus within art 37(2) and, in consequence, prima facie entitled to the immunity from criminal prosecution contained in art 31(1). Having been dismissed it would seem that he is likely to return to Ruretania; in principle he is entitled to his immunity until he leaves the country: art 39(2). Since the allegations against Alphonso relate to the abuse of the diplomatic bag, then it is arguable that they concern the improper performance of his duties and are subject to the longer time limit provided by art 39(2).

Our advice to Alphonso is that he is likely to be able to raise a plea of diplomatic immunity in the proposed criminal proceedings. No such proceedings are likely to be brought because the allegations relate to the abuse of the diplomatic bag and Swabia, in producing such evidence, might be forced to acknowledge breaches of art 27. A note that Alphonso is persona non grata under art 9 of the Vienna Convention is likely to be served.

In respect of Bertram it would appear that he is within art 1(g) of the Vienna Convention. The only relevant immunity is that contained within art 37(3), and Bertram cannot avail himself of it because: (i) he is a national of the receiving State; and (ii) distributing drugs in the locality is not an act performed in the course of his duties as a cook. It would therefore seem that Bertram is not immune from criminal proceedings in Swabia.

In respect of Alphonso a marginal point arises as to whether there has been any waiver of immunity by the Ruretanian ambassador under arts 32(1) and (2). This is most unlikely given that Alphonso's conduct relates to the sensitive issue of abuse of the diplomatic bag.

Civil action in the courts of Swabia

The second matter that we are asked to consider is whether Alphonso and Bertram can bring an action for wrongful dismissal in the courts of Swabia. In such an action the plaintiffs would be Alphonso and Bertram, while the defendant would be the Republic or Kingdom of Ruretania. This aspect of the problem raises the question of State immunity and its relationship with the law of diplomatic immunity.

The short answer is that the law will be contained in whatever legislation exists in Swabia in relation to State immunity. Most States have some form of legislation based on the restrictive theory of State immunity: eg State Immunity Act 1978 (UK); Foreign Sovereign Immunities Act 1976 (US); Foreign States Immunities Act 1985 (Australia). The broad approach of such legislation is to confer immunity subject to limited exceptions. It is certainly true that a contract of employment might be an exception, but in respect of members of the mission the usual course is to render any exception subject to the terms of the Vienna Convention: see ss4 and 16(1)(a) State Immunity Act 1978.

We do not have precise details of the legislation in Swabia, but it is clear from cases elsewhere that any case of wrongful dismissal would involve an examination of the alleged breach of contract and an investigation into the internal workings of the embassy and, in particular, the use of the diplomatic bag. To reach a final determination it would be necessary to pass judgment on the conduct of the ambassador in dismissing the two individuals. It is quite clear that such a claim would attract immunity in the United Kingdom: see ss4 and 16(1)(a) State Immunity Act 1978. While we do not have details of the legislation in Swabia, there is every reason to believe that a court in that jurisdiction would be influenced by the same considerations that caused the court in *Sengupta* v *Republic of India* [1983] ICR 221; 64 ILR 352 to uphold a claim for immunity. The cases of Alphonso and Bertram, as co-conspirators, cannot be determined separately. It is also obvious that a claim for wrongful dismissal cannot be determined without an extensive investigation as to the internal workings of the embassy. The courts in Swabia are likely to allow a plea of State immunity if it is entered by Ruretania. The assertion that Bertram as a national of Swabia should be treated differently for the purposes of employment legislation is likely to be rejected because he is a 'member of a mission' for the purposes of art 1 of the Vienna Convention on Diplomatic Relations 1961: see *Ahmed* v *Government of the Kingdom of Saudi Arabia* [1996] 2 All ER 248. The courts of Swabia are likely to decline jurisdiction and to allow the plea of immunity.

Conclusion

Our conclusion in this matter must be that Alphonso is immune from criminal jurisdiction but Bertram is not. Any civil proceedings for wrongful dismissal brought in the courts of Swabia are likely to attract a plea of State immunity.

QUESTION TWO

a) 'The Vienna Convention on Diplomatic Relations, 1961, requires radical revision.'

   Discuss.

b) State A's authorities suspect that Edvard, a member of the staff of State B's diplomatic mission to State A, is engaged in drug smuggling activities. Assuming that both States are parties to the Vienna Convention on Diplomatic Relations, 1961, advise State A's authorities as to whether they may:

   i) subject the diplomatic bag of State B to electronic surveillance;

   ii) search the private residence of Edvard and of his driver, Maria, who is a national of State A;

   iii) arrest Edvard and Maria when they attend a meeting with suspected drug dealers outside the capital of State A; and

   iv) expel the ambassador of State B for failing to prevent the alleged drug smuggling activities.

University of London LLB Examination
(for External Students) Public International Law June 1996 Q4

General Comment

The question is neatly divided up into two sections. The answer to part (a) may be utilised to help answer the problems presented in part (b).

Part (a) invites a discussion of the main areas of diplomatic immunity relating to the misuse of diplomatic missions, of personal diplomatic immunity and of the diplomatic bag. The answer should also include a defence of the Vienna Convention and the importance of diplomatic immunity in the international system.

Skeleton Solution

a) Introduction: status of Vienna Convention – abuse of the functions of a foreign embassy: Libya and Sun Yat Sen incidents – actions of diplomatic staff – diplomatic bag and its misuse – conclusion and necessity of diplomatic immunity.

b) i) Article 27(3) Vienna Convention.

   ii) Article 30 and private residence of diplomats – status of private residence of service staff.

   iii) Article 26 and freedom of movement – immunity from arrest of categories of staff.

   iv) Persona non grata and workings of art 9.

Suggested Solution

a) The Vienna Convention codified the rules on diplomatic immunity. More than 150 states have ratified it and it is recognised as being in accordance with customary international law. It can therefore be used as evidence of customary international law even in situations involving a State which is not party to the convention.

Diplomatic immunity was a feature of the ancient Greek system of city States and is regarded as 'essential for the relations between states as accepted by nations of all creeds and political complexions': *United States Diplomatic and Consular Staff in Tehran Case* (1980) ICJ Rep 3. Diplomatic representation and diplomatic relations are not a requirement in international law but the vast majority of states have some form of diplomatic representation abroad and receive diplomats on their territory.

Why, then, is there a demand that the Vienna Convention be fundamentally redrawn? The disquiet with the Convention and its workings originates in the abuse of the diplomatic norms by some States. Article 3 of the Convention outlines the main functions of a diplomatic mission and these involve representation of the sending State, protection of its interests and nationals and, importantly, the promotion of friendly relations. This not always the case. A foreign embassy may involve itself in actions which are hostile to the interests of the receiving State. The most notable example of this took place in London on 17 April 1984 during a peaceful demonstration outside the Libyan Embassy. Shots were fired from the Embassy at a group of demonstrators opposed to the government of Libya. One of the shots killed a policewoman who was marshalling the demonstrators. Following this event the United Kingdom ordered the closure of the Libyan Embassy and the expulsion of her diplomats. The Embassy staff and organisation were obviously not involved in promoting friendly relations between Britain and Libya, but the receiving State was unable to vet the activities of the embassy. Similarly, in the Sun Yat San incident a Chinese national was kidnapped and held against his will in the Chinese Embassy. Although the British government expressed its displeasure to the government of China the court in the United Kingdom refused to intervene.

It is, however, with the activities of diplomatic staff outside their embassy that most disquiet has been expressed. Diplomatic agents have complete immunity from the criminal jurisdiction of the receiving State and immunity from the civil jurisdiction save in respect of, inter alia, actions relating to private real property or succession under a will. A diplomat is therefore immune from the criminal law in relation to, for example, murder or theft. Abuses of this immunity have been a cause for concern. Parking offences in London are the most common examples of errant behaviour but diplomats have also indulged in other areas. Dixon (*International Law* (3rd ed), p182) quotes the statistic that in 1996 29 diplomats were found to be responsible for 'serious offences'. The receiving State may of course exercise its discretion and declare the diplomat 'persona non grata', but what it cannot do is punish the diplomat. Article 41 places an obligation on diplomats to obey the receiving State's laws, but by the same article the receiving State is prevented from interfering with the privileges and immunities of the diplomat. The only option open to the receiving State is either to utilise art 32 and ask for the diplomat's immunity to be waived or else, as mentioned above, declare the individual persona non grata. Administrative and technical staff also enjoy immunities similar to the diplomatic staff with the exception that their civil immunity is limited to their official duties: art 37(2). Such individuals are therefore free to engage in potentially unlawful activities in the receiving State. The most common example during the cold war was, of course, spying.

Under art 27 the receiving State is obliged to protect free communications for all official purposes and the sending State is authorised to use codes to communicate with its home State. The receiving State is also forbidden to open or detain the diplomatic bag: art 27(3). The image of the diplomatic bag is, however, at variance with the reality, and it may consist of large wooden crates rather than a hand-held bag. As long as the item has visible external marks identifying it as a diplomatic bag it cannot be opened or detained. This aspect of diplomatic immunity has been the subject of much debate owing to its misuse for the smuggling of drugs or even in the case of Nigeria, people: discussed in (1985) 34 ICLQ 602. Dikko, a former Nigerian government Minister was kidnapped by Nigerian agents, drugged and placed in a crate, a diplomatic bag, destined for Nigeria. The crate was examined following insufficient official paperwork and was found to contain Dikko and his kidnappers. The United Kingdom government justified this breach of diplomatic protocol on the basis that a receiving State is entitled so to do where there is a threat to an individual's wellbeing.

Against this background diplomatic immunity, or its extent, has been called into question, particularly in relation to the diplomatic bag. The United Kingdom, for instance, would like to have the authority to open the bag in the presence of an official of the embassy and if this is refused then to have the authority to order the return of the bag to the sending State. However, certain countries have given a flexible interpretation of when they may violate diplomatic premises or hinder the workings of a diplomatic mission. In 1984 following the closure of the Libyan

Embassy the building was searched by the British police in the presence of a Saudi diplomat. This would appear to be in breach of art 45(a) which states that after a break in diplomatic relations 'the receiving State must ... respect and protect the premises of the mission'. The United Kingdom argued that does not mean that the premises continue to be inviolable, and one may argue that the search could be justified as a right of self-defence.

It is, however, when the consequences of abandoning diplomatic immunity are considered that the present system looks most satisfactory. The invasion and seizure of the hostages in the American Embassy in Tehran provide a vivid example of the dangers (see case above), as does the possibility of diplomats being arrested on false charges.

b) i) Under art 27 the receiving State is obliged to permit and protect free communications for all official purposes. The diplomatic mission may, however, only install and use a wireless transmitter with the consent of the receiving State: art 27(1). State A may therefore be using an electronic surveillance system in order to ascertain whether the diplomatic bag contains a wireless transmitter. If State B has no permission to use a wireless transmitter and is so doing then State A is justified in complaining to State B. What is not permissible is to open or detain the diplomatic bag to confirm or refute this belief.

ii) Whether a search of the private residence of Edvard is permitted would depend upon his status. One is only told that he is a member of staff.

If Edvard is a diplomatic agent then his private residence is inviolable: art 30. The private residence enjoys the same inviolability as the diplomatic mission. This also true of the diplomatic agent's papers. If Edvard is a member of the administrative and technical staff then similar immunities will apply as long as he is not a national of State A nor permanently resident in State A. However, Maria is a national of State A so even if she is classed as technical and administrative staff she will attract no immunity to her residence which will not be inviolable.

Equally, no immunity will apply to Maria's residence if she is a member of the service staff or a private servant, which is likely in the case of a driver.

iii) Edvard is permitted to journey outside the capital of State A. Under art 26 the receiving State is obliged to ensure freedom of movement for all members of the mission provided the area is not a prohibited zone which is designated as such on grounds of national security.

The arrest of Edvard will not be lawful if he is a diplomatic agent; that is if he is head of the mission or a member of the diplomatic staff of the mission. A diplomatic agent is completely immune from the criminal jurisdiction of the receiving state (art 31) and cannot be detained. If Edvard is a member of the administrative and technical staff, for example a clerk or radio operator, he will also enjoy complete immunity from criminal jurisdiction: art 37(2). If he is a member of the service staff he will enjoy immunity only in respect of acts performed in the course of his duties: art 37(3). The meeting with suspected drug dealers is unlikely to fall into this category.

As a national of State A and presumably a member of the service staff or a private servant, Maria will enjoy no immunities: art 37(3) and (4).

iv) The ambassador may be declared persona non grata by State A. If this happens, he should either be recalled by State B or have his functions with the mission terminated: art 9. State A is not obliged to furnish any explanation when notifying State B of its decision to declare a member of State B's diplomatic staff persona non grata. If State B refuses or fails to carry out its resulting obligations then State A may refuse to recognise the ambassador as a member of the mission: art 9(2).

QUESTION THREE

a) 'Recent years have seen some important developments concerning the immunity of foreign states before domestic courts.'

Discuss.

b) Your client seeks your advice concerning the failure of Alcoholico, a state trading entity in an East European state, to honour its contractual obligation to deliver a consignment of vodka to London in time for the Christmas trade. He has been informed by the London Office of Alcoholico, situated in the embassy of the state concerned, that state immunity will be claimed if he institutes proceedings against Alcoholico.

Advise your client.

Written by the Author

General Comment

An interesting two-part question on immunity from jurisdiction, which requires knowledge of the relevant case law.

Skeleton Solution

a) Sovereign immunity – principles – qualified immunity – State Immunity Act 1978 – relevant case law.

b) Attitude of courts to claim for state immunity – application of s3 State Immunity Act 1978 – conclusion.

Suggested Solution

a) In international law, since states are independent and equal, no state may exercise jurisdiction over another state without its consent. This sovereign immunity rests upon two principles. Firstly the principle of par in parem non habet imperium: whereby legal persons of equal standing cannot have their disputes settled in the courts of one of them, and secondly, the principle of non-intervention in the internal affairs of other states. However, while international law recognises the doctrine of sovereign immunity there is dispute as to its extent.

As long as state activity was restricted to governmental matters the principle of sovereign immunity and the application of absolute immunity in relation to such matters found universal toleration. However, recently there has taken place a dramatic expansion of state activity. States are becoming increasingly involved in commercial activities and enterprises and the advent of communism and socialism has meant that today most state economies have a state controlled public sector. The problem therefore became whether states should enjoy the same absolute immunity in respect of their commercial activities as they did in respect of their government activities.

Many states, in response to this extension of state activity, began to distinguish between the various acts of government, acts jure imperii, acts of a commercial or less essential nature and acts jure gestionis. While allowing absolute immunity to states in respect of their governmental acts, absolute immunity was denied or restricted in respect of the states' commercial activities. At common law the United Kingdom courts have abandoned absolute immunity in favour of the doctrine of restrictive immunity. In *Trendtex Corporation* v *Central Bank of Nigeria* [1977] QB 529, Lord Denning extended the doctrine of qualified immunity to actions in personam, the immunity attaching to actions in rem having been declared qualified in *The Philippine Admiral* [1977] AC 373. This approach was given statutory effect by the State Immunity Act 1978 which provides that a state is not immune as respects proceedings relating to a commercial transaction entered into by the state.

The UK courts have greatly elaborated on the principles behind the State Immunity Act (SIA) 1978 in a series of recent cases. Essentially, the statute limits the immunity of states when they engage in commercial transactions as defined in s3(3) SIA 1978. Other exceptions to the absolute immunity of a state to proceedings relate to claims for personal injury, death or loss or damage to tangible property in the UK, proceedings concerning immovable property situated in the UK, proceedings relating to infringement of intellectual property rights, and proceedings concerning liability to tax.

The courts have recently closely examined many of these exceptions to the principle of state immunity. For example, in *A Company Ltd* v *Republic of X* [1990] 2 Lloyd's Rep 520 a court was asked whether a company could obtain an injunction to prevent the disposal of assets held by the government of a state in the United Kingdom in order to enforce a decree obtained in an action for non-payment for a consignment of rice ordered by the government. The court dismissed the action on the grounds that, even if the bank account could be subject to an injunction, no decree could be enforced against a state without its consent.

The question of a state's liability to UK income tax was raised in *R* v *IRC, ex parte Camacq Corp* [1990] 1 All ER 173 where it was held that there is no immunity for liability for UK income tax assessed in income accruing on earnings due to foreign governments from investments in the UK.

Other decisions recently rendered by the courts in the interpretation of this statute have concerned questions relating to the status of money in bank accounts held by states for commercial purposes (*Alcom Ltd* v *Republic of Colombia* [1984] 2 All ER 6), the issue of whether a plea of diplomatic immunity is a preliminary or substantive matter for the courts to decide and the possibility of registering a local land charge over an embassy.

It is clear that a considerable body of law has recently developed regarding the application of the principles under SIA 1978. However, a considerable number of provisions still remain to be interpreted by the courts and no doubt will be subject to scrutiny by the courts in due course.

b) Clearly the success of any action against Alcoholico will depend upon the attitude of the courts to the claim for state immunity. If that immunity is successfully claimed, it will amount to a bar to my client's action.

At common law the Court of Appeal has held in *Trendtex Trading Corporation* v *Central Bank of Nigeria* that as a matter of international law and therefore as a matter of English municipal law, immunity will only apply to acts jure imperii. If Alcoholico can be regarded as a separate legal entity which carries on commercial activities for a state then it is an agent not an organ of government. Therefore, it can be said with some confidence that a claim to state immunity supported by the Eastern European Government will not simply be accepted by the courts as it was in *The Porto Alexandre* [1920] P 30. The court will undoubtedly acknowledge that trading in vodka is not a function that would normally be regarded as one of government.

The approach of Lord Denning in *Trendtex* (above) is now given statutory effect in SIA 1978 which provides that a state is not immune as regards proceedings relating to a commercial transaction entered into by the state. By s3(3) SIA 1978 a 'commercial transaction' is defined as including 'any contract for the supply of goods and services'. Further, under s3(1)(b) a state is not immune as respects proceedings relating to an obligation of the state which by virtue of a contract (whether a commercial transaction or not) falls to be performed wholly or partly in the United Kingdom.

Therefore, assuming that the matter is covered by SIA 1978, the contract to deliver a consignment of vodka to London, being a contract for the supply of goods and therefore a commercial transaction within the meaning of the State Immunity Act means that Alcoholico will be unable to rely on any general state immunity as a bar to the action.

QUESTION FOUR

Outline the principles behind the doctrine of sovereign immunity from jurisdiction as applied by the English courts. In particular, to what extent has the law been altered by statutory enactments?

Written by the Author

General Comment

This question requires a descriptive discussion of the principles of immunity as recognised and applied by the English courts.

Skeleton Solution

The rationale for sovereign immunity – the movement from absolute to restrictive interpretation – discussion of the State Immunity Act 1978 – case law.

Suggested Solution

Originally, sovereign immunity was granted by the English courts on an absolute basis. In *The Parlement Belge* (1879) 4 PD 129, it was held that a mail packet vessel belonging to the Belgian King was entitled to absolute immunity from jurisdiction. This principle was upheld in subsequent cases, including *The Porto Alexandre* [1920] P 30; *Krajina* v *Tass Agency* [1949] 2 All ER 274; and *Baccus SRL* v *Servicio Nacional del Trigo* [1957] 1 QB 438. However, the absolute approach to sovereign immunity presupposed that state governmental activities remained in the public sphere of international activities and did not extend into the private aspects of international life, such as trade and commerce.

States have increasingly moved into areas once considered outwith the traditional scope of state concern. This is particularly the case as regards business and commercial matters. As a result of this expansion of state governmental activities, the restrictive theory of sovereign immunity began to gather momentum.

The British courts were rather reluctant to adopt the restrictive approach to sovereign immunity, preferring to uphold the absolute doctrine. This produced a number of inequitable decisions. In *Baccus SRL* v *Servicio Nacional del Trigo*, the court held that the defendants, although a separate legal person under Spanish law from the government were in effect a department of state of the Spanish government and therefore entitled to immunity. Lord Justice Singleton, in a dissenting opinion, condemned the extension of immunity to separate legal entities on a de facto as opposed to de jure basis.

In order to remedy this undesirable situation, in a series of cases, the English courts adopted the restrictive approach to sovereign immunity on a fragmented basis. In *The Philippine Admiral* [1977] AC 373, the Privy Council, hearing the case on appeal from the Supreme Court of Hong Kong, reviewed the legal situation and concluded that it would not follow earlier cases. This decision was made on the rationale, inter alia, that the trend of opinion was against the absolute immunity doctrine, and also because the absolute doctrine did not recognise the fact that sovereigns often could be sued in their own municipal courts by their own citizens, eg Crown Proceedings Act 1947. The Privy Council held that, where a state-owned merchant ship was involved in ordinary commerce, it would not be entitled to sovereign immunity, and the case proceeded to the merits.

The restrictive doctrine of sovereign immunity was completely embraced by the English court in *Trendtex Trading Corp* v *Central Bank of Nigeria* [1977] QB 529, where all three judges of the Court of Appeal upheld the validity of the restrictive doctrine.

Since the restrictive doctrine of sovereign immunity is accepted in British judicial reasoning, it therefore becomes necessary to distinguish between acts of a governmental nature (jure imperii) and acts of a commercial nature (jure gestionis). In order to differentiate between governmental activities in these dimensions, the plaintiff has an onus to establish that the relevant act which forms the basis of the claim was an act jure gestionis, or in other words 'an act of a private law character such as a private citizen might have entered into'. This requires an evaluation of the nature of the actions at issue to ascertain whether they are within or without the realm of trading activities. This was the test established by Lord Wilberforce in *I Congreso del Partido* [1983] 1 AC 244.

The position at common law has been modified by the State Immunity Act 1978. According to this statute, a state cannot plead sovereign immunity in relation to:

a) a commercial transaction entered into by a state. A 'commercial transaction' is defined by s3(3) to include:

   i)   a contract for the supply of goods;

   ii) a loan or other transaction for the provision of finance and any other connected guarantees or indemnities; and

   iii) any other commercial, industrial or financial or similar transaction or activity which is not an exercise of sovereign authority.

b) a contractual obligation to be performed wholly or partly within the United Kingdom, unless the contract (not being a commercial transaction) was made in the territory of the state concerned and the obligation in question is governed by its administrative law.

In addition, immunity is restricted in cases relating to death or injury caused by foreign state activities in the United Kingdom; questions of immovable property in the United

Kingdom; patent and trademark cases; disputes arising from membership of corporate bodies; and actions in rem against commercial ships.

The UK courts have greatly elaborated on the principles behind the State Immunity Act 1978 in a series of recent cases. Essentially, the statute limits the immunity of states when they engage in commercial transactions as defined in s3(3) of the statute. Other exceptions to the absolute immunity of a state to proceedings relate to claims for personal injury, death or loss or damage to tangible property in the UK, proceedings concerning immovable property situated in the UK, proceedings relating to infringement of intellectual property rights, and proceedings concerning liability to tax.

The courts have closely examined some of the exceptions to the principle of state immunity. For example, in *A Company Ltd* v *Republic of X* [1990] 2 Lloyd's Rep 520, a court was asked whether a company could obtain an injunction to prevent the disposal of assets held by the government of a state in the United Kingdom in enforcing a decree obtained in an action for non-payment for a consignment of rice ordered by the government. The court dismissed the action on the grounds that, even if the bank account could be subject to an injunction, no decree could be enforced against a state without its consent.

The question of a state's liability to UK income tax was raised in *R* v *IRC, ex parte Camacq Corp* [1990] 1 All ER 173, where it was held that there is no immunity for liability for UK income tax assessed on income accruing on earnings due to foreign governments from investments in the UK.

Other decisions rendered by the courts in the interpretation of this statute have concerned questions relating to the status of money in bank accounts held by states for commercial purposes (*Alcom Ltd* v *Republic of Colombia* [1984] 2 All ER 6), the issue of whether a plea of diplomatic immunity is a preliminary or substantive matter for the courts to decide (*Maclaine Watson & Co* v *Department of Trade and Industry* [1988] 3 All ER 257), and the possibility of registering a local land charge over an embassy: *Westminster City Council* v *Iran* [1986] 3 All ER 284. *A Ltd* v *B Bank* (1996) The Times 15 August is a recent illustration of the exception to the doctrine of sovereign immunity where a state is involved in commercial activities.

Two particular matters require more detailed attention. Firstly, s13(2) of the State Immunity Act 1978 declares that, in the absence of consent from the foreign state, relief may not be given against a state by way of injunction or order for specific performance or for the recovery of land. Secondly, the same section provides that the property of a state may not be subject to any process for the enforcement of a judgment or arbitration award or, in an action in rem, for its arrest, detention or sale. This second restriction was strictly construed by Lord Diplock in *Alcom Ltd* v *Republic of Colombia*, in a case involving attachment of a bank account of a diplomatic mission. Such an account could be attached if it could be demonstrated that 'the bank account was earmarked by the foreign state solely ... for being drawn on to settle liabilities incurred in commercial transactions'.

British courts therefore appear to embrace a restrictive approach to the question of sovereign immunity. However, the uneasy co-existence of statutory and common law will eventually give rise to a number of complex and confusing issues.

QUESTION FIVE

INTERSAT is an international organisation established under the terms of the 'Satellite Communications Treaty 1985' for the purposes of owning and operating satellite communications on behalf of member states and commercial customers. Superlectric plc has supplied to INTERSAT large quantities of equipment for which payment is still outstanding. Superlectric has recently commenced proceedings in the English courts in order to recover the debt. Assume that the United Kingdom is a party to the 1985 Treaty and also that the 'Satellite Act 1985' provides that INTERSAT should have the capacity of a body corporate.

Advise:

1) Whether INTERSAT's plea of immunity from suit is likely to succeed; and

2) Whether INTERSAT's assets in the United Kingdom would be available for settlement of any judgment debt.

How would you answer the same question if the 1985 Act had provided that INTERSAT should enjoy the immunities conferred upon a state by the State Immunity Act 1978?

University of London LLB Examination
(for External Students) Public International Law June 1987 Q7

General Comment

This problem question requires analysis of the principles of immunity applicable to international organisations from an international law perspective.

Skeleton Solution

Introduction: does immunity extend to international organisations? – is INTERSAT entitled to immunity?; is this general immunity or restrictive immunity? – the use of INTERSAT's assets for settlement of judgment debts – the position under the State Immunity Act 1978.

Suggested Solution

There is no multilateral convention regulating the legal status of international organisations in general and it is uncertain to what extent international organisations enjoy immunity under customary international law. In practice, the matter is usually regulated by treaty, an example being the General Convention on the Privileges and Immunities of the United Nations 1946. One would therefore look to the Satellite

Communications Treaty 1985 to ascertain whether or not INTERSAT had immunity before the municipal courts of member states. For the purposes of immunity before the British courts, the provisions of the International Organisations (Immunities and Privileges) Act 1950 should be examined.

In the absence of specific provisions regulating the legal status of INTERSAT, the only alternative basis on which immunity might be conferred would be by analogy to the concept of sovereign immunity in British law. This would, at the outset, require a certificate from the Foreign Office verifying the status of INTERSAT for the purposes of immunity before the British courts. Section 21 of the State Immunity Act 1978 confers authority for such determinations upon the Secretary of State.

Assuming that INTERSAT was eligible for immunity before municipal courts, one would have to consider whether or not the immunity was general or restrictive. In contemporary state practice, a distinction is made between the acts of government jure imperii, and acts of a commercial or less essential nature, jure gestionis. The doctrine of restrictive immunity was recognised by the British courts in the case of *Trendtex Trading Corporation* v *Central Bank of Nigeria* [1977] QB 529 and codified by s3 of the State Immunity Act 1978. This statute allows general immunity subject to numerous exceptions which accord to the doctrine of restrictive immunity.

Applying the same principles to INTERSAT, it is necessary to decide whether its activities were commercial or governmental. This requires examination of the functions of the organisation and the way in which it is controlled. The function of INTERSAT is to own and operate satellite communications equipment on behalf of member states and also commercial customers. It could be argued that the presence of customers indicates that the functions of the organisation are not wholly concerned with the governmental activities of the member states but are commercial in nature and are therefore not subject to immunity. It is unclear from the facts presented to what degree control over INTERSAT is exercised by member states. One would probably classify the supply of technical equipment to INTERSAT by Superlectric as a commercial transaction. All that one can therefore say is that the doctrine of restrictive immunity will apply and that, if INTERSAT is held to be entitled to immunity and is engaged in activities jure imperii, then the plea of immunity from suit is likely to succeed. On the other hand, if its activities are held to be jure gestionis then its plea will fail.

Concerning the question whether INTERSAT's assets in the United Kingdom would be available for the settlement of any judgment debts, the position remains unsettled. It could be argued that, if INTERSAT was held entitled to immunity but for the fact that its activities are commercial, then the court could order the assets available in the United Kingdom to be used to settle any judgment debt. However, it could also be argued that, as regards the execution of judgment, absolute immunity still applies and a separate act of waiver of immunity from execution is required before execution can be levied even in respect of commercial activities.

If the Satellite Act 1985 provided that INTERSAT should enjoy the immunities conferred on a state by the State Immunity Act 1978, then the Organisation would be entitled to general immunity from suit subject to the exceptions stipulated in s3. In this respect, the statute provides that a state is not immune as respects proceedings relating to commercial transactions entered into by the state. Section 3(3) of the Act defines a 'commercial transaction' as: (a) any contract for the supply of goods and services; (b) any loan or other transaction for the provision of finance and any guarantee or indemnity in respect of such transaction or of any other financial obligation; and (c) any other transaction or activity (whether of a commercial, industrial, financial, professional or other similar character) into which a state enters or in which it engages otherwise than in the exercise of sovereign authority.

On this basis the supply of equipment to INTERSAT by Superlectric will be classed as a contract for the supply of goods and no immunity from suit may therefore be claimed. Further, under s13 of the State Immunity Act 1978, any property of INTERSAT in the United Kingdom for the time being in use or intended for use for commercial purposes may also be available for the settlement of outstanding judgment debts.

Chapter 9

State Responsibility

9.1   Introduction

9.2   Key points

9.3   Key cases and legislation

9.4   Questions and suggested solutions

9.1 Introduction

State responsibility refers to the liability of states for conduct in violation of the rules of international law and resulting in injury to other states. It is a complex, and often little understood aspect of the syllabus. Confusion arises in part due to the lack of consensus behind some of the more important principles involved, but also as a result of the complicated nature of the fundamental concepts involved. The following discussion will emphasis the distinctions made within this branch of the law and will concentrate on highlighting the difficulties involved in the application of basic principles.

9.2 Key points

All legal systems create rights and impose duties upon the subjects which they regulate and in this respect international law is no different. Infringement or denial of a right owed to another state creates a duty to redress the violation or to make reparation. In the *Spanish Zones of Morocco Claim* (1925) 2 RIAA 615, Umpire Huber expressed the concept of state responsibility in the following terms:

> 'Responsibility is the necessary corollary of a right. All rights of an international character involve international responsibility. If the obligation is not met, responsibility entails the duty to make reparations.'

The International Law Commission (ILC) Draft Articles on State Responsibility (Yearbook of the ILC, 1979, II, p90), represent an authoritative statement of the principles regulating this topic, in particular in relation to the content, forms and degrees of state responsibility. This is supplemented by a considerable amount of case law on the subject generated within the last century.

It is noteworthy that the ILC adopted a final text of the Draft Articles on Responsibility of States for Internationally Wrongful Acts in August 2001. It is uncertain whether the

Draft will be incorporated into a treaty or whether it will take the form of a declaration aopted by the General Assembly.

Distinction between civil and criminal responsibility

Although there is little doubt that international responsibility has both civil and criminal dimensions, the nature and scope of criminal responsibility remains highly controversial while civil responsibility is regulated on more settled principles.

Civil liability

In general, state responsibility is synonymous with civil liability and the principles discussed in the subsequent key points of this chapter relate exclusively to civil liability. International law does not subdivide civil responsibility into contractual and delictual (or tortious) liability, and when the terms 'international delict' or 'international tort' are employed, this has a wider meaning than the common law terms. All unlawful violations of international law, including breaches of treaty, are considered to be international delicts or torts.

According to the ILC Draft, 'any internationally wrongful act which is not an international crime ... constitutes an international delict': Draft art 19(4). This allows for a relatively simple distinction: an act or omission prohibited by international law constitutes an international delict where it is not a recognised international crime.

Criminal liability

Article 19(2) of the Draft Articles defines an international crime as:

> 'An internationally wrongful act which results from the breach by a state of an international obligation so essential for the protection of fundamental interests of the international community that its breach is recognised as a crime by that community as a whole ...'

Four practices are expressly identified as international crimes, although these are merely illustrative and not exhaustive. These are:

a) a serious breach of the international rules created for the preservation of international peace and security, such as the rules prohibiting aggression;

b) a serious infringement of the principles which safeguard the right of self-determination of peoples, such as the rule prohibiting the establishment or maintenance by force of colonial domination;

c) a serious breach on a widespread scale of an international obligation of essential importance for safeguarding human beings, such as those prohibiting slavery, genocide and apartheid; and

d) a serious breach of an international obligation of essential importance for the safeguarding and preservation of the human environment, such as those prohibiting mass pollution of the atmosphere or of the seas.

Other unlawful actions falling within the definition of an international crime, but which are not included within this list, are feasible.

International criminal law remains inchoate. No sanctions or penalties have been prescribed for criminal conduct, and no tribunals with jurisdiction over international crimes have been established, with the exception of the ad hoc Nuremberg Tribunal. Further, it is unclear whether international crimes are perpetrated by individuals or by states. Brownlie claims that 'the state is only liable for delicts ... (while) ... the individual directly responsible for a crime against peace in liable to trial and punishment: *International Law and the Use of Force by States* (1963), p15. However, in their commentary on the Draft Articles, the ILC declared that 'in adopting the designation "international crime" the Commission intends only to refer to "crimes" of the state, to acts attributable to the state as such'.

In June 1998, the UN's Secretary General officiated at a full-scale diplomatic conference in Rome, in respect of the establishment of an International Criminal Court (ICC). In July 1998, 120 delegations voted to approve a treaty and statute which would establish such a court. The statute, called the Rome Statute of the International Criminal Court, is anticipated to enter into force by 2006. The court will be based in The Hague but may sit elsewhere when appropriate. The ICC will have international legal personality.

Imputability

The actions of a number of state organs, agencies and representatives must be attributed to the state for the purposes of determining international responsibility. Direct or indirect responsibility will devolve to the state for:

a) Acts of the executive, legislative and judicial branches of the government: Draft art 6.

b) Any actions of the political sub-division of the state, such as individual federal states or provinces: Draft art 5.

c) An action of any organ, state employee or other agent of the government functioning within their official capacity: Draft art 8.

Acts which are lawful under municipal law, but unlawful under international law, attract international responsibility and it is no defence to an international delict that such action was legitimate under municipal law. As the Court pointed out in the *Certain German Interest in Polish Upper Silesia Case* (1926) PCIJ Rep Ser A No 7:

'... municipal laws are merely facts which express the will of and constitute the activities of states in the same manner as do legal decisions or administrative measures.'

Imputability for actions of agents and employees of the state extends in particular to the police and the armed forces. In this respect, the following principles are important:

a) A state is liable for the official actions of all agents no matter how minor in rank: Draft art 6. In the *Massey Case* (1927) 4 RIAA 15 Commissioner Nielsen declared:

> 'To attempt by some broad classification to make a distinction between some "minor" or "petty" officials and other kinds of officials must obviously at times involve practical difficulties ... In reaching conclusions in any given case with respect to responsibility for acts of public servants, the most important considerations ... are the character of the acts alleged to have resulted in injury to persons or to property, or the nature of functions performed whenever a question is raised as to their proper discharge.'

b) A state is also liable for the conduct of an individual or group if it can be established that such a person or group was in fact acting on behalf of the state, or the individual or group was in fact exercising elements of governmental authority, in the absence of official permission, in circumstances which justified the exercise of those elements of authority: Draft art 8.

c) A state is liable for the actions of its agents even when these are ultra vires of their authority. Article 10 of the ILC Draft proposals states:

> 'The conduct of an organ of the state, of a territorial governmental entity empowered to exercise elements of the governmental authority, such organ having acted in that capacity, shall be considered as an act of the state under international law even if, in the particular case, the organ exceeded its competence according to international law or contravened instructions concerning its activity.'

In the *Youman's Claim* (1926) 4 RIAA 110, Mexico was held liable for the actions of militia responsible for the murder of American citizens, even although the soldiers had acted unlawfully and outwith their powers. Similarly, in the *Caire Claim* (1929) 5 RIAA 516, Commissioner Verzijl declared:

> 'The state, in international affairs, [bears] the responsibility of all acts committed by its officials or organs which constitute offences from the point of view of the law of nations, whether the official or organ has acted within or exceeded the limits of his competence.'

d) A state is not liable for the acts of foreign states or international organisations performed within its territory: Draft arts 12 and 13.

e) A state is not liable for the actions of revolutionary forces: Draft art 14. In the *Sambaggio Claim* (1903) 10 RIAA 499, Umpire Ralston declared that 'the government [of a state] should not be held responsible for the acts of revolutionaries ... Revolutionaries are not the agents of the government, and a natural responsibility does not exist.'

However, should a revolutionary government overthrow the incumbent government, then responsibility devolves on those authorities for their actions in the civil conflict: Draft art 15.

f) A state is not responsible for the conduct of persons or groups not acting on behalf of the state: Draft art 11. Actions by nationals or private individuals not related to the state do not impute liability to the state.

The basis of responsibility

Two contending theories purport to describe the basis for the operation of responsibility:

a) Objective responsibility

According to this theory, strict liability is conferred upon states for the commission of international delicts by itself of its agents. It is therefore unnecessary to establish fault or intention on behalf of the officials alleged to have perpetrated the unlawful act. This is supported by a number of cases. In the *Caire Claim* (1929) 5 RIAA 516 the Mixed Claims Commission advocated the application of:

> '... the doctrine of the objective responsibility of the state, that is to say, a responsibility for those acts committed by its officials or its organs ... despite the absence of fault on their part.'

b) Subjective responsibility

This approach emphasises the requirement of fault or negligence on the part of the state or its officials for the determination of international responsibility. In the *Home Missionary Society Claim* (1920) 6 RIAA 42, the arbitral tribunal declared:

> 'It is a well-established principle of international law that no government can be held responsible for the act of rebellious bodies of men committed in violation of its authority, where it is itself guilty of no breach of good faith, or of no negligence in suppressing insurrection.'

In the *Lighthouses Arbitration* (1956) 12 RIAA 217, the Permanent Court of Arbitration held that the damage to a lighthouse was neither a foreseeable nor a normal consequence of the evacuation, nor attributable to any want of care on the part of Greece. Liability for the act on the part of Greece was denied.

Although it is unclear whether fault, negligence or intention is a necessary attribute for state responsibility, strict liability may be imputed by treaty. See, for example, the Convention on International Liability for Damage Caused by Space Objects 1972 (10 ILM 965).

Defences and justifications for the commission of international delicts

The International Law Commission Draft Articles on State Responsibility distinguish between defences and justifications. A state may be allowed to plead the following in defence of an otherwise unlawful action.

a) The alleged wrongful act was committed by a state subject to the power or control of another state and coerced into the action.

b) The state alleging the violation of international law consented to the commission of the act.

c) The actions constituted legitimate countermeasures under international law (not including the use of force).

d) A situation of force majeure or extreme distress occasioned the unlawful act and there was an absence of willingness on the part of the officials concerned: Draft art 30.

In addition, two grounds may be adduced to justify the commission of illegal acts.

a) A state of necessity may justify an otherwise illegal action where (i) the act was the only means of safeguarding the vital interests of the state against grave and imminent peril; and (ii) the act did not seriously impair the essential interests of the state harmed: Draft art 33.

b) Actions taken by a state in conformity with lawful measures of self-defence under the United Nations Charter do not entail international responsibility: Draft art 34.

Reparations

A violation of international obligations invariably establishes a duty to make reparations. In the *Chorzow Factory Case (Indemnity) (Merits)* (1928) PCIJ Rep Ser A No 17, the International Court clearly enunciated that 'any breach of an engagement involves an obligation to make reparation'. Reparation should be made through restitution in kind which must, as far as possible, wipe out the consequences of the illegal act and re-establish the status quo ante. Where this is not possible, according to the Court in the above case, monetary compensation is required which:

'… corresponds to the value which a restitution in kind would bear; the award, if need be, of damages for loss sustained which would not be covered by restitution in kind or payment in place of it – such are the principles which should serve to determine the amount of compensation due for an act contrary to international law.'

Although the international law of damages is little settled, a few points seem to have been established. In *British Petroleum* v *Libya* (1974) 53 ILR 297 the arbitrator made it clear that:

'… when by the exercise of sovereign power a state has committed a fundamental breach of a concession agreement by repudiating it through a nationalisation of the enterprise … in a manner which implies finality, the concessionaire is not entitled to call for specific performance [of the contract] … but his sole remedy is an action for damages.'

The quantum of damages was considered in the *Norwegian Shipowners Claim* (1922) 1 RIAA 307, in which a Mixed Tribunal enunciated the principle that:

'Just compensation implies a complete restitution of the status quo ante, based, not upon future gains … but upon the loss of profits of the Norwegian owners as compared with owners of similar property.'

Compensation must cover the damage caused by the illegal act and that which is likely to result from it. However, remote or 'speculative' damages are unlikely.

Nationality of claims

For a state to espouse an international claim against another state for violation of international law, it must prove that the injury was occasioned against a national. In the *Panevezys-Saldutiskis Railway Case* (1939) PCIJ Rep Ser A/B No 76 the Permanent Court stated:

> 'In taking up the case of one of its nationals … a state is in reality asserting its own right … This right is necessarily limited to intervention on behalf of its nationals because…it is the bond of nationality between the state and the individual which alone confers upon the state the right of diplomatic protection … Where the injury was done to the national of some other state, no claim to which such injury may give rise falls within the scope of diplomatic protection which a state is entitled to afford nor can it give rise to a claim which that state is entitled to espouse.'

This rule is firmly enshrined in the Rules regarding International Claims issued by the British Foreign and Commonwealth Office in 1971. Rule 1 states: 'Her Majesty's Government will not take up the claim unless the claimant is a United Kingdom national and was so at the date of the injury'.

Establishing nationality

Each state is at liberty to determine, in accordance with its domestic laws, those individuals who will be conferred with nationality. As the Permanent Court pointed out in the *Nationality Decrees in Tunis and Morocco Case* (1923) PCIJ Rep Ser B No 4, 'in the present state of international law, questions of nationality are in principle within the reserved domain [of a state's domestic jurisdiction]'. This principle was confirmed in the *Nottebohm Case* (1955) ICJ Rep 4, where the ICJ stated:

> 'It is for Lichtenstein, as it is for every sovereign state, to settle by its own legislation the rules relating to the acquisition of its nationality, and to confer that nationality by naturalisation granted by its own organs in accordance with that legislation …'

Nationality is generally determined by reference to two principles.

a) Jus sanguinis: nationality is conferred, according to this principle, by the nationality of the father or mother. Thus, the British Nationality Act 1981 permits the grant of nationality by descent for one generation through either parent for legitimate children and through the mother for illegitimate children.

b) Jus soli: nationality is conferred on this basis where the child was born in the territory of a state.

In addition, nationality may be acquired through naturalisation – application to the appropriate immigration authorities – or by marriage.

Although a state has unilateral discretion to determine the rules according to which it confers nationality, this authority is circumscribed in relation to claims against other states. In the *Nottebohm Case* the International Court established the principle that:

> 'A state cannot claim that the rules it has thus laid down (for the grant of nationality) are entitled to recognition by another state unless it has acted in conformity with this general aim of making the legal bond of nationality accord with the individual's genuine connection with the state ...'

In order to determine the existence of a genuine link at the international level, the Court continued to define nationality as:

> '... a legal bond having as its basis a social fact of attachment, a genuine connection of existence, interests and sentiments, together with the existence of reciprocal rights and duties. It may be said to constitute the juridical expression of the fact that the individual upon whom it is conferred, either directly by the law or as a result of an act of the authorities, is in fact more closely connected with the population of the state conferring nationality than with that of any other state.'

Although the rules for granting nationality remain relatively simple, despite the existence of this additional test at the international level, special circumstances often arise in which two or more states are involved in the determination of nationality. In this respect, a number of special situations merit consideration.

Dual nationality

Where a person possesses dual nationality, either state may institute proceedings against third states. The dicta of the arbitral tribunal in the *Salem Case* (1932) 2 RIAA 1161 is particularly instructive in this respect:

> 'The rule of international law [is] that in a case of dual nationality a third power is not entitled to contest the claim of one of the two powers whose national is interested in the case by referring to the nationality of the other power.'

In relation to claims between the two states of which the nationalities are held, in the *Merge Claim* (1955) 22 ILR 443 it was held that a test of 'effective nationality' was relevant to the determination of whether one state could initiate a claim against the other. In order to establish the prevalent nationality in individual cases, habitual residence can be one of the criteria of evaluation, but not the only one. The conduct of the individual in his economic, social, political, civic and family life, as well as the closer and more effective bond with one of the two states must also be considered.

This test was upheld in the Iran-United States Claims Tribunal where the full tribunal held that it had jurisdiction over claims against Iran by a dual national when the 'dominant and effective nationality' was American. See the *Islamic Republic of Iran* v *United States* (1984) 78 AJIL 912.

Companies and legal persons

The general rule is that a company has the nationality of the state under whose laws it was incorporated and in whose territory it has its registered office. This was confirmed in the *Barcelona Traction, Light and Power Co Case* (1970) ICJ Rep 3, where the ICJ stated:

> 'In allocating corporate entities to states for purposes of diplomatic protection, international law is based, but only to a limited extent, on an analogy with the rules governing the nationality of individuals. The traditional rule attributes the right of diplomatic protection of a corporate entity to the state under the laws of which it is incorporated and in whose territory it has its registered office. These two criteria have been confirmed by long practice and by numerous international instruments.'

As a result, a state is precluded from initiating an international claim against another state on behalf of its nationals merely by virtue of their possessing shares in a foreign company.

Nationality of ships

The Geneva Convention on the High Seas 1958, art 5, states the rule in relation to the nationality of ships:

> 'Ships have the nationality of the state whose flag they are entitled to fly. There must exist a genuine link between the state and the ship; in particular, the state must effectively exercise its jurisdiction and control in administrative, technical and social matters over ships flying its flag.'

This rule is confirmed by art 91 of the Convention on the Law of the Sea 1982. The rules for conferring British nationality on a ship are contained in the Merchant Shipping Act 1894, ss1–2.

Nationality of aircraft

The nationality of aircraft is governed by art 17 of the Chicago Convention on International Civil Aviation 1944 (15 UNTS 295) which provides that 'aircraft have the nationality of the state in which they are registered'. In British law, this is regulated by the Civil Aviation Act 1949, s8.

Exhaustion of local remedies

In order to reduce both the number of international claims and friction between states caused by the institution of proceedings, a customary rule of international law has been established to the effect that, before recourse is made to international processes, the state alleged to be responsible for the unlawful act must be given an opportunity to remedy the alleged violation through processes, both judicial and administrative, available within the state itself. This was ably restated in the *Ambatielos Arbitration* (1956) 12 RIAA 83, in which the principle was enunciated that:

> 'A state against which an international action is brought for injuries suffered by private individuals has the right to resist such an action if the persons alleged to have been injured have not first exhausted all the remedies available to them under the municipal law of that state.'

The principle extends to the whole system of redress established by the municipal law of the state in question, and not only judicial processes. However, it is restricted in that only effective remedies need be exhausted. For example, in the *Finnish Ships Arbitration* (1934) 3 RIAA 1479, the arbitrator ruled that appeal to the highest court in the land was unnecessary because that tribunal could not overturn the decision because it was restricted to considerations of law and the controversy in question was one of fact.

The International Court has made a further erosion of this principle. In the *Elettronica Sicula SpA Case* (1989) ICJ Rep 15, the Court held that local remedies were exhausted if the claim in question is inappropriate for resolution by national courts or tribunals and is in fact a matter for an international court or body. As the Court pointed out:

> 'The local remedies rule does not, indeed cannot, require that a claim be presented to the municipal courts in a form, and with arguments, suited to an international tribunal, applying different law to different parties; for an international claim to be admissible, it is sufficient if the essence of the claim has been brought before the competent tribunals and pursued as far as permitted by local law and procedures, and without success ...'

Common international delicts

Maltreatment of aliens

In the *Mavrommatis Palestine Concessions Case (Jurisdiction) Case* (1924) PCIJ Rep Ser A No 2 the International Court stated the customary principle that:

> '[I]t is an elementary principle of international law that a state is entitled to protect its subjects, when injured by acts contrary to international law committed by another state, from whom they have been unable to obtain satisfaction through ordinary channels.'

At the same time, a state is not automatically responsible for all criminal acts committed against aliens within its territory. In the *Noyes Claim* (1933) 6 RIAA 308, the following rule was elaborated:

> 'The mere fact that an alien has suffered at the hands of private persons ... does not make a government liable for damages under international law. There must be shown special circumstances from which the responsibility of the authorities arises; either their behaviour in connection with the particular occurrence, or a general failure to comply with their duty to maintain order, to prevent crimes or to prosecute and punish criminals.'

However, the exact nature of the obligation to treat aliens in national territory remains unclear. Two formulations of duty have been asserted.

a) International minimum standard

This standard has been maintained by the developed states. It is a minimum standard that must be upheld regardless of how a state treats its own nationals. In the *Neer Claim* (1926) 4 RIAA 60 it was held that 'the propriety of governmental actions should be put to the test of international standards', while in the *Certain*

German Interests in Polish Upper Silesia Case (1926) PCIJ Rep Ser A No 7, the Permanent Court recognised the existence of a certain minimum standard of treatment in international law. See also the *Garcia Case* (1926) 4 RIAA 119 and the *Roberts Claim* (1926) 4 RIAA 77.

b) National treatment standard

Developing states assert that foreign nationals need only be treated in the same manner, and to the same standard, as nationals of the state into which they enter.

Expropriation

It is a recognised attribute of state sovereignty that property within the territory of a state may be nationalised or expropriated. Only the processes and compensation of the practice raise differences in formulating principles.

a) Public purpose

In the *Certain German Interests in Polish Upper Silesia Case* (1926) PCIJ Rep Ser A No 7 the International Court observed that expropriation must be for 'reasons of public utility, judicial liquidation and similar measures'. This standard was reiterated in the 1962 General Assembly Resolution on Permanent Sovereignty over Natural Resources, although it was omitted in the subsequent 1974 Charter of Economic Rights and Duties of States.

b) Non-discrimination

Expropriation must involve no discrimination between national and foreign property: see the *Oscar Chinn Case* (1934) PCIJ Rep Ser A/B No 63 and the *Anglo-Iranian Oil Co Case* (1952) ICJ Rep (Pleadings) 93.

c) Compensation

The original formulation for appropriate compensation was made by US Secretary of State Hull on the occasion of Mexican expropriations, where the formula of 'prompt, adequate and effective' was established. This was adopted in the 1962 Resolution on Permanent Sovereignty over Natural Resources. However, the 1974 Charter of Economic Rights and Duties of States declares that compensation is a matter to be determined by national law.

9.3 Key cases and legislation

- *Barcelona Traction, Light and Power Co Case* (1970) ICJ Rep 3
  Nationality of corporations

- *Case Concerning the Gabcikovo-Nagymaros Project (Hungary v Slovakia)* (1998) 37 ILM 62
  The ICJ considered the efficacy of the defence of necessity

- *Chorzow Factory Case (Indemnity) (Merits)* (1928) PCIJ Rep Ser A No 17
  Detailed judgment on the legality of expropriation

- *Elettronica Sicula SpA (ELSI) Case (United States v Italy)* (1989) ICJ Rep 15
  Application of the exhaustion of domestic/local remedies rule

- *Interhandel Case* (1959) ICJ Rep 6
  Exhaustion of local remedies

- *Nottebohm Case* (1955) ICJ Rep 4
  Leading case on the issue of nationality of individuals

- *Texaco* v *Libya* (1977) 53 ILR 389
  Rules of reparation and commission of international delicts

- International Law Commission (ILC) Draft Articles on Responsibility of States for Internationally Wrongful Acts 2001 – sets out an authoritative statement of principles governing this topic

- International Law Commission (ILC) Draft Articles on State Responsibility 1979

9.4 Questions and suggested solutions

QUESTION ONE

Relying on the International Law Commission's Draft Articles on State Responsibility and any relevant cases, comment on the issues of state responsibility arising from each of these.

a) Ahmed leads 'Our Father Land', a revolutionary group in the State of Arcadia. In 1996, he instigated members of the group to attack foreigners living in Arcadia. In the resulting uprising, petrol bombs were thrown and considerable damages were done. Some foreigners were killed. In 2000, a new Government assumed office in Arcadia, formed by a coalition of groups, including 'Our Father Land'.

b) Negara and Brazal are friendly States maintaining diplomatic relations at ambassadorial level. Both States are parties to the 1961 Vienna Convention on Diplomatic Relations including its Protocol on the Compulsory Settlement of Disputes. During a major soccer competition in Haka, the Eagles of Negara defeated Brando, the national football team of Brazal, by 3–0. At the suggestion of an official of the National Sports Council of Brazal who was facing the prospect of redundancy due to the unprecedented defeat, the group marched towards the building housing the Embassy of Negara in Kramo, the capital city of Haka, setting it ablaze. The Hakan police officers were stationed to guard the Embassy all disappeared from the scene on seeing the approaching crowd.

University of London LLB Examination
(for External Students) Public International Law June 2000 Q2

General Comment

It is quite common to include a question on the principles of state responsibility. A well prepared candidate will need to be aware of the relevant principles as well as the First and Final Drafts of the International Law Commission's Draft Articles on State Responsibility (1996 and 2001). In this question the candidate is required to apply the relevant law to two concrete situations.

Skeleton Solution

Assess the general principles of the law on state responsibility – the relevance of the ILC Draft Articles – methods of resolving or determining the issue of state responsibility – remedies if applicable.

Suggested Solution

In broad terms this question concerns the law of state responsibility. A preliminary point arises in respect of the wording; the candidate is asked to take into account the International Law Commission Draft Articles on State Responsibility. It is proposed here to consider two drafts; the first appeared in 1996 and the final in August 2001. It is therefore sensible to answer this question by reference to: (a) the position under the general law, and (b) the impact of the International Law Commission Drafts of both 1996 and 2001. With these circumstances in mind one can now turn to the problems set.

The problem in Arcadia

In this instance the Government of Arcadia was, after 1996, subject to terrorist outrages by a revolutionary group that was in the habit of attacking foreigners. The general principle that one begins with is that a state will not normally be liable for the acts of terrorists or insurgents, provided it has acted with good faith and due diligence in seeking to maintain law and order: see *Home Missionary Society Claim: USA v Great Britain* (1920) 6 RIAA 42. Liability will not normally arise unless it can be shown that the Government failed to act when warnings were given. However, all that is irrelevant now because we are told that in the year 2000 a new Government assumed office, including 'Our Father Land'.

In circumstances such as these, where the revolutionaries later join the Government, liability may arise for the prior acts in the period 1996–2000. However, to establish such liability it will be necessary to show that the acts were committed by agents of 'Our Father Land' rather than by mere supporters: *Bolivian Railway Company Case* (1903) 9 RIAA 445; *Short v Iran* (1987) 16 Iran–US CTR 76; 82 ILR 148.

This approach was followed in art 15(1) of the First Draft of the International Law Commission Draft Articles on State Responsibility 1996, which stipulates that 'the act of an insurrectional movement which becomes the new government of a State shall be considered as an act of that State'. This approach is continued in art 10 of the Second Draft of the International Law Commission Draft Articles 2001 which reads: 'The conduct of an insurrectional movement which becomes the new government of a State shall be considered an act of State under international law.'

Thus it would seem that, under the general principles of customary law and under the International Law Commission Draft Articles, the relevant foreign governments may make claims against the Government of Arcadia in respect of acts arising in the period 1996–2000, provided it can be shown that such acts were undertaken by agents of the revolutionary movement.

The burning of the Embassy of Negara in Kramo

We are asked in this question to consider the legal consequences of the burning of the Embassy of Negara in Kramo, the capital city of Haka. In broad terms Negara are the sending State and Haka are the receiving State. Difficulties have arisen after a football competition taking place in Haka in which the Eagles of Negara defeated Brando, the national football team of Brazal. It is sensible to take the relevant questions in order.

a) Is Brazal liable in the law of state responsibility for the activities of the mob?

On this issue the evidence is at best equivocal. The mob may have been urged to march on the Embassy by an official of the National Sports Council of Brazal. It is arguable that the National Sports Council is an arm of government. In some states football authorities are separate corporate entities; in others they may be part of the executive branch of government. If at this stage we assume that it was an arm of government this does not carry matters much further. It is doubtful whether the official urged the mob to burn the building; the mob themselves were not agents of the Brazal Government. At best they were supporters of the football team; the State of Brazal is in principle not liable for the acts of its private citizens when abroad. Unless it can be shown that the official urged action against the Embassy, then it is difficult to imagine that Brazal are liable in the law of state responsibility. However, those responsible for burning the Embassy would be liable under the criminal law of Haka.

b) Is Haka answerable for the burning of the Embassy?

Haka is the receiving State under the terms of the Vienna Convention on Diplomatic Relations 1961 and is under a duty, under art 22 and under customary law, to take appropriate steps to protect the premises of the mission. This was confirmed by the judgment of the International Court of Justice in the *Hostages Case: USA* v *Iran* (1980) ICJ Rep 3. The State of Haka failed in its duty by allowing the security personnel to withdraw in the face of the oncoming mob. The security personnel were aware that the Embassy was being threatened but, far from strengthening the security presence, they chose to withdraw. The actions of the security personnel are attributable to the State of Haka. This is confirmed by art 5 of the International Law Commission Draft Articles of 1996 and art 4 of the International Law Commission Draft Articles of 2001.

It is therefore strongly arguable that Haka are liable either because of a failure of due diligence under the general law of state responsibility, and also because of a failure to discharge their duty as a receiving State under customary law relating to the protection of diplomatic premises. It is well recognised that international football competitions are often attended by civil disorder; this was certainly not the day to allow the removal of all security protection from the Embassy. The wording of the question indicates that the personnel were police officers; clearly such actions were at variance with their duties. However, it will be no defence that the decision of the security personnel was ultra vires: see *Youman's Claim: USA v Mexico* (1926) 4 RIAA 110.

c) The relevance of the International Law Commission Draft Articles

It is sensible to draw together a number of relevant provisions. Articles 5 and 6 the International Law Commission Draft Articles 1996 and art 4 of the International Law Commission Draft Articles 2001 indicate that whether the National Sports Council of Brazal is to be regarded as an organ of state depends on it status on the internal law of the state. However, as indicated above there seems to be no causal link with the burning of the Embassy. There is a distinction between urging individuals to march on the Embassy and the actual burning of the Embassy.

d) Resolution

In summary, serious damage has been done to the Embassy of Negara. This will be expensive and it is arguable that the principal liability rests with Haka for failing to properly protect the premises. The responsibility of Brazal depends not only on the status of the National Sports Council, but also whether the official can be said to have urged violent action against the Embassy. In principle all three States should agree to a method of peaceful resolution of the dispute. It seems that Negara and Brazal are parties to the 1961 Protocol on the Compulsory Settlement of Disputes; if Haka is as well, then the entire matter could be considered by the International Court of Justice. However, if Haka is not, then the International Court of Justice will be unable to rule on the conduct of a third party: see the *Monetary Gold Case* (1954) ICJ Rep 19.

QUESTION TWO

The States of Nordistan and Austiland share a common border formed in part by the river Tranqua. In 1995 they concluded the Tranqua Navigation and Conservation Treaty which provides in art 4 that:

'Any dispute regarding the management and conservation of the Tranqua shall be settled with due regard to international environmental standards and the principles of state responsibility under international law.'

In late 1997 the People's Liberation Front, a group seeking to overthrow the Government of Nordistan, planted a bomb in a privately owned oil refinery located on the banks of the Tranqua. The bomb was identified by refinery staff, and, although

Nordistan Army bomb disposal experts were called to defuse it, the experts were delayed by the failure of their helicopter, and the bomb detonated before they arrived. The explosion caused the release of thousands of barrels of oil which flowed into the Tranqua, causing extensive damage to the Austiland fishing industry. The Austiland Fishing Company sued the refinery owner and the Government of Nordistan in the courts of Nordistan, but was denied compensation on the grounds that the damage was caused by a terrorist group. The Company now seeks advice on the possibility of bringing a claim in international law.

Advise the Company.

University of London LLB Examination
(for External Students) Public International Law June 1999 Q8

General Comment

It is very rare for a paper on public international law to be set without a question on the general area of state responsibility. In recent years, it has become common to add some reference to environmental law because of the increasing number of disputes in this area. The student is then asked to comment not only on the traditional and limited rules of state responsibility, but also to exhibit some knowledge of emerging principles of international environmental law. A sensible candidate may also make reference to the question as to whether the new principles have yet attained the status of rules of customary international law.

Skeleton Solution

Introduction – locus standi – exhaustion of internal remedies – the law of state responsibility – relevance of treaty obligations – international environmental protection – the question of compensation – matters of procedure.

Suggested Solution

This is a rather curious question which turns on the relationship between the international law of state responsibility, the emerging international law of the environment and the relevance of the principles of municipal law. By the conclusion of the question, the following events have taken place: (a) the bomb has exploded in the premises of a privately owned oil refinery, (b) the escape of the barrels of oil has damaged the river Tranqua and its marine life, (c) the Austiland Fishing Company and its shareholders have suffered financial loss, and (d) the Austiland Fishing Company has failed in a legal action in the Nordistan courts. It is important to note that we are principally concerned to advise the Austiland Fishing Company in respect of a claim in international law. However, it is sensible to take the various matters arising in turn.

Damage to the refinery itself

It is sensible to dispose of this preliminary point. The privately owned refinery would have an action in the municipal law of tort in Nordistan against those responsible for planting the bomb; however, it is more likely in the present instance that the claim will be met by the insurers of the premises, as it is unlikely that the People's Liberation Front are in a position to satisfy any judgment. It also follows that the acts themselves will attract criminal liability under the law of Nordistan.

The Austiland Fishing Company

It would seem that the Austiland Fishing Company is a corporate body incorporated and having its principal place of business in Austiland. Thus the state of Austiland and its Foreign Ministry are entitled to take up its case on the international plane. In principle there seems no reason why the Austiland Foreign Ministry should not take up the case of any other business based in Austiland that has suffered financial loss caused by the pollution of the river Tranqua.

The exhaustion of internal remedies

It would seem on the facts that the Austiland Fishing Company have exhausted all possible remedies in the municipal law of Nordistan. It is of course necessary to consider whether all internal appeals have been exhausted. If that is the case then there is no reason why the Austiland Fishing Company should not request Austiland to bring a claim on the international plane: see the *Ambatielos Arbitration: Greece* v *UK* (1956) 12 RIAA 83. If such a claim is to be brought then it involves consideration of three aspects, namely: (a) the law of state responsibility, (b) the law of treaties, and (c) international environmental law. It is necessary to take each in turn.

Causation and the law of state responsibility

The environmental damage was caused by the escape of the oil; the escape of the oil was caused by the explosion of the bomb. The explosion of the bomb was caused by those revolutionaries who placed and primed it to go off. In the traditional law of state responsibility it would be argued that, in the absence of negligence or bad faith, a state would not be liable for the acts of the rebels: see the *Home Missionary Society Claim: USA* v *Great Britain* (1920) 6 RIAA 42 and *Youman's Claim: USA* v *Mexico* (1926) 4 RIAA 110. This principle was reaffirmed in art 14 of the 1996 First Draft of the International Law Commission Draft on State Responsibility. While a state would not be in general liable for the acts of revolutionaries, the exception under the law of state responsibility was if state agencies had acted negligently or in bad faith. However, while it is acknowledged that all the cases cannot be harmoniously reconciled, the general tendency has been only to hold the state liable if it showed a reluctance to act over a period of time: see the *Neer Claim: USA* v *Mexico* (1926) 4 RIAA 60. In the present case the bomb disposal experts did not arrive in time. However, it has to be recognised that occasionally helicopters experience difficulties, and even if the bomb disposal experts had arrived on site in time it is by no means certain that they could have defused the device on time and without damage. Bomb disposal is a very hazardous task, not least in the confines of an oil refinery. The rational conclusion must be that under the traditional law of state responsibility it would have been difficult to affix blame to the State of Nordistan.

The relevance of the treaty obligations

It is clear under the treaty that Nordistan has accepted obligations in respect of the management and conservation of the river Tranqua, and that any dispute should (under art 4) be resolved by reference to international environmental standards and the principles of state responsibility. It is therefore necessary to consider the relevance of international environmental standards as developed in the emerging field of international environmental law.

International environmental protection

In the last quarter of a century there is no doubt that international environmental law has modified the principles of the traditional law on state responsibility. Under the law on state responsibility, it was normally necessary to show that a state agency was at fault before responsibility could be held to arise. In international environmental law the emphasis has been upon the obligation to protect the environment, and there is a greater readiness to impose strict liability. This is done by reference to a number of principles that may not yet have acquired the status of rules of customary international law, but have nevertheless acquired a wide degree of general acceptance. In particular, one can note 'the principle of the good neighbour' or 'the precautionary principle', as well as the general duty arising under Principle 21 of the Stockholm Declaration 1972, whereby states must ensure 'that activities within their jurisdiction or control do not cause damage to the environment of other states or of areas beyond the limits of national jurisdiction'. Further, it is also well established in customary law that states must co-operate together to mitigate transboundary environmental risks: see *Lac Lanoux Arbitration: France* v *Spain* (1957) 24 ILR 101 and Principle 24 of the Stockholm Declaration 1972.

If we apply this developing jurisprudence to the present facts, we can see that Nordistan allowed an oil refinery to operate close to a major river boundary in circumstances where, if oil barrels escaped, pollution was inevitable. It is strongly arguable that in the light of emerging international standards, Nordistan did not take proper precautions against such an eventuality, and in any event did not consult with its fellow boundary state. It might be argued that some of the corpus of international environmental law comprises simple principles; however, in the present case Nordistan has bound itself by treaty to Austiland. So if Austiland bring a complaint against Nordistan, then any arbitrator is bound to pay regard to international environmental standards, including the obligation to take precautions against foreseeable harm. The rational conclusion is that a claim has a reasonable prospects of success.

Compensation

Where pollution has been caused, physical damage and loss of trading profit may arise. There seems to be no good reason why Austiland should not make a claim under both heads, as well as demanding that Nordistan pay the costs or undertake the burden of remedial works. The number of reported cases has been small, but the likely result is that Austiland will receive a lump sum and Nordistan may be ordered to carry out essential 'clean up' works; the tendency in past cases has been to approach the matter on a pragmatic basis: see the *Trail Smelter Arbitration: USA* v *Canada* (1941) 3 RIAA 1905. Having regard to the wide definition of pollution in the Law of the Sea Convention 1982 (art 1(4)) the obligations of Nordistan in respect of restoring the marine environment are likely to be considerable.

The position of the Company

As the company seems to have exhausted any possibility of action in the courts of Nordistan, the sensible course is to ask Austiland to take up the case on the international plane. Austiland will wish to receive details of losses suffered by other fishing companies and then a total claim can be made. Nordistan is likely to settle the claim by payment of a lump sum to be divided between the various fishery interests. That task is likely to be carried out by a tribunal in Austiland equivalent to the Foreign Compensation Commission in the United Kingdom.

QUESTION THREE

Explain the significance of the law of state responsibility of the following:

a) the *Chorzow Factory (Indemnity)* case;

b) the *Youman's* claim;

c) the *Nottebohm* case;

d) the *Barcelona Traction* case.

University of London LLB Examination
(for External Students) Public International Law June 1997 Q7

General Comment

The well prepared student, being aware of the salient facts in each case, will be concerned to stress the relevant legal propositions that can be extracted from each judgment. The most difficult of the four cases to deal with is the *Nottebohm Case* because a number of criticisms were made of both the judgment and the seeming width of its language. The examiner will be interested to note whether candidates are aware of any of the criticisms made of the judgment and of attempts made in subsequent cases to narrow the ratio. The most sensible way of approaching the question is to deal with each case separately and then to draw all four cases together in the form of a general conclusion. The question is a perfectly fair one because extracts from the cases are available in the relevant cases and materials books.

Skeleton Solution

Introduction – the *Chorzow Factory (Indemnity) Case* – the *Youman's Claim* – the *Nottebohm Case* – the *Barcelona Traction Case* – conclusion.

Suggested Solution

We are asked in this question to consider a number of cases and to determine the significance of the rulings in respect of the law of State responsibility.

The law of State responsibility is concerned with the determination of whether a particular act or omission is wrongful and whether a specific State may be held responsible. In general terms the case law indicates that the following problems arise, namely: (a) the question as to when can State A bring a claim against State B; (b) in what circumstances are acts attributable or 'imputable' to a State?; (c) does any form of fault need to be established or is liability absolute?; and (d) how should compensation be assessed? With these considerations in mind one can consider the specific cases.

The Chorzow Factory (Indemnity) Case *(1928) PCIJ Rep Ser A No 17*

The case concerned the expropriation by Poland of a factory in Upper Silesia. The court had earlier determined that such conduct was at variance with the Geneva Convention of 1922 between Germany and Poland on the status of Upper Silesia. The question for the court was whether compensation was payable and, if so, upon what principle. In effect the court ruled that there was a distinction between a lawful expropriation and an unlawful expropriation, and that in the case of an unlawful expropriatory act the State must, in addition to paying the compensation due in respect of a lawful expropriation, also pay damages in respect of any loss by the third party.

The long term effect of the case has been to stress the remedial nature of international law. Dicta in the case stress the importance of making restitution for breaches of international law. Thus, in the *Temple of Preah Vihear Case* (1962) ICJ Rep 6 the International Court of Justice could order Thailand to return to Cambodia religious objects unlawfully removed from the Temple of Preah Vihear.

The distinction drawn between lawful and unlawful expropriation is relevant today because in the former case compensation as a 'going concern' may be sufficient, but in the latter case a claim may be made for loss of profit from the time of seizure to the date of determination.

The Youman's Claim *(1926) 4 RIAA 110*

The *Youman's Claim* was determined by the US-Mexican General Claims Commission. A mob had gathered around a house in Mexico in which there were three US nationals. The mayor of the town was called and he ordered an officer and troops to put down the disturbance. When the troops arrived they joined with the mob in killing the three US citizens. The United States made a claim for compensation.

The tribunal rejected the argument advanced that the State was not liable because the troops were acting ultra vires. While the tribunal accepted that the conduct of the troops went beyond their actual authority, they were nevertheless, acting within their ostensible or apparent authority and thus acting within the performance of their duties. Acting under the authority of a serving officer they were acting within the scope of their duties and thus their acts were imputable to the State. The tribunal acknowledged that if the troops had been off duty then the position might well have been different.

The case is authority for two propositions relating to State responsibility, namely that military forces are in principle the agents of the state and that acts beyond the actual authority but within the apparent or ostensible authority will render the State liable.

The Nottebohm Case *(1955) ICJ Rep 4*

This was a case brought by Liechtenstein before the International Court of Justice. The first phase of the case concerned jurisdiction. The substantive case was heard in 1955 when Liechtenstein brought the action against Guatemala on behalf of one Friedrich Nottebohm. Nottebohm had been a German national from his birth in 1881 but had resided in Guatemala since 1905. In October 1939 he renounced German citizenship and acquired that of Liechtenstein. In 1943 he was arrested by the Guatemalan authorities and deported to the United States where he was interned; much of his property was subject to litigation.

In 1946 Nottebohm was refused permission to return to Guatemala; at a later date his property was confiscated. From 1946 Nottebohm resided in Liechtenstein. In 1951 Liechtenstein instituted legal proceedings before the International Court of Justice against Guatemala.

In reply to the claim by Liechtenstein it was argued on behalf of Guatemala that Nottebohm had acquired his citizenship invalidly under Liechtenstein law, and even if he had not done so his nexus with Liechtenstein was so limited that Liechtenstein was unable to bring a claim on the international plane because claims for diplomatic protection were contingent on a genuine link existing between the national and the claimant State.

The International Court of Justice ruled that it was a matter for each State to set out the terms of its own citizenship laws, but before a claim could be presented on the international plane a State would be required to demonstrate that a genuine connection existed between the national and the claimant state. The International Court of Justice ruled that no claim could be brought by Liechtenstein unless evidence of a genuine link existed. The judgment was subject to criticism on the following grounds: (a) that it confused questions of citizenship with those of nationality; (b) that the judgment was too dualist in tone; (c) that its effect would be to curtail the right of diplomatic protection; (d) that the spirit of the judgment was at variance with art 15 of the Universal Declaration of Human Rights 1948; and (e) that the Court had transferred the requirement of 'effective link' from the context of dual nationality to a situation involving one nationality. The view that the judgment should be interpreted narrowly and confined to its particular facts was propounded in the later case of *United States, ex rel Flegenheimer* v *Italy* (1958) 25 ILR 91.

Having regard to the subsequent criticisms and the reservations expressed in later cases the *Nottebohm Case* is probably authority for the limited proposition that a State may not espouse a claim on behalf of a national who has no effective link with that State in circumstances where the claim is against another State with which he does have such a link.

The Barcelona Traction, Light and Power Co Case *(1970) ICJ Rep 3*

The Barcelona Traction, Light and Power Company was incorporated in Canada in 1911 and operated in Spain. In 1948 it was declared insolvent by the Spanish courts in circumstances where questions arose as to claims against the Spanish authorities. The Company was placed in receivership in Canada. For a time the Canadian authorities made representations to the Spanish government on behalf of the company. At a later date, when it became clear that over 80 per cent of the shares in the company were held by Belgian nationals, Belgium began an action against Spain in the International Court of Justice. Spain argued that Belgium lacked locus standi to bring the action as the damage was done to the company as a legal person distinct from its shareholders.

The International Court of Justice ruled: (a) that the company being in receivership legally still existed; (b) that the legal person to whom the damage was done was the company; (c) that the shareholders had no independent right of action; and (d) that the appropriate State to make a claim would be Canada not Belgium, since the company was created under the terms of the municipal law of Canada and remained subject to its laws.

Conclusion

In respect of the law of state responsibility it is safe to conclude that both the *Nottebohm Case* and the *Barcelona Traction Case* are concerned with locus standi to claim. The *Youman's Claim* is concerned with the extent of liability for ultra vires acts, while the *Chorzow Factory (Indemnity) Case* is concerned to establish the broad principle that breaches of international law give rise to the obligation to make appropriate restitution.

QUESTION FOUR

Pestikill operates a herbicide factory within the territory of Polyland, adjacent to the border of Unoland. The Polyland Factories Act 1990 requires the factory to be inspected every two years for compliance with applicable health and safety standards. However, Pestikill has bribed the Polyland Factory Inspector to turn a blind eye to blatant violations of those standards. In late 1992 the Pestikill factory leaked into the atmosphere a large amount of herbicide which was spread by prevailing winds on to the territory of Unoland, destroying a crop of trees owned by Arborgrow plc. Arborgrow is a company which is incorporated under the laws of Unoland, but which is entirely owned by nationals of Infiland. Arborgrow has filed a suit for damages in the

Polyland courts, but is reliably informed that it cannot expect a hearing for at least five years. The Unoland government has advised Arborgrow that is not prepared to raise the matter internationally.

Prepare a memorandum considering any claims that might arise under international law in respect of the loss of trees.

University of London LLB Examination
(for External Students) Public International Law June 1994 Q9

General Comment

This question revolves around a problem which involves the application of the principles applicable to the law of state responsibility in relation to a hypothetical situation. Consideration of diplomatic protection in respect of corporations is also required.

Skeleton Solution

Diplomatic protection: *Mavrommatis Palestine Concessions Case* – nationality of claims: *Barcelona Traction* and corporate nationality – direct international wrongs: *Trail Smelter* – exhaustion of local remedies: *Robert E Brown Case* – denial of justice: imputability; ILC Draft articles.

Suggested Solution

In drafting this memorandum, it is important first to isolate the claims that might arise under international law for the loss of Arborgrow plc's trees. The possible domestic claims – Arborgrow's action against Pestikill in the Polyland courts; and, perhaps, Arborgrow's action in the Unoland courts challenging the refusal of diplomatic protection – may be discounted, save to the extent that they have consequences for the relevant international claims. As to these latter, although Unoland has advised Arborgrow that it is not prepared to raise the matter internationally, that advice may change in the light of the circumstances to be considered. Unoland would also seem to have a claim in its own right against Polyland for the environmental damage done. Finally, Infiland might wish to claim either against Polyland on behalf of Arborgrow, hoping to persuade the International Court of Justice (ICJ) to depart from its earlier decision in the *Barcelona Traction Case* (1970) ICJ Rep 3 or, perhaps, against Unoland.

In the *Mavrommatis Palestine Concessions Case* (1924) PCIJ Rep Ser A No 2 the Permanent Court of International Justice (PCIJ) explained that it is:

> '... an elementary principle of international law that a State is entitled to protect its subjects, when injured by acts contrary to international law committed by another State, from whom they have been unable to obtain satisfaction through the ordinary channels. By taking up the case of one of its subjects and by resorting to diplomatic action or international judicial proceedings on his behalf, a State is in reality asserting its own

rights – its right to ensure, in the person of its subjects, respect for the rules of international law.'

A number of common elements thus underpin the claims considered here.

First, a state is 'entitled to protect its subjects'. However, 'it is the bond of nationality between the State and the individual which alone confers upon the State the right of diplomatic protection': *Panevezys-Saldutiskis Railway Case* (1939) PCIJ Rep Ser A/B No 76. The issue of Arborgrow's nationality thus becomes central. In *Barcelona Traction*, on similar facts, the ICJ held that the nationality of a company was to be determined by reference to its state of incorporation, in that case Canada. The fact that the majority of the shareholders in the company were Belgian was insufficient to give rise to a right of diplomatic protection in Belgium. It would seem therefore that Infiland would be unable to claim on behalf of Arborgrow as against Polyland. There is, however, some difference in the facts and it may be that *Barcelona Traction* could be distinguished on the grounds that, first, Arborgrow is 'entirely owned' by nationals of Infiland and, second, there is no evidence of a 'close and permanent connection' between Arborgrow and Polyland.

The ICJ might be persuaded to reconsider its rejection of the extension to corporations of the 'genuine connection' theory for the attribution of nationality to individuals in cases of dual nationality. Judge Gros in *Barcelona Traction* did argue that the Court should have examined whether on the facts there was a genuine connection: who really controlled the company? On the facts given here, it is probably arguable that there is such a genuine connection between Arborgrow and Infiland. The argument does not seem strong, however, at least for a claim against Polyland.

The second element from the *Mavrommatis Case* is that the acts complained of must be 'contrary to international law [and] committed by another State'. In the *Trail Smelter Arbitration* (1941) 3 RIAA 1905 the Tribunal held that in international law 'no State has the right to use or permit the use of its territory in such a manner as to cause injury by fumes in or to the territory of another or the properties of persons therein, when the case is of serious consequence and the injury is established by clear and convincing evidence'. This element appears to be satisifed on the facts here. Assuming, too, that the damage to the trees is of 'serious consequence' and that there are no evidential problems, it would seem that Unoland could present a claim against Polyland, not for injury done indirectly through one of its nationals, but rather for the direct injury through damage to its territory.

The third element is that the national has been 'unable to obtain satisfaction through the ordinary channels'. Arborgrow must therefore first exhaust local remedies in Polyland by pursuing its domestic action through Polyland's courts before Unoland could take up its claim. In the *Robert E Brown Case* (1923) 6 RIAA 120 the Tribunal explained that a 'claimant in a foreign State is not required to exhaust justice in such State where there is no justice to exhaust'. It may be that the refusal to list a hearing date for the action for five years thus constitutes a denial of justice, although one would have to have regard to the standard required of Polyland. Since, according to art 6 of the ILC's Draft Articles on State Responsibility, the conduct of the judiciary 'shall be considered as an act of that State under international law', any such denial would be imputable to Polyland on the ordinary principles of state responsibility. It may be that Unoland could reconsider its refusal. In any event, this argument would be equally applicable were Infiland entitled to claim on Arborgrow's behalf.

Finally, it is worth mentioning that Infiland could perhaps claim against Unoland, on the grounds that the latter's refusal to exercise its right of diplomatic protection in respect of Arborgrow has caused indirect injury to Infiland, through the medium of its nationals, the shareholders in Arborgrow. Here, too, apart from the 'genuine connection' problem (which would clearly be different from the situation in *Barcelona Traction*), Arborgrow would have to establish that it had exhausted domestic remedies in Unoland, no doubt through pursuing its challenge to Unoland's refusal through the courts there.

This concludes the memorandum.

QUESTION FIVE

Thomas is a national of State T. State V's secret services suspect that, in 1990, Thomas passed secret information relating to State V's armaments industry to State W's intelligence services. In 1992 State V's secret services learned that Thomas was living in State T. They then sent some of their agents to State T in order forcibly to abduct him and bring him back him to State V. This mission was successful. Nothing has been heard of Thomas since.

Outraged, State T has demanded that State V's government return Thomas, apologise for the actions of their secret services and punish the agents who abducted Thomas.

State V's government has refused to comply with any of these demands; but it has indicated that it is prepared to pay 'compensation' of £500,000 to State T.

Advise State T.

How, if at all, would your answer have differed if Thomas had been a national of State U?

University of London LLB Examination
(for External Students) Public International Law June 1993 Q9

General Comment

A clearly defined problem, as it deals specifically with kidnapping by secret services and consequent state responsibility for direct international wrongs. As such it is not difficult to answer, although the issue must not be mistaken for one of jurisdiction; as long as that pitfall is avoided the answer becomes quite straightforward.

Skeleton Solution

Abduction as a direct international wrong – state responsibility for the violation of another state's territorial sovereignty – the effect of abduction on jurisdiction – state claims for harm done to individuals – reparations – the nationality of claims doctrine.

Suggested Solution

At issue in this case are the options open to State T following the abduction of Thomas, one of its nationals, by the secret service of State V. There can be no doubt that the act of abduction (as an exercise of one state's sovereignty on the territory of another state without the latter's consent) is a violation of the territorial sovereignty of the state where it occurred, and as such it constitutes a 'direct international wrong' (or 'international delict') under art 19(4) of the International Law Commission Draft Articles on State Responsibility 1979. As an international delict it automatically gives rise to state responsibility on the part of the abducting state.

Recourse to kidnapping in order to obtain custody of a wanted fugitive is regrettably common in international affairs. The precedent was set by Israel in 1960 when agents of the Mossad (the Israeli secret service) kidnapped the Nazi war criminal Adolf Eichmann in Argentina and smuggled him out of the country to stand trial in Israel for genocide and crimes against humanity under the Nazis and Nazi Collaborators (Punishment) Law 1951. Argentina complained to the United Nations Security Council, which passed a rather tepid Resolution condemning Israel's violation of Argentina's territorial sovereignty and requiring Israel to make reparations to Argentina. Even closer to the scenario of this problem is another action by Israel; the abduction from Italy of Mordechai Vanunu by Israeli secret agents in 1986. Vanunu was a former nuclear research scientist who disclosed information to the *Sunday Times* of London concerning Israel's nuclear programme. This information was classified top secret by the Israelis, and after kidnapping Vanunu in Rome they tried him in camera and sentenced him to 18 years' imprisonment for betraying state secrets. Again the Israeli recourse to abduction attracted widespread condemnation, but to date no apology or reparation has been offered by the Israeli authorities.

Nevertheless, the principle remains that the act of abduction in a foreign state is a violation of that state's territorial sovereignty and incurs responsibility on the part of the state which committed the act. A succession of cases on this subject only reinforce the point in a singularly unhelpful fashion by commenting that even though the custody of the suspect was obtained in violation of international law, the court hearing the case cannot be deprived of jurisdiction. Thus in *Attorney-General for Israel* v *Eichmann* (1962) 36 ILR 5 the District Court of Jerusalem stated:'It is an established rule of law that a person being tried for an offence … may not oppose his trial by means of the illegality of his arrest'; and in *R* v *O/C Depot Battalion, RASC Colchester, ex parte Elliott* [1949] 1 All ER 373 Goddard LCJ said that as long as an accused is charged under the law correctly applicable to the case, '[the] court cannot dismiss the charge at once without its being heard'.

The net result of this is that State V, having custody of Thomas (albeit illegally obtained), will do what it chooses with him. This brings the problem to the inter-state level. In the *Eichmann* case the Israeli court commented that:

'... the question of the violation of international law by the manner in which the accused was brought into the territory of a country arises at the international level, namely, the relations between the two countries concerned alone, and must find its solution at such level.'

The District Court of Jerusalem quoted approvingly from the judgment of the Supreme Court of Palestine in *Afouneh* v *Attorney-General for Palestine* (1942) 10 AD 327: 'It belongs exclusively to the government from whose territory [the accused] was wrongfully taken to complain of the violation of its rights'. Similarly, in *Re Argoud* (1964) 45 ILR 90 the French Court of Cassation noted that only the Federal Republic of Germany (from which the accused had been kidnapped by the French secret service) would have a valid claim to reparation (the German authorities chose in the event to turn a blind eye to the incident).

The right of State T to bring a claim against State V for reparation is clearly established by these cases and the general doctrine of the nationality of claims; in the *Panevezys-Saldutiskis Railway Case: Estonia* v *Lithuania* (1939) PCIJ Rep Ser A/B No 76 the Permanent Court of International Justice said:

'... In taking up the case of one of its nationals, by resorting to diplomatic action or international judicial proceedings on his behalf, a State is in reality asserting its own right, the right to ensure in the person of its nationals respect for the rules of international law.'

The PCIJ had made an almost exactly identical ruling earlier in the *Mavromattis Palestine Concessions Case: Greece* v *UK* (1924) PCIJ Rep Ser A No 2.

The purpose of reparations in such cases was stated in the *Chorzow Factory Case (Indemnity): Germany* v *Poland* (1928) PCIJ Rep Ser A No 17 as being 'as far as possible, [to] wipe out all the consequences of the illegal act and re-establish the situation which would, in all probability, have existed if that act had not been committed'. The *Chorzow Factory Case* was concerned with expropriation of property, not treatment of individuals, so the second part of the quoted statement obviously could not apply to an abduction, but the spirit of the statement is equally applicable to all claims for compensation under the theory of state responsibility. It is now generally believed (and advocated by the International Law Commission) that there is a duty to pay compensation for an illegal act entailing state responsibility.

State T therefore has every right to demand reparations from State V and, if they are not forthcoming, to register diplomatic protests (if the two states have diplomatic relations) or commence a claim for compensation. Unfortunately, State V cannot be compelled to release Thomas and we know that it has refused to do so. State V has, however, offered to pay State T a lump sum of £500,000 by way of compensation. Unsatisfactory and inadequate though this undoubtedly is, acceptance of this offer is the only practical option open to State T as lump sum settlement agreements (usually effected by bilateral treaty) have since 1945 become the standard way of settling claims for wrongful treatment of nationals at the hands of another state.

Had Thomas been a national of State U the position would have been different. Under the doctrine of the nationality of claims a state can only intervene on behalf of its own nationals, not those of other states. This was made clear in the *Panevezys-Saldutiskis Railway Case*:

> 'Where the injury was done to the national of some other State, no claim to which such injury may give rise falls within the scope of the diplomatic protection which a State is entitled to afford nor can it give rise to a claim which that State is entitled to espouse.'

Note that there are certain very limited circumstances in which a state may protect persons not having its nationality, as hinted at in the *Reparations for Injuries Suffered in the Service of the United Nations Case* (1949) ICJ Rep 174, but it is thought that those exceptions only apply to protected persons, members of a foreign state's armed forces and crew members of a foreign state's merchant ships. They would certainly not be applicable in this case. It follows from this that State T would not have been entitled to bring a claim on Thomas's behalf if he had been a national of State U.

Chapter 10

The Law of Treaties

10.1 Introduction

10.2 Key points

10.3 Key cases and legislation

10.4 Questions and suggested solutions

10.1 Introduction

Procedures for negotiating, concluding, observing, terminating, suspending and ratifying treaties are relatively settled and non-controversial matters. Other issues such as reservations and rights of non-parties to treaties remain contentious. However, it is the extensive scope and detailed contents of this subject that together cause problems for students trying to familiarise themselves with this topic. Students must not only understand the main substantive rules of this subject, but should also be prepared to address issues involving application of less familiar principles in the law of treaties.

10.2 Key points

International conventional obligations, both bilateral and multilateral, are all regulated by the same general principles of international law. For the greater part, these are contained in the Vienna Convention on the Law of Treaties 1969 ((1969) 8 ILM 679). Although this treaty did not enter into force until 1980, and technically applies only between parties to the agreement, certain elements represent a codification of the law of treaties, carried out under the auspices of the International Law Commission: see the *Namibia Case* (1971) ICJ Rep 16 at 47. This agreement has been revised and will ultimately be replaced by the Vienna Convention on Law of Treaties between States and International Organisations or between International Organisations 1986 (25 ILM 543 (1986)).

Definition and force of treaties

The Vienna Convention is limited in application to treaties between states, although this does not preclude principles embodied in the treaty being applied as customary international law to agreements between non-state entities such as international organisations: art 3.

The Convention defines the term 'treaty' as 'an international agreement concluded between states in written form and governed by international law, whether embodied in a single instrument or in two or more related instruments and whatever its particular designation': art 2. The term is therefore a generic one, which encompasses all international agreements, protocols, exchanges of notes, declarations, etc regardless of designation.

Although the Convention only refers to written agreements, valid obligations may also be constituted on an oral basis. In two separate cases the ICJ held that legal obligations could be created by oral undertakings.

a) The *Legal Status of Eastern Greenland Case* (1933) PCIJ Rep Ser A/B No 53: a declaration by a Norwegian Foreign Minister that 'the Norwegian Government would not make any difficulty' over the Danish claim to sovereignty over Eastern Greenland was held to constitute a valid legal obligation since it was 'beyond all dispute that a reply of this nature given by the Minister ... on behalf of his government in response to a request by a diplomatic representative of a foreign power, in regard to a question falling within his province, is binding'. However, it is unclear whether the decision was reached on the basis of an oral treaty or through the application of estoppel.

b) The *Nuclear Test Cases* (1974) ICJ Rep 253: public statements made by French Ministers in relation to a matter of international concern were declared obligatory because states could be bound by unilateral acts coupled with the intention of voluntarily restricting state actions. However, it is likely that these statements did not constitute a treaty since neither state affected by the French actions had accepted these undertakings.

The Convention promotes the use of written agreements in order to discourage oral agreements which are more susceptible to mistinterpretation. In practice, unwritten agreements are limited by art 102 of the UN Charter which stipulates that 'every treaty ... entered into by any Member of the United Nations ... shall as soon as possible be registered with the Secretariat and published by it ... (and) ... no party to any such treaty ... which has not been registered ... may invoke that treaty or agreement before any organ of the United Nations'.

The legal force of treaties is derived from the principle pacta sunt servanda. This fundamental norm is reiterated in art 26 of the Convention, according to which 'every treaty in force is binding upon the parties to it and must be performed by them in good faith'. One aspect of this principle is that 'a party may not invoke the provisions of its internal law as justification for its failure to perform a treaty': art 27. This is a restatement of the decision in the *Polish Nationals in Danzig Case* (1931) PCIJ Rep Ser A/B No 44 at p24, where the Court declared that 'a state cannot adduce as against another state its own constitution with a view to evading obligations incumbent upon it under international law or treaties in force'. See also art 13 of the Draft Declaration on Rights and Duties of States 1949.

Capacity and authority to negotiate treaties

Authority to enter into binding legal engagements is a matter for the internal constitutional foundation of each individual state. At the international level, a plenipotentiary is either expressly or impliedly granted full powers from the appropriate national authorities to enter into binding obligations.

Article 6 of the Convention recognises that all sovereign states have full capacity and power to conclude treaties, while art 7(1) provides that an individual is deemed to possess authority to represent a state if:

a) appropriate full powers are produced; or

b) it appears from the practice of the states concerned or from other circumstances that such a person is intended to represent a state for this purpose.

In addition, according to art 7(2), a number of individuals are presumed to have authority to enter into certain obligations without having to produce full powers. These include:

a) heads of state, heads of government and ministers for foreign affairs, for the purposes of performing all acts relating to the conclusion of a treaty;

b) heads of diplomatic missions, for the purpose of adopting the text of a treaty between the accrediting state and the state to which they are accredited;

c) representatives accredited by states to an international conference or to an international organisation or one of its organs, for the purpose of adopting the text of a treaty in that conference, organisation or organ.

A treaty entered into by a person without appropriate authority is void ab initio, and is without legal effect unless subsequently confirmed by the state: art 8.

Consent to be bound by a treaty and ratification

In order for a treaty to be valid, it must be adopted by the free consent of the contracting parties. Consent may be expressed by signature, exchange of instruments constituting a treaty, ratification, acceptance, approval or accession, or by any other means if so agreed: art 11. The important point is that the means selected to express consent should be recognised and acknowledged by all the parties. Signature, exchange of instruments or ratification will be binding if the text provides that these actions are to have that effect. Equally, signature, exchange or ratification express consent if this has been agreed to elsewhere than in the agreement by the parties. Where signature, exchange or ratification is made subject to approval or acceptance, then these actions do not represent consent to be bound.

Article 2 of the Convention defines ratification as 'the international act … whereby a state establishes on the international plane its consent to be bound by a treaty'. This is generally manifested by the approval from the head of state or government of the signature of the plenipotentiary. By ratification a state acknowledges the assumption of international rights and duties. In procedural terms, ratification involves two stages: the act of the appropriate organ of state, which is the Crown in the United Kingdom; and the exchange or deposit of instruments of ratification at the international level.

In British practice, there is no rule requiring treaties to be approved by Parliament prior to ratification. In constitutional theory the Crown is at liberty to ratify any treaty without the consent of Parliament, because the adoption of treaty obligations is a matter of the Crown prerogative. However, a constitutional convention has evolved, called the 'Ponsonby rule', according to which the text of every treaty subject to ratification is laid before Parliament for a period of 21 days before ratification. But, as observed by Lord Atkin, in *Attorney-General for Canada* v *Attorney-General for Ontario* [1937] AC 326:

> 'Within the British Empire there is a well-established rule that the making of a treaty is an executive act, while the performance of its obligations, if they entail alteration of the existing domestic law, requires legislative action ... The stipulations of a treaty duly ratified do not ... by virtue of the treaty alone, have the force of law.'

Article 24 of the Convention stipulates that a treaty enters into force in accordance with the terms provided in the treaty, eg at a certain date or when a certain number of states become parties to the agreement. A treaty becomes binding on parties subsequently acceding to the agreement at the moment that consent of the state to be bound by its provisions is expressed.

Reservations to treaties

The question of reservations to treaties involves a conflict between two desirable objectives in international negotiations:

a) the desirability of having near-universal participation in the multilateral treaty-making processes; and

b) the need to maintain consistency and uniformity in the creation of legal obligations on a universal basis.

A reservation is defined by art 2(1)(d) of the Convention as a 'unilateral statement, however phrased or named, made by a state, when signing, ratifying, accepting, approving or acceding to a treaty, whereby it purports to exclude or modify the legal effect of certain provisions of the treaty in their application to that state'.

Under traditional international law, a state could not make a reservation to a treaty unless it was accepted by all the parties signing the agreement. In the absence of unanimous consent to the reservation, it would be null and void, and the state would fail to become a party to the treaty. This was the clear policy of the League of Nations when acting as depository for the registration of treaties.

Increasing state participation in the processes of multilateral treaty-making rendered this approach impractical and in the *Reservations to the Convention on Genocide Case* (1951) ICJ Rep 15 the ICJ enunciated a compromise series of principles. The Court held that a state making a reservation to a treaty to which one or more, but not all, of the parties to the treaty had raised an objection, could be considered a party to the treaty so long as the reservation was compatible with 'the object and purpose of the treaty'. In relation to (a) states objecting to the reservation; and (b) those accepting the reservation, the Court laid down the following rules.

a) If a party to the Convention objects to a reservation which it considers to be incompatible with the object and purpose of the Convention, it can consider the reserving state not to be a party to the Convention.

b) If, on the other hand, a party accepts the reservation as being compatible with the object and purpose of the Convention, it can consider the reserving state to be a party to the Convention.

The Court introduced a new test of 'compatibility' which, according to the Court, was to be applied individually by states on a subjective basis.

On the whole, the Vienna Convention follows the rules laid down in the *Genocide Case*. It distinguishes between 'permissible' and 'impermissible' reservations. Article 19 allows a state to formulate a reservation when signing, ratifying, accepting, approving or acceding to a treaty, unless the reservation is 'impermissible' which occurs when:

a) the reservation is prohibited by the treaty. An example of this is art 64 of the European Convention on Human Rights 1950 which specifically prohibits 'reservations of a general character': see *Belilos* v *Switzerland* (1988) 10 EHRR 466;

b) the treaty provides that only specified reservations, which do not include the reservation in question, may be made; or

c) in cases not falling under sub-paragraphs (a) and (b), the reservation is incompatible with the object and purpose of the treaty.

If a reservation is permissible, art 20 regulates the occasions on which a reservation requires acceptance by other parties. Two rules are important:

a) a reservation expressly authorised by a treaty does not require any subsequent acceptance by other parties unless specifically stipulated; and

b) when it appears from the limited number of parties and the object and purpose of the treaty that the application of the treaty in its entirety between all parties is an essential condition of the consent of each one to be bound by the treaty, a reservation requires acceptance by all the parties.

The effect of a reservation depends on whether it is accepted or rejected by the other parties in accordance with the rules described above. The relations between reserving state and other parties to the treaty are governed by the following rules.

a) Acceptance by another contracting state of a reservation constitutes the reserving state a party to the treaty in relation to that other state if or when the treaty is in force for those states.

b) An objection by another contracting state to a reservation does not preclude the entry into force of the treaty as between the objecting and reserving states unless a contrary intention is definitely expressed by the objecting state.

c) An act expressing a state's consent to be bound by the treaty and containing a reservation is effective as soon as at least one other contracting state has accepted the reservation.

The actual legal obligations of a state making a reservation are modified in accordance with principles enunciated by art 21. Where a permissible reservation has been properly constituted and accepted according to the rules prescribed, it:

a) modifies for the reserving state in its relations with that other party the provisions of the treaty to which the reservation relates to the extent of the reservation; and

b) modifies those provisions to the same extent for that other party in its relations with the reserving state.

However, the reservation is ineffective in relation to the contractual relations of other parties to the treaty.

Effect of treaties on third parties

As a general principle, a treaty does not establish rights or duties for third states without their consent: art 34. This rule is expressed in the maxim pacta tertiis nec nocent nec prosunt, and is supported by a number of international decisions. See, especially, the *Free Zones of Upper Savoy and the District of Gex Case* (1932) PCIJ Rep Ser A/B No 46.

A number of exceptions to this rule have been established both under the Convention and also in customary law. Cumulatively, these include the following.

a) A duty arises for a third state from a provision of a treaty if the parties to the treaty intend the provision to be the means of establishing the duty and the third state has expressly accepted this obligation in writing: art 35.

b) A right arises for a third state from the provision of a treaty if the parties to the treaty intend the provision to accord that right either to a third state, or to a group of states to which it belongs, or to all states, and the third state assents thereto. Its assent shall be presumed so long as the contrary is not indicated, unless the treaty provides otherwise: art 36.

c) Multilateral treaties declaratory of customary law will apply to non-parties, although in fact they are not bound by the treaty itself, but rather the underlying customary principles: see the *North Sea Continental Shelf Cases* (1969) ICJ Rep 3.

d) Multilateral treaties which are instrumental in the creation of new customary rules may ultimately bind third parties on a customary basis, for example, the Hague Convention on the Rules of Land Warfare 1907.

e) Certain multilateral conventions which are intended to have near-universal operation may require application to non-parties. For example, art 2(6) of the United Nations Charter provides that the Organisation shall ensure observance of the principles of the Charter by states which are not members of the United Nations.

Validity of treaty obligations

The Vienna Convention is deemed to exhaust all possible criteria on which the application of a treaty may be discontinued. Article 42 declares that a treaty may only be terminated under the terms of the Convention itself. Further, where an agreement is terminated under the Convention's rules, this is specifically declared not to relieve a state of duties embodied in a treaty which either codified or created customary principles of law which are independently imposed: art 43.

Where avoidance of a treaty is permitted, it is not usually possible to divide the provisions of a treaty into applicable and inapplicable provisions. Consequently the treaty must stand or fall as a whole and cannot be divided into operative and inoperative sections. The main exception to this rule is that, where the reason for invalidity can be attributed to specific provisions and not the treaty as a whole, then division may be possible if:

a) the provisions are separable with regard to their application;

b) acceptance of these provisions was not an essential basis for the procurement of the other party's consent; and

c) continued performance of the obligations in the remaining sections of the treaty would not be unjust: art 44(3).

Under art 45 of the Convention, if a state party to a treaty has knowledge of a reason for vitiating an agreement, but either consents to, or acquiesces in, the continuation of the agreement, then the right to terminate the treaty on that ground is lost.

Under the Convention, a number of reasons and causes may justify a treaty being declared invalid.

Error

Article 48 stipulates that 'a state may invoke an error in a treaty as invalidating its consent to be bound by a treaty if the error relates to a fact or situation which was assumed by that state to exist at the time when the treaty was concluded and formed an essential basis of its consent to be bound by the treaty'.

However, where a state contributed or caused the error to arise, consent cannot be invalidated. In the *Temple of Preah Vihear Case* (1962) ICJ Rep 6 the International Court declared:

'It is an established rule of law that the plea of error cannot be allowed as an element vitiating consent if the party advancing it contributed by its own conduct to the error, or could have avoided it, or if the circumstances were such as to put that party on notice of a possible error.'

Fraud

If a state has been induced to enter into a treaty by the fraudulent misrepresentations of another state, the deceived state may invoke the fraud as a reason for invalidating its consent to the obligated: art 49. This is not thought to be a particularly important principle in actual practice.

Corruption

Expression of a state's consent to be bound by a treaty procured by the corruption of its representative during the negotiation process and directly or indirectly perpetrated by another negotiating state, allows that state to invoke such corruption as a justification for withdrawing its consent to be bound: art 50.

Coercion

Consent on the part of a state to a contractual obligation shall have no legal effect if it was procured:

a) by the coercion of the representative of the state (art 51); or

b) by the threat or use of force in violation of the principles of international law embodied in the United Nations Charter: art 52.

In the *Fisheries Jurisdiction Case (Jurisdiction)* (1973) ICJ Rep 14, the International Court observed that:

> 'There can be little doubt, as is implied in the Charter of the United Nations and recognised in Article 52 of the Vienna Convention on the Law of Treaties, that under contemporary international law an agreement concluded under the threat or use of force is void. It is equally clear that a court cannot consider an accusation of this serious nature on the basis of a vague general charge unfortified by evidence in its support.'

The Court displayed a similarly restrictive approach to the application of this principle in *Case Concerning the Territorial Dispute between Libya and Chad* (1994) ICJ Rep 6. In this case Libya had argued that a treaty negotiated in 1955 between itself and France, although valid, should be interpreted favourably towards Libya because, at the time of negotiation, Libya lacked the necessary experience in this type of negotiations. The Court rejected this allegation of coercion and refused to recognise this factor as a justification for interpreting the treaty in favour of Libya.

Jus cogens

A treaty is void if, at the time of its conclusion, it conflicts with a peremptory norm of general international law: art 53. A peremptory norm of general international law is a norm accepted and recognised by the international community as a whole as a norm from which no derogation is permitted. Such norms may only be modified by the creation of a subsequent and equally authoritative norm of general international law having the same character.

In the *Barcelona Traction, Light and Power Co Case* (1970) ICJ Rep 3, at 32, the majority judgment of the International Court drew a distinction between the obligations of states among themselves and the obligations of states owed to the international community as a whole. In relation to the latter, the Court stated:

> 'Such obligations derive, for example, in contemporary international law, from the outlawing of acts of aggression, and of genocide, as also from the principles and rules concerning the basic rights of the human person, including protection from slavery and racial discrimination.'

This is generally taken to be a statement of the present content of the concept of jus cogens.

Interpretation of treaty obligations

In traditional international law, three methods or techniques have been suggested as being appropriate for the interpretation of treaties. In summary these are:

a) the 'intention of the parties method' which attempts to give effect to the obligations intended by the parties at the time of concluding the agreement;

b) the 'textual' or 'ordinary meaning of the word method' which seeks to avoid referring to extra-textual elements by restricting analysis to the terms of the text in the light of the meaning ordinarily attibuted to them; and

c) the 'teleological method' which looks to the objectives of the treaty in order to construe and apply the terms of the agreement.

In the *Interpretation of the Peace Treaties Case* (1950) ICJ Rep 65, the International Court adopted the 'ordinary meaning method' when it refused to allow the object and purpose of a treaty to override the clear language of the text.

However, the Court has been prepared to look to the purposes and objects of a treaty where the terms of an agreement are not explicit or clear. Thus, in the *Reparations Case* (1949) ICJ Rep 174, in which the Court derived the international legal personality of international organisations, and the *Certain Expenses Case* (1962) ICJ Rep 151, where the Court determined the role of the General Assembly in relation to the United Nations organisation, evidence of this approach is obvious.

Article 31 of the Vienna Convention adopts a qualified ordinary meaning approach by declaring that 'a treaty shall be interpreted in good faith in accordance with the ordinary meaning to be given to the terms of the treaty in their context and in the light of its object and purposes'. Although the primary method of interpretation remains the 'ordinary meaning method', the treaty's object and purpose are not irrelevant.

Article 31(2) emphasises that the primary source for the interpretation of a treaty remains the text of the agreement itself, but may also extend to:

a) an agreement between the parties made in connection with the conclusion of the treaty itself; and

b) any instrument, ie a letter or declaration, made by parties in connection with the negotiation and conclusion of the agreement;

c) subsequent agreements and practice of the parties in relation to the implementation of the treaty under examination: art 31(3).

Article 32 of the Convention does not preclude reference to the travaux preparatoires made in connection with the negotiation of the treaty, but implies that such documentation may only be referred to as a 'supplementary means of interpreation' in order to 'confirm the meaning resulting from the application of Article 31', or to determine the meaning of the treaty when the 'ordinary meaning method' produces an ambiguous or obscure meaning or leads to a result which is manifestly absurd or unreasonable.

Where a treaty has been negotiated in two or more languages which have both been afforded equal authenticity, art 33(4) recommends that the interpretation which 'best reconciles the texts, having regard to the object and purpose of the treaty' is to be favoured. This permits scope for an extensive interpretation to treaty obligations in such circumstances.

Modification, suspension and termination of treaty obligations

A number of reasons may be advanced to justify the conclusion of an international agreement. The Vienna Convention identifies a number of such grounds.

Mutual consent

A treaty will terminate where this eventuality is specifically envisaged in the agreement itself, on the occurrence of certain conditions or at a certain time. Such an event may also be manifested by the collective consent of the parties after consultations with all relevant contracting parties. Similarly, amendment and modifications of obligations may also be achieved on the basis of mutual consent.

Material breach

Article 60(1) specifies the applicable rule in relation to material breach of a bilateral treaty by one party. In such circumstances, the other party is at liberty to terminate the treaty, either in whole or in part.

A material breach of a multilateral treaty by one party entitles:

a) the other parties, by unanimous agreement, to suspend the operation of the agreement in whole or part or to terminate it either in the relations between themselves and the defaulting state or among all parties;

b) a party specially affected by a breach is permitted to invoke it as a ground for suspending the operation of the agreement in whole or in part in the relationship between itself and the state in default; and

c) any party other than the one in default may invoke the breach as a ground for suspending the agreement in whole or in part with respect to itself where the treaty is of such a character that a material breach by one party radically changes the position of every other party to the agreement.

A material breach of a treaty includes a repudiation of the treaty or a violation of a provision essential to the accomplishment of the object or purpose of the treaty: art 60(3).

Supervening impossibility

Article 61(1) of the Convention permits a state to terminate or withdraw from an agreement if it has become impossible to perform as a consequence of 'the permanent disappearance or destruction of an object indispensable for the execution of the treaty'. However, temporary impossibility merely gives rise to suspension of the obligations of the treaty.

A party is precluded from invoking this defence to non-performance of the agreement where the supervening impossibility has been brought about by the failure of that party to perform its international obligations.

Fundamental change of circumstances

The concept of rebus sic stantibus is framed in the negative by the Convention. A fundamental change of circumstances which was not foreseen by the parties, may not be invoked as a ground for terminating or withdrawing from a treaty unless:

a) the existence of those circumstances constituted an essential basis of the consent of the parties to be bound by the treaty; and

b) the effect of the change is radically to transform the extent of obligations still to be performed under the treaty.

Notwithstanding these rules, a fundamental change of circumstances may never be relied upon as a ground for terminating a treaty which establishes a boundary or where the change is a consequence of the actions of a party in breach of its obligations under the treaty: art 62(2).

Emergence of a jus cogens

Article 64 of the Convention stipulates that, where a new peremptory norm of general international law has emerged, any existing conflicting conventional obligations are terminated.

Note that a number of circumstances are specifically precluded from permitting the termination of an agreement. In particular, according to art 63, the severance of diplomatic or consular relations between two states does not affect the legal relations established between them on the basis of treaties.

State succession to treaties

The Vienna Convention on Succession of States in Respect of Treaties 1978 (17 ILM 1488 (1978)) attempts to deal with this problem. Article 8 declares that, where one state succeeds another as the internationally responsible person for that territory, the treaty obligations of the previous state do not automatically bind the succeeding state unless these obligations relate to boundaries or other territorial demarcations. Under this regime, the successor state has discretion in relation to assuming the obligations of certain treaties and rejecting others.

Treaties by international organisations

The Vienna Convention on the Law of Treaties between States and International Organisations or between International Organisations 1986 regulates the procedures for negotiating treaties between states and international organisations and among international organisations themselves. For the most part, the 1986 Convention repeats the rights and duties contained in the Vienna Convention on the Law of Treaties 1969, relating to matters such as the formalities and negotiating procedures for making treaties, validity, the application of treaties, the amendment and modification of treaties, interpretation and termination.

10.3 Key cases and legislation

* *Belilos* v *Switzerland* (1988) 10 EHRR 466
  Interpretation of reservation by the European Court of Human Rights in the case of the European Convention on Human Rights

* *Case Concerning the Gabcikovo-Nagymaros Project (Hungary* v *Slovakia)* (1998) 37 ILM 162
  Examined the circumstances precluding wrongfulness

* *Case Concerning the Territorial Dispute between Libya and* v *Chad* (1994) ICJ Rep 6
  ICJ rejected the doctrine of unequal treaties as illegal

* *Fisheries Jurisdiction Case (Jurisdiction)* (1973) ICJ Rep 14 at 16–20
  Discussion of the concept of rebus sic stantibus

* *Free Zones of Upper Savoy and the District of Gex Case* (1932) PCIJ Rep Ser A/B No 46
  Consideration of the rights of third parties to treaties

- *Interpretation of Peace Treaties Case* (1950) ICJ Rep 65
  The leading pre-Convention case on the subject of the interpretation of treaties

- *Reservations to the Convention on Genocide Case* (1951) ICJ Rep 15
  Advisory opinion of the International Court on the subject of reservations to multilateral agreements

- Vienna Convention on the Law of Treaties 1969

- Vienna Convention on Succession of States in Respect of Treaties 1978

- United Nations Charter – provides the framework within which the law of treaties effectively operate

10.4 Questions and suggested solutions

QUESTION ONE

'Modern legal arrangements between states cover a huge range of issues and concerns involving routine bilateral road transport agreements, highly sensitive defence arrangements, global trade and environmental compacts, comprehensive codification exercises, constitutions of international organisations and many others. It has proved necessary to adapt traditional treaty law principles and procedures to meet these challenges so that certainty has been sacrificed in favour of flexibility.'

Critically analyse this statement.

University of London LLB Examination
(for External Students) Public International Law June 1999 Q7

General Comment

It is rare for a paper on public international law not to include a question on the law of treaties. The problem is that this is a very wide subject, allowing the examiner to focus on a particular area. In this question the emphasis is on changes in treaty practice. As with other areas, the well-prepared candidate will be able to illustrate their answer with reference to particular treaty provisions.

Skeleton Solution

Introduction – the three elements of the question – the wide range of issues covered by treaty law – the adapting of treaty principles – the attempt to strike a balance between certainty and flexibility – conclusions.

Suggested Solution

The treaty is a device for conducting relations between states and while it can be traced back to Graeco-Roman times, it acquired increased prominence in Europe after the Peace of Westphalia in 1648. Since then the volume of treaty law has steadily grown in part reflecting the increased complexity of international society. By the nineteenth century its role was well established so it could be taken as a source of international law in 1920, and its status is confirmed in the list of sources set out in art 38 of the Statute of the International Court of Justice 1945. Writers have pointed out for many years that the treaty has to serve as an all purpose vehicle; it may operate in similar form to a statute, as in law-making treaties such as the Vienna Convention on Diplomatic Relations 1961, but it may also operate in a manner akin to a contract in a simple bilateral agreement.

None of the foregoing is new and much is trite law. The quotation itself requires us to comment on three matters, namely: (a) that modern legal arrangements between states cover a huge range of issues, (b) that traditional treaty law principles have had to be adapted, and (c) that certainty has been sacrificed in favour of flexibility. It is sensible to take each of these aspects in turn.

In respect of the first element, it is correct that international society has witnessed an increase not only in the number of states, but also in the areas in which some form of international regulation is required. Areas such as the law of the air, the law of the sea, the law of outer space and the environment are increasingly regulated by treaty provision in a manner inconceivable in the time of Professor Oppenheim. Not only are there more treaties, but these treaties embrace a larger number of states and concern a much wider range of issues. The emphasis on detailed provision has been accommodated either by including detailed schedules to the treaty (as with the Law of the Sea Convention 1982), or by the device of the Framework Convention and subsequent Protocol. In areas such as environmental law it has proved sensible to try and reach agreement in matters of principle in a Framework Convention and then to deal with matters of detail in the subsequent Protocol. This is a sensible way of proceeding where scientific opinion is still evolving, as illustrated by the Framework Convention on Climate Change 1992 and the Kyoto Treaty 2002 (which comes into effect in 2008).

The reason why there has been such a proliferation of treaties is in part due to the realisation that the rules of customary international law are in many areas vague and inadequate. Since 1947 the International Law Commission has been concerned to strengthen international law through codification and progressive development. Second, many of the 180 states in the world are those created after 1945; many of these reject the Euro centric rules of customary international law, but are prepared to accept rules voluntarily agreed in treaty form. As the quotation indicates, states may enter into agreements on matters of road transport or defence as well as those well-known codification exercises, such as the Vienna Convention on Diplomatic Relations 1961. Of particular interest in the post war period are those treaties often termed statutes which act as the constitution of an international organisation: there are more of such documents for the simple reason that since 1945 there has been a steady increase in the number and variety of regional and international organisations.

The second aspect of the question flows from the first. The emphasis on multilateral law-making treaties has had the effect that the interests of individual states have had to be accommodated. In some instances it is not merely a question of obtaining a certain number of ratifications, but of securing the consent of important states. The emphasis here has been on flexibility. A good example is afforded by the Law of the Sea Convention 1982; after the text was agreed in 1982 there was a serious possibility that the Convention would come into force without the consent of the United States and other important maritime powers. International negotiations continued in the period 1982–1994, resulting in the conclusion of the New York Implementation Agreement 1994, which modified the contents of Part XI of the Convention and enabled those states who had been reluctant in 1982 to ratify the Convention. The 1994 Implementation Agreement was an unorthodox method of modifying the original Convention so as to secure the object of near universal participation.

Under this head one should also note those circumstances – normally of a bilateral nature – where states choose not to draw up a treaty at all, but to proceed by a memorandum of understanding (MOU); such documents have the advantage of lacking formality, being easy to amend and have the virtue of confidentiality. Such a method of proceeding may be appropriate in technical matters and may in certain instances avoid constitutional difficulties. Such MOUs are of advantage in bilateral matters of a quasi-contractual nature.

The third aspect of the question refers to the concern that certainty may have been sacrificed in the interests of flexibility. There is no doubt that there has been a change of practice since 1945. Generally, prior to that date the rule was that any state wishing to make a reservation to a treaty had to obtain the consent of all other state parties. This view, which was grounded in analogies drawn from the law of contract, gave way to the more liberal approach propounded in the *Reservations to the Convention on Genocide Case* (1951) ICJ Rep 15; under the liberal approach a state may be regarded as a party to the Convention if the reservation is compatible with the object and purpose of the Convention. This later flexible approach is continued in arts 19 and 20 of the Vienna Convention on the Law of Treaties 1969, which draw a distinction between those reservations prohibited or incompatible with a treaty and those that are not. Allied to a more flexible approach to reservations, one can note the steady increase in the employment of interpretative declarations. It is of course important that such declarations should not in substance be disguised reservations. Sometimes a treaty may provide for interpretative declarations to be made (see art 310 Law of the Sea Convention 1982), and such a declaration may be an element in the interpretation of the treaty, provided it is not in substance a disguised reservation: see arts 31 and 32 of the Vienna Convention on the Law of Treaties 1969.

Thus, taking a rounded view, there is no doubt that the law of treaties has expanded in scope partly because of the need to regulate. It is also true that traditional principles of the law of treaties have had to be modified and a degree of flexibility has been introduced. However, that flexibility in the law of treaties has been with the object of securing certainty within the wider field of international law. To take an example: the law of the sea is now much clearer today than in 1956 simply because over 100 states have accepted the Law of the Sea Convention 1982. Furthermore, 80 per cent of the 'Sea States or Ports' now subscribe to the International Maritime Organisation, which has a regulatory framework in operation in respect of the laws governing the sea. That certainty would not have been possible had not some flexibility been shown in the process of ratification. In essence the purpose of the law of treaties is to foster consent and co-operation. In a world of over 180 states, with different economic and social circumstances, a degree of flexibility is required if a draft document is to emerge as an agreed treaty.

QUESTION TWO

In what circumstances, if any, are the rights and obligations enshrined in a multilateral treaty binding upon states not party to the treaty?

University of London LLB Examination
(for External Students) Public International Law June 1997 Q1

General Comment

A difficult question in so far as the examiner is clearly seeking to test the knowledge of the student on a particular aspect of the law of treaties. The candidate seeking to answer this question would need to be familiar with the general approach of customary international law, as well as being aware of the specific provisions of the Vienna Convention on the Law of Treaties 1969. It is clear that the examiner expects some reference to the relationship between multilateral law-making treaties and the rules of customary international law. Manifestly, the examiner is not seeking a general discussion on the law of treaties but an analysis of the position of non-parties.

Skeleton Solution

Introduction: the nature of treaties – the provisions of the UN Charter 1945 – the stipulation of benefits in favour of non-parties – the imposition of burdens upon non-parties – dispositive treaties – the relationship between multilateral law-making treaties and the rules of customary international law.

Suggested Solution

We are asked in this question to analyse the circumstances in which the rights and obligations enshrined in a multilateral treaty might be binding on a State not itself a party to the treaty (ie a non-party State).

The first preliminary point concerns definitions. A treaty is defined in art 2(1)(a) of the Vienna Convention on the Law of Treaties 1969 as 'an international agreement concluded between States in written form and governed by international law, whether embodied in a single instrument or in two or more related instruments'. A multilateral treaty may be broadly defined as 'a treaty with three or more parties'. It is often the case that a multilateral treaty is a law-making treaty designed to establish general rules of common application; indeed, since 1946 several thousand such treaties have been deposited with the United Nations under the terms of art 106 of the UN Charter.

As is implied in the question, the general rule in international law is that agreements bind only the parties to them. As a broad principle this rule applies in many municipal legal systems. The rule is often expressed in the maxim 'pacta tertiis nec nocent nec prosunt'. This long-standing rule is reflected in art 34 of the Vienna Convention which reads 'A treaty does not create either obligations or rights for a third State without its consent'.

In respect of the question there are five matters that require to be discussed:

a) the particular provisions of the UN Charter;

b) treaties that expressly stipulate benefits in favour of non-party States;

c) treaties that impose obligations on non-party States;

d) dispositive treaties; and

e) the relationship between multilateral law-making treaties and customary international law.

The United Nations Charter 1945 contains a number of provisions that apply to non-Member States. In particular, art 2(6) imposes obligations on non-Members, while arts 32, 35(3) and 50 confer rights. It might be argued that the UN Charter is a particular form of global constitution whose fundamental objective in preserving peace would be frustrated if the reach of the treaty did not extend to non-Members.

In respect of the general position under the law of treaties, the rules are more restricted. It has been accepted for more than a century that a treaty might confer benefits on a non-party, although particular questions did arise as to: (i) whether the third party could claim directly or merely through a contracting party; and (ii) whether the parties to the treaty could abolish the stipulation without the consent of the third party.

The matter of rights 'in favorem tertii' was considered by the PCIJ in the *Free Zones of Upper Savoy and the District of Gex Case* (1932) PCIJ Rep Ser A/B No 46; 6 ILR 362 where the court ruled that for a benefit to arise in favour of a third party: (i) the treaty must be examined to determine whether a right has been created; (ii) it must then be determined whether the right has been accepted by the third party; and (iii) in certain circumstances the right might not be terminated without the consent of the third party. The general tenor of the judgment is reflected in art 36(1) of the Vienna Convention which reads:

> 'A right arises for a third State from a provision of a treaty if the parties to a treaty intend the provision to accord that right either to the third State, or to a group of States to which

it belongs, or to all States and the third State assents thereto. Its assent shall be presumed so long as the contrary is not indicated, unless the treaty otherwise provides.'

In general, customary international law favoured the stipulation of benefits in favour of non-parties and examples can be found in art 1 of the Constantinople Convention 1888 governing the Suez Canal and art 380 of the Treaty of Versailles 1919 that governed the Kiel Canal.

However, customary international law was hostile to the concept of a treaty imposing obligations upon a non-party. This reluctance is now reflected in art 35 of the Vienna Convention which reads as follows:

'An obligation arises for a third State from a provision of a treaty if the parties to the treaty intend the provision to be the means of establishing the obligation and the third State expressly accepts that obligation in writing.'

It should be noted that both in respect of obligations arising under art 35, or rights arising under art 36, the Vienna Convention provides in art 37 for a regime of revocation by consent.

In respect of the fourth matter indicated above some jurists have argued that there is a distinct category of 'dispositive' treaties that create an objective legal regime binding upon third States. Examples of such treaties would be those that govern international waterways (eg, Permanent Neutrality and Operation of the Panama Canal Treaty 1978), or those that determine boundaries. It is arguable that treaties creating international organisations fall within this category, although it is probably sensible to regard the UN Charter 1945 as a treaty sui generis.

Fifthly, it is asserted that a multilateral treaty may create legal effects for a non-party if: (a) it is declaratory of customary international law; or (b) it establishes new customary law. However, it is clear from judgments in the *North Sea Continental Shelf Cases* (1969) ICJ Rep 3 and *Nicaragua* v *United States (Merits)* (1986) ICJ Rep 14 that a heavy onus probandi lies on the party so asserting. In any event, in such circumstances the non-party State will be bound not by the treaty but by the customary rules.

Finally, it might be argued that international law has evolved in a hesitant and uncertain fashion when dealing with the rights of non-party States. However, this is hardly surprising when one remembers that in the major municipal legal systems of the world there is a division of opinion between stipulations 'in favorem tertii' and the opposite principle of 'alteri nemo stipulari potest'.

QUESTION THREE

a) Why was the incorporation of the concept of jus cojens into the Vienna Convention on the Law of Treaties 1961, a source of controversy?

b) In 1996, Arcadia, a former colony of Imperia, obtained independence after a long struggle for national liberation. The new foreign minister of Arcadia seeks your advice on the following matters:

i)   Arcadia's obligations, if any, in respect of a treaty concluded in 1982 by Imperia under which a substantial part of the then colony of Arcadia was transferred to the neighbouring state of Sindaria in return for military assistance against the Arcadian Liberation Front;

ii) Arcadia's wish to become a party to a United Nations Convention on Compulsory Dispute Settlement subject to a reservation excluding disputes with Imperia in respect of any matters arising before Arcadia's independence.

University of London LLB Examination
(for External Students) Public International Law June 1996 Q7

General Comment

A question divided into three parts, the first section of which invites a discussion of the meaning of jus cogens. Because there is no definitive answer, this answers the question as to why its incorporation was a source of controversy.

The remaining parts of the question relate to the issue of jus cogens in seeking a solution to the problems. The issue of self-determination and its possible inclusion as a peremptory norm of international law needs to be discussed.

Part (b)(ii) includes a consideration of reservations to treaties and the Vienna Convention on Succession of States in Respect of Treaties 1978.

The writer has assumed that 1961 is a misprint as the Vienna Convention on the Law of Treaties is 1969.

Skeleton Solution

a) Jus cogens and peremptory norms: where do they come from? – what are they? – moral content of law – conclusion.

b) i)   Self-determination: the importance of the rule – the source of self-determination – the relationship to the problem.

    ii) Significance of reservations – Vienna Convention Treaties: *Genocide Case* – Vienna Convention on Succession of States – conclusion.

Suggested Solution

a) Jus cogens refers to the body of peremptory norms of international law. Being peremptory no derogation from them is permitted and any derogation will involve the treaty being declared invalid.

Article 53 of the Vienna Convention 1969 defines a peremptory norm of international law as:

> '... a norm accepted and recognised by the international community of States ... and which can be modified only by a subsequent norm of general international law having the same character.'

Article 64 of the Vienna Convention goes on to say:

> 'If a new peremptory norm of general international law emerges, any existing treaty which is in conflict with that norm becomes void and terminates.'

Such is the effect of violating a norm of international law. What is less clear is what amounts to a peremptory norm and where do they originate? Article 64 talks about peremptory norms 'emerging', which would indicate that they might come from customary law, only being deemed to exist once the world community of States has accepted them. They might also originate from a treaty which has received universal approval or, more likely, a treaty which has served to codify customary international law, the Vienna Convention on Diplomatic Relations 1961 being an example.

Peremptory norms may emerge from a UN General Assembly Resolution which has been passed by a large majority with no votes against it, the Universal Declaration of Human Rights and Res 1514 on the Granting of Independence to Colonial Peoples being examples – their passage may have resulted in peremptory norms of human rights and self-determination for peoples. The problem with this area of international law is that not only is the definition of a peremptory norm unclear, (for example, who constitute 'peoples' entitled to self-determination?), but also may a definitive list of such norms be drawn up at any one time?

It is submitted that there are now a limited number of peremptory norms of international law such as the prohibitions on the slave trade and piracy. It is easy to predict that a treaty authorising either would be void as both constitute international crimes. Other examples of the same genre which have emerged in the post-war era include the possibility of a treaty to effect genocide (the prohibition thereof being found in a treaty: Convention on the Prevention and Punishment of the Crime of Genocide 1948) and a treaty which might involve crimes against humanity.

Other areas are more opaque. The principle of non-discrimination on the grounds of race and the prohibition of racial discrimination might possibly be categorised as a norm of international law. It has not, however, been suggested that the treaty between the United Kingdom and the People's Republic of China be declared void, even though the treaty takes into account ethnic origins in determining who is entitled to Chinese citizenship after 1997.

It has been argued that the:

> '... rules of jus cogens will encompass rules based more on "morality" or "natural law" than the traditionalist "positivist" rules.' (Dixon *International Law* (3rd ed), p68.)

As such they can be hard to define, and supporting the contention that a treaty is against jus cogens introduces an element of uncertainty into international practice and jurisprudence.

b) i) In its former status of a colony of Imperia, Arcadia was denied the right to self-determination. This right is referred to in art 1(2) of the UN Charter which states that one of the organisation's purposes is to develop friendly relations among nations based upon respect for the principle of equal rights and self-determination. Article 55 of the Charter also makes reference to self-determination, as do the International 'Human Rights' Covenants 1966. Moreover, Res 1514 might be a contributory factor in this area. Judicial discussion of the principle of self-determination is found in the *Namibia Advisory Opinion (Legal Consequences for States of the Continued Presence of South Africa in Namibia (South West Africa) Case* (1971) ICJ Rep 16) and the *Western Sahara Case: Advisory Opinion* (1975) ICJ Rep 12.

It is against this background that we must consider the contention that the 1982 treaty represents a rule of jus cogens. The treaty between Imperia and Sindaria would appear to violate the right of self-determination for the people of Arcadia. The doctrine of self-determination is designed to facilitate the independence of colonial peoples within already existing colonial boundaries. This is not the case here, and in fact the treaty appears to be designed to thwart the wishes of the people of Arcadia in that the neighbouring State of Sindaria has helped in the suppression of the Arcadian Liberation Front. Further, while the act of secession is not against international law it presumably will be an expression of self-determination, which is not the situation in this case. An act of secession is permissible in international law but in this case a substantial part of Arcadia was transferred to the State of Sindaria by Imperia without the consent of the Arcadian population. A substantial part of Arcadia was transferred by the colonial power, without, one would surmise, the consent of the population of Arcadia.

Arcadia should be advised that the treaty is in violation of jus cogens and will not be valid. It is void from its inception.

ii) It is permissible in international law to enter a reservation concerning a treaty. A reservation is defined in art 2 Vienna Convention on the Law of Treaties as a statement by a State which purports to 'exclude or to modify the legal effect of certain provisions of the treaty in their application to that State'.

The significance of a reservation was discussed in an Advisory Opinion of the ICJ in *Reservations to the Convention on Genocide Case* (1951) ICJ Rep 15. The Court was of the opinion that:

'... a State may be regarded as being a party to the Convention if the reservation is compatible with the object and purposes of the Convention.'

What is or is not compatible with the Convention is, according to the *Genocide Case*, to be decided by States individually. The effect of this in practice means that a State may be a party to the treaty in the eyes of some States but not of others.

Articles 19–21 of the Vienna Convention follow the opinion in the *Genocide Case*, except in cases where by art 20(2):

> '... it appears from the limited number of States and the object and purpose of the treaty that the application of the treaty in its entirety between all the parties is an essential condition of the consent of each one to be bound by the treaty.'

In this instance it is most unlikely that only a limited number of States would become a party to a UN Convention.

Arcadia will be seen in international law as the successor to Imperia over its territory. The standard rule is that 'new' or recently independent States are not bound by treaties made on their behalf by the former sovereign or colonial power. This is put forth in the Vienna Convention on Succession of States in Respect of Treaties 1978. There is an exception, however, in relation to boundaries. Articles 11 and 12 of the Succession Convention cover boundaries and provide that territorial boundaries are binding on the new State.

Arcadia should therefore be advised that she is not bound by any treaty altering her territory as this goes against a rule of jus cogens, namely self-determination. The territorial question is likely to be the main item of dispute with Imperia. Arcadia should enter a reservation in case of any other disputes with Imperia, but the dispute over the transfer of territory should not be part of Arcadia's reservation as any agency established under the said UN Convention on Dispute Settlement is likely to rule in favour Arcadia that the treaty between Imperia and Sindaria is against a rule of jus cogens and therefore void.

QUESTION FOUR

A problem requiring the application of certain principles of the law of treaties to a hypothetical factual situation.

a) Article 100 of State X's constitution provides that treaties providing for the stationing of foreign military forces on State X's soil must first be approved by State X's legislature. In 1990 representatives of State X and State Y met to negotiate a treaty which would define the jurisdictional rights which State X and State Y might exercise over members of State Y's army who are stationed in State X in accordance with a treaty which was concluded between the two States in 1950. They adopted and signed a treaty. The treaty provides that it 'will enter into force upon the exchange of instruments of ratification'. In 1991 the treaty was submitted to State X's parliament for approval. The parliament approved it. In 1992 State X and State Y exchanged instruments of ratification. State Y's instrument of ratification was accompanied by certain statements to the effect that certain clauses of the treaty 'must be interpreted' in a particular manner.

A member of State X's parliament seeks your advice as to whether State X is bound by the treaty and, if so, whether it may free itself from it.

b) What role or roles, if any, may be accorded to the travaux préparatoires (preparatory work) of a treaty in the interpretation of that treaty? When, if at all, can they be used to give to a treaty a meaning different from that which is suggested by an examination of its text?

University of London LLB Examination
(for External Students) Public International Law June 1993 Q4

General Comment

A question in two parts, each of them concentrating on a different aspect of the law of treaties. Care must be taken properly to focus on the exact aspects required for each part, although fortunately each is quite separate from the other and both relate to their aspects in a narrow way which makes it easy to exclude irrelevant material.

Skeleton Solution

a) The effect of a second treaty succeeding the first one – the effect of ratification – the effect of reservations – the possibility of withdrawal.

b) The interpretation of treaties – the effect of travaux préparatoires on interpretation.

Suggested Solution

a) The Treaty of 1990 between State X and State Y was made in the shadow of the original treaty of 1950 between the two States and relates to much the same subject-matter. Under art 30(3) of the Vienna Convention on the Law of Treaties 1969 the 1990 treaty can effectively be regarded as superseding the 1950 one in view of the fact that the earlier treaty has not apparently been terminated or suspended. Thus the fact that the earlier treaty was made before the enactment of the Vienna Convention in 1969 is irrelevant, notwithstanding art 4 of the Convention relating to the non-retroactivity of the Convention with respect to treaties concluded before 1969; the 1990 treaty to all intents and purposes replaces the 1950 one on the subject-matter in question.

There is no problem with the provision in the treaty that it shall enter into force 'upon the exchange of instruments of ratification' – art 24(1) of the Convention states: 'A treaty enters into force in such a manner and upon such a date as it may provide or as the negotiating States may agree.' Thus the exchange of instruments of ratification between State X and State Y has the effect of rendering the treaty operative.

The main problem concerns State Y's inclusion in its instrument of ratification of what amounts to a reservation to the treaty concerning its interpretation. State X is bound by the treaty by the act of accepting State Y's instrument of ratification (in accordance with art 14 of the Convention), so the question is whether State X can invoke State Y's reservation as justification for unilaterally withdrawing from the treaty. Article 19 of the Convention expressly allows the formulation of a reservation upon ratification and adds that in the absence of any provision in the treaty dealing with reservations – which appears to be the case here – reservations are only prohibited if they are incompatible with the 'object and purpose' of the treaty, so prima facie State X seems to have no right to protest.

However, it is considered that the effect of reservations on a bilateral treaty in fact amounts to a counteroffer which can be accepted or rejected by the other party, so State X's best course of action would be to express its objections to State Y's reservations and suggest a return to the negotiating table to attempt an amicable solution to the problem. It follows that it would be pointless and self-defeating of State X to withdraw from the treaty as that would have the effect of rendering the whole treaty null and void due to a material breach under art 60(3)(a) of the Convention; such a move by State X would be ill-advised, unless of course it is State X's intention to nullify the whole treaty ... which is unlikely. This course of action might also result in State Y going to the International Court of Justice. It would in any case be very difficult for State X to justify withdrawal in the terms of art 56 of the Convention, assuming that the treaty contains no provisions for withdrawal.

b) The difficult problem of the interpretation of treaties is the subject of three main jurisprudential theories: the first goes back to the intentions of the parties as the most important consideration; the second stresses the ordinary meaning of the words in the actual text of the treaty, regarding them as sacrosanct; and the third prefers to consider the aims and objectives of the treaty as a whole. The three theories are not intended to be mutually exclusive.

The principal provision on treaty interpretation contained in the Vienna Convention is to be found in art 31(1), which lays particular emphasis on good faith in conjunction with the second and third theories. So good faith, the ordinary meaning of the words 'in their context ... in the light of' the treaty's object and purpose are paramount. International case law, on the whole, has varied the focus of art 31(1) slightly: in the *Interpretation of Peace Treaties Case (Second Phase)* (1950) ICJ Rep 65, the International Court of Justice refused to consider the object and purpose of the treaty in such a way as to override the clear meaning of the text; and in the *Ambatielos Arbitration: Greece* v *UK* (1956) 12 RIAA 83 the ICJ applied the same approach in a less extreme formulation.

The specific question to be addressed here is the effect of the travaux préparatoires in interpreting a treaty – and, in particular, whether consideration of the travaux préparatoires can in any way supplant the ordinary meaning of the words in the text of the treaty. Article 32 of the Convention states that 'supplementary means of interpretation' (including travaux préparatoires) may be used either to confirm the meaning resulting from an application of art 31 or to determine the meaning when an art 31 interpretation either leaves the meaning 'ambiguous or obscure' or leads to a result which is 'manifestly absurd or unreasonable'. The Vienna Conference eventually decided not to permit the use of travaux préparatoires on an equal footing with the formula adopted in art 31(1), but instead to classify them as a supplementary aid of particular use in cases where art 31 proves inadequate.

From this we can deduce that perhaps the greatest value of travaux préparatoires is as evidence of the intentions of the parties when drafting and negotiating a treaty. However, it should be noted that there are one or two pitfalls to be avoided with this technique: in the *Territorial Jurisdiction of the International Commission of the River Oder Case* (1929) 5 AD 339, the Permanent Court of International Justice ruled part of the travaux préparatoires of the Treaty of Versailles in 1919 to be inadmissible because not all the parties to the case had participated in the drafting of the treaty. An even more serious interpretational problem would arise if the travaux préparatoires, resorted to for the purposes of confirmation, actually contradicted the clear meaning of the text outright. (On the other hand, logically, there would not be any need at all to resort to the travaux préparatoires for confirmation if the text were already 'clear', as such a scenario implies – why bother to confirm something that is already adequately clear?)

The most satisfactory resolution of this controversy seems to be that, when interpreting a treaty, travaux préparatoires can only be used in such a way as to deviate from the apparent meaning of the text if the conditions of art 32 are met: namely, that an art 31 interpretation is totally unsatisfactory.

QUESTION FIVE

a) In 1988 twenty States concluded the Treaty on the Suppression of Racketeering. Article 2 of the Treaty requires parties to the Treaty to make racketeering a criminal offence. Article 3 imposes on each party an obligation either to prosecute, or else to extradite to a State which requests it, any person found within its territory whom there is reasonable cause to suspect of having committed acts of racketeering. Article 12 provides that the Treaty will enter into force once it has been ratified by ten states.

In January 1992 State K sent to the depositary of the Treaty an instrument of ratification. This instrument includes a statement to the effect that, notwithstanding its ratification of the Treaty, State K is to remain free not to apply Articles 2 and 3 to persons who are engaged in a struggle of national liberation. State K is the tenth State to send to the depositary an instrument ratifying the Treaty. In June 1992 State L, which ratified the Treaty in 1989, sends to the depositary a letter stating that the statement contained in State K's instrument of ratification is 'so repugnant to the spirit of the Treaty that State L is unable to accept State K's ratification as valid until that statement is withdrawn'.

Advise State M: (i) whether the Treaty is now in force; and (ii) what are the actual or potential effects of State K's statement and State L's note.

b) In 1985 State N and State O, together with fifty other states, concluded the Treaty on Laser Weapons. Article 2 provides that parties to the Treaty undertake to refrain from the design, development, testing and deployment of laser weapons. Article 15 provides that the Treaty is to remain in force indefinitely. State N signed the Treaty in 1985 and ratified it in 1990. State O acceded to the Treaty in 1986.

State O has recently learned that, between 1987 and 1989, State N designed and built a laser weapon and that it tested that device in 1991. Fearing that State N's army has gained a laser weapon capability and wishing to develop laser weapons of its own, State O's army enquires of the foreign ministry what steps, if any, might be taken to free State O from its commitment in Article 2 of the Treaty.

Advise State O's foreign ministry.

University of London LLB Examination
(for External Students) Public International Law June 1992 Q8

General Comment

This is a two-part problem-based question requiring a descriptive analysis of the principles applicable to the law of treaties. A thorough knowledge of the Vienna Convention on the Law of Treaties 1969 is required.

Skeleton Solution

a) Principles regulating reservations formulated by the ICJ in the *Reservations to the Convention on Genocide Case* – the test of 'compatibility' – arts 19 and 20 of the Vienna Convention on the Law of Treaties – potential effects of the reservation and the corresponding note.

b) Entry into force of the treaty; difference between signature and ratification; legal effects – modification of treaty obligations in the event of a material breach of its provisions: art 60(1) – fundamental change of circumstances: art 62(2).

Suggested Solution

a) The statement made by State K in its instrument of ratification is a reservation. A reservation is defined in art 2(1) of the Vienna Convention on the Law of Treaties 1969 as a unilateral statement, however phrased, made by a state, when signing, ratifying, accepting or acceding to a treaty, whereby it purports to exclude or to modify the legal effect of certain provisions of the treaty in their application to that state. The effects of the reservation have to be assessed according to the rules of law elaborated by the International Court in the *Reservations to the Convention on Genocide Case* (1951) ICJ Rep 15 and those contained in the 1969 Convention.

In the *Genocide Case* the International Court held that a state which has made a reservation to an international agreement which has been objected to by one or more of the parties to the convention, but not by all the parties to the agreement, can be regarded as a party to the convention if the reservation is compatible with the object and purpose of the agreement.

The Court also introduced the test of 'compatibility' which allowed individual states to determine their relationship to states making reservations to treaties. If a party objects to the reservation on the basis that it is incompatible with the object and effect of the convention, it can consider the country making the reservation not to be a party to the convention. If, on the other hand, a party accepts the reservation, it must consider the reserving state to be a party to the convention.

The Vienna Convention largely codified these principles but contains more detailed rules to assist determination of the effects of reservations.

To allow a distinction to be drawn between those reservations that are compatible with the object and purpose of a convention from those that are incompatible, art 19 establishes a distinction between permissible and impermissible reservations. Impermissible reservations are reservations that are expressly prohibited by the treaty, or which do not fall within the scope of the specific reservations permitted by the convention, or which are incompatible with the objects and purpose of the convention.

But there are no guidelines to help determine whether a reservation is incompatible with the object and purpose of a treaty. While State L asserts that the reservation is repugnant to the spirit of the treaty, no other state has made such an assertion. Certainly State M does not consider this to be the case otherwise it would have adopted a more aggressive posture towards the making of the reservation.

If the reservation is incompatible with the spirit and purpose of the treaty, it would constitute an impermissible reservation and would render State K's instrument of ratification null and void in which case the treaty would not have entered force and State K would not be a party to the agreement.

If the reservation is compatible, and therefore permissible, art 20(4) of the convention provides that a reservation entered by one contracting party will not prevent the entry into force of an agreement so long as at least one other contracting party accepts the reservation. It is therefore open to State K, or any other contracting party for that matter, to accept the reservation which will bring the treaty into force. If State K does not accept the reservation, the treaty will not enter force.

Acceptance by a contracting party of a reservation constitutes a binding obligation between accepting and reserving states as regards the terms contained in the treaty. So, in these circumstances, State K and State M are both legally bound by the terms of the treaty.

The position is slightly different as regards State K and State L. An objection by a state to a reservation precludes the entry into force of the treaty as between the objecting and reserving states if the intention is expressed by the objecting state that no legal obligation will exist between them. In other words, State L will not be able to enforce the terms of the convention against State K.

Naturally, State K's reservation is ineffective in relation to the contractual obligations among the other contracting parties vis-a-vis themselves. It is only the legal relationship between the remaining states and State K that are affected by the reservation.

As regards State L's note, it is unlikely that it would act as a reservation to State L's instrument of ratification simply because it is a statement of intention to object to State K's reservation. It is not intended to be a reservation itself. In the *UK/France Continental Shelf Arbitration* (1979) 54 ILR 6, the international tribunal held that statements could be held to be reservations but only if they were intended to be interpretative. It is unlikely that State L's note would have such an effect.

b) State N and State O, along with 50 other states, are parties to the Treaty on Laser Weapons. State N was an original signatory, but did not deposit its instrument of ratification until five years later, while State O is bound by accession to its terms.

The first question raised is whether State N was entitled to engage in development of laser weapons after it had signed the agreement but before it deposited its instrument of ratification. This depends to a large extent on the express terms of the Treaty itself. Article 11 of the Vienna Convention on the Law of Treaties 1969 provides that the consent of a state to be bound by a treaty may be expressed by signature, exchange of instruments constituting a treaty, ratification, acceptance, approval or accession. In other words, a treaty enters force the moment that a sufficient number of states comply with its provisions regarding the expression of consent.

Signature of an agreement may indicate mere authentication of a text. At the same time, where signature is subject to ratification, acceptance or approval, the signature of a head of state to an agreement does not establish consent to be bound. In the *North Sea Continental Shelf Cases* (1969) ICJ Rep 3 the Federal Republic of Germany had signed the 1958 Convention on the Continental Shelf but had not ratified it. The International Court held that Germany was not bound by the terms of that agreement because the treaty expressly declared that signature was a preliminary step and ratification was required. Since Germany had merely signed and not ratified, it was not bound by the terms of the convention provisions.

Since State N deposited an instrument of ratification in 1990, it is likely that the treaty contained a provision making the signature of the agreement ineffective pending ratification. In these circumstances, State N was not legally bound by the terms of the treaty until 1990.

The only exception to this rule is where a treaty is declaratory of customary law. In other words, if the Treaty on Laser Weapons created a principle of custom, then State N would be bound by that principle at the moment it signed the treaty.

Whether or not the Treaty establishes such a principle depends on the number of contracting parties, their significance relative to weapons development, and whether the parties acted in the belief they were creating a rule of law.

While the actions of State N do not violate its obligations under the Treaty, it is liable for breach of the obligation of good faith. Article 18 of the Vienna Convention stipulates that the act of signing a treaty establishes an obligation of good faith on the part of a signatory. This duty extends to refraining from acts designed to frustrate the objects of the treaty. Since the treaty in question was intended to prevent research and development of laser weapons, it is clear that State N has frustrated the objects of the agreement by developing such a weapon.

State O may also be able to argue that the treaty is at an end by virtue of State N's conduct on two grounds: termination of a treaty through material breach; and termination by virtue of a fundamental change in circumstances.

It is generally recognised that a material breach of a bilateral treaty by one party entitles the other party to the treaty to invoke the breach as a ground for terminating the agreement: art 60(1) of the Vienna Convention. The position is more complicated in the case of multilateral agreements. Article 60(2) of the Convention establishes two consequences for a material breach of a multilateral agreement by a party. First, the other parties to the agreement may agree to suspend the operation of the treaty in whole or in part as long as there is unanimous agreement to this effect. Second, a party specially affected by a breach can invoke this as a ground for suspending the operation of the treaty in the relations between itself and the defaulting state.

In addition, the breach of the treaty must be deemed material to warrant repudiation. Under art 60(3) of the Vienna Convention a material breach consists of a repudiation of the treaty or a violation of a provision essential to the accomplishment of the object or purpose of the treaty. Clearly a material breach has occurred since the treaty itself was originally intended to prevent the development of laser weaponry which State N has subsequently done.

State O has therefore two alternatives in this respect. First, it can obtain the unanimous agreement of the remaining 49 parties to the Treaty to terminate the application of the Treaty to State N. Alternatively, State O can suspend the operation of the agreement as between itself and State N. Naturally, however, any development of laser weapons would place State O in violation of its obligations vis-a-vis the other parties to the Treaty.

The second possibility of terminating the Treaty arises from the principle of rebus sic stantibus which allows states to terminate the agreement if a fundamental change of circumstances arises. Article 62 of the Vienna Convention defines a fundamental change of circumstances as a situation which could not be foreseen by the parties at the time the negotiations were conducted. In the event that such a situation exists, a party can terminate an agreement if two conditions are met. First, the existence of the circumstances prevailing before must constitute an essential basis for the consent of the parties to be bound. Second, the effect of the changed circumstances is to radically transform the extent of the obligations still to be performed under the treaty.

The criteria for establishing the existence of a fundamental change of circumstances are therefore very stringent. However, it is likely that State O could legitimately argue that the non-existence of laser weapons at the time the treaty was negotiated constituted a situation which would continue given the nature of the terms of the agreement. The Treaty would have prevented the development of such weapons indefinitely and therefore the creation of such devices can validly be seen as a situation that was not envisaged at the time the Treaty was agreed. It is the nature of the absolute prohibition on development that gives this argument strength.

At the same time, the non-existence of such weapons obviously provided the essential basis for the negotiation of the agreement. No state would have consented to an absolute ban on the development of such weapons had they been aware that such weapons would be built in the very near future. Similarly the nature of the obligation contained in the Treaty has been radically transformed by this development.

Chapter 11
Human Rights

11.1   Introduction

11.2   Key points

11.3   Key cases and legislation

11.4   Questions and suggested solutions

11.1 Introduction

The individual has only gradually been acknowledged as a candidate for international legal rights and this recognition has been confined, on the whole, to the protection of human rights. Unfortunately, even human rights law still remains aspirational and hortatory. Effective mechanisms to remedy violations of human rights have only been established on a regional basis. As a result, the substantive and procedural processes of regional redress have grown in significance. However, this phenomenon should not be allowed to obscure the importance of the movement towards the universal protection of human rights with which students should remain acquainted.

11.2 Key points

Post-1945 protection of human rights

Throughout the nineteenth and early twentieth centuries, a number of limited attempts were made on an ad hoc basis to prohibit many of the most flagrant abuses of human rights.

Slavery

The General Act of the Brussels Conference for the Repression of the African Slave Trade 1890 confirmed that 'trading in slaves is forbidden in conformity with the principles of international law': see *Le Louis* (1817) 2 Dods 210. These principles were codified in the Slavery Convention 1926, 60 LNTS 253 (as amended by the Supplementary Convention on the Abolition of Slavery 1953, 266 UNTS 3).

The laws of war

These rules are designed to prevent excessive brutality in periods of armed conflict and developed in the customary practices of belligerents, eventually being codified in a series of Hague Conventions negotiated between 1899 and 1907. These have been extended by a number of instruments including the four Geneva Red Cross Conventions 1949 and the two Geneva Protocols 1977.

Protection of workers

Part XIII of the Treaty of Versailles 1919 founded the International Labour Organisation (ILO) which had as a mandate the promotion of better standards and conditions for workers. This organisation is empowered to draft conventions for the achievement of these goals and to supervise the application of these instruments.

Protection of minorities

The 1919 peace agreements with Austria, Bulgaria, Hungary and Turkey incorporated terms designed to protect minority groups within these states. In the *Minority Schools in Albania Case* (1935) PCIJ Rep Ser A/B No 64, the International Court observed:

'The idea underlying the treaties for the protection of minorities is to secure for certain elements incorporated in a state, the population of which differs from them in race, language or religion, the possibility of living peaceably alongside that population and cooperating amicably with it, while at the same time preserving the characteristics which distinguish them from the majority, and satisfying the ensuing special needs.'

However, although the League of Nations Council was empowered to determine infringements of these obligations, individual minorities had no locus standi as such before either the Council or the Permanent Court. In this context it is noteworthy that, in December 2003, the United Nations General Assembly requested the International Court of Justice to 'urgently render an advisory opinion' on the possible legal consequences that arise from the construction of the wall being built by Israel in the Occupied Palestinian Territory.

UN Protection of Human Rights: The Universal Declaration of Human Rights 1948

Article 55 of the UN Charter states that 'the United Nations shall promote ... universal respect for, and observance of, human rights and fundamental freedoms for all without distinction as to race, sex language, or religion'. As a first stage towards the implementation of this goal, the Universal Declaration of Human Rights was adopted by General Assembly Resolution 217A (III) on 10 December 1948 by a vote of 48 to 0, with eight abstentions (including the USSR, Saudi Arabia and South Africa).

The 30 articles of the Declaration deal with an extensive number of matters including: the liberty and security of the person (art 3); prohibitions on torture (art 5); equality before the law (art 7); effective remedies in law (art 8); due processes of law (arts 9 and 10); freedom from arbitrary interference with privacy (art 12); protection of the freedom of movement (art 13); protection of the freedom of expression (art 18); the right to work and equal pay (art 23); the right to social security (art 25); and the right to education: art 26.

The Declaration was not intended to be a legally binding treaty and the preamble clearly describes the document as 'a common standard of achievement for all peoples and nations'. However, it is less clear whether the Declaration represents, or has subsequently become binding as, customary law.

At the adoption of the Declaration, Eleanor Roosevelt, the chairperson of the UN Commission on Human Rights, expressly stated that the Declaration 'is not, and does not purport to be a statement of law or legal obligation' and she reiterated that the Declaration was intended as a common standard of achievement for all nations. Since the Declaration represents the first attempt to identify, on a universal basis, the law relating to the protection of human rights, it seems reasonably clear that the Declaration did not state or codify existing customary principles.

The Declaration has undoubtedly had a profound influence on the drafting of the constitutions of many states and also in the formation of subsequent human rights instruments. With these developments in mind, in the *Namibia (South-West Africa) Case* (1971) ICJ Rep 55, Vice-President Ammoun stated:

> 'Although the affirmations of the Declaration are not binding qua international convention ... they can bind states on the basis of custom ... whether because they constituted a codification of customary law or because they have acquired the force of custom through a general practice accepted as law.'

However, dicta from other sources have tended to refute this possibility. In the case *M v United Nations and Belgium* (1966) 45 ILR 446, a Belgian civil court declared:

> 'The Universal Declaration does not have the force of law. Its sole aim is to express the common ideal to be attained by all peoples and all nations, in order that by instruction and education respect for these rights and freedoms may be developed and that measures may be taken progressively to ensure that they are recognised and universally and effectively applied in the future ...'

Since 1966, two Protocols on Human Rights have been created which provide vehicles for full expression and participation of states in the protection of human rights. The Declaration has often been adduced to support other instruments in an attempt to prove a rule of customary law: see *Filartiga v Pena-Irala* 630 F 2nd 876 (1980) and *Sei Fujii v California* 38 Cal 2nd 718 (1952).

The Commission on Human Rights was not established by the Universal Declaration, but was created by the UN Economic and Social Council (ECOSOC) in 1946. This Commission receives private allegations of human rights violations and the governments concerned are invited to reply after being informed as to the nature of the complaint. The Commission may appoint ad hoc observer groups to investigate specific situations of human rights violation. In addition, the Commission performs drafting functions and prepares texts which codify and develop human rights law.

In the United Kingdom, the Human Rights Act 1998, which became effective on 2 October 2000, incorporated the European Convention on Human Rights into English law.

UN Protection of Human Rights: International Covenants on Human Rights 1966

In order to give binding force to the principles enunciated in the Universal Declaration, two treaties were drafted by the UN Commission on Human Rights: the International Covenant on Civil and Political Rights 1966 and the International Covenant on Economic, Social and Cultural Rights 1966, both of which entered into force in 1976.

Covenant on Civil and Political Rights 1966

This Covenant binds the parties as a treaty and gives force of law to the civil and political rights originally propounded in the Universal Declaration. The terms of the Covenant extend to 'all individuals within (a state's) territory and subject to its jurisdiction'. Rights guaranteed by the Covenant include: the right of self-determination (art 1); the right to non-discriminatory treatment (art 2); the right to life (art 6); prohibitions on torture and slavery (arts 7 and 8); the right to liberty and security of the person (art 9); and the right to freedom of movement: art 12.

A Human Rights Committee (HRC) was created in accordance with Part IV of the Covenant. This body consists of eighteen expert and independent members elected for terms of four years and with representation of the principal forms of civilisation in mind. The Committee receives reports from the parties to the Covenant which detail the measures adopted by these states in relation to the implementation of the rights under the Covenant. Initial reports are required within the first year of entry into force of the Covenant for the state in question and subsequent reports are required every five years. These reports are discussed by the Committee and state representatives, with consideration also being given to informal or unofficial reports from alternative sources. The Committee, under art 40(4), is permitted to make 'general comments as it may deem appropriate'.

State parties may recognise the competence of the Committee to entertain inter-state complaints where declarations have been made to that effect by both the defendant and complaining state under art 41. All domestic processes for settlement must be exhausted for the complaint to be valid. The Committee will attempt to resolve the issue, but, ultimately, art 42 allows for the appointment of an ad hoc Conciliation Commission with the consent of both parties. There is no provision for settlement by judicial processes.

The Optional Protocol to the Civil and Political Rights Covenant ((1967) 6 ILM 383) empowers the committee to receive communications from individuals alleging violations of the Covenant by parties to the Protocol. Neither the United Kingdom nor the United States has accepted the Optional Protocol. A competent communication must not be anonymous, it must concern a violation of a right under the Covenant and it must not relate to a matter already the subject of international processes: see the *Mauritian Women Case* (1981) Report of the Human Rights Committee, 114 and the *Weinberger Case* (1981) Report of the Human Rights Committee, 134.

The Secretary-General collates all the relevant materials and presents them to the Working Group on Communications of the Committee which decides the issue of admissibility. The Committee itself may hear issues relating to both the admissibility and the merits of the case. Proceedings are based on written submissions, there being no provision for oral hearings. The Committee fulfils an investigatory role by formulating views on the question of whether or not a violation of the Covenant has occurred and submits these to both the state concerned and the complainant. The views of the Committee are not binding, and no processes for enforcement or redress are contained in the Protocol.

Covenant on Economic, Social and Cultural Rights 1966

The provisions of this treaty do not have immediate effect, since art 2 provides that each state party need only implement measures to the maximum of its available resources 'with a view to achieving progressively the full realisation of the rights recognised in the ... Covenant'.

The rights endorsed in the Covenant include the right to self-determination (art 1), the right to work (arts 6 and 7), the right to social security (art 9), right to an adequate standard of living (art 11), right to education (art 13), the right to participate in cultural life and to enjoy the benefits of scientific progress: art 15.

State parties to this Covenant are required to submit reports 'in stages, in accordance with a programme to be established by the Economic and Social Council (ECOSOC) within one year of the entry into force of the present Covenant after consultation with the state parties and the specialised agencies concerned'. These reports are not submitted to the Human Rights Committee, but to ECOSOC, an organ of the United Nations. This reporting procedure is the only supervisory machinery provided for this agreement.

ECOSOC has the authority to transmit these reports to the UN Commission on Human Rights for studies, in order to make general recommendations, or as appropriate for information. Further, it may also submit to the General Assembly, from time to time, comments of a general nature made on state reports.

Additional United Nations human rights intruments

An extensive edifice has been created under United Nations auspices for the preservation of human rights in one form or another. Some establish independent bodies for investigation of allegations, whilst others remain silent on this issue.

a) Convention for the Prevention and Punishment of the Crime of Genocide 1948

According to this treaty, genocide, whether committed in times of war or peace, constitutes an international crime. No independent enforcement mechanism was established by the Convention, and persons charged with genocide may be tried by a competent tribunal in the state where the act was committed or by an international penal tribunal.

b) Convention for the Suppression of Traffic in Persons and of the Exploitation or the Prostitution of Others 1950

c) Convention on the Status of Refugees 1951

d) International Convention on the Elimination of All Forms of Racial Discrimination 1965

Under the terms of this agreement, a committee of eighteen experts was established to oversee the proper application of the agreement. State parties are required to submit reports on progress made towards the stated goals and the Committee may make recommendations and suggestions based on the reports. Article 11 allows for inter-state complaints.

e) International Convention on the Suppression of the Crime of Apartheid 1973

f) Declaration on the Protection of All Persons from Torture and Other Cruel, Inhuman or Degrading Treatment or Punishment 1975

g) Convention on the Elimination of All Forms of Discrimination Against Women 1979

A Committee is established under Article 22 of this agreement to ensure the proper implementation of the obligations assumed by states. Again reports must be submitted by the state parties and these are submitted with comments to the UN General Assembly.

Regional human rights arrangements

A number of arrangements for the protection of human rights have been consummated on a regional basis. Of these, the most important include:

a) The European Convention for the Protection of Human Rights and Fundamental Freedoms 1950 (including additional Protocols)

b) The Inter-American Convention on Human Rights 1969

This is administered by the Inter-American Commission on Human Rights (established by the Organisation of African States).

c) The Helsinki Declaration 1975

Adopted on August 1, 1975, by over 30 European states, Canada and the United States at the conference on Security and Co-operation in Europe, this document recognises in Part VII the need to respect human rights and fundamental freedoms.

d) The African Charter on Human and Peoples' Rights 1981

This instrument was adopted by the Organisation of African Unity (OAU) and creates an African Commission on Human and Peoples' Rights. This organ has a quasi-judicial status, dealing with both inter-state and individual petitions.

e)   The European Economic Communities

Respect for fundamental human rights has been recognised in both the Treaties establishing the European Communities and in the jurisprudence of the European Court of Justice. See *National Panasonic (UK)* v *EC Commission* [1980] ECR 2033. In the case *Nold* v *EC Commission* [1974] ECR 491, the European Court of Justice recognised that:

> 'Fundamental rights form an integral part of the general principles of law which [the Court] enforces ... The international treaties on the protection of human rights in which the member states have co-operated or to which they have adhered can also supply indications which may be taken into account within the framework of Community law.'

European Convention on Human Rights 1950

The European Convention for the Protection of Human Rights and Fundamental Freedoms was signed by the members of the Council of Europe on 4 November 1950, and entered into force in 1953. The Convention has a total of eight protocols.

The Convention establishes three organs:

a)   a Committee of Ministers;

b)   a European Commission on Human Rights; and

c)   a European Court of Human Rights.

Each party to the Convention appoints one member to the Commission, each to serve for a period of six years. This body is competent to receive both inter-state petitions (art 24) and individual applications: art 25. An individual application is only competent where the state being complained against has declared that it recognises the competence of the Commission to receive such complaints. Sixteen states have made declarations recognising this jurisdiction.

Where individual applications are competent, domestic remedies must be exhausted and the petition must be lodged with the Commission within six months of the final decision being rendered by the national tribunal. See *Donnelly* v *United Kingdom* (1973) (unreported, but cited at p212 of the Yearbook of the European Court of Human Rights). Article 27 requires that the Commission reject the application if:

a)   the application itself is anonymous;

b)   the complaint contains substantially the same subject matter as previously considered by the Commission;

c)   the grounds of complaint are incompatible with the Convention or the complaint is manifestly unfounded; or

d) the complaint is tantamount to an abuse of rights.

If the complaint is competent, the Commission examines the source of the alleged violation and is obliged by art 28 to attempt to achieve a friendly settlement of the dispute. If a solution is not reached, a comprehensive report is submitted to the Committee of Ministers in accordance with art 31 of the Convention. The Committee may then make a determination of its own on the merits of the matter and will indicate which corrective measures should be adopted by the state complained against. However, the Commission, within three months of the submission of the report, may also refer the matter to the European Court of Human Rights for a decision.

The European Court may only hear cases brought by the Commission or by a state party. But no case may be entertained by the Court unless jurisdiction has been recognised as compulsory in a declaration by the accused state or unless that state submits to jurisdiction. Individuals do not have direct access to the European Court and individual complaints must be adopted, processed and brought by the Commission. Over the past three decades, the Court has built up a substantial volume of jurisprudence in relation to human rights law.

Although art 53 of the Convention provides that 'the High Contracting Parties undertake to abide by the decision of the Court in any case to which they are parties', ultimately, the European Convention has only the sanction of public opinion pressure. No enforcement procedures have been established by the Convention in order to ensure the observance of decisions. Further, the European Convention does not form part of British law, and the judgments cannot be enforced in the British courts. See the dictum of Lord Denning in *R* v *Chief Immigration Officer, ex parte Bibi* [1976] 3 All ER 843 and also *Malone* v *Metropolitan Police Commissioner (No 2)* [1979] Ch 344.

The substantive rights contained in the European Convention

The Human Rights Act 1998 incorporates the ECHR into English law. Of particular importance are ss2 and 3 of the HRA 1998. Section 2 requires all courts and tribunals to take on board the jurisprudence of the European Court and the Human Rights Commission. Section 3 requires primary and secondary legislation to be read and given effect in a way which is compatible with Convention rights.

Article 1 of the European Convention requires contracting parties to extend the protection of the Convention to all persons within their respective jurisdictions. This protection takes the form of a guarantee that a number of basic human rights will be respected within their territories. These rights expressly include:

a) The right to life: art 2.

b) The right to freedom from torture and slavery (arts 3 and 4): see *Soering* v *United Kingdom* (1989) 11 EHRR 439.

c) The right to liberty and security of the person: art 5.

d) Right to due process of law (arts 6 and 7): see *Brogan and Others* v *United Kingdom* (1989) 11 EHRR 117 and *Golder* v *United Kingdom* (1975) ECHR Ser A No 18.

e) Right to privacy: art 8.

f) Right to freedom of thought, conscience and religion: art 9.

g) Freedom of expression (art 10): see *Observer & Guardian* v *United Kingdom* (1992) 14 EHRR 153.

h) Freedom of assembly and association: art 11.

i) The right to marriage and a family: art 12.

j) The right to an effective remedy in law: art 13.

k) The right to the non-discriminatory application of these rights and freedoms.

While exceptions to these general principles are applicable in certain circumstances, on the whole such exceptions must be proportionate to the objectives sought to be achieved and based in law.

The coming into force of the Human Rights Act 1998 has witnessed a distinct willingness on the part of the English courts to consider judgments by the European Court of Human Rights. An indication of the changing mood is examplified by *Barclays Bank plc* v *Ellis* (2000) The Times 24 October.

11.3 Key cases and legislation

* *Barclays Bank plc* v *Ellis* (2000) The Times 24 October
  The court applied Convention rights as a direct result of the Human Rights Act 1998

* *Brogan and Others* v *United Kingdom* (1989) 11 EHRR 117
  Considered the implications of art 5 of the European Convention

* *Democratic Republic of Congo* v *Belgium* (2002) 41 ILM 536
  National changes must be put in place in order to comply with international standards

* *Golder* v *United Kingdom* (1975) ECHR Ser A No 18
  The right to a fair and impartial trial under art 6 of the European Convention involved the right of a prisoner to free communication with legal counsel

* *Ireland* v *United Kingdom* (1978), ECHR Ser A No 25
  The only inter-state application to date considered by the Court

* *Observer & Guardian* v *United Kingdom* (1992) 14 EHRR 153
  The court assessed the implications of art 10 of the European Convention, ie freedom of expression

* *Soering* v *United Kingdom* (1989) 11 EHRR 439
  Held that art 3 of the European Convention is absolute and unqualified

- *Sunday Times (Thalidomide) Case* (1979) ECHR Ser A No 30
  An injunction obtained from the House of Lords contravened art 10 of the European Convention since it infringed on the freedom of expression

- European Convention on Human Rights 1950 – sets out basic human rights on a universal basis

- Human Rights Act 1998 – incorporates the European Convention on Human Rights into English law

- United Nations Charter 1945 – also provides for the protection of fundamental human rights

11.4 Questions and suggested solutions

QUESTION ONE

To what extent has the developing law of human rights eroded the 'reserved domain of domestic jurisdiction' as given expression in art 2(7) of the United Nations Charter?

University of London LLB Examination
(for External Students) Public International Law June 2000 Q6

General Comment

It is not unusual for a paper on public international law to focus upon a particular provision of the United Nations Charter 1945. The well prepared student should be able to say something about why the provision was included, and how it has been subsequently interpreted. To do this the candidate will need to know a little about the history of the United Nations in the years since 1945, and the circumstances in which the provisions of art 2(7) have been set aside in favour of other provisions in the United Nations Charter. The well structured answer will terminate with clear conclusions as to the circumstances in which it will not be possible to rely on art 2(7).

Skeleton Solution

Brief description of reasons to include art 2(7) – examine how human rights law has developed – examples of regional instability – principles of humanitarian intervention and its effects.

Suggested Solution

We are asked in this question to consider the terms of art 2(7) of the United Nations Charter. The precise words of the sub article read as follows:

'Nothing contained in the present Charter shall authorise the United Nations to intervene in matters which are essentially within the domestic jurisdiction of any State or shall require Members to submit such matters to settlement under the present Charter; but this principle shall not prejudice the application of enforcement measures under Chapter VII.'

This provision has given rise to more problems than perhaps any other under the United Nations Charter 1945; it should be borne in mind at the outset that it is not an original provision and it had its predecessor in art 15(8) of the Covenant of the League of Nations 1919. It is sensible to reflect on why such a provision was carried over in 1945 and inserted in the United Nations Charter. First, at the time the United Nations Charter was being drafted, a number of important states were still in control of colonial empires and were unwilling to submit to external probing, particularly as to the speed with which they were prepared to grant independence. Second, the provision itself was consistent with the general principle in public international law that a state was sovereign within its own territory. Third, the provision did contain an express exclusion in respect of enforcement measures taken under Chapter VII. Fourth, it has to be noted that the human rights movement was not as influential in 1945 as it is today. Lastly, the draftsmen of the Charter needed the co-operation of the Soviet Union; such a regime was unwilling to participate unless there were clear guarantees of non-interference in domestic affairs.

In considering the question of domestic jurisdiction it is necessary to differentiate the provisions of art 2(7) from those cases where one or other state party argues that the International Court of Justice should not determine a matter, because it is within the domestic jurisdiction of a state: see *Nationality Decrees in Tunis and Morocco* (1923) PCIJ Ser B No 4. One distinguishing feature of art 2(7) from the prior art 15(8) is that there is no reference to domestic jurisdiction being determined in accordance with international law. There had been some debate on this at San Francisco in 1945, but it was decided to omit any reference in the Article to international law. This has had little practical effect because it is for the relevant United Nations organs to determine whether a state is able to rely on art 2(7).

The meaning of art 2(7) has had to be worked out as a matter of practice. The general tendency has been to interpret the exclusion narrowly. Partly, this is a matter of logic and common sense. If a state is subject to criticism and United Nations action is urged, then the state with nothing to hide will normally defend the matter on the merits. Article 2(7) tends to be invoked by the state fearful of an independent investigation of the facts. For this reason, interpretation of art 2(7) has tended to be strict. This tendency began early in the history of the United Nations when the General Assembly wished to discuss aspects of decolonisation or the apartheid regime in South Africa. There was, in the early years, something of a dilemma; many new states had only recently been created out of colonial empires and were jealous of their newly acquired sovereignty. At the same time, apartheid was regarded as a uniquely objectionable social system and therefore outside art 2(7). In these circumstances South Africa was not able to successfully invoke art 2(7) to preclude discussion. Similarly, liberation conflicts in Algeria or Portuguese colonial territories were held to be outside art 2(7). Today, apart from the express exclusion, a matter will not be regarded as within the domestic jurisdiction if it represents a threat to regional peace, an infringement of international law or a violation of human rights. While of course votes in the General Assembly or Security Council are of influenced by 'political' considerations, the general tendency has been to determine 'domestic jurisdiction' as having a very narrow scope. The principle of intervention on humanitarian grounds has generally come to be accepted.

One can certainly note that the developing law of human rights has had an important impact on the interpretation of art 2(7). This development must be seen in the wider context; the basis of the nineteenth century Law of Nations had been that a state was sovereign within its own territory and not subject to interference by other states or by other international organisations. However, the basis of the development of international human rights law has been that a state agrees by treaty to meet certain standards and to submit to external authority. It is important to note that the United Nations Charter 1945 itself contains a number of references to human rights law, so it is clear that even in the original document, reliance on art 2(7) could only be limited. This ambiguity is explained by the fact that the United States was anxious to pursue policies of self-determination and decolonisation, but required the consent of colonial powers to establish the organisation. As many have noted there is a contradiction in the original document. Article 2(7) looks back to the nineteenth century Law of Nations, while other provisions anticipate the development of a modern law of human rights.

In considering art 2(7) it is sensible to remember that it excludes matters that might be the subject of a Chapter VII action. Since 1945 any form of aggression or international misconduct that is likely to cause regional instability cannot be regarded as a matter of domestic jurisdiction alone. As the quotation indicates, the scope of human rights law has increased considerably since 1945. Many of the provisions of the Universal Declaration of Human Rights 1948 have acquired the status of rules of customary international law. Further, even if this were disputed, many states have voluntarily entered into regional human rights treaties or signed instruments, such as the International Covenant on Civil and Political Rights 1966; such documents often provide for state reporting and individual applications. Increasingly the United Nations has taken the view that if a state has voluntarily entered into obligations on human rights (other than those in the United Nations Charter itself) then it is estopped from raising art 2(7) when questions of its own conduct arise for discussion. It is worth noting that this form of estoppel argument was one that appealed to the House of Lords in *R v Bow Street Metropolitan Stipendiary Magistrate, ex parte Pinochet Ugarte (No 3)* [2001] 1 AC 147 although in a slightly different context. It is also relevant to observe that, under the international economic structures put in place after Bretton Woods in 1944, many states will be receiving some form of financial assistance from United Nations agencies. In these circumstances it is felt that states should not be allowed to benefit from the efforts of international institutions without meeting minimum standards of conduct. If one examines the content of human rights law it is clear that many states have voluntarily agreed to submit to reporting obligations, to inter state complaints and to individual applications; in these circumstances it would be anomalous if their conduct could not even be discussed for fear of offending art 2(7).

A more technical point is that enforcement action is already specifically exempted under Chapter VII. As the draftsmen of the United Nations Charter realised, those states that abuse human rights are those that most threaten their neighbours. The connection between human rights abuse and regional instability was expressly stated by President Truman in his closing speech to the San Francisco Conference. First, abuses of human rights may lead to refugees and regional instability. Second, history since 1945 indicates that states that threaten their neighbours often do not hesitate to abuse their own citizens (eg Argentina in 1982). It may be today that the problem can only be discussed but, as in Chechnya, if a state raises art 2(7) this will not prevent the United Nations Commissioner on Human Rights seeking to visit, and international institutions may be urged to review funding arrangements. Indeed it is strongly arguable, as the Chechnya case illustrates, that art 2(7) is to some extent redundant. If a state behaves badly it is not necessary for the United Nations to intervene; it may react instead by imposing sanctions and influencing international agencies to withdraw support.

If one examines the history it is clear that the motivation for action has often been to sustain human rights, but the legal basis has been a Resolution passed under Chapter VII. As this is specifically provided for under art 2(7) it is clear that this provision was not intended to act as a barrier to action in appropriate cases. So Security Council Resolution 418 (1977) could impose an arms ban on South Africa as part of the attempt to persuade that State to end its apartheid system. Secondly, in 1991 the Kurdish population of Iraq were protected under Security Council Resolution 688 and Iraqi sovereignty was restricted because of evidence of human rights violations. In more recent times action has been taken on Somalia (Security Council Resolution 751 (1992)), Rwanda (Security Council Resolution 929 (1994)), and Haiti (Security Council Resolutions 841 (1993); 861 (1993); 867 (1993); 873 (1993); 875 (1993); and 940 (1994)). In all these cases the legal basis has been under Chapter VII and art 2(7) has not constituted an obstacle. What is equally important is that in all the cases the motivation was to try and restrain abuses of human rights. This tendency was continued in the numerous Resolutions passed in respect of Yugoslavia or Kosovo. All the evidence of the last three decades is that, where a humanitarian problem arises, then art 2(7) will not act as an obstacle. Indeed much of the debate in international law in recent years has not been about any infringement of sovereignty, but a failure of certain powers to provide the military forces to implement the Security Council Resolutions that have been passed.

If one returns to the precise quotation, a number of conclusions can be attempted. First, art 2(7) was inconsistent with other provisions of the United Nations Charter. Second, the development of human rights law has made it almost impossible to shield behind art 2(7). Third, the readiness to use powers under Chapter VII to authorise humanitarian intervention has further limited the force of art 2(7); so much so that the main complaint today is often not that sovereignty has been infringed, but that the United Nations has decided to intervene in some areas and not in others. This, however, is inevitable because states have different views on the need to intervene: strategic interests may differ, and in some cases public opinion will demand action and in others it will be indifferent. As some writers have indicated, there is a danger that intervention will be embarked upon when public opinion is outraged by media reports. If the violations take place far from Europe in a place inaccessible to the Western media, then pressure to act will not be so great. There is unlikely to be a universal standard for all occasions. The experience of the last two decades indicates that art 2(7) is of limited relevance. What is of relevance is the nature of the humanitarian problem and the willingness of powerful states to provide the resources to enable United Nations action to be effective. The most damaging outcome for international law is where Resolutions are passed, but resources are not made available to enforce the will of the Security Council. It is noteworthy that the last two Secretary Generals of the United Nations have expressed concern about the willingness to pass Resolutions and the reluctance of some states to make military contributions.

Our conclusion on this matter is that the importance of art 2(7) has been displaced by a number of pressures, including the desire to curb regional instability, the wish to promote human rights and the present enthusiasm for humanitarian intervention.

QUESTION TWO

The State of Imperia is ruled by a military junta which scheduled an election for February of this year as part of a plan to transfer power to civilian rule. In January there were two demonstrations which led to violent clashes between police and political party workers. Shortly thereafter the Government cancelled the election, citing the 'malign influence of subversive elements threatening law and order'. Mr Pax, a newspaper publisher, criticised the Government on the front page of his newspaper, arguing that his 'human right to multiparty elections' had been violated by the cancellation. The next day his newspaper was closed down by the police invoking powers under the Public Order Act. Mr Pax unsuccessfully sought to challenge the closure before the local Federal Court, but has not brought an appeal before the Constitutional Court because he has been advised by a friend that the Constitutional Court is 'packed with junta men'. He now seeks your advice on remedies which may be available to him under international human rights law.

Imperia is party to the International Covenant on Civil and Political Rights 1966, the Optional Protocol to the Covenant, and the African Charter on Human and Peoples' Rights 1981.

Advise Mr Pax.

University of London LLB Examination
(for External Students) Public International Law June 1999 Q5

General Comment

It is normal for a paper on public international law to include a question on human rights law. In this particular question the candidate is expected to know a little about both the International Covenant on Civil and Political Rights 1966 (ICCPR) and the African Charter on Human and Peoples' Rights 1981 (ACHPR). Those who answer the question will need to know about the various methods by which a human rights treaty may be enforced. In brief these are (a) by reporting mechanisms, (b) by inter state complaint, and (c) by individual action. The question also raises the difficult issue of the obligation to exhaust internal remedies, as Mr Pax has failed to avail himself of a method of appeal that was open to him.

Skeleton Solution

The Government of Imperia – the conduct of the newspaper– rights of property – action under the ICCPR – action under the ACHPR– exhaustion of internal remedies – conclusion.

Suggested Solution

We are asked in this matter to advise Mr Pax in respect of the various problems that have arisen. We are informed that Imperia is a signatory to the International Covenant on Civil and Political Rights 1966 (ICCPR) and the African Charter on Human and Peoples' Rights 1981 (ACHPR). It is sensible to take each of the various matters in chronological order.

The Government of the State of Imperia

The United Nations has from the outset favoured representative government. Imperia has operated a military junta which violates ICCPR 1966 (art 25) and ACHPR 1981: art 13. In a functioning democracy it is reasonable to allow political demonstrations and this is acknowledged by ICCPR 1966 in arts 18, 19 and 21 which respect the right of assembly, and also ACHPR 1981 in arts 9 and 11. The decision to cancel the intended elections violates ICCPR 1966 (art 25) and ACHPR 1981: art 13.

The conduct of the newspaper

The freedom of the press is viewed as an important aspect of representative government; the conduct of the Government violates ICCPR 1966 (art 19(2)) and ACHPR 1981: art 9(2). It is arguable that the Government might seek to rely on the national security limitations contained in ICCPR 1966 (art 19(3)) and ACHPR 1981: art 29.

Rights of property

It is arguable that the closure of the newspaper represents an interference with property rights. Although these are not expressly stated in the ICCPR 1966, a right of enjoyment of property is included in art 14 of the ACHPR 1981 which provides that it may only be encroached upon 'in the interest of public need or in the general interest of the community'. In principle any limitation on the general presumption of a right to property should be interpreted narrowly.

Action in the courts of Imperia

It appears that Mr Pax has failed in his action before the local Federal Court. In principle he should have exercised his right of appeal to the Constitutional Court. Rather than act on legal advice, Mr Pax has paid attention to the opinions of a friend. The relevance of this is that it is a general principle of international law, and of human rights treaties, that available internal remedies should be exhausted. I will return to this point below.

Action on the international plane

It seems that the two basic grievances of Mr Pax are (a) the cancellation of the elections, and (b) the closing down of his newspaper. It is sensible to distinguish between action under the ICCPR and action under the ACHPR; we shall look at each matter in turn.

Action under the ICCPR 1966

Imperia will be subject to reporting obligations under art 40 of the ICCPR 1966: it would be possible for Mr Pax or his supporters to supply information to the Human Rights Committee. If Imperia has made a declaration under art 41 then another state may bring a complaint to the Human Rights Committee alleging that Imperia has failed to meet its obligations under the treaty. Further, as Imperia has signed the Optional Protocol, then an individual complaint may be made, although this depends on exhausting all internal remedies: see art 2, First Optional Protocol.

Action under the ACHPR 198

A state party to the African Charter on Human and Peoples' Rights 1981 may make a complaint under arts 47–49; this may be done by communicating with Imperia or the Secretary General of the Organisation of African Unity, or the Chairman of the African Commission on Human and Peoples' Rights. It is also possible for an individual complaint to be made directly to the African Commission on Human and Peoples' Rights: see arts 55–56. However, once again there is a requirement that there should have been an attempt to exhaust internal remedies: see arts 50 and 56(6).

The failure to exhaust internal remedies

Action on the international plane normally depends on the applicant having exhausted internal remedies, and this principle is restated in both the International Covenant on Civil and Political Rights 1966 and the African Charter on Human and Peoples' Rights 1981. In each case it is a question of fact and degree, but this requirement remains an important principle of international law: see the *ELSI Case* (1989) ICJ Rep 15. It must be open to question as to whether Mr Pax has done so, and the onus of showing he has done so will fall upon him. First, there is no objective evidence that an appeal was obviously futile: see *Finnish Ships Arbitration: Finland v Great Britain* (1934) 3 RIAA 1479. Second, Mr Pax did not act on legal advice but on the personal non-expert opinion of a friend. Third, there seems no evidence that an appeal to the Constitutional Court would have been unduly delayed. Fourth, there seems to be no evidence that the Constitutional Court lacked the authority to overrule the Federal Court. It seems that there was still a possibility of appeal: see the *Interhandel Case: Switzerland v USA* (1959) ICJ Rep 6. Fifth, all the evidence indicates that the claim Mr Pax wishes to pursue on the international plane is identical to that he was bringing in Imperia. Lastly, the advice of the friend was incomplete. In many legal systems the executive branch plays a role in nominating judges to the highest court: indeed this is so even in the United States. What matters is not who appointed such judges, but whether the important constitutional principle of the independence of the judiciary is in operation.

Conclusion

Our advice to Mr Pax is that a claim brought on the international plane might be very difficult because of the failure to exhaust internal remedies. Although the time for appeal has now passed, he should apply for leave to apply out of time to the Constitutional Court in Imperia. If the application is granted he should argue his appeal. If the application is refused he could consider action on the international plane.

QUESTION THREE

Redland and Beigeland are parties to the International Covenant on Civil and Political Rights, as well as the First Optional Protocol. Blueland is not party to the Covenant.

Johnson, a national of Beigeland, is alleged to have killed the parents of his employer in the state of Blueland. He was subsequently arrested in Redland and his extradition was sought to Blueland, which has a mandatory death penalty for murder. Were he to be extradited to Blueland, Johnson might face the death penalty and the usual wait of six to eight years on death row prior to execution. The Blueland state prosecutor has secured an extradition order in a lower court of Redland, but Johnson has appealed to the Redland Supreme Court on the grounds that extradition to Blueland would result in cruel, inhuman and degrading treatment in violation of Article 7 of the Covenant. He is advised that his appeal may take up to six years and that he would be entitled to legal aid, although he has no private means to employ counsel. He has expressed a desire to be tried in the criminal courts of Beigeland, which may exercise jurisdiction over his case by reason of his nationality. He now seeks your advice on whether a complaint lodged with the Human Rights Committee under the First Optional Protocol will meet with success.

Advise Johnson.

University of London LLB Examination
(for External Students) Public International Law June 1997 Q6

General Comment

Given the importance of the law of human rights it is unusual for a paper in public international law not to contain a question on some aspect of the subject. The problem for the student is that the subject is so broad that the examiner has such a wide area to pick from. In this question the examiner requires the candidate to give practical legal advice to Johnson as to the options open to him. The sensible approach in advising an individual is to go through the case in chronological order and identify the possible grounds of legal challenge. A candidate would find this question much easier to deal with if he were familiar with the facts of *Soering* v *United Kingdom*.

This was a case decided under the European Convention on Human Rights, but it indicates that the correct advice to give to Johnson is to pursue all remedies available to him. In answering the question the student should be aware of the general requirement in the law of extradition for the requesting State to produce evidence of a prima facie case.

Skeleton Solution

The extradition request by Blueland – Johnson's presence in Redland – making a complaint under the International Covenant on Civil and Political Rights 1966 – the attitude of Beigeland – the attitude of the Human Rights Committee.

Suggested Solution

We are asked in this problem to advise Johnson in respect of a number of matters. Johnson, a national of Beigeland, is now subject to an order of a lower court in Redland that he be extradited to Blueland to stand trial for the unlawful killing of two persons. To preserve his position, Johnson should give immediate notice of appeal to the Supreme Court of Redland. In advising Johnson we can isolate a number of aspects.

The extradition request by Blueland

In accordance with normal principles relating to criminal jurisdiction, Blueland are entitled to assert the right to try crimes committed within their territory. Provided a valid extradition treaty is in force, and provided prima facie evidence has been submitted, then it is not unreasonable for the lower court in Redland to have made the order that it did.

Johnson's presence in Redland

It is unclear whether any implementing legislation has been passed in Redland to implement any regional human rights treaty. In any event the executive of Redland should be informed that they have responsibilities towards Johnson as a person present within the territory: see art 2 International Covenant on Civil and Political Rights (ICCPR) 1966. Therefore, Johnson should first lodge notice of appeal to the Supreme Court of Redland, and then request a hearing date for the appeal. If it is confirmed that no appeal can be heard for six years then Johnson should proceed to the next step.

Making a complaint

In the absence of satisfaction Johnson should bring an individual complaint against Redland by virtue of art 1 of the First Optional Protocol. It is correct that in normal circumstances one must exhaust internal remedies, but in cases of unreasonable delay this is not required: art 5(2)(b) First Optional Protocol.

It is certainly arguable that the inexplicable delay of six years constitutes a failure to treat with dignity (art 10 ICCPR), and a failure to offer any form of legal representation in an appeal concerning a capital offence is likely to be viewed most seriously: see art 14

ICCPR; *Robinson* v *Jamaica* (1989) MRC Rep 241. The possible extradition to Blueland, where there is a mandatory death sentence in all convictions for murder, may be regarded as a potential infringement of art 7 by Redland. A breach of art 7 ICCPR is one of the grounds of appeal to the Redland Supreme Court, but the validity of that ground within the municipal law of Redland will be determined by the content of the internal law. For such a ground to be valid in Redland, implementing legislation would in all likelihood have to have been passed. In these circumstances the sensible course is for Johnson to make a complaint to the Human Rights Committee.

The attitude of Beigeland

We are not told whether Redland and Beigeland have made declarations under art 41 ICCPR. If such declarations have been made then Beigeland could bring a complaint against Redland in respect of both the substance and the procedural delay. The excessive delay would enable a complaint to be made even though internal remedies have not been exhausted: art 41(1)(c) ICCPR.

A second matter arises as to the possible trial venue. It is highly unlikely that Beigeland is appropriate. Following the approach in *Soering* v *United Kingdom* (1989) 11 EHRR 439 it is possible to form a view as to the relevant factors. The crime was committed in Blueland, all the available evidence is in Blueland and the first request for extradition was made by Blueland.

There is, however, a more important practical consideration. In international law the normal practice is for an extradition treaty to stipulate that the State seeking extradition should provide prima facie evidence of a crime; this evidence cannot be presented by Beigeland. We will therefore be obliged to advise Johnson that there is no principle that allows the accused to determine the trial venue and that he will eventually be tried in Blueland.

The attitude of the Human Rights Committee

On the available facts it is clear that the Human Rights Committee are likely to consider the case of Johnson. We should demand that Redland agree that no extradition take place pending a ruling by the Human Rights Committee and a determination of the appeal in Redland. We will, however, have to advise Johnson that, as in the *Soering* case, the best outcome that he can hope for is that he is extradited by Redland to Blueland after Blueland has been forced to give an assurance that the death penalty would not be sought by the prosecution.

QUESTION FOUR

To what extent do individuals possess procedural capacity in global and regional regimes established for the protection of human rights?

University of London LLB Examination
(for External Students) Public International Law June 1996 Q6

General Comment

This is a rather narrow question which involves an analysis of the various procedural devices by which an individual may raise the issue of human rights violations and possibly seek compensation. The candidate should be familiar with the main international and regional treaties in this area. In addition knowledge of the avenues available before UN committees and commissions is needed.

Skeleton Solution

Introduction: theory of the individual as a subject in international law – UN Charter and the human rights provisions therein: UDHR – First Optional Protocol, Civil and Political Covenant and workings thereof – UN Commission on Human Rights: Res 1503 – ECHR: art 25 and the workings thereof; art 26 – American Convention on Human Rights – conclusion.

Suggested Solution

The traditional theory of international law from the time of the Peace Treaty of Westphalia 1648 until the end of the 1914–18 war subscribed to the view that only States were subjects of international law. This standpoint has, however, been challenged since the end of the 1914–18 War. Under the 'minority treaties' enacted under the umbrella of the 1919 Peace Agreement individuals were given standing and in its Advisory Opinion relating to the *Danzig Postal Service* ((1925) PCIJ Rep Ser B No 11) the Permanent Court of International Justice (PCIJ) stated that there was nothing in international law to prevent individuals from being granted rights under a treaty.

It was with the end of the Second World War that individuals were granted a significant increase in the number of instances in which they could initiate proceedings in order to protect their rights. This was, however, a gradual process and at first the UN contented itself with establishing international standards for the protection of human rights. Reference to the concept of human rights is found in the UN Charter. The Preamble to the Charter states that the Peoples of the UN reaffirm their 'faith in fundamental human rights ... in the equal rights of men and women'. Article 1(3) of the Charter lists among the main purposes of the UN the achievement of international cooperation:

> 'In promoting and encouraging respect for human rights and for fundamental freedoms for all without distinction as to race, sex, language or religion.'

Article 55 States that the UN shall promote:

> 'Universal respect for and observance of human rights and fundamental freedoms for all without distinction as to race, sex, language or religion.'

Article 56 talks about members of the UN pledging themselves to take joint and separate action in co-operation with the organisation to achieve the purposes set out in art 55.

Further, the Universal Declaration of Human Rights (UDHR) set out a 'charter' of those rights which it was hoped would be respected by the world community. It was a standard-setting document and was not intended to be legally binding. The Member States of the UN were reluctant to establish any enforcement mechanisms for the protection of human rights and moreover the (then) Soviet Union and the countries of the 'Eastern Bloc' (as it was then known) denied that individuals were subjects of international law. Any procedural capacity of individuals in this area, the Soviet Union argued, would be a violation of national sovereignty and would conflict with art 2(7) of the UN Charter which forbids intervention in the domestic affairs of States.

The UN therefore proceeded cautiously in this area and separated the issue of putative individual capacity form that of standard setting and inter-state complaints. The International Covenant of 1966 on Civil and Political Rights reflects this approach. The First Optional Protocol to the Civil and Political Covenant is just that. This is a separate document and requires separate ratification from the Covenant. The Protocol establishes the procedure whereby an individual may make a complaint to the 18-person Human Rights Committee (HRC) established under the Covenant. The individual will have to make out a case that his/her rights as set out in the Covenant have been violated: if this is not the case then the application may be declared inadmissible. The individual has to comply with the requirement of exhausting local remedies, which is a standard requirement before international proceedings are initiated: *Ambatielos Arbitration (Greece v United Kingdom)* (1956) 12 RIAA 83.

The international procedure is not, however, comparable to an individual bringing a case before a domestic tribunal, as the Human Rights Committee is not a court and it has no power to compel the allegedly errant State to appear or to provide the necessary documentation. Further, any decision that the Committee may reach does not bind the State. Thus the individual has procedural capacity to bring his case before the Committee if the State so wishes and has ratified the Optional Protocol, but that does not guarantee any resolution of the action.

The UN has also attempted to put in place other means of human rights enforcement (in the broad sense of the word) to assist the individual. This has been initiated by means of investigation and reporting without the necessity of a State having had to ratify a treaty or covenant. Since 1971 the Commission on Human Rights has been able to debate complaints submitted to it by the Sub-Commission on Prevention of Discrimination and Protection of Minorities. The Sub-Commission is authorised by Res 1503 to form a working group to examine individual petitions relating to violations of human rights received by the Secretary General of the UN, and to then report to the Sub-Commission the violations which appear to reveal a 'consistent pattern of gross and reliably attested violations of human rights'. Reference on to the Commission could then follow. Whether or not this is a worthwhile procedure for the individual to follow is open to question. The standards of application of this procedure have not been universal and any attempt to introduce alternative procedures other than judicial or even quasi-judicial raises an issue of political pressure.

The regional picture, at least in Europe, is much more satisfactory. By art 25 the European Convention on Human Rights entitles the European Commission on Human Rights to receive petitions from individuals. Firstly the Commission must decide whether the petition is admissible. The individual must be a victim. The applicant cannot complain of a violation to which he is a 'stranger'. This issue was discussed in *Dudgeon* v *United Kingdom* (1981) 4 EHRR 149 in which the applicant, a United Kingdom citizen resident in Northern Ireland, was subject to a police search of his flat for evidence relating to illegal possession of drugs. When lawfully present in his flat they seized material concerning his homosexual activities (then a criminal offence in Northern Ireland). The police returned the material and decided not to prosecute. He nevertheless convinced the Court (ECHR), by a majority, that the possibility of a prosecution for homosexual activities made him a victim, although no prosecutions had been brought in the immediate years proceeding this case.

The victim must also have exhausted all domestic remedies (art 26), a requirement which is relatively easy to fulfil as regards the United Kingdom because the absence of a Bill of Rights means that the issue may be conclusively dealt with by a court of first instance.

The majority of cases brought before the Commission are, however, declared inadmissible as they do not raise an issue within the terms of the European Convention or the matter is substantially the same as a matter which has already been examined by the Commission: art 27(1)(b). Moreover, only States or the Commission may refer a case to the Court: art 44. It is, however, proposed that individuals will have the right to bring a case before the Court. It should be stressed though that the capacity of the individual to bring a case before the Commission and the subsequent hearings by the Court has provided a stronger impetus to the development of the jurisprudence of the Convention than the inter-State procedure.

Those States which have ratified the European Convention cannot opt out of the inter-State complaint procedure but may choose not to make an optional declaration allowing individual petition, while the reverse is true with the American Convention on Human Rights. On ratification of the American Convention the States agree to the compulsory nature of the individual petition procedure whereby the matter is dealt with by the Inter-American Commission of Human Rights. The jurisdiction of the Courts is, however, optional and, as with all treaties, the rights of the individual (whether substantive or procedural) depend upon whether the State concerned wishes to ratify the treaty in the first place.

The trend in international human rights organisations and even international institutions with a wider brief is to grant individuals locus standi in matters concerning the interpretation of their rights under a treaty. The European Council, for instance, proposed in Protocol 11 to make a citizen's direct right of appeal mandatory, thereby allowing automatic access to the European Court of Human Rights, while the UN Human Rights Commission and its Sub-Commission have been active in hearing allegations from individuals which allegedly show 'widespread and serious human rights abuses'. All the above should nevertheless be treated with caution – individuals are not tenants in the international legal system but rather licencees functioning by the largesse of States and institutions.

QUESTION FIVE

Françoise claims that her freedom of speech has been violated by the British Government. She has brought an action before the High Court to vindicate her freedom, but it has been rejected by that court. She now wishes to invoke the machinery of the European Convention for the Protection of Human Rights and Fundamental Freedoms to protect and vindicate her right.

Advise her of the steps which she must take and the procedures which she must follow in order to do this. Warn her of any pitfalls which she must avoid if she is to have any chance of success.

University of London LLB Examination
(for External Students) Public International Law June 1993 Q2

General Comment

A straightforward question on the procedure to be followed when seeking to pursue a claim of a human rights violation, with particular reference to the rules on the exhaustion of local remedies. Specialised knowledge of human rights law and procedure is not necessary to any great extent as the rules are mostly identical to those of general public international law.

Skeleton Solution

Introduction to human rights procedure – the exhaustion of local remedies rule – other admissibility requirements in human rights – further procedure after the preliminary decision.

Suggested Solution

The problem facing Françoise in pursuing her claim is one of procedure, not of law. The fact that this is in the specific field of human rights does not create any additional difficulties as basic human rights procedure is identical to that in general public international law – there are only a few extra requirements laid down by human rights instruments in addition to the standard international law ones.

The procedure for an individual petition to the European Commission of Human Rights is laid down in arts 25, 26 and 27 of the European Convention for the Protection of Human Rights and Fundamental Freedoms 1950. The basic framework is contained in art 25: individuals (along with certain other clearly defined bodies) may submit petitions to the Commission as long as the state against which they are lodging the complaint has accepted the competence of the Commission to hear individual petitions:

art 25(1). The state party in this case is the United Kingdom, which initially accepted the competence of the Commission under art 25 in 1966 for a period of five years; the acceptance has been renewed since then at regular intervals. The only other proviso attached to art 25 is that the individual in question must personally be the victim of a violation: abstract complaints or complaints relating exclusively to other individuals are inadmissible. Thus art 25 poses no obstacle to Françoise's application.

The Commission can therefore examine in detail the admissibility of Françoise's case, it having been established that it is prima facie admissible as an individual petition under art 25. The most important condition which falls to be satisfied here is that Françoise must have exhausted all available remedies under domestic law – this is required by arts 26 and 27(3). Article 26 includes the phrase 'according to the generally recognised rules of international law': therefore the criteria here are those established in the classic international law *Ambatielos Arbitration: Greece* v *UK* (1956) 12 RIAA 83. The relevant question here is whether a failure on Françoise's part to appeal from the High Court to the Court of Appeal would constitute non-exhaustion of local remedies. The answer is provided by the *Finnish Ships Arbitration: Finland* v *UK* (1934) 3 RIAA 1479, in which the arbitrator ruled that an appeal to the Court of Appeal would be 'obviously futile' as that court can only consider questions of law, not of fact; therefore, if the High Court's rejection of Françoise's case was based on a question of fact, she need not bother to go to the Court of Appeal. This situation is supplemented by the *Panevezys-Saldutiskis Railway Case: Estonia* v *Lithuania* (1939) PCIJ Rep Ser A/B No 76, in which the Permanent Court of International Justice said: 'There can be no need to resort to the municipal court if ... the result must be a repetition of a decision already given'.

The position of the Commission on all this is that only 'effective and sufficient' domestic remedies need be pursued, as stated in *Nielsen* v *Denmark* (1957) 11 EHRR 175. It follows that the reasons for the High Court's decision are crucial to establishing whether or not Françoise should go to the Court of Appeal. Much will also turn on the opinion of Françoise's counsel, who can make a decision on an appeal to the Court of Appeal or House of Lords which will be accepted by the Commission as final. Since no further details are provided in the question it is futile to pursue this particular point any further.

The only other condition appended to art 26 on the exhaustion of local remedies is that not more than six months may elapse between the date of the final decision in the domestic courts and the application to the Commission, otherwise the complaint becomes time-barred. The calculation of the time limit for Françoise obviously depends on the answer to the questions raised in relation to appeals within the English legal system.

The other specific requirements for a petition to be admissible before the Commission are as follows: the application must not be anonymous (art 27(1)(a)); it must not be 'substantially the same as a matter which has already been submitted to the Commission or has already been submitted to another procedure of international investigation or settlement and if it contains no relevant new information' (art 27(1)(b));

it must not be incompatible with the provisions of the Convention, manifestly ill-founded or an abuse of the right of petition: art 27(2).

The only conditions requiring any explanation here are those of art 27(2), as the others are quite obvious in their ambit. The Commission assumes incompatibility with the provisions of the Convention to mean one of the following: if the application falls outside the scope of the Convention ratione personae, ratione materiae, ratione loci or ratione temporis; if the individual application is in contravention of art 25(1); or if the application aims at the destruction of one of the rights and freedoms guaranteed in the Convention, contrary to art 17. The phrase 'manifestly ill-founded' has been indicated in the *De Becker Case* (1956) 2 YBECHR 214 to mean that the complaint does not disclose any prima facie violation of the Convention, in the sense that the facts as alleged evidently do not constitute such a violation, or cannot be proved and cannot justify the complaint, or are obviously incorrect. Abuse of the right of petition is ill-defined, but seems to consist primarily of the object the applicant wishes to attain – for instance, if the application is made exclusively or predominantly for political reasons. The best example is perhaps *Koch* v *West Germany* (1961) 5 YBECHR 134, in which the wife of the former Commandant of Buchenwald concentration camp demanded that her conviction for crimes against humanity be quashed, without invoking a single specific provision of the Convention or supporting any of her accusations or complaints with the Convention. The applicant's conduct can also constitute an abuse, in a way analogous to 'frivolous and vexatious' claims in English law – for example, 'querulous applicants' or those who attempt to mislead the Commission, use threatening or insulting language in the petition, fail to provide information repeatedly requested and so on.

None of these various criteria appear to be applicable in the case of Françoise; the sole pitfall of which she must be wary, therefore, is the question of whether all available domestic remedies will have been exhausted in the absence of an appeal within the English legal system from the decision of the High Court. Assuming that this criterion also is in fact satisfied, she will be able successfully to petition the Commission, who will then examine the merits of her complaint and attempt a 'friendly settlement' under art 28; if no such settlement is reached the Commission can then draw up a Report (art 31) and refer the case to the European Court of Human Rights (art 48) or the Committee of Ministers of the Council of Europe: art 32.

Chapter 12

The Peaceful Settlement of International Disputes

12.1   Introduction

12.2   Key points

12.3   Key cases and legislation

12.4   Questions and suggested solutions

12.1 Introduction

The relative importance of judicial processes is often over-emphasised in relation to the international settlement of disputes, particularly at the expense of alternative means of resolving international disagreements. Although adjudication remains important in the theoretical application of international law, in practice, resolution of disputes is often achieved through political processes such as negotiation, mediation or by the intercession of international organisations. Students should be familiar with the spectrum of processes through which international disputes are settled. In addition, a basic familiarity with the jurisdiction of the International Court remains essential.

12.2 Key points

Forms of international dispute resolution

Article 2(3) of the United Nations Charter obliges all members to pursue peaceful means of settling their international disputes, in order to ensure that international peace, security and justice are not endangered. This obligation is fortified by art 33 which regulates the pacific settlement of international disputes and which compels members to settle disputes in the following terms:

> 'The parties to any dispute, the continuance of which is likely to endanger the maintenance of international peace and security, shall, first of all, seek a solution by negotiation, enquiry, mediation, conciliation, arbitration, judicial settlement, resort to regional agencies or arrangements, or other peaceful means of their own choice.'

Negotiations

Negotiations are discussions held directly between the contending parties with a view to finding a solution through dialogue without requiring reference to third parties. Political considerations, rather than legal arguments, permeate such discussions, but legal arguments are often adduced to support the negotiating positions of the parties.

In the *Mavrommatis Palestine Concessions Case* (*Jurisdiction*) (1924) PCIJ Rep Ser A No 2, the Permanent Court declared that negotiations should be exhausted before a case is brought before the Court. Negotiations are the most common form of dispute resolution and frequently, where these processes are successful, the resulting compromise is embodied in a document which is given legal force, such as a treaty.

Enquiry

Contending states may, on occasion, agree to appoint an impartial body to carry out an investigation or enquiry into the facts surrounding a matter. The object of such a factual report is to facilitate a negotiated settlement. The Hague Conventions for the Pacific Settlement of Disputes 1899 and 1907 both contain provisions which expedite the setting up of commissions of enquiry. This procedure does not involve the making of specific recommendations for the settlement of the problem.

General Assembly Resolution 2329 (XXII), of 1967, urged members of the Organisation to make greater use of enquiry procedures in the settlement of international disputes. However, the utility of such investigations is recognised by the international community to be limited, particularly where the facts surrounding an issue are not in dispute.

Good offices

An offer of good offices involves the possibility of intercession by a third neutral party into a dispute in order to establish direct contacts between the parties, ultimately leading to direct negotiations. The tendering of good offices may be made by an individual, such as the Secretary General of the United Nations, or an agency such as the Security Council. By providing good offices, the objective of the third party is to bring the parties together to facilitate discussions, without actually becoming involved in the negotiations.

Mediation

Mediation involves a greater degree of third party participation than good offices, but essentially is an attempt to bring the parties together and to suggest and, subsequently communicate, alternative proposals for the solution of the dispute and to attempt to reconcile the positions of the parties. Suggestions of mediators do not have a binding effect. A recent illustration of mediation was the successful efforts of the US in establishing peaceful relations between Israel and Palestine.

Conciliation

Conciliation involves the participation of impartial or neutral third parties in the formulation of proposals for the resolution of international disputes. This procedure often requires an attempt to reconcile the views of the contending parties although again the proposals of conciliators have no binding effect in law.

The Hague Conventions for the Pacific Settlement of International Disputes 1899 and 1907 contain mechanisms and rules for the creation of conciliation commissions. Such bodies may only be constituted with the mutual consent of the parties in contention and are commonly given the mandate of investigating and reporting the facts surrounding the matter. In contemporary international relations, a number of international organisations have adopted this procedure as a principal means of dispute resolution, eg specialised agencies of the United Nations such as the GATT.

Settlement through the United Nations

The United Nations has, as a primary objective, the maintenance of international peace and security and must ensure that disputes are settled through peaceful resolution. Chapter VI of the Charter details the steps to be taken by members to assure the pacific settlement of international disputes.

However, in addition to the obligations placed on individual states, certain organs of the United Nations are empowered to take specified actions to facilitate the resolution of certain types of disputes. Article 33(2) permits the Security Council to call on parties to a dispute which threatens the maintenance of international peace to settle the issue by the methods prescribed in art 33(1). The Security Council may also investigate any dispute which might cause international friction and, under art 36, may recommend appropriate measures or procedures for the settlement of such a dispute. Article 37 requires the parties to such a dispute to refer the matter to the Council where settlement by the means indicated in art 33 proves impossible.

Under art 35, any dispute which is a threat to international peace may be brought to the attention of the Security Council or the General Assembly by any member. This provision extends to notification by non-participants in the dispute.

Arbitration

Arbitration has been defined by the International Law Commission (ILC) as 'a procedure for the settlement of disputes between states by a binding award on the basis of law and as a result of an undertaking voluntarily accepted': (1952) II YBILC 202. Arbitration differs from adjudication in two important respects:

a) arbitration gives the parties freedom to select the tribunal in contrast to judicial settlement where the composition of the Court is beyond the control of the parties; and

b) arbitration allows the parties to select the applicable law whereas the International Court is bound to apply principles of international law, even where a decision is permitted ex aequo et bono.

International arbitration originated in the procedures established under the Jay Treaty 1794 between the United States and the United Kingdom for the settlement of bilateral disputes. This procedure was successfully invoked throughout the nineteenth century by the parties, culminating in 1872 with the *Alabama Claims Arbitration* (1892) 1 Moore Int Arb 485. In this case, under the terms of the Treaty of Washington 1871, the parties agreed to submit alleged breaches of neutrality by the United Kingdom during the American Civil War to binding arbitration.

Arbitration may be carried out by a single arbitrator, on an ad hoc basis, or by reference to a panel of arbitrators. The Hague Convention for the Pacific Settlement of International Disputes 1899 originally established the Permanent Court of Arbitration, but the organisation and composition of this body was substantially revised by the 1907 Hague Convention of the same name. The Permanent Court of Arbitration is not a continuous institution nor a court of law. It is a panel of 300 nominees from the various contracting parties who may be selected as arbitrators for the settlement of a particular dispute. The Court has a permanent Bureau which fulfils administrative functions. In total, the Court has settled 25 cases, but since the Second World War, the role of this body has been limited.

A state cannot be compelled to arbitrate a matter without its consent, a factor which remains a fundamental prerequisite for the initiation of these processes. If both parties consent to arbitrate a matter, a compromis must be agreed. This instrument embodies the consensus between the parties to arbitrate a matter and forms the basis of the tribunal's jurisdiction. A compromis must specify a number of details, including:

a) the identity of the arbitrators and their number;

b) the questions which the tribunal is expected to address;

c) the law and procedure which is to be applied by the tribunal; and

d) the period within which the award must be rendered.

In order to facilitate the drafting of such agreements, model rules on arbitration procedure have been formulated. Of these, the most important include:

a) The model rules on arbitration under the Hague Conventions 1899 and 1907;

b) The General Act on the Pacific Settlement of International Disputes 1928; and

c) The Model Rules on Arbitral Procedures 1958, adopted by the General Assembly, on the recommendation of the ILC.

Arbitral awards are generally binding on the parties as stipulated in the compromis and compliance with arbitration awards in extremely high: see the *Ambatielos Case (Merits)* (1953) ICJ Rep 19.

Normally arbitration between states is intended to be final and the award binding as a final settlement of a dispute. The general principle is that the decision of the arbitral tribunal should not be disturbed except in the event of a manifest error of law or fact.

Appeal of an arbitral award to the ICJ is permitted in certain circumstances. For example, in *Guinea-Bissau* v *Senegal* (1991) ICJ Rep 53 the ICJ clarified a number of points concerning the grounds on which such appeals may be made. There are three separate grounds on which an appeal against the decision of a tribunal panel may be made.

a) Exces de pouvoir – if an arbitral body exceeds its competence, its decision is null and void. Arbitrators only have such powers as the parties have conferred on them in the document by which they refer the matter to the panel. If a tribunal failures to respect these limits, it exceeds its own competence and the decision can be declared void.

b) Failure to reach a decision by true majority – if the vote passing the decision of the tribunal does not amount to a true majority the decision cannot be given legal effect.

c) Insufficiency of reasoning – the decision of the arbitral body must be supported by adequate legal arguments. However, a statement of reasoning, although relatively brief and succinct, if clear and precise, does not amount to an insufficiently of reasoning.

In the event that an arbitral decision is overturned on one of these three grounds, the award of the tribunal is null and without binding force on the parties concerned.

In contemporary international relations, resort to arbitration has been generally confined to the settlement of private claims of nationals against foreign states. In particular, the Iran-United States Claims Tribunal has been especially active.

International judicial settlement: The PCIJ and the ICJ

The Permanent Court of International Justice (PCIJ) was the forerunner to the International Court of Justice (ICJ). It was established pursuant to art XIV of the League Covenant, which conferred on the Court jurisdiction over any issue which the parties 'recognise as suitable for submission to it for arbitration'. The Statute of the PCIJ was drafted by a Commission of Jurists and bears a remarkable similarity to the subsequent Statute of the ICJ. The Court was ultimately dissolved in 1946 on the dissolution of the League of Nations and international judicial procedure was resurrected in the form of the International Court of Justice.

The International Court of Justice is the principal judicial organ of the United Nations and its Statute forms an annex to the United Nations Charter itself. The Statute is, in reality, an adaptation of the Statute of the PCIJ, with little amendment. The jurisprudence of the PCIJ, even in relation to jurisdiction and procedure, remains relevant to the continuing functioning of the ICJ. The judges to the Court were elected at the first meeting of the UN General Assembly.

The primary function of the ICJ is the peaceful settlement of the disputes between states and a recent illustration is provided by the *Case Concerning Questions of Interpretation and Application of the 1971 Montreal Convention Arising from the Aerial Incident at Lockerbie (Jurisdiction and Admissiblity)* (1998) ICJ Rep 9. See also *Case Concering the Application of the Convention on the Prevention and Punishment of the Crime of Genocide (Bosnia and Herzogovina* v *Yugoslavia) (Admissibility and Jurisdiction)* (1996) ICJ Rep 1.

Composition of the International Court of Justice

The Court is composed of fifteen judges who are elected by an absolute majority in separate and simultaneous meetings of the Security Council and the General Assembly: art 4. Candidates must be nominated by national groups appointed for this purpose in the Permanent Court of Arbitration. Only persons 'of high moral character, who possess the qualifications required in their respective countries for appointment to the highest judicial offices, or are jurisconsults of recognised competence in international law' are eligible for appointment.

Although the Statute of the Court states that judges are to be elected without regard to nationality, in practice an equitable geographical representation has been sought, and as a result of political reality, the five permanent members of the Security Council, except China, have been continuously represented on the Court. Judges are appointed for a five-year period and are eligible for re-election. Elections for appointments are staggered, with five vacancies arising every three years. The judges themselves elect both a President and a Vice-President.

A judge is not prohibited from hearing a case involving his national state, although the Rules of Court dictate that, if a national is President of the Court, he will refrain from exercising his Presidential functions in that case. If a state party to a dispute does not have a judge of that nationality, a judge ad hoc may be appointed for that specific case. If the Court has no nationals of either party, both may exercise their right to appoint a judge ad hoc.

Cases are decided by the majority of judges present and in the event of a tied vote, the President has a casting vote. The judgment of the Court, as well as separate opinions and dissenting judgments, are published.

A case may be heard by a full Court (in which case the quorum is nine) or by a Chamber of three or more judges. In January 1982, the Court created a special Chamber for the first time to adjudicate on the Gulf of Maine dispute between Canada and the United States: see the *Delimitation of the Maritime Boundary in the Gulf of Maine Area Case* (1984) ICJ Rep 246.

Contentious and non-contentious jurisdiction

The Court has both a contentious jurisdiction and an advisory jurisdiction.

Contentious jurisdiction

The contentious jurisdiction of the Court refers to its capacity to adjudicate disputes between two or more states. Access to the Court for the settlement of international differences is limited by the principle that only states may be parties in cases before the Court: art 34. As a result, international organisations may not litigate matters before the Court, nor may non-state entities. Only states may be parties to the Statute of the Court and in this respect the following principles apply:

a) All UN members are ipso facto parties to the Statute;

b) A non-UN member may become a party to the Statute if it is prepared to give:

   i) an acceptance of the provisions of the Statute;

   ii) an agreement to accept and enforce the Court's judgments; and

   iii) an undertaking to contribute to the Court's expenses

   Switzerland, Liechtenstein and San Marino have become parties to the Statute through this procedure.

c) A state may become a party to the Statute by lodging a special declaration with the Court's registry, according to which it accepts the obligations of the Statute and art 94 of the UN Charter. Declarations may be general, accepting the Court's jurisdiction in respect of all disputes, or particular, which restricts jurisdiction to the case in hand. The Court has recently had to consider the standing of newly independent states which have only limited recognition from the international community. In *Case Concerning the Application of the Convention on Genocide (First Request for the Indication of Provisional Measures)* (1993) ICJ Rep 3 the Court accepted an application made by Bosnia-Herzegovina against the former state of Yugoslavia (Serbia and Montenegro) but declined to analyse in detail how an application was admissible from a state with only limited international recognition.

Although a state is a party to the Statute and is entitled by right to utilise the judicial processes of the Statute, no state may be compelled to litigate a matter unless it consents to do so. The Security Council may recommend that parties submit a dispute to the ICJ, but such a recommendation cannot compel the states to litigate their differences. State consent forms the basis of the contentious jurisdiction of the Court. An example of this is where jurisdiction by way of a special agreement arises. This was the basis on which the ICJ held that it had jurisdiction in the *Case Concerning Maritime Delimitation and Territorial Questions between Qatar and Bahrain (Jurisdiction and Admissibility)* (2001) ICJ Rep 16.

The Court may exercise contentious jurisdiction only where the consent of the parties has been established. This may be done in a number of ways.

a) Article 36(1)

This provision allows states to voluntarily submit a dispute to the jurisdiction of the Court. In particular, it is specifically declared that:

> 'The jurisdiction of the Court comprises all cases which the parties refer to it and all matters specially provided for in the Charter of the United Nations or in treaties and conventions in force.'

It is clear that jurisdiction may be founded not only where the mutual consent of the parties after the dispute has arisen, but also by prior consent expressed in a treaty. Among the instruments which refer questions and disputes to the Court, are treaties of Commerce and Economic Co-operation, numerous bilateral Air Services Agreements and the European Convention for the Peaceful Settlement of Disputes 1957. In the *Iran Hostages Case* (1980) ICJ Rep 3, the Court accepted jurisdiction on the referral provision in the bilateral Treaty of Amity, Economic Relations and Consular Rights between the two parties and in the protocols to the multilateral Vienna Convention on Diplomatic Relations 1961 and the Vienna Convention on Consular Relations 1963.

Where parties are submitting a dispute to the Court on a bilateral basis, in order to initiate legal processes under this provision, the parties must agree on the terms of a compromi, which is a bilateral agreement detailing the consensus of the parties to litigate. The compromi must be lodged with the Court.

An example is provided by the *Case Concerning the Aerial Incident of 10 August 1999 (Pakistan v India) (Jurisdiction)* (2000) ICJ Rep 21.

b) Forum prorogatum

Prorogated jurisdiction arises when, at the initiation of proceedings, only one state has expressly consented to jurisdiction, but the consent of the other party may be implied. In the *Corfu Channel (Preliminary Objection) Case* (1948) ICJ Rep 15 the Court accepted the contention that a letter from the Albanian Deputy Minister for Foreign Affairs expressed the consent of Albania. Further, consent to submit to jurisdiction may be adduced from the actions of a State. In the *Rights of Minorities in Polish Upper Silesia* (1928) PCIJ Rep Ser A No 15 the Court stated that jurisdiction may be 'inferred from acts conclusively establishing it … (such as) the submission of arguments on the merits, without making reservations in regard to the question of jurisdiction'. See also the *Monetary Gold Case* (1954) ICJ Rep 19.

However, the existence of jurisdiction on the ground of forum prorogatum has encouraged states to refrain from behaviour which could be construed as implied consent to the jurisdiction of the Court.

c) Article 36(2) – the optional clause.

Article 36(2) of the Statute of the Court provides:

> 'The state parties to the present Statute may at any time declare that they recognise

as compulsory ipso facto and without special agreement, in relation to any other state accepting the same obligation, the jurisdiction of the Court in all legal disputes concerning:

(a) the interpretation of a treaty;

(b) any question of international law;

(c) the existence of any fact which, if established, would constitute a breach of an international obligation;

(d) the nature and extent of the reparation to be made for the breach of an international obligation.'

States are not required to make a declaration under Article 36(2) solely by becoming a party to the Statute. However, once a declaration has been properly made, the jurisdiction of the Court is mandatory in relation to the matters specifically detailed. Article 36(5) of the Statute provides that declarations made under the Statute of the PCIJ are to continue under the Statute of the ICJ. In the *Case Concerning the Aerial Incident of 27 July 1955 (Preliminary Objections)* (1957) ICJ Rep 127 the Court deemed that former declarations may only be transferred if made by state parties to the ICJ Statute. Article 36(3) permits declarations to be formulated on an unconditional basis, or subject to the condition of reciprocity. At present 46 states have made declarations under this provision.

Declarations are made for specific periods, normally five years, with provision for renewal, and may be terminated on notice, but cannot be terminated retroactively. Consequently, where the Court is seized of a case, a state cannot withdraw by revoking its declaration: see *Nicaragua* v *United States (Jurisdiction) Case* (1984) ICJ Rep 392.

Although art 36(2) does not specifically grant such a right, states frequently make declarations subject to reservations. The most common reservations relate to:

i)   disputes in which another forum for resolution is specified;

ii) disputes arising before a specific date, which is generally the date of the declaration;

iii) disputes arising as a result of hostilities;

iv) disputes arising in relation to certain categories of states, ie Commonwealth nations, Central American states;

v)   disputes relating to matters falling within the domestic jurisdiction of the declaratory state, as determined by international law or even by the state itself.

The issue of reservations to compulsory jurisdiction arose in the *Norwegian Loans Case* (1957) ICJ Rep 9. In this case, the Court allowed Norway to invoke, as a bar to jurisdiction, the automatic self-judging reservation of the French government. Although the Court itself has not directly pronounced on the legitimacy of such reservations, the practice has been the subject of adverse comment in a number of separate opinions and dissenting judgments. See also the *Interhandel Case* (1959) ICJ Rep 6.

The practice of making reservations has created problems for the Court in trying to ascertain the exact scope of the subject matter over which states have consented by declaration. Since declarations are made on the basis of reciprocity, the Court has jurisdiction only over those areas which fall within the areas in which the declarations of parties overlap. This involves the application of the principle of 'reciprocity'. As a result, the jurisdiction of the court under art 36(2) may be circumscribed in two respects:

i)   a party may rely on a reservation made by itself to limit the jurisdiction of the Court; and

ii) a party may rely on a reservation made by the party trying to establish jurisdiction, on the basis of reciprocity, as a limitation on jurisdiction. See the *Interhandel Case (Preliminary Objections)* (1959) ICJ Rep 6.

Advisory jurisdiction

Article 96 of the UN Charter states:

'(1) The General Assembly or the Security Council may request the International Court of Justice to give an advisory opinion on any legal question.
(2) Other organs of the United Nations and specialised agencies, which may at any time be so authorised by the General Assembly, may also request advisory opinions of the Court on legal questions arising within the scope of their activities.'

The counterpart provision of the Statute is art 65 of the UN Charter which states that 'the Court may give an advisory opinion on any legal question at the request of whatever body may be authorised by or in accordance with the Charter of the United Nations to make such a request'.

Where the question posed is not within the functions of the body requesting the opinion, the Court does not have jurisdiction to give an advisory opinion: *Legality of the Use by a State of Nuclear Weapons in Armed Conflict (Request for Advisory Opinion by the World Health Organisation)* (1996) The Times 18 July. Here, the Court could not give an opinion because WHO was not concerned with the legality of nuclear weapons but with their effect upon health.

Advisory opinions are not legally binding on the body requesting the legal opinion of the Court. In practice, however, bodies have treated such opinions with a considerable degree of reverence and certain advisory opinions have undoubtedly contributed to the development of international law: eg *Reparations Case* (1949) ICJ Rep 174, *Certain Expenses Case* (1962) ICJ Rep 151 and the *Western Sahara Case* (1975) ICJ Rep 12.

Two problems have arisen in relation to the exercise of advisory jurisdiction.

a) The suitability of subjects for an advisory opinion

In the *Conditions for Admission of a State to Membership of the United Nations Case* (1948) ICJ Rep 57, the International Court made it clear that reference to 'any legal question' permitted the Court to give an advisory opinion to questions qualifying as 'an essentially judicial task'. However, the political dimensions of requests for certain advisory opinions cannot be ignored: see the *Namibia Case* (1971) ICJ Rep 16.

b) The propriety of rendering an advisory opinion

The Court has expressed concern at the use of requesting advisory opinions which are, in fact, means by which states are circumventing the requirement of state consent to adjudication: see the *Eastern Carelia Case* (1923) PCIJ Rep Ser B No 5 and the *Western Sahara Case* (1975) ICJ Rep 12.

Limitation periods for international actions

The Statute of the International Court contains no express provision relating to a period within which a case must be brought to its attention. However, this is not to say that such a period of limitation does not exist.

In the *Certain Phosphate Lands in Nauru Case (Preliminary Objections)* (1992) ICJ Rep 240 the Court acknowledged that a delay in initiating proceedings might render an application inadmissible if the delay prejudices the rights of the other party. The overriding principle was to decide 'in the light of the circumstances of each case whether the passage of time renders an application inadmissible'.

A number of factors have to be taken into consideration in assessing whether the circumstances of the case render the application inadmissible, including the relationship between the parties and the steps that had been taken prior to litigation to resolve the matter.

Interim measures of protection

The requirements for obtaining interim protection from the ICJ were discussed at length by the Court in the *Case Concerning Questions of Interpretation and Application of the 1971 Montreal Convention Arising from the Aerial Incident at Lockerbie (Provisional Measures): Libya v UK* (1992) ICJ Rep 3.

The Court confirmed that two pre-conditions were required for interim protection, namely the existence of a prima facie case for the exercise of jurisdiction by the Court over the merits of the dispute and the existence of a risk of imminent irreparable damage to the rights of the party seeking protection.

In the event that a state fails to implement an interim protection order of the Court, no sanctions can be imposed by the Court to compel compliance. The Court merely has power to reiterate the terms of its earlier order through a subsequent order. For example, in *Case Concerning the Application of the Convention on the Prevention and Punishment of the Crime of Genocide (Second Request for the Indication of Provisional Measures)* (1993) ICJ Rep 325, where Yugoslavia had effectively ignored the Court's first order, the Court could only order Yugoslavia to give immediate and effective implementation to the earlier order. No additional steps could be taken to enforce the terms of the original order.

12.3 Key cases and legislation

- *Case Concerning Maritime Delimitation and Territorial Questions between Qatar and Bahrain (Jurisdiction and Admissibility)* (2001) ICJ Rep 16
  Jurisdiction established by way of special agreement

- *Case Concerning Questions of Interpretation and Application of the 1971 Montreal Convention Arising from the Aerial Incident at Lockerbie (Jurisdiction and Admissibility)* (1998) ICJ Rep 9
  Considered jurisiction and interim measures

- *Case Concerning the Aerial Incident of 10 August 1999 (Pakistan v India) (Jurisdiction)* (2000) ICJ Rep 21
  Considered the implications of art 36(3) of the Statute of the ICJ

- *Case Concerning the Application of the Convention on the Prevention and Punishment of the Crime of Genocide (Bosnia and Herzogovina v Yugoslavia) (Admissibility and Jurisdiction)* (1996) ICJ Rep 1
  Considered the 'extra territorial' jurisdiction of the ICJ

- *Certain Phosphate Lands in Nauru (Nauru v Australia) (Preliminary Objections)* (1992) ICJ Rep 240
  Limitation periods for international actions

- *Corfu Channel Case (Preliminary Objection)* (1948) ICJ Rep 15
  Statements made in relation to prorogation to jurisdiction

- *Guinea-Bissau v Senegal* (1991) ICJ Rep 53
  The principles behind the appeal of arbitral decisions to the ICJ

- *Interhandel Case* (1959) ICJ Rep 6
  Dicta relating to the legality of reservations to optional declarations

- *Legality of the Use by a State of Nuclear Weapons in Armed Conflict (Request for Advisory Opinion by the World Health Organisation)* (1996) The Times 18 July
  An opinion was given on the justifications required of a state in using nuclear weapons.

- *Lockerbie Case (Libya v United Kingdom/United States)* (1992) ICJ Rep 3
  Conditions required for the application of preliminary measures

- *Nicaragua* v *United States (Jurisdiction)* (1984) ICJ Rep 392
  Complex case involving extensive discussion of the principles underlying the jurisdiction of the Court

- *Norwegian Loans Case* (1957) ICJ Rep 9
  Cross application of reservations to jurisdiction

- *Nuclear Test Cases (Interim Protection)* (1973) ICJ Rep 99
  Leading case on the jurisdiction of the court in relation to measures of interim protection

- *Rights of Passage over Indian Territory Case (Preliminary Objections)* (1957) ICJ Rep 125
  Consideration of the concept of 'reciprocity' in declarations made under art 36(2) of the Statute of the ICJ

- *United States Diplomatic and Consular Staff in Tehran Case* (1980) ICJ Rep 3
  Legal consequences of non-appearance before the Court

- Jay Treaty 1794

- Statute of the International Court of Justice 1945

- UN Charter 1945

Note: these provide the framework within which peaceful settlement of disputes between states at international level is effected.

12.4 Questions and suggested solutions

QUESTION ONE

The Government of the State of Yuga is controlled by the Sean majority ethnic group which dominates the armed forces. There has been mistreatment by the Government of Yuga of the members of the Ogona minority ethnic group who are agitating for their own homeland within Yuga, a safer environment and an increased control of the natural resources extracted from Ogonaland, which are the mainstay of Yuga's national revenue.

To show its strong disapproval of the agitation, the Government of Yuga sends troops into Ogonaland. In the ensuing confrontation, many Ogona ethnic group were injured. There was mass murder, forced labour and kidnapping of the Ogonas. Their leader campaigning against the 'gross injustice, persecution and ethnic cleansing by this undemocratic and repressive Government' as well as the environmental damage caused by the activities of oil companies in Ogona, was hanged after a secret trial by a tribunal composed of military and police officers appointed by the President of Yuga.

The North Action Organisation (ACO) is a defensive military arrangement established to give military assistance to its members suffering armed attack as recognised by art 51 of the UN Charter. It has a membership of 18 States (all members of the United Nations and three of which are permanent members of the UN Security Council). ACO adopted a resolution 'condemning the gross violation of human rights taking place in Yuga against the Ogona peoples'. After attempts by ACO to negotiate the situation in Ogonaland with the Yuga Government had failed, ACO threaten to use force to dislodge the repressive Government in Yuga, to prevent the grave violations of human rights there and to up-hold the right of the people of Ogonaland to self-determination. Accordingly, between March and May 1999, ACO, without prior resort to the United Nations, carried out multilateral air strikes which destroyed much of the military infrastructure of Yuga, led to enormous human casualties and to the destruction of the Embassy of Zamunda which is a permanent member of the UN Security Council.

The Yuga and some other States argued that ACO's action was illegal in general international law and under the UN Charter.

Consider the legal issues arising from the above facts and assess the legal validity of ACO's action.

University of London LLB Examination
(for External Students) Public International Law June 2000 Q8

General Comment

As an examination question this is a difficult problem. The examiner has put together elements of the situation in Nigeria with aspects of the Kosovo problem to form a challenging question. The original text seems to contain a number of misprints but, be that as it may, the examination candidate has to read the question quickly and seek to identify the salient elements. In such circumstances it is sensible to read the entire question through and then to re-read it, seeking to identify the central legal issues. The question raises the complex problem of how an outside regional organisation can intervene in a civil war to restrain excesses without making the situation worse. The question is generally phrased requiring the candidate to 'consider the legal issues' and 'the legal validity of ACO's action'.

Skeleton Solution

Treatment of ethnic minority – methods of negotiation in international law – breach of human rights – role of UN Security Council – human rights law – international personality (ACO) – legality of military action – peaceful settlement of disputes.

Suggested Solution

We are asked in this matter to consider a number of issues arising from the facts of the question. In reviewing the entire question, the relevant legal issues can be summarised as follows.

1. Has there been mistreatment of the Ogona minority?

2. Are the demands of the Ogona people consistent with international law?

3. The sending of troops into Ogonaland.

4. The execution of the leader of the Ogona people.

5. The status of the ACO.

6. The legality of the military action of the ACO.

7. The destruction of the Embassy of Zamunda.

It is necessary to consider each of these aspects in turn.

1. Has there been mistreatment of the Ogona minority?

It is clearly the case that the Government of Yuga will be in breach of any regional human rights treaties that they may have signed in that they have manifestly abused and discriminated against a minority. On the facts, there are clear breaches of arts 2, 3, 9 and 18 of the Universal Declaration of Human Rights 1948. It is also evident that such conduct violates art 27 of the International Covenant on Civil and Political Rights as well as the letter and spirit of both the International Covenant on Economic, Social and Cultural Rights 1966 and the Declaration on the Rights of Persons Belonging to National, Ethnic, Religious and Linguistic Minorities 1992. In broad terms there is no doubt that the Government of Yuga is in breach of the United Nations Charter and accepted principles of international law.

2. Are the demands of the Ogona people consistent with international law?

International society has tended to be hostile to any form of secession from an established state (eg Biafra in 1967); it is arguable that only in the case of Bangladesh in 1971 has such conduct been encouraged. The general thrust of international law is that ethnic minorities within existing states should be accorded constitutional guarantees of equal treatment and non-discrimination. As is set out in the 1970 Declaration on the Principles of International Law (General Assembly Resolution 2625), and as exemplified by the initial response in respect of Yugoslavia in 1991, the international community tends to be reluctant to take any action that would lead to the disintegration of existing states. The Government of Yuga should have sought a negotiated solution that involved a degree of autonomy and respect for cultural rights. Clearly this has not been done.

3. The sending of troops into Ogonoland

It is arguable that this is the critical development because, while a state may take such action, it is likely that any refugees created will cause regional instability. This will entitle the Security Council to act under Chapter VI and Chapter VII of the United Nations Charter. The reports of mass murder, forced labour and the kidnapping of members of the Ogona ethnic group represent very serious breaches by the Government of Yuga of international human rights law. In such circumstances the Security Council would have been entitled to act, but they do not appear to have done so; it is clearly established that where regional instability has been created, art 2(7) does not act as an obstacle to Security Council action.

4. The execution of the leader of the Ogona people

Although some human rights systems provide for the outlawing of the death penalty (see Sixth Protocol to the European Convention 1983 and the Second Optional Protocol to the International Covenant on Civil and Political Rights 1990), the general view is that punishment is for the criminal justice system of each member state. However, international human rights law does provide for certain procedural safeguards, amongst which are: (a) an open public trial, (b) by an independent judiciary, (c) a requirement of relevant evidence of serious criminal acts, (d) an entitlement to appoint independent defence counsel, (e) the entitlement to cross examine witnesses, and (f) a reasoned finding of guilt. These procedural safeguards vary in regional human rights systems but are traceable back to arts 10 and 11 of the Universal Declaration of Human Rights 1948. On the given facts, there appear to have been serious breaches of arts 6 and 14 of the International Covenant on Civil and Political Rights 1966. Lastly, a capital sentence appears to have been imposed not because of evidence of a serious criminal offence, but because of political opposition to the Government of Yuga.

5. The status of the ACO

It appears the ACO is a treaty based regional defence organisation operating within the general terms of arts 51–54 of the United Nations Charter 1945. The propriety of the resolution passed by ACO depends on the internal constitution of ACO. There seems no reason to believe that it was ultra vires. In accordance with art 33 of the United Nations Charter there then appears to have been some attempt to seek a peaceful solution. More worryingly, when negotiations failed there appears to have been no attempt to refer the entire matter to the Security Council.

6. The legality of the military action of the ACO

One begins with the general proposition that such military action against another state is unlawful under the terms of art 2 of the United Nations Charter. Manifestly such action has not been authorised by the Security Council; it cannot be said to be a lawful exercise of self-defence because there has been no formal request from the Government of the State of Yuga: see the *Nicaragua Case: Nicaragua* v *United States (Merits)* (1986) ICJ Rep 14. Thus there is a twofold question: (a) does international law recognise a right of international humanitarian action and subject to what conditions, and (b) is such intervention justified on the present facts?

Whether international law recognises a right of humanitarian intervention is a matter of considerable dispute amongst writers. According to Professor Lowe and Professor Greenwood, there are probably three requirements, namely: (a) prior determination by the Security Council of a grave crisis, (b) imminent humanitarian catastrophe, and (c) military intervention as the only practicable means to avoid serious loss of life. Unlike the Kosovo crisis, where the Security Council had passed a number of critical resolutions, no such action has been taken in the present case. It is correct that the ACO has a membership of 18 states and the Security Council has a membership of only 15 states. However, under the United Nations Charter the Security Council is the guardian of peace within the international community and it should have been given an opportunity to pass judgment on the crisis. The objective of the United Nations Charter is to ensure that force is not employed outside the terms of the Charter; there is a danger of allowing regional organisations to act without reference to the Security Council. So it is arguable that the conditions for humanitarian intervention have not been met.

The next question that arises is whether the means employed are consistent with international law. In principle any military attack must be: (a) necessary, (b) proportionate, (c) directed to military objectives, and (d) not directed at civilians or civilian targets. The reference to numerous civilian deaths would appear to indicate that the rules in customary international law, and those set out in arts 48–60 of the First Additional Protocol 1977 to the Geneva Convention 1949, have not been observed. In these circumstances it is open to serious doubt as to whether the decision to employ force, and the manner of its use, is consistent with international law.

7. The destruction of the Embassy of Zamunda

The premises of the Embassy of Zamunda are located in the State of Yuga and are subject to the normal protections afforded by the Vienna Convention on Diplomatic Relations 1961, in particular art 22. As a matter of the law of state responsibility Zamunda is entitled to seek financial compensation from the state responsible for the damage to the Embassy. In the case of the Kosovo conflict, where the Chinese Embassy in Belgrade was damaged and three citizens killed, the United States communicated an apology and made an offer of financial compensation. As an innocent party there is no defence to a claim by Zamunda.

The conclusions in this matter can be briefly stated. The launching of a humanitarian mission without any reference to the Security Council is probably a breach of international law. The heavy loss of human life may indicate that the laws of war have not been sufficiently observed.

QUESTION TWO

Alpha and Beta have both made unconditional declarations accepting the jurisdiction of the International Court of Justice (ICJ) under Article 36(2) of the Statute of the Court. Gamma has made a similar declaration, accepting the jurisdiction of the Court except in any dispute relating to the integrity of Gamman territory. Two years ago the government of Gamma seized Silvana, an island governed by Alpha since 1919 but populated mainly by persons of Gamman ethnicity, on the grounds of 're-uniting the Gamman people'. Alpha immediately imposed trade sanctions upon Gamma, and, invoking the provisions of a bilateral Treaty of Friendship and Co-operation with Beta, called upon Beta to do the same. Before Beta could act, the government of Gamma froze all Betan assets within its jurisdiction. Beta has demanded that Gamma release the assets of its nationals, but the Government of Gamma has stated that it will only do so if Beta recognises its legitimate title to Silvana. The Government of Delta, which has recognised the territorial claims of Gamma to the island, has offered to mediate in the dispute between Gamma and Beta.

The Secretary-General of the United Nations Organisation seeks your advice on BOTH of the following issues:

a) the legality of Gamma's territorial claim to Silvana; and

b) the most effective means of resolving the various disputes through either judicial or non-judicial means.

Advise the Secretary-General.

University of London LLB Examination
(for External Students) Public International Law June 1997 Q4

General Comment

This is an interesting question that embraces a number of elements. In essence the student is required to discuss three matters: (a) how Gamma might formulate a claim in international law to the territory of Silvana; (b) the unlawful seizure of Silvana; and (c) the various mechanisms by which such disputes can be resolved in public international law. The sensible candidate will realise that there are some disputes arising in the international community that require action by both the Security Council and the International Court of Justice. It is clear from the question that we are asked to advise the Secretary-General so that any advice will have to be consistent with the rights and obligations arising under the UN Charter. The student should also make some mention of the problems that arise in respect of the jurisdiction of the International Court of Justice.

Skeleton Solution

The claim by Gamma to the territory of Silvana: the limits to the principle of self-determination; the unlawful seizure of Silvana – the resolution of the various disputes: the role of the Security Council; the role of the International Court of Justice; the role of conciliation and arbitration.

Suggested Solution

We are asked in this problem to consider two distinct, but related, matters. It is sensible to take each in turn.

The legality of Gamma's territorial claim to Silvana

It is clear beyond doubt that Gamma's acquisition of Silvana by force is unlawful under international law. Territory cannot be lawfully acquired by force. Such conduct is a violation of the UN Charter (art 2(4)) and would be so even if Gamma were not a Member State: art 2(6). The prohibition on this form of conduct is also clearly set out in the Declaration on the Principles of International Law Concerning Friendly Relations and Co-operation among States in Accordance with the Charter of the United Nations 1970 (GAR 2625 (XXV)). There can be little doubt that the appropriate course would be for the Security Council to meet and pass a resolution in similar form to that passed during the Kuwait crisis (ie, Resolution 660). Such a resolution would demand withdrawal by Gamma, and declare any annexation null and void. It is likely that such a resolution would ask States not to recognise any purported annexation.

It might be argued that Gamma has a valid claim to Silvana which should be considered by the International Court of Justice. It would seem that such a claim is based on the principle of self-determination. On the assumption that such a legal right is capable of existing in international law, a number of difficulties arise. First, there is no evidence of any request by the people of Silvana. Second, in those international instruments in which the right to self-determination has been asserted (UN Charter 1945; Declaration on the Granting of Independence to Colonial Territories and Peoples 1960 (GAR 1514 (XV)); Declaration of the Principles of International Law 1970 (GAR 2625 (XXV))) it has always been accepted that the right to self-determination only existed in respect of non self-governing States and was not to be employed to damage the territory of existing States. Even if such a right were appropriate it cannot be enforced by force (art 2(4) UN Charter). It is relevant to observe that since Alpha acquired Silvana in 'the Wilson year' of 1919 it is highly unlikely that it acquired it in a colonial capacity. Moreover, where a right to self determination exists it is vested in the people of the territory; it certainly does not vest in an adjoining state: see *Western Sahara Case* (1975) ICJ Rep 12. It therefore follows that Gamma's claim to the territory of Silvana has little prospect of success, and its conduct in resorting to force represents a serious breach of art 2(4) of the UN Charter.

The resolution of the various disputes

We are asked in this second aspect of the problem to advise the Secretary-General of the United Nations as to how the various disputes should be resolved. In giving advice we must be mindful that any dispute should be resolved in accordance with the broad principles of the UN Charter. Taking the various matters in turn.

a) The Security Council should be required to meet to discuss the situation in Silvana. A resolution should be drawn up under Chapter VII of the United Nations Charter: (i) condemning the use of force; (ii) demanding the withdrawal by Gamma; (iii) declaring the purported annexation null and void; (iv) requiring that no state recognises the seizure; and (v) threatening economic sanctions in the event of refusal. Such a course would be in line with the precedent of August 1990 (the Kuwait crisis).

b) Alpha and Gamma should be requested to consent to the dispute as to Silvana being determined by the International Court of Justice as it is pre-eminently a question of international law: see art 36(3) UN Charter; art 36(2)(b) ICJ Statute. It must, however, be borne in mind that a resolution to this effect by the Security Council does not of itself confer jurisdiction on the Court: see *Corfu Channel Case (Preliminary Objection)* (1948) ICJ Rep 15.

c) Since both Alpha and Gamma have made unconditional declarations then prima facie Alpha would be able to bring the matter before the International Court of Justice. A difficult question arises as to the validity of the reservation lodged by Gamma. It is arguable that such a reservation is 'self-judging' and thus not effective as being incompatible with the power of the Court to determine jurisdiction: see art 36(6) ICJ Statute. It is also open to argument that such a form of reservation is at variance with the principle of acceptance of jurisdiction within art 36(2) of the ICJ Statute: see *Norwegian Loans Case* (1957) ICJ Rep 9; *Interhandel Case (Preliminary Objections)* (1959) ICJ Rep 6.

d) The fact that the dispute about the territory of Silvana may be subject to the good offices of the Secretary-General, or be subject to Security Council consideration, does not prevent the International Court of Justice from having jurisdiction: *US Diplomatic and Consular Staff in Tehran Case* (1980) ICJ Rep 3; *Nicaragua* v *United States (Jurisdiction and Admissibility)* (1984) ICJ Rep 392.

e) In respect of the seizure of property belonging to Betan citizens, there is little doubt that the discriminatory nature of the act renders it contrary to the rules of customary international law. In essence Beta will have two objectives, namely to secure the lifting of the freezing order and to obtain compensation for those citizens whose businesses have incurred loss. In respect of the first aspect there are probably four options: (i) to begin legal action in the municipal courts of Gamma; (ii) to apply to International Court of Justice seeking interim measures against Gamma on the basis that a legal dispute is in existence and the relevant reservation is inapplicable; (iii) to request that the Security Council pass a resolution demanding a lifting of the freezing order; and (iv) to request the government of Delta to exercise its good offices and, if Gamma is willing, to adopt a more formal role as mediator.

At a later date when the assets have been unfrozen it is clear that some Betan nationals will be seeking compensation. This is a matter suitable for arbitration; it would seem that a citizen from Delta would be most appropriate as chairman of the arbitral tribunal.

f) In respect of all the disputes there is no reason why the Secretary-General should not use his good offices to encourage the parties to reach a negotiated settlement.

g) The difficulty with the present problem is that the forces of Gamma have physically seized Silvana. As the Falkland Islands dispute (1982) and the Kuwait crisis (1990) indicate, the Security Council is likely to demand full withdrawal by Gamma before the long-term future of Silvana can be resolved. Above all else the Security Council will be anxious to ensure that the principle enshrined in art 2(4) of the UN Charter is fully maintained.

QUESTION THREE

To what extent, if at all, has the International Court of Justice made an effective contribution to the settlement of international disputes? How, if at all, could the effectiveness of the Court be enhanced?

University of London LLB Examination
(for External Students) Public International Law June 1992 Q2

General Comment

A broad general question requiring a narrative and descriptive answer. In essence, the examiner is looking for specific factors affecting the ability of the ICJ to effect settlement of international disputes.

Skeleton Solution

Volume of cases; rate of successful implementation – delaying and avoiding tactics: the *Nicaragua Case* – effectiveness: problem of lack of compulsory jurisdiction; limitations on the jurisdiction – enhancement: compulsory jurisdiction; sanctions for non-compliance.

Suggested Solution

Adjudication of disputes at the international level is not as common a phenomenon as in most developed national legal systems. In part, this reflects the fact that the rule of law in the international community is less dominant than inside states. As a result, the role of the International Court of Justice (ICJ) in the settlement of international disputes has been relatively passive and its contribution to the effective enforcement of international law limited.

As a means of settling disputes, adjudication in this form is not as significant as the resolution of conflicts through political processes such as negotiation, mediation and the intervention of international organisations such as the agencies and organs of the United Nations. In terms of volume of cases, the ICJ rarely renders more than around six or seven decisions on the merits of cases each year. This figure contrasts sharply with settlements established through political dialogue, negotiation and discussion.

Even if a dispute has been presented to the Court for adjudication, this does not mean that the matter will be resolved by the Court. There are many devices that states may employ to delay or to deny effect to adverse rulings. One illustration of the deployment of such tactics was the conduct of the United States government in the two decisions of the Court in *Nicaragua* v *United States (Jurisdiction)* (1984) ICJ Rep 392 and *Nicaragua* v *United States (Merits)* (1986) ICJ Rep 14.

In the first case, which related to the court's jurisdiction over the subject matter, the United States government argued that, firstly, the Court had no jurisdiction on a number of technical legal grounds and, secondly, that the matter was a political one and therefore non-justiciable in the Court. Both these arguments were rejected by the Court which held that it had jurisdiction to hear the merits of the case.

In response to this ruling, the United States government withdrew from participation in the arguments on the merits. It took no further part in the arguments in the Court and declared that it considered the Court to have exceeded its jurisdiction. For its part, the Court had no authority to compel the United States to return to argue its case even though it had ruled that it could exercise jurisdiction over both parties.

Not only did the United States refuse to continue to participate in the case, but also it rejected the final decision of the Court awarding compensation to Nicaragua for unlawful acts attributed to the United States. This decision of the Court has never been complied with by the United States since the International Court has no power to make the United States pay appropriate levels of compensation.

In this dispute it is clear that the overriding considerations were not legal but political. The Reagan administration found the Sandinista government of Daniel Ortega to be politically repugnant and support for the Contra insurgents, while flagrantly incompatible with international law, was considered the most expeditious method of overthrowing the incumbent government. Since legal considerations did not influence the government's original behaviour, it is not therefore surprising that the International Court, which applies legal principles, was unsuccessful in deterring the United States from its activities merely through the application of rules of international law.

In the past, states have also simply refused to appear at all in the Court to argue their cases when they disagree with the Court's findings on jurisdiction. For example, France refused to appear before the Court in the *Nuclear Test Cases* (1974) ICJ Rep 253 and Iran declined to appear in the *Iran Hostages Case* (1980) ICJ Rep 3. In cases where states refuse to appear, it is of course extremely unlikely that they will comply with the final decision of the court.

The limited contribution of the International Court to the settlement of international disputes stems from the shortcomings in the Statute of the Court.

The Statute distinguishes between contentious and non-contentious (advisory) jurisdiction. The contentious jurisdiction of the Court refers to its powers to decide disputes between two or more states. This jurisdiction is, however, considerably fettered because, in the absence of the application of the Optional Clause contained in art 36(2), the Court is only entitled to hear disputes that are voluntarily submitted to it.

Disputes may be referred to the Court on an ad hoc basis, that is when such disputes develop between parties, or by the prior consent of the parties as manifested in an earlier international agreement. The important point is that, in all cases, the mutual consent of the parties is required before a dispute can be submitted. This element of mutual consent is often missing in international differences of opinion and therefore states often fail to agree on the terms of a reference to the Court or to submit the matter to the Court at all. In general, states have demonstrated a reluctance to expose themselves to the possibility of adverse judgments and have instead preferred to reserve the right of making decisions to themselves.

The most important exception to the requirement of mutual consent for the submission of disputes is the Optional Clause contained in art 36(2). This provides that states may declare the Court's jurisdiction compulsory without any special agreement, as regards jurisdiction over all legal disputes concerning the interpretation of treaties, questions of international law, the existence of breaches of international law, and the nature and extent of reparations to be made for breaches of international obligations. While this provision has the potential of expanding the compulsory jurisdiction of the Court, in practice it has not had this effect primarily for three reasons.

First, states are not required to make a declaration under art 36(2) when they become a party to the Statute. A separate procedure is employed in order to prevent participation in the Statute from automatically having the effect of establishing compulsory jurisdiction. Thus, of the present parties to the Statute, less than half have made declarations under art 38(2).

Second, declarations are made for specific periods, normally five years, and may be terminated on notice. Even although some provide for automatic renewal in the absence of notice of termination, in the past states have attempted to terminate these notices once an undesirable reference has been made: see *Nicaragua* v *United States (Jurisdiction)*.

Third, while art 36(2) does not specifically allow for the possibility of reservations to declarations, in practice states frequently do so. Thus, states frequently exclude disputes arising from particular factual circumstances such as, in the case of the United States declaration, disputes arising with Central American states and disputes falling within the domestic jurisdiction of the state.

The effect of such reservations has been exacerbated by the International Court itself which has held that it will only exercise jurisdiction under art 36(2) when the subject matter of the dispute in question falls within the overlap between the relevant declarations. In other words, the Court will decline jurisdiction where the matter in contention is covered by reservations in declarations by either contesting state. Thus, in the *Norwegian Loans Case* (1957) ICJ Rep 9 the Court allowed Norway to invoke, as a bar to jurisdiction, the automatic self-judging reservation of the French government, the latter country being the state attempting to bring the dispute before the Court.

Since the issues of the non-enforceability of the judgment of the Court and the lack of compulsory jurisdiction of the Court are the two most significant factors undermining the effectiveness of the Court, any proposed improvements to the functioning of the Court must address both these matters.

To secure effective compliance with the decisions of the Court, some form of international sanctions must be made available to ensure that states abide by the rulings of the Court. The power to fine a state, or to require the adoption of particular measures to compel a state to comply with a ruling, could be made available directly to the Court. Alternatively, a political body such as the Security Council could be charged with the responsibility of ensuring compliance. This latter solution could however be undermined if political considerations in these organs were allowed to interfere with the proper sanctioning of maverick states.

To empower the Court with any semblance of compulsory jurisdiction would require significant amendments to the Statute. Article 36 of the Statute would need substantial alteration and, in particular, the requirement of mutual consent for the submission of disputes should be supplanted by a provision imposing mandatory jurisdiction. Equally, the Optional Clause must be deleted to ensure that states do not continue to abuse its terms.

QUESTION FOUR

In 1980, State N deposited with the UN Secretary-General a declaration accepting the jurisdiction of the International Court of Justice under Article 36(2) of the Court's Statute. This declaration does not contain any provision relating to its termination or providing for its withdrawal.

In 1983, State O deposited a similar declaration with the UN Secretary-General. However, this declaration provides that, by notifying the Secretary-General, State O might, at any time, exclude from the scope of its declaration any dispute or category of disputes, such exclusion to be effective from the moment that it was notified to the Secretary-General.

On 1 January 1986, State N and State O concluded a Treaty of Friendship. Article 20 of this treaty provides that, if any dispute should arise between the two States, then it shall be referred to the International Court of Justice at the request of any one of the parties. Article 21 excludes from the scope of Article 20 disputes arising out of or relating to acts or facts occurring before 1 January 1986.

In 1982, State N cancelled a concession which it had granted in 1978 to Oluwole, a national of State O. Oluwole tried and failed to obtain redress in State N's courts for this action. In 1989, he asked the Government of State O to take up his case against State N. Negotiations relating to Oluwole's case took place between State N and State O; but, on 31 December 1990, State O declared further negotiations to be pointless and submitted the dispute to the International Court of Justice.

On 29 December 1990, State N sent a note to the UN Secretary-General. This note stated that State N wished to withdraw, with immediate effect, its declaration accepting the jurisdiction of the International Court of Justice. The note also stated that, if and in so far as it might not be possible to withdraw its declaration with immediate effect, then, in the alternative, State N wished to exclude from the scope of its declaration disputes relating to its treatment of foreign nationals. On 31 January 1991, State N sent a note to the Registrar of the International Court stating that the Court did not have jurisdiction over its dispute with State O both by reason of its note of 29 December 1990 and because the dispute was excluded from the jurisdiction of the Court by Article 21 of the treaty of 1986.

Advise State O.

University of London LLB Examination
(for External Students) Public International Law June 1991 Q8

General Comment

A problem question which appears to be tricky. Students should be familiar with issues relating to jurisdiction under art 36 of the Statute of the ICJ and methods of peaceful settlements of international disputes.

Skeleton Solution

Two grounds for jurisdiction: art 36(2) and the Friendship Agreement – the principle of reciprocity – the impacts of exclusion clauses and terminations of declarations – Treaty of Friendship; importance of the receipt of the complaint – the relevant factual circumstances.

Suggested Solution

Article 36(2) of the Statute of the International Court of Justice provides that states may declare that they recognise the compulsory jurisdiction of the Court in relations to disputes concerning the interpretation of treaties, the application of international law, the determination of a set of facts which, if established, would constitute a breach of an international obligation, and the nature or extent of reparation to be made for a breach of an international obligation.

Declarations made under art 36(2) may be made conditionally or unconditionally. Often declarations also contain provisions which allow the states making the declaration to terminate their obligations under art 36(2) upon the expiry of a specified period of time. Similarly, a state may exclude particular subject matters from the compulsory jurisdiction of the Court. For example, the United Kingdom excludes all disputes arising after 1945, together with disputes between the United Kingdom and Commonwealth countries.

Therefore, the fact that State O has specified that the terms of its declaration may be changed by notification is not ipso facto inconsistent with art 36(2).

From the facts of the question, there are two possible grounds for the exercise of compulsory jurisdiction by the International Court: (a) on the basis of the declarations under art 36(2); and (b) under the terms of the 1986 Friendship Agreement.

As regards the declaration made under art 36(2), the International Court applies the principle of reciprocity in deciding whether it may exercise its compulsory jurisdiction. A state accepting the jurisdiction of the ICJ under the optional clause does so only in relation to other states accepting the same obligation. Therefore, states that are brought before the International Court under art 36(2) may rely on reservations made in the declarations of their opponents as a defence to the jurisdiction of the court.

This has in fact occurred in a number of cases. For example, in the *Norwegian Loans Case* (1957) ICJ Rep 9, in which Norway was allowed to invoke the reservation made by France as a bar to the jurisdiction of the Court. France had reserved matters deemed to be essentially within the national jurisdiction of the French government and therefore Norway was allowed to do the same thereby effectively preventing the claim.

State O subsequently attempts to limit the scope of its obligations under its declaration. In the *Military and Paramilitary Activities in and against Nicaragua Case (Jurisdiction)* (1984) ICJ Rep 392, the Court made it clear that if a declaration contains a term which delays the coming into effect of an exclusion of a category of disputes, this would allow states to escape from the general obligation, but only after the expiry of the prescribed period. But, since State N has made no express provision in its declaration, it is likely that the Court will give effect to its proposed withdrawal of its declaration.

However, if State O has lodged a complaint with the ICJ prior to the receipt of the notice of withdrawal, it is possible that the Court will accept jurisdiction to decide the merits of the case. Once the Court is seized of a case, a state cannot later withdraw its acceptance of the compulsory jurisdiction on a retroactive basis: *Rights of Passage over Indian Territory Case* (1957) ICJ Rep 125.

According to the facts set out in the question, State O submitted the complaint on 31 December 1990, but State N withdrew its declaration of 29 December. Therefore it is unlikely that State N will be subject to the contentious jurisdiction of the Court on this basis.

This leaves the matter of jurisdiction under the 1986 Friendship Treaty to be resolved. There are a number of illustrations of bilateral agreements giving rise to the compulsory jurisdiction of the Court. In the *Iran Hostages Case* (1980) ICJ Rep 3, the United States was able to bring the taking of US embassy staff in Iran before the International Court on the basis of a bilateral Friendship Treaty, although two multilateral conventions were also relied upon in the American pleadings.

Similarly, the International Court brought the United States before it by means of a bilateral treaty obligation in the *Military and Paramilitary Activities in and against Nicaragua (Jurisdiction) Case*. Further, it is unlikely that a bilateral undertaking to prorogate to the jurisdiction of the Court can be modified by way of a unilateral denunciation. Therefore, the note by State N revoking its consent to the jurisdiction of the Court under the friendship treaty is probably irrelevant.

State O would still have to overcome the argument that the facts of the case arose prior to 1 January 1986, events before which are excluded under art 21 of the treaty. In this case, State O would be best advised that the action is admissible because, until 1989, Oluwole's claim could not be adopted because he was engaged in exhausting the local remedies in State N. Until this was done, no claim could be submitted, and therefore in fact the relevant facts did not surface until after 1 January 1986.

QUESTION FIVE

Compare and contrast the effectiveness of the rules of jurisdiction procedure of the International Court of Justice and the International Centre for the Settlement of Investment Disputes in providing compensation to foreign-owned corporations in the context of public international law.

Written by the Author

General Comment

This question requires consideration of two primary issues, namely the comparative rules as between the International Court of Justice and the International Centre for the Settlement of Investment Disputes in relation to the granting of compensation.

Skeleton Solution

A brief outline of the procedural differences that exist between the ICJ and the ICSID – distinguish between their primary jurisdiction – discuss the concept of nationalisation and extra-territoriality and discuss how compensation is awarded under the ICJ rules and under the ICSID rules – are the current rules satisfactory? – any suggestions or comments for reform?

Suggested Solution

The International Court of Justice (ICJ) is the main judicial organ of the United Nations. It is located in The Hague, Netherlands. It was created in 1945, and started operations in 1946, replacing what was then known as the Permanent Court of International Justice (PCIJ). The PCIJ functioned as an organ of the League of Nations from 1920 to 1939. The United Nations Charter declares that all the member states of the UN are automatically included into the Statute of the ICJ: the ICJ is composed of 15 judges, each elected to nine-year terms of office. The United Nations General Assembly and Security Council is responsible for designating the terms in office. Elections are held every three years for one-third of the seats.

The ICJ has jurisdiction in two main scenarios. First, it is able to settle any legal disputes between states. This, however, has to be in accordance with international law regulations. This first scenario is known as contentious jurisdiction. Second, it is able to provide advisory opinions regarding any legal questions that certain agencies of the United Nations might inquire about. This is known as advisory jurisdiction.

For the ICJ to hear a contentious case, all the parties involved with the proceedings must acknowledge that the Court has contentious jurisdiction. This is usually achieved on an ad hoc basis. This means that both parties involved in the dispute agree that the ICJ will decide the case before it actually takes place. Sometimes, however, these agreements can be made permanent through a bilateral treaty. Another way in which the Court can acquire jurisdiction is through unilateral declarations made by each party. This is usually a less common approach as it is more controversial.

The ICJ's advisory jurisdiction exists so that the Court may provide opinions regarding any international law matters that agencies within the UN might want to inquire about. However, if the request for an opinion has the effect of making a state included in a dispute without its consent, then the Court will simply reject the request.

With regards to any case brought before the ICJ, it may be concluded in one of three ways.

a) The parties involved may tell the Court that they have reached a settlement between themselves. The Court will then proceed to remove the case from its list by issuing an Order.

b) The applicant state may withdraw its suit. The Court will then order the case to be removed from its list.

c) The Court may simply deliver a judgment.

Once the parties have presented their statements in relation to the case at hand, it is up to the Court to then proceed to make a judgment. Since the Court is made up of several jurists, each one is allowed to express their opinion on the matter to ensure that there is equal opportunity for all members participating in the case. Once a decision or judgment has been concluded, it is final. As arts 59 and 60 of the Statute of the ICJ suggest, 'the judgment is final and without appeal. The decision of the Court has no binding force except between the parties and in respect of that particular case.' This means that the Court's decision should not reflect any other cases occurring, even if they are of similar history. However, the Court's decisions have no precedential value. This means that the condition of letting the decision stand, or stare decisis, does not apply. The Court is always allowed to depart from its previous decisions. But, as history states, it seldom does so, often citing past cases as precedent for present or future ones. One of the ways in which a party can suggest to the Court to review its final decision is if new evidence, previously unseen, comes to light. This request must be made within six months after the evidence is uncovered, and within ten years of the delivery of the original document.

As previously mentioned, the Court's decisions are final and may not be challenged by the parties. However, in reality there have been cases where certain parties have simply ignored the Court's decisions. For instance, in *Corfu Channel Case (Merits)* (1949) ICJ Rep 4, Albania refused to pay damages awarded to the United Kingdom for the injuries suffered by their ships in the Corfu Channel in 1946. Also relevant is *Military and Paramilitary Activities in and against Nicaragua (Jurisdiction)* (1984) ICJ Rep 392 and *(Merits)* (1986) ICJ Rep 14, whereby the United States ignored the Court's decision when it was helping the Contras overthrow the Nicaraguan government. The US aided the Contras by planting mines in harbours along Nicaragua. When an innocent fishing trawler was sunk by one of the mines, the Court made a decision against the US, who simply ignored it.

There are other ways of settling disputes between parties. Certain agencies have been created to assist in this procedure. The World Trade Organisation (WTO), for instance, is responsible for implementing and enforcing international rules regulating trade between nations. Put simply, its goal is to 'help producers of goods and services, exporters and importers conduct their business'. The basis for all the rules and regulations that make up the WTO was created in agreements such as the General Agreement on Tariffs and Trade (GATT), etc.

Each of the agreements created had three main objectives: to help trade flow as freely as possible, to achieve further liberalisation gradually through negotiation, and to set up an impartial means of settling disputes. The WTO is an example of an organisation that was set up to settle disputes, with those disputes being trade ones. Other organisations that have been set up to settle disputes may have different rules and regulations, but the main aim is essentially the same, that is to straighten out any difficulties encountered by parties.

Another organisation that was set up to settle investment disputes is the International Centre for the Settlement of Investment Disputes (ICSID). It was created in 1966 at a conference in Washington DC. The convention was named the Settlement of Investment Disputes between States and Nationals of Other States. It has now been ratified by 131 states, and was created to alleviate some of the burden of dispute settlements previously undertaken by the World Bank and the President himself. The main purpose of the ICSID is to encourage private investment in underdeveloped nations. It is also on hand to settle any disputes between the governments of these nations and foreign investments. The Centre is comprised of an Administrative Council, a Secretariat and two panels of experts. The Council is chaired by the President of the World Bank. This shows that there is a strong link between the World Bank and the ICSID. The budget of the Centre is obviously also controlled by the World Bank.

There are three ways in which the ICSID can assist parties to settle any disputes they might have:

a) arbitration;

b) conciliation; and

c) mediation.

The Administrative Council regulates how any arbitrations and conciliations are to begin by laying down certain rules, known as institutional rules. It also monitors the conduct of arbitrations and conciliations through arbitration rules and conciliation rules.

Arbitration

An arbitration is the process by which parties to a dispute submit their differences to the binding judgment of an impartial third person or group selected by mutual consent. The party wishing to make a complaint does so by addressing the Centre, which then sends out what amounts to a summons to the other party. The person chairing the dispute must be unrelated to either of the parties. This person is usually taken from an international organisation such as the International Monetary Fund (IMF) or the WTO. It usually takes place at the ICSID's headquarters in Washington DC; however, the parties can mutually elect to have the arbitration at a different office of the ICSID (ie the Permanent Court of Arbitration at The Hague). An arbitral hearing is usually less costly, less time-consuming, less rigid and less formal than normal litigation. Another advantage is that one does not require a lawyer to be present when in an arbitral hearing. Arbitrations are common in the shipping industry, where multi-national and trans-national contracts are regularly used.

Conciliation

If an arbitral hearing is not an adequate form of settlement in the view of the ICSID, they will adopt a conciliation approach. A conciliation is the process by which an impartial third party makes an independent investigation and suggests a solution to the dispute. The two parties involved come to a compromise to resolve the issue. It is evidently observed by the Centre (being the third person), and any advisory opinions are given out to the parties. It is slightly less cost-friendly than arbitration and usually takes more time to resolve. It is usually seen in building and surveying dispute scenarios.

Mediation

Mediation involves bringing about a peaceful settlement or compromise between parties to a dispute through the benevolent intervention of an impartial third party. It is the least common method of the three mentioned. When a mediator offers only his point of view (ie informal approach), it is known as him offering good offices. Anything more formal than that is regarded as conciliation.

In terms of the jurisdiction of the ICSID, it must rule over both parties involved and also over the subject matter of the dispute. Sometimes, a personal jurisdiction is enforced. This is when a tribunal is agreed to have power over both parties before it hears the dispute. In reality, though, there have been many cases where the jurisdiction of the ICSID has been completely ignored. In those instances, the 'guiltless' party is able to take the matter up further with the ICJ or the Permanent Court of International Justice (PCIJ) which is located in Geneva.

With any dispute there is always a solution. International disagreements are obviously more complicated than domestic ones. The two organisations mentioned above (the ICJ and the ICSID) have been set up specifically to eliminate any disputes that occur between international parties. The ICJ uses a more formal approach to settling disputes compared to the ways of the ICSID. The ICJ's jurisdiction is more apparent than that of the ICSID. The decision of the ICJ carries more weight and therefore more parties will respect it and adhere to it. Similarly, parties dealing with the ICSID tend to be informal and involve communications with each other, and so breaching the final judgment is said to be rare.

However, in reality certain international parties do not have to pay attention to the jurisdictions of these organisations. They are able to break the rules and regulations with little concern for the consequences (should there even be any). This is a result of the heavy political powers that the parties might have. However, disputes must be resolved, be it investment disputes or otherwise, for there to be healthy relationships between states around the world.

Chapter 13

The Law of the Sea

13.1   Introduction

13.2   Key points

13.3   Key cases and legislation

13.4   Questions and suggested solutions

13.1 Introduction

The international law of the sea is regulated for the most part by international conventions. Customary law remains a relatively unimportant factor in determining of the content of the law in contrast to its role in other areas. However, codification has not completely clarified the situation. On the contrary, a number of outstanding issues remain controversial and unsettled. Students should be prepared for these issues to arise in questions, and must be familiar with the different perspectives involved in determining the content of the law of the sea.

13.2 Key points

Attempts at codification

The original attempt to codify the law of the sea was undertaken at the League of Nations Codification Conference in 1930. Although this proved unsuccessful, attempts at codification were resurrected in the work of the International Law Commission (ILC), between 1950 and 1956. This culminated in the UN Conference on the Law of the Sea, held in Geneva in 1958. Four conventions were produced at this session:

a) The Geneva Convention on the Territorial Sea and the Contiguous Zone;

b) The Geneva Convention on the High Seas;

c) The Geneva Convention on the Continental Shelf; and

d) The Geneva Convention on Fishing and Conservation of the Living Resources of the High Seas.

These Conventions bind the parties to them by way of multilateral treaty obligation. However, non-parties may be bound in two ways:

a) if a Convention can be shown to declare the existing customary principles of that period; or

b) if a Convention has had such an effect on the development of customary law that it can be said to represent the present customary position: see the *North Sea Continental Shelf Cases* (1969) ICJ Rep 3.

However, these Conventions did not settle a number of important points, including the permissible width of the territorial sea, and a second Geneva Conference on the Law of the Sea was convened in 1960. However, this meeting was abandoned as unsuccessful without adopting any agreements.

The third United Nations Law of the Sea Convention (UNCLOS) was signed in 1982, and finally came into force in November 1994. This treaty was the product of almost ten years' negotiations and includes a comprehensive coverage of most subjects relating to the law of the sea. The delay before UNCLOS entered into force was because Part XI (which includes the proposed regime for the mining of the ocean floor) was unacceptable to most of the developed world. An impasse was resolved by a UN General Assembly Resolution (Res 48/263), in the form of an 'Implementing Agreement', which effectively revised Part XI, making it more commercially viable and market-orientated, thus enabling the United States and others to ratify the Convention. Although the Convention does not have force of law through treaty, it may be adduced in order to substantiate principles of customary law.

Internal waters

Internal waters such as lakes, rivers, canals and other landlocked bodies of water are considered entirely within the sovereign authority of the state by virtue of forming a part of the territory of the state.

In strict legal terms, jurisdiction over ships in internal waters falls to the territorial state and it is therefore subject to the laws and courts of that state. In practice this jurisdiction has been circumscribed by a rule of comity which has developed whereby a state will prorogate jurisdiction over many matters to the flag state. However, this rule will be ignored where:

a) a request has been made by the flag state to exercise territorial jurisdiction; or

b) action by the territorial state is necessary to preserve the internal order of that state.

See the *Wildenhus Case* 120 US 1 (1887) and *R v Anderson* (1868) 11 Cox Cr Cases 198.

The territorial sea

Article 1 of the Territorial Sea Convention 1958 and art 2 of UNCLOS defines a territorial sea as that belt of sea adjacent to the coast of a state and over which the state exercises sovereignty.

In customary international law, the width of the territorial sea was originally recognised as three miles, although this has been modified by art 3 of UNCLOS which stipulates:

'Every state has the right to establish the breadth of its territorial sea up to a limit not exceeding 12 nautical miles, measured from the baselines determined in accordance with this Convention.'

States therefore exercise discretion in relation to the width of their territorial sea, although this cannot exceed 12 miles. To date, a total of 25 states, maintained a territorial sea of three miles, while 88 states claimed a territorial sea of 12 miles. Twelve states claimed to have territorial seas of greater than 12 miles.

The territorial sea is measured from the baselines, which are identified in art 3 of the Territorial Sea Convention 1958 in the following terms:

'[T]he normal base-line for measuring the breadth of the territorial sea is the low-water line along the coast marked on large-scale charts officially recognised by the coastal state.'

This rule is confirmed in art 5 of UNCLOS. However, exceptions to this rule may be made in the following cases.

a) Straight baselines

Where the coast of a state is deeply indented and cut into, or if there is a fringe of islands along the coast in its immediate vicinity, straight baselines joining the appropriate points may be employed in order to ascertain the breadth of the territorial sea: art 4 1958 Convention, art 7 UNCLOS. See the *Anglo-Norwegian Fisheries Case* (1951) ICJ Rep 116.

b) Bays

A special method of drawing baselines is applicable in the case of bays, and is regulated by art 7 of the 1958 Convention and art 10 of UNCLOS. A bay is defined as 'a well-marked indentation whose penetration is in such proportion to the width of its mouth as to contain landlocked waters and constitutes more than a mere curvature of the coast'. An indentation shall not, however, be regarded as a bay unless its area is as large, or larger than, that of the semi-circle whose diameter is a line drawn across the mouth of that indentation. In any case, the width of a bay must not exceed 24 miles in order to qualify under this rule.

Where the baseline is drawn across the mouth of an historic bay and the bay is in the territory of only one state, the waters inside the bay are considered to be part of the internal waters of that state.

In the event that the bay falls within the territory of two or more states, the status of these waters falls to be determined in light of the special circumstances of the case. For example, in *Case Concerning Land, Island and Maritime Frontier Dispute* (1992) ICJ Rep 351 the International Court held that a bay with three adjacent coastal states was subject to the joint authority of all three states except for a three-mile maritime belt along the coast.

c) Historic bays

A historic bay is one whose mouth is greater than 24 nautical miles, but which has been regarded for some time as part of the coastal state's internal waters. Canada, for example, claims that Hudson's Bay is a historic bay.

Within the territorial sea, the coastal state exercises sovereignty, subject only to the rights of other states under international law. The coastal state is given exclusive rights to exploit the resources of the territorial sea and subsoil and to enact health and welfare regulations, customs administration and navigation requirements.

However, the rights of the coastal state to exercise civil and criminal jurisdiction within the territorial sea are circumscribed by the concept of 'innocent passage'. Article 14 of the 1958 Convention declares that 'ships of all states shall enjoy the right of innocent passage through the territorial sea'. For this purpose, passage means navigation through the territorial sea for the purposes of either traversing that sea without entering internal waters, or of proceeding to internal waters, or if making for the high seas from internal waters. Passage remains innocent so long as it does not prejudice the peace, good order or security of the coastal state.

Where a ship is engaged in innocent passage, the coastal state may only exercise limited criminal jurisdiction. Article 20 of the 1958 Convention precludes civil jurisdiction by providing:

'The coastal state should not stop or divert a foreign ship passing through the territorial sea for the purpose of exercising civil jurisdiction in relation to a person on board the ship.'

Similarly, art 19 of the same Convention restricts criminal jurisdiction over a ship engaged in innocent passage by providing:

'The criminal jurisdiction of the coastal state should not be exercised on board a foreign ship passing through the territorial sea to arrest any person or to conduct any investigation in connection with any crime committed on board the ship during its passage, save only in the following circumstances:
(a) If the consequences of the crime extends to the coastal state; or
(b) If the crime is of a kind to disturb the peace of the country or the good order of the territorial sea; or
(c) If the assistance of the local authorities has been requested by the captain of the ship or by the consul of the country whose flag the ship flies; or
(d) If it is necessary for the suppression of illicit traffic in narcotic drugs.'

According to art 15 of the 1958 Convention, 'the coastal state must not hamper innocent passage through the territorial sea', although the coastal state is at liberty to 'take the necessary steps in its territorial sea to prevent passage which is not innocent'. Article 19 of UNCLOS specifies a number of activities which preclude passage being innocent.

The continguous zone

Article 33 of UNCLOS 1982 provides:

'(1) In a zone of the high seas contiguous to its territorial sea, the coastal state may exercise the control necessary to:
(a) Prevent infringement of its customs, fiscal, immigration or sanitary regulations within its territory or territorial sea;
(b) Punish infringement of the above regulations committed within its territory or territorial sea.'

The contiguous zone cannot extend beyond 24 nautical miles from the baseline from which the breadth of the territorial sea is measured: art 33(2) UNCLOS.

The continental shelf

The original concept of the continental shelf was espoused by US President Truman in 1945. He defined the continental shelf as 'an extension of the land mass of the coastal nation and thus naturally appurtenant to it'. Henceforth, the United States would regard 'the natural resources of the subsoil and seabed of the continental shelf beneath the high seas but contiguous to the coast of the United States as appertaining to the United States, subject to its jurisdiction and control'.

The Geneva Convention on the Continental Shelf 1958 attempted to regulate this matter. Article 1 of this Convention states:

'The term "continental shelf" is used as referring (a) to the seabed and submarine areas adjacent to the coast but outside the area of the territorial sea, to a depth of 200 metres or, beyond that limit, to where the depth of the superjacent waters admits of the exploitation of the natural resources of the said areas.'

Article 2 of the 1958 Convention confers upon the coastal state sovereign rights for the purposes of exploring and exploiting the natural resources of the continental shelf. Articles 1 and 2 of this Convention are generally accepted as representing customary international law. In the *North Sea Continental Shelf Cases* (1969) ICJ Rep 3 the International Court declared:

'The Court entertains no doubt [that] the most fundamental of all the rules of law relating to the continental shelf enshrined in Article 2 of the 1958 Geneva Convention, though quite independent of it, (is) that the rights of the coastal state in respect of the area of the continental shelf that constitutes a natural prolongation of its land territory into and under the sea exists ipso facto and ab initio, by virtue of its sovereignty over the land, and as an extension of it in an exercise of sovereign rights for the purpose of exploring the seabed and exploiting its natural resources. In short, there is an inherent right. In order to exercise it, no special legal process has to be gone through, nor have any special legal acts to be performed.'

Article 76 of UNCLOS provides a more specific definition of the continental shelf:

'The continental shelf of a coastal state comprises the sea-bed and subsoil of the submarine areas that extend beyond its territorial sea throughout the natural prolongation of its land territory to the outer edge of the continental margin, or to a distance of 200 nautical miles from the baselines from which the breadth of the territorial sea is measured where the outer edge of the continental margin does not extend up to that distance.'

A complex, and non-customary, formula is stipulated in art 76(4) as a means to establish the edge of the continental margin in areas exceeding 200 miles.

The rules regulating the division of the continental shelf are undoubtedly the most complex aspect of the law in this field. The Geneva Convention 1958, art 6, provides two rules for the delimitation of the continental shelf:

a) 'Where the same continental shelf is adjacent to the territories of two or more states whose coasts are opposite each other, the boundary of the continental shelf appertaining to such states shall be determined by agreement between them. In the absence of agreement, and unless another boundary line is justified by special circumstances, the boundary is the median line, every point of which is equidistant from the nearest point of the baselines from which the breadth of the territorial sea is measured.'

b) 'Where the same continental shelf is adjacent to the territories of two adjacent states, the boundary of the continental shelf appertaining to such states shall be determined by agreement between them. In the absence of agreement, and unless another boundary line is justified by special circumstances, the boundary shall be determined by application of the principle of equidistance from the nearest point of the baselines from which the breadth of the territorial sea of each State is measured.'

However, these rules do not represent customary international law. See the *North Sea Continental Shelf Cases* (1969) ICJ Rep 3. In this case, the Court held that the apportionment should be made:

'... in such a way as to leave as much as possible to each party all those parts of the continental shelf that constitute a natural prolongation of its land territory ... without encroachment on the natural prolongation of the land territory of the other.'

A number of factors could be taken into account in this determination, including:

a) the general configuration of the coasts as well as the presence of any special or unusual features;

b) physical or geological structures and the natural resources of the continental shelf; and

c) a reasonable degree of proportionality between the extent of each state's continental shelf area and the length of its coast.

These principles have been expanded upon in a series of cases which include the following:

a) *Anglo-French Continental Shelf Case* (1979) 18 ILM 387;

b) *Libya-Tunisia Continental Shelf Case* (1982) ICJ Rep 3;

c) *Gulf of Maine Case* (1984) ICJ Rep 246;

d) *Libya-Malta Continental Shelf Case* (1985) ICJ Rep 12;

e) *Maritime Delimitation in the Area between Greenland and Jan Mayen (Denmark v Norway)* (1993) ICJ Rep 38.

The deep seabed and ocean floor

The status of the deep seabed and ocean floor has been described both as res nullius and as res communis. However, the Declaration of Principles on the Seabed and Ocean Floor appears to favour the concept of the 'common heritage of mankind', which assimilates to res communis.

UNCLOS contains detailed provisions in relation to the seabed and ocean floor which comprise arts 133–191. The following are the basic principles involved in the operation of this regime:

a) the resources of the seabed are declared to be the province of all mankind;

b) the status of the seabed does not affect the status of the superjacent high seas;

c) the seabed is to be exploited in accordance with the regime established by the 1982 Convention; and

d) a number of conditions are placed on exploitation by multinational corporations, including provisions for work plans, contracts, parallel development, transfer of technology, tenure of contracts and review of contracts.

A number of states have adopted unilateral measures for the exploitation of the seabed, including the United States, the United Kingdom, Russia and Germany. Indeed, the regime proposed under the Convention is the primary reason for the non-ratification of the agreement by developed states.

The high seas

Article 2 of the 1958 Convention on the Law of the High Seas declares:

'The high seas being open to all nations, no state may validly purport to subject any part of them to its sovereignty. Freedom of the high seas is exercised under the conditions laid down by these articles and by the other rules of international law. It comprises, inter alia, both for coastal and non-coastal states:
(1) Freedom of navigation;
(2) Freedom of fishing;
(3) Freedom to lay submarine cables and pipelines; and
(4) Freedom to fly over the high seas.'

These freedoms are maintained by UNCLOS in art 87.

Jurisdiction over the high seas is regulated by art 6 of the Geneva Convention 1958. This provides:

'Ships sail under the flag of one state only and, save in exceptional cases expressly provided for in international treaties or in these Articles, shall be subject to its exclusive jurisdiction on the high seas.'

This is an established principle of customary international law, which is codified in art 92 of UNCLOS. The following are the exceptions to this rule.

a) Collisions and other incidents of navigation: see the *SS Lotus Case* (1927) PCIJ Rep Ser A No 10.

b) The right of visit for the purpose of preventing piracy and the slave trade, art 22 of the 1958 Convention: see *Molvan v Attorney-General for Palestine* [1948] AC 351.

c) Hot pursuit, under art 23 of the 1958 Convention: see *The I'm Alone* (1935) 3 RIAA 1609.

The Exclusive Economic Zone

Article 55 of the UNCLOS defines the EEZ as 'an area beyond and adjacent to the territorial sea, subject to the specific legal regime established by this Part'. Article 57 provides that an EEZ shall not exceed 200 nautical miles from the baselines from which the breadth of the territorial sea is measured.

Article 56(1) sets out the rights of the coastal state in relation to the EEZ and provides:

'(1) In the exclusive economic zone, the coastal state has:
(a) sovereign rights for the purpose of exploring and exploiting, conserving and managing the natural resources, whether living or non-living, of the waters superjacent to the seabed and of the seabed and its subsoil, and with regard to other activities for the economic exploitation and exploration of the zone, such as the production of energy from the water, currents and wind;
(b) jurisdiction as provided for in the relevant provisions of this Convention with regard to:
(i) the establishment and use of artificial islands, installations and structures;
(ii) marine scientific research;
(iii) the protection and preservation of the marine environment.'

13.3 Key cases and legislation

- *Anglo-Norwegian Fisheries Case* (1951) ICJ Rep 116
  Illustrates the working of the doctrine of consolidation

- *Case Concerning Land, Island and Maritime Frontier Dispute (El Salvador v Honduras, Nicaragua intervening)* (1992) ICJ Rep 351
  Determination of the legal status of internal waters within an historic bay

- *Corfu Channel Case (Merits)* (1949) ICJ Rep 4
  Considered the jurisdiction of the ICJ based on forum prorogatum

- *I'm Alone, The* (1935) 3 RIAA 1609
  Considered the question of reparations by states responsbile for international wrongs

- *Maritime Delimitation in the Area between Greenland and Jan Mayen* (1993) ICJ Rep 38
  A case relating to the impact of different relative coastlines in the delimitation of the continental shelf and fishery zones between adjacent countries

- *North Sea Continental Shelf Cases* (1969) ICJ Rep 3
  Addressed the contentious jurisdiction of the ICJ

- Deep Sea Mining (Temporary Provisions) Act 1981

- Geneva Conventions 1958 – provide the framework within which the law of the sea operates at an international level

- Geneva Convention on the Law of the Sea 1982

- Territorial Sea Act 1987

13.4 Questions and suggested solutions

QUESTION ONE

The State of Arcadia consists of two islands some 20 nautical miles apart and 50 nautical miles from the coast of the State of Batavia. Between the two Arcadian islands lies the Swift Strait, much used for international navigation, particularly by Batavian shipping. Recently, relations between Arcadia and Batavia have deteriorated owing to disputes about the exploitation of off-shore oil and gas resources and Batavian warships have carried out frequent patrols through the Swift Strait. The Arcadian Government has announced the following measures:

a) a prohibition on all Batavian warships from using the Swift Strait and from entering other parts of Arcadian territorial waters without advance permission from the Arcadian authorities;

b) a prohibition on submarines of all states from using the Swift Strait for submerged transit;

c) a prohibition on Batavian military aircraft from overflying the Swift Strait;

d) a ban on all Batavian-registered civil aircraft from overflying Arcadian territorial waters; and

e) the suspension of the right of passage of all foreign vessels using the Swift Strait and certain other parts of Arcadia's territorial sea 'for reasons of national security' where such vessels are proceeding to Batavian ports.

Assuming that Arcadia and Batavia are both parties to the United Nations Convention on the Law of the Sea 1982, advise the Batavian Government as to the legality of the Arcadian Government's measures.

University of London LLB Examination
(for External Students) Public International Law June 2000 Q9

General Comment

It would be a poor examination on public international law that did not contain a question on the law of the sea. The law of the sea has been one of the most important aspects of international law since at least the time of Hugo Grotius (1583–1645). The coming into force of the United Nations Law of the Sea Convention 1982 in 1994 has provided a degree of clarity and codification in this most important area of law. Past experience indicates that examiners in public international law often set a problem question on the topic of the law of the sea, rather than a discussion question. Such questions are popular with those students who are familiar with the various maritime zones. In such questions it is often sensible for the candidate to draw a quick sketch prior to drafting his answer; this avoids any confusion as to the various zones.

Skeleton Solution

Examine each of the measures taken by the Government of Arcadia – determine whether they are consistent with the requirements of public international law – discuss the general position – conclusions about the legality of the measures taken.

Suggested Solution

On the assumption that Arcadia and Batavia are both parties to the United Nations Law of the Sea Convention 1982 we are asked to advise the Batavian Government as to whether the measures taken by Arcadia are consistent with international law.

Generally

Batavia is an independent State and is in principle entitled to its own maritime zones. Arcadia is an independent State comprising two islands 50 nautical miles from the coast of the State of Batavia. It is therefore an archipelagic state within the broad meaning of art 46 of the Law of the Sea Convention 1982 (LOSC 1982). It therefore follows that it may draw straight archipelagic baselines joining the outermost points of the two islands (see art 47 Law of the Sea Convention 1982), and such baselines will serve for determining the maritime zones of Arcadia. So we are dealing with two independent States each entitled to their own maritime zones. After 1945 a number of archipelagic states in the Carribean, Indian and Pacific Ocean became independent, so it was not surprising that special provision should be made in the 1982 Convention. Water within the archipelagic baselines will in principle be either archipelagic waters (see art 49) or internal waters if closing lines have been drawn across river mouths: see art 50. With these general considerations in mind we can turn to the specific problems.

The ban on Batavian warships using the Swift Strait and entering parts of Arcadian territorial waters

It is clear that Swift Strait is part of archipelagic waters and is in principle subject to the rights of innocent passage of third parties: LOSC 1982, art 49. Since 1958 it as been assumed that the right of innocent passage extends to warships. Thus Batavian warships have a right of innocent passage in archipelagic waters: LOSC 1982, arts 49 and 52 when read with arts 19 and 20. It is correct that the right of passage in archipelagic waters may be suspended (see art 53) but this must only be done: (a) after prior publication, (b) be non discriminatory, and (c) be for the protection of security. These requirements have not been met in this instance. The right of innocent passage must be exercised in accordance with the terms of the Convention: LOSC 1982, arts 39 and 54.

In respect of the territorial waters of Arcadia, the warships have in principle a right of innocent passage: see LOSC 1982, arts 19 and 20. There is a limited entitlement to suspend the right of innocent passage in territorial waters, but such suspension must be non discriminatory and essential for security: see LOSC 1982, art 25(3). The right of innocent passage must be exercised in a manner consistent with the Convention: LOSC 1982, arts 19 and 20. The sensible conclusion must be that the prohibitions announced by Arcadia are at variance with the requirements of international law.

The prohibition on submarines of all States from using the Swift Strait for submerged transit

As indicated above Swift Strait constitutes archipelagic waters (see LOSC 1982, art 49) so that a right of innocent passage arises under art 52. However, that right is referable to the requirements in Part II, section 3 of the Law of the Sea Convention. It is stipulated in art 20 that, for the purposes of the exercise of the right, submarines must navigate on the surface and show their flag. It would therefore seem that this prohibition by Arcadia is consistent with the requirements of international law.

The prohibition on Batavian military aircraft overflying the Swift Strait

As indicated above the waters of the Swift Strait are archipelagic waters and the sovereignty of the archipelagic State extends to the airspace over the archipelagic waters: LOSC 1982, art 49(2). It is correct that art 52 confers a right of innocent passage through archipelagic waters, but only for ships; aircraft have no such right. It may be that Arcadia has designated an air route under art 53(1) as a 'right of archipelagic sea lanes passage'; if that has been done then it may be used by any aircraft under the terms of art 53(2), which would include Batavian military aircraft. So the Batavian military aircraft have no right of overflight unless Arcadia has declared a designated air route under the terms of art 53. If such an air route has been designated, then its subsequent withdrawal on a discriminatory basis would seem to be unlawful having regard to the Law of the Sea Convention 1982: art 54 when read with art 44.

The fact that Batavian aircraft have been overflying in the past would seem to indicate that there had been a designated air route, so that its withdrawal would have been unlawful.

A ban on all Batavian registered civil aircraft from overflying Arcadian territorial waters

It is clear that Arcadia has sovereignty over its own territorial waters (LOSC 1982, art 2) and that such sovereignty extends to the superjacent airspace: LOSC 1982, art 2(2). No right of innocent passage for aircraft exists, so that in the absence of specific international agreement, Batavian registered civil aircraft have no right to overfly Arcadian territorial waters. This legislative ban would thus seem to be consistent with international law.

The suspension of the right of passage of foreign vessels in the Swift Strait and certain other parts of Arcadia's territorial sea

In this part we have two suspensions; one in respect of the archipelagic waters and the other in respect of the territorial sea. In the case of archipelagic waters, a state has the entitlement to suspend the right of innocent passage temporarily provided that it is: (a) without discrimination, (b) if it is essential for the protection of security, and (c) if it has been subject to prior publication: LOSC 1982, art 52(2). In the present instance the suspension is not temporary and it discriminates against those foreign vessels proceeding to Batavian ports. In these circumstances this is not a lawful suspension of the right of innocent passage through archipelagic waters.

In the case of parts of the territorial sea, the right of innocent passage may be suspended temporarily, but such a suspension must be: (a) without discrimination among foreign vessels, (b) essential for the security of the coastal state, and (c) be subject to a requirement of prior publication: LOSC 1982, art 25(3). Manifestly the suspension by Arcadia is discriminatory; it is not temporary and has not been subject to prior publication. The sensible conclusion is that the suspension in respect of innocent passage in the territorial sea is contrary to international law.

Conclusions

In giving advice to the Batavian Government as to the legality of the measures taken by Arcadia, it is strongly arguable that in respect of the specific heads (a)–(e) in the question, the position may be expressed as follows: (a) the measures are contrary to international law, (b) the prohibition is consistent with international law, (c) if there is a designated air route then the measures may be contrary to international law, (d) the ban is consistent with the requirements of international law, and (e) the measures taken are contrary to international law.

Resolution

A final matter arises as to how Batavia and Arcadia may settle their dispute. The dispute itself relates to exploitation of off-shore oil and gas resources; presumably the dispute relates to the continental shelf. It would seem that the solution is probably to be found by an equitable determination of the continental shelf. Under the terms of art 279 of the Law of the Sea Convention 1982, parties are required to settle the dispute peacefully; in these circumstances an agreed reference to the International Court of Justice seems the appropriate course.

QUESTION TWO

The State of Arabia has a coastline which includes a fringe of small adjacent islands, the Miniers, and two major indentations known as the Gulf of Fortune and the Bay of Plenty. The Gulf of Fortune is 200 nautical miles wide at the mouth and the Bay of Plenty is 22 miles wide at the mouth. The territory of Erubia also includes the island known as 'Piscia Rock' some 50 miles from the coast. Erubia has drawn baselines enclosing its internal waters from the outer fringe of the islands, including waters once part of the high seas, and across the mouths of the two bays. Erubia has also extended its exclusive economic zone and continental shelf for 200 miles from the seaward side of Piscia Rock.

The neighbouring State of Felbonia has fiercely contested Erubia's claims and a number of recent incidents have exacerbated tension between the two states. A Felbonian passenger vessel was arrested by the Erubian coastguard while in passage between the Erubian coastline and the Miniers; Erubian aircraft fired on a Felbonian aircraft carrier while the latter was launching its aircraft 20 miles within the Gulf of Fortune; the Erubian navy has arrested a Felbonian vessel for fishing 100 miles seaward of Piscia Rock. Felbonia has alleged that all these acts constitute flagrant breaches of international law and the two states have agreed to refer the disputes to arbitration.

Assuming that both states are parties to the Law of the Sea Convention 1982, outline the findings of the arbitrator on the merits.

University of London LLB Examination
(for External Students) Public International Law June 1999 Q9

General Comment

It is very unusual for a paper on public international law not to contain a question on the law of the sea. In all such questions the candidate has to know how the baselines are drawn and how the maritime zones are determined. Once that has been done, the candidate is able to form a view as to whether particular conduct is consistent with international law. The problem for a candidate is that a question often embraces more than one maritime zone, so the candidate is required to have a good grasp of the entire area. In this particular problem the candidate will need to know about the provisions relating to the drawing of baselines in respect of maritime bays.

Skeleton Solution

Determine the status of each of the maritime zones – examine each of the specific incidents – following arbitral practice, set out conclusions at the end.

Suggested Solution

On any basis this is an interesting question. It brings to mind a remark of the late Lord Denning (in a case on the law of easements) that it is the type of problem that cannot be properly understood without a map. The question itself involves an arbitration in respect of three specific incidents. However, the correct legal analysis in respect of these incidents depends on forming a judgment about particular maritime zones, so that the arbitrator is first required to reach a conclusion about the relevant maritime zones. In all questions concerning the law of the sea one has to first determine the maritime zone before reaching a conclusion on specific rights. The questions that fall for consideration may be listed as follows.

1. The drawing of baselines from the outer fringe of the islands (the Miniers).

2. The drawing of baselines in respect of the Gulf of Fortune.

3. The drawing of baselines in respect of the Bay of Plenty.

4. The drawing of baselines from Piscia Rock.

5. The arrest of the Felbonian passenger vessel.

6. The firing on the Felbonian aircraft carrier by Erubian aircraft.

7. The arrest of the Felbonian fishing vessel by the Erubian navy.

8. Conclusions.

The first preliminary matter is to consider whether arbitration is a suitable method for the resolution of the dispute. Under the terms of art 287 of the United Nations Law of the Sea Convention 1982, it is one of the methods available for the resolution of disputes. Second, it is important to point out that as both states are probably members of the United Nations and certainly parties to the Law of the Sea Convention 1982, they are under a fundamental duty to resolve their disputes peacefully: see art 33(1) United Nations Charter 1945 and art 279 of the Law of the Sea Convention 1982.

1. The drawing of the baselines from the outer fringe of the islands (the Miniers)

   The drawing of the baselines is of crucial importance in the determination of maritime zones. The law on this point has been developed through the judgment in the *Anglo-Norwegian Fisheries Case: UK v Norway* (1951) ICJ Rep 116 and the Territorial Sea Convention 1958. The relevant law is now to be found in arts 5 and 7 of the Law of the Sea Convention 1982. The normal method is the drawing of the baseline by reference to the low watermark line along the coast: see art 5 of the 1982 Convention. However, by art 7 it is provided that the straight baseline method may be employed 'where the coastline is deeply indented and cut into, or if there is a fringe of islands along the coast in its immediate vicinity'. It would seem from the words of the problem that Erubia was entitled to draw straight baselines from appropriate points on the on the Miniers. It is clear that the fringe of islands must be in the immediate vicinity of the coast and cannot embrace Piscia Rock: see art 7 of the 1982 Convention.

2. The drawing of baselines in respect of the Gulf of Fortune

   It would seem that Erubia are not entitled to draw straight baselines across the mouth of the Gulf of Fortune. Even if it could be said that the Gulf of Fortune met the requirements of a 'bay' under art 10(2), it is clear that with a mouth wider than 24 nautical miles, a straight baseline cannot be drawn across: see art 10(4) of the 1982 Convention. The second aspect is whether such baselines could be justified because this is a historic bay. In the *Land, Island and Maritime Frontier Case (El Salvador v Honduras)* (1992) ICJ Rep 351 the International Court of Justice ruled that such claims should be approached with caution. In general, a state must be able to show: (a) it has for a considerable time claimed the bay as internal waters, (b) it has continuously exercised its authority, and (c) during that time the claim has received the acquiescence of other states. It would seem that these criteria cannot be met in the present case, so that the decision to draw a straight baseline across the Gulf of Fortune was probably contrary to international law.

3. The drawing of baselines in respect of the Bay of Plenty

    Given the name employed and having regard to art 10(1) of the Law of the Sea Convention 1982, the question arises as to whether the Bay of Plenty is in law a 'bay'. It will be if its 'area is as large as, or larger than, that of the semi-circle whose diameter is a line drawn across the mouth of that indentation'. If that is the case then it will in law be a bay, and a straight baseline may be drawn across its mouth, because the width does not exceed 24 nautical miles: see art 10(4) of the 1982 Convention. This means that such waters in the Bay of Plenty are internal waters.

4. The drawing of baselines from Piscia Rock

    We are given to understand that Piscia Rock is part of the territory of Erubia. Prima facie it would seem that it is an island (see art 121(1) of the 1982 Convention) and entitled to its own maritime zone (see art 121(2) of the 1982 Convention), unless it cannot sustain human habitation or economic life: see art 121(3) of the 1982 Convention. If Piscia Rock cannot sustain human habitation or economic life it is unable to claim an Exclusive Economic Zone or a Continental Shelf. This matter is returned to below.

5. The arrest of the Felbonian passenger vessel

    If the baselines are drawn at the Miniers as indicated above then on traditional principles water landward of the baselines represents internal waters. In principle a state enjoys full territorial sovereignty over its internal waters so that no right of innocent passage arises in international law. However, where the straight baseline method has been adopted to enclose water not previously internal waters, then a right of innocent passage arises: see art 8(2) of the 1982 Convention. To give a definitive answer one would need to know at what date Erubia adopted the straight baseline method which was validated in the *Anglo-Norwegian Fisheries Case: UK v Norway*; this is because the provisions in art 8(2) of the 1982 Convention repeats provisions in the Territorial Sea Convention 1958: art 5(2). It would seem that in the circumstances a right of innocent passage may have arisen, and interference by Erubia was a breach of international law.

6. The firing on the Felbonian aircraft carrier by Erubian aircraft

As indicated above, the Gulf of Fortune is probably not a historic bay so that straight baselines cannot be drawn across its mouth to confer the status of internal waters upon the Gulf. Instead the baseline would have to be drawn in the manner indicated in art 10(5) of the 1982 Convention. This has the effect that the aircraft carrier may be either in territorial waters or in the Exclusive Economic Zone. If the aircraft carrier is within territorial waters, then its conduct would not constitute innocent passage: see arts 19(a), 19(b), 19(c) and 19(d) of the 1982 Convention. If such aircraft are launched into the airspace above the territorial waters of Erubia, then that would be a breach of art 2(2) of the 1982 Convention. If, however, it is in the Exclusive Economic Zone, then it is arguable that, if it is not interfering with marine life, then it is immune from action: see arts 56, 58(2) and 95 of the 1982 Convention. In any event Erubia is under an obligation to settle the matter peacefully.

7. The arrest of the Felbonian fishing vessel by the Erubian navy

The legality of such an arrest depends on determining the correct maritime zone. If Piscia Rock is capable of sustaining human habitation or economic life, then it is entitled to its own maritime zones (see arts 121(1) and 121(2) of the 1982 Convention) and Erubia would have the right to regulate fishing within any Exclusive Economic Zone see art 56 of the 1982 Convention. If however, as seems likely, Piscia Rock cannot support human habitation or economic life, then it is not entitled to an Exclusive Economic Zone: see art 121(3) of the 1982 Convention. Any such fishing vessel would therefore be on the high seas and prima facie have the right to fish subject to the terms of any regional fishing treaty: see arts 63–67 and 116 of the 1982 Convention.

8. Conclusions

Our conclusions in this matter on the available facts are as follows.

a) The arrest of the Felbonian passenger ship is probably a breach of international law.

b) The firing on the Felbonian aircraft carrier is a breach of international law.

c) Whether the arrest of the fishing vessel is a breach of international law depends on whether Piscia Rock is entitled to an Exclusive Economic Zone within art 121 of the Law of the Sea Convention 1982.

QUESTION THREE

What is the significance for both the law of treaties and the law of the sea of the Agreement on the implementation of Part XI of the Law of the Sea Convention, 1982?

University of London LLB Examination
(for External Students) Public International Law June 1997 Q9

General Comment

There is little doubt that this is the most difficult question on the paper. The law of the sea is a central area of public international law, but this question is directed to a number of technical questions. A well prepared student would be required to know: (a) why the original provisions of the Law of the Sea Convention 1982 were unacceptable to many developed nations; (b) how those objections were formulated; (c) the dangers posed to a universal system by the Reciprocating States Regime; (d) the social and political changes in the years 1982 until 1994 that made compromise possible; (e) the terms of that compromise; (f) the mechanism by which the New York Agreement became provisionally effective; and (g) the extent to which the procedure adopted was consistent with the general law of treaties.

The second difficulty with the question lies in its wording. There is a danger that the student reading the paper quickly might think that the answer required a detailed analysis of the entire Law of the Sea Convention; it is quite clear that the examiner is interested only in the relevant provisions of Part XI of the Law of the Sea Convention. The examiner is clearly seeking to discover whether the student is aware of the compromises that had to be made to ensure that the comprehensive Law of the Sea Convention was able to obtain universal participation.

Skeleton Solution

Introduction – Part XI of the Law of the Sea Convention – concerns of the developed States – precise objections of the United States – the Reciprocating States Regime – negotiations 1990–1994 – the New York Agreement 1994 and General Assembly Resolution 48/263 – conclusion.

Suggested Solution

From the time of Grotius it has been accepted that the law of the sea was one of the cardinal concerns of public international law and likely to be the focus of competing claims by States. The subject itself has grown very considerably since 1945 as the process of decolonisation began to gather pace, and as technological advances made deep sea exploration possible. As with so many areas of public international law there is a need to accommodate the viewpoints of States at different stages of economic development. The Law of the Sea Conference that took place between 1974 and 1982 was charged with drawing up a comprehensive treaty on the law of the sea. The final draft in 1982 received 130 votes in favour with 17 abstentions. Under art 308 the Convention would come into force one year after 60 instruments of ratification had been deposited.

From the outset of the negotiations certain important developed States (eg, Unites States, Germany, United Kingdom) expressed concern about the provisions of Part XI (arts 133–181) as they related to the international sea bed or area, namely, the seabed and ocean floor beyond national jurisdiction. The Convention made detailed provisions in respect of activities within the area. In broad terms the area was to be governed by the International Sea Bed Authority (comprising an Assembly and Council). A Preparatory Commission was established to make arrangements for the establishment of both the International Sea Bed Authority and the International Tribunal of the Law of the Sea.

Although the general scheme was popular with developing nations it did not obtain an enthusiastic welcome elsewhere. The objections of the developed nations were, broadly, concerns about the bureaucratic structure, the share in decision-making and access to sea bed materials, and misgivings about the limitations placed on free market principles.

From the outset the problem had always been that the Law of the Sea Convention would need to be universal if it was to be successful. However, the developed nations made it clear that they were unlikely to ratify the Convention if the provisions in Part XI were allowed to stand.

In January 1982 President Reagan had listed the precise objections of the developed nations to the provisions of Part XI. In general terms these objections were concentrated upon: the process of decision-making within the International Seabed Authority; limitations upon production; mandatory technology transfer; access to qualified applicants; the privileged position of the Enterprise (a separate organ of the International Seabed Authority intended to engage in commercial prospecting and mining); financial provisions; regulatory burdens; distribution of revenues; and the amendment powers of the review conference. These objections were prompted by the influence of free market thinking in certain developed countries.

In the years following 1982 two developments took place. First, the countries most affected by the provisions of Part XI entered into international agreements (the 1982 Agreement Concerning Interim Arrangements Relating to Polymetallic Nodules of the Deep Seabed and the 1984 Provisional Understanding Regarding Deep Sea Mining) and enacted their own legislation. Commencing with the United States' Deep Seabed Hard Mineral Resources Act 1980, and continuing with the United Kingdom's Deep Sea Mining (Temporary Provisions) Act 1981, individual States enacted legislation to enable their own nationals to exploit the seabed. Provision was made for the mutual recognition of licences and the payment of royalties into a central fund. This regime became known as the Reciprocating States Regime. The danger was that when the Law of the Sea Convention finally entered into force there might be two legal regimes in respect of the international seabed.

The second development was that from 1990 the UN Secretary-General (Javier Perez de Cuellar) began active negotiations to obtain a compromise. Such a compromise was possible for three reasons: the end of the Cold War resulted in a greater willingness to accept market-based solutions; the bureaucratic structure of Part XI seemed less necessary; and the fall in metal prices made the problem less pressing. By 1992 negotiations had resulted in agreement on the substantive issues and the particular concerns of developed nations. The problem was how to modify the Law of the Sea Convention 1982 and yet enable it to enter into force on 16 November 1994.

These objectives were accomplished by the complex documentation drawn up in New York in 1994. The Agreement on the Implementation of Part XI of the Law of the Sea Convention ('The New York Agreement') contained a detailed Annex which effectively amended Part XI to meet the concerns of the developed nations. The Agreement was to be provisionally effective from 16 November 1994, and fully in force when 40 States had given consent. A liberal consent regime was included (arts 4, 5 and 6) and no further ratifications of the Convention were possible without consenting to the Agreement. To enable the Law of the Sea Convention to be brought into force on 16 November 1994, and to enable the Agreement to be provisionally effective from that date, General Assembly Resolution 48/263 was passed.

In respect of the law of the sea, the New York Agreement: (a) gave effect to the desire to obtain a comprehensive law-making treaty that would attract universal participation; (b) the Annex to the Agreement effectively amended Part XI of the Law of the Sea Convention to meet the concerns of developed States; (c) while the Treaty and Agreement were to be interpreted together, in the event of inconsistency in respect of Part XI the Agreement would prevail; and (d) the Agreement avoided the possibility of two legal regimes operating in respect of the seabed.

In respect of the law of treaties the entire episode indicates that: flexibility can be achieved in procedure where there is clear international will to achieve a particular objective; the provisions of art 12 of the Vienna Convention on the Law of Treaties are given effect to in the consent provisions of the Agreement; the Agreement in being provisionally applicable is consistent with art 25 of the Vienna Convention of the Law of Treaties; the Agreement is evidence of the practice of employing an agreement (which itself is provisionally applicable) in order to adapt a Convention to changed circumstances; and in effect those that have ratified and those that require an adaptation have agreed that certain provisions of the Convention should be provisionally applicable.

The conclusion must be that the adoption of the Agreement to bring the Convention into force does not represent a radical departure in the law of treaties. The consequences for the law of the sea are more profound. From the early 1970s efforts had been made to achieve a comprehensive treaty that was capable of universal participation. The entire history of the law of the sea since the Truman Proclamations of 1945 testifies to the need to make compromises between States at different stages of economic development. The entire episode illustrates that the social and economic changes since 1982 made the 1994 Agreement possible. It is arguable that the most important change in the Annex to the Agreement is the modification of the decision-making process of the Assembly to meet the concerns of the United States. In any event it was clear from 1982 that the price of universal participation was a degree of compromise with the developed nations in respect of Part XI. The entire Law of the Sea Convention represents a package deal. To a large extent the Agreement represents the end of the negotiating process. The more detailed provisions on maritime pollution will come into force with the Convention, while the dreadful prospect of two legal regimes pertaining to the international sea bed has been avoided.

QUESTION FOUR

'The 1994 Agreement relating to the "implementation" of the United Nations Convention on the Law of the Sea, 1982, represents a victory for states opposed to the principles originally embodied in Part XI of the Convention.'

Discuss.

University of London LLB Examination
(for External Students) Public International Law June 1996 Q9

General Comment

This is a rather narrow question involving a detailed knowledge of Part XI of the Law of the Sea Convention 1982, which relates to the deep seabed. The candidate should be aware of the background to the original section of the convention dealing with the deep seabed and how the General Assembly Resolution in this matter influenced the original draft.

The reasons for the opposition to the original draft should be understood and how the opposition of the developed world influenced the 1994 Agreement.

Skeleton Solution

Nature and status of deep seabed – GA Res 2749 and its influence on the Convention – the terms of the 1982 Convention and the International Sea-Bed Authority – the role of the 'Enterprise'; transfer of technology – opposition of developed world – the terms of the 1994 Agreement – conclusion.

Suggested Solution

Part XI of the Convention is addressed to the 'Area' and it is this geographical entity, and its legal definition and the rights of exploitation which have been the source of controversy in the international community and which delayed the coming into force of the Law of the Sea Convention 1982. The 'Area' refers to the deep seabed and was the subject of disagreement in international law as to its status. The two opposing theories were that, on the one hand, the seabed was res nullius and therefore capable of occupation and appropriation and, on the other hand, that the seabed shared the same characteristics as the high seas and could not be appropriated by either States or other legal entities. The reason for this subject matter taking on a controversial character was the possibility of exploiting the deep seabed and the minerals therein. The General Assembly saw fit to pass a resolution on the matter before even a definition of the area in question was reached. General Assembly Res 2749 (1970) refers to an area of the seabed and the ocean floor beyond the limits of national jurisdiction the precise limits of which are yet to be defined.

The controversy did not, however, centre so much on the definition of the area as on who was to receive the fruits of the exploitation. The resolutions in art 1 to the resources of the seabed, beyond the national jurisdiction, as being the common heritage of mankind. Article 7 speaks of the exploration of the area and its resources being carried out for the benefit of mankind as a whole. The precise legal status of this resolution is unclear and although the resolution did not attract any votes against it, nevertheless it was not authoritatively argued that the resolution represented customary international law.

The Resolution nevertheless acted as a spur to the matter being placed on the agenda at United Nations Convention on the Law of the Sea 1982 (UNCLOS III). Article 9 of the Resolution called for an international regime to apply to the area and the setting-up of international machinery 'to give effect to its provisions ... established by an international treaty'.

The Law of the Sea Convention attempted to establish such an international regime. The deep seabed was firstly defined (the 'Area') as the seabed, ocean floor and subsoil beyond the limits of national jurisdiction: art 1 Law of the Sea Convention. The Convention then went to state that the 'Area and its resources are the common heritage of mankind': art 136. An International Seabed Authority was proposed as the organisation through which activities in the Area were to be controlled and organised. Membership of the Authority was to include all States parties to the Convention: art 156. The Convention then went on to propose that the financial and other economic benefits derived from activity in the Area should be applied by the Authority for the benefit of mankind as a whole, irrespective of the geographical location of States, whether coastal or land locked, taking into particular consideration the interests and needs of developing States: art 149.

The above presented issues of conflict between the developed world and the developing world. Because they had the economic capability, the developed States wished exploitation in the Area to be conducted by their own national enterprises, while the developing States argued for the establishment of an international body to regulate exploitation of the Area's resources. The Convention put forward a Solomonic compromise. The International Seabed Authority delegated the activity of exploitation of the seabed to one of its institutions, the 'Enterprise', with the other half going to a commercial enterprise; this was known as the parallel access basis. The Convention also stated in art 44 that there should be a transfer of technology relating to activities in the Area, from the developed countries and their mining companies to the Authority and the developing States. Articles 150 and 151 sought to regulate the development of the Area with the object of controlling and stabilising mineral prices and thereby protecting those developing countries and their economies which are dependent on the export of raw materials.

The above proposals were unacceptable to the developed world. The developed world argued that the effect would be harmful to their economic well-being as their companies were the most advanced technologically and the most able to exploit and benefit from the exploitation of the seabed. It was an undertaking involving a considerable expenditure of capital, and the proposed regulation of prices went against their free-market principles. On 29 January 1982 President Reagan put forward a number of amendments necessary to effect a United States ratification of the treaty. He argued against restriction of deep sea mining in order to control prices and demand. The United States also stated its opposition to the mandatory transfer of technology. The viewpoint of the United States was also shared by other western States such as Germany and the United Kingdom, which together with the United States refused to sign the treaty while, for instance, France, Russia and Japan refused to ratify the agreement. Moreover the developed world enacted legislation enabling its companies to engage in exploration and exploitation of the deep seabed. Further, the developed world in some instances reached arrangements with each other so as to prevent them granting overlapping national licences: *Starke's International Law* (11th ed), p254.

This refusal of the developed world, with the exception of Iceland, resulted in an impasse.

The opposition of Part XI of the Law of the Sea Convention led to a rethinking of the concepts and ideas behind Part XI. This was put forward by a UN General Assembly Resolution in 1994 (GA Res 48/263). The Resolution addressed itself to the implementation of Part XI. The Resolution urged the States to adopt a revised version of Part XI. The effect of this 'Implementing Agreement' is to accommodate the views of the developed world. The assertion that the deep seabed is the common heritage of mankind is still present but the workings of the Agreement reflect the demand for a market-oriented system. The role of the Enterprise which was to carry out exploration on a parallel access basis (half the seabed to be exploited by commercial enterprises and the other half by the Enterprise) has been diminished. The Enterprise was originally placed in an advantageous position in that the commercial operation was saddled with the initial exploration costs. Under the terms of the Implementation Agreement this obligation is no longer present. Moreover the transfer of technology is no longer a bureaucratic directive, rather it is governed by market principles.

The effect of the above was to allay the fears of the developed world and it led to the ratification of the Law of the Sea Convention by, for example, the United States in July 1994, and the treaty came into force in November 1994. The 1994 Agreement is an effective 'rewrite' of the original. The 'dirigiste' character of the original has been changed. The dropping of a mandatory transfer of technology and of arbitrary limits on production reflects not only the importance and influence of the developed world in this area but also the acceptance of a market-oriented system since the original was drafted.

QUESTION FIVE

The UN Convention on the Law of the Sea 1982 came into force in November 1994. Discuss whether and, if so, the extent to which this event will modify the international legal regime relating to:

a) mining of the deep seabed; and

b) pollution of the marine environment.

Adapted from University of London LLB Examination
(for External Students) Public International Law June 1994 Q5

General Comment

A direct essay question addressing the relevant principles applicable to the law of the sea. Knowledge of recent developments affecting this area of law is necessary to do well in this question.

Skeleton Solution

Implementing Agreement relating to Part XI; US and UK practice – marine pollution: UNCLOS III Part XII; general conventional law and the relationship with UNCLOS III; improvements under UNCLOS III – enforcement.

Suggested Solution

The Third United Nations Convention on the Law of the Sea 1982 (UNCLOS III) came into force on 16 November 1994, more than a decade after it was originally signed.

There had been considerable opposition by Western States to Part XI dealing with deep seabed mining, and after concerted efforts during 1993 and 1994 to negotiate a solution to the problem of non-universal participation in the Convention, such an agreement was reached on 3 June 1994. The Implementing Agreement includes numerous alterations to the provisions on deep seabed mining, to make them more acceptable to the Western powers. Thus, licensing costs have been reduced considerably; there is to be less discrimination in favour of the Enterprise; there is to be no mandatory transfer of technology; nor arbitrary limits on production; and Western states, concerned over financial implications, have blocking powers over certain decisions : see *The Times*, 6 July 1994, p12; I A Shearer, *Starke's International Law* (11th ed, 1994), pp259–60.

These momentous developments have thus obviated the real problems that could have arisen had the Convention come into force over the opposition of the Western powers. Such a situation would have given rise to a lack of certainty as to the applicable legal regime for deep seabed mining which could have significantly affected the likelihood of the mining industry being willing to make investment plans for the exploration and exploitation of deep seabed mineral resources in the absence of a firm legal basis. They also ensure that earlier concerns of conflict between two parallel regimes for deep seabed mining, the one under UNCLOS III, and the other between the non-participating Western states, should not now arise: 'Provisional Understanding Regarding Deep Sea-bed Matters 1984' (1984) 23 ILM 1354; see, generally, D J Harris, *Cases and Materials on International Law* (4th ed, 1991), pp445–9. The regime of deep seabed mining that has come into force is that contained in Part XI, subject to such modifications as are contained in the Implementing Agreement. This carries with it implicit acceptance of the concept of the common heritage of mankind in art 136.

Much the same comments may be made with respect to the provisions in Part XII concerning the Protection and Preservation of the Marine Environment. Thus, were UNCLOS III not to achieve universal participation, the applicable legal regime for the control of marine pollution would have become rather complex. The obligations on states under the Geneva Conventions of 1958 were rather limited in scope and the relevant rules of customary international law of little efficacy. UNCLOS III provides for the first time that states have a general obligation 'to protect and preserve the marine environment': UNCLOS III, art 192.

It would be a mistake, however, to assume that the coming into force of the Convention will drastically modify the legal regime for the control of marine pollution. Indeed, this particular area has been one of the most fertile in the past 50 years or so for state practice; there are now a large number of international conventions, both general and regional, dealing with marine pollution from virtually all sources: see, generally, R R Churchill & A V Lowe, *The Law of the Sea* (2nd ed, 1988), pp241–87. In many respects, the Convention will supplement these several conventions. It does, however, adopt a global approach to the extent that, under art 194, states parties are to deal with 'all sources of pollution of the marine environment'; the approach under UNCLOS III is thus more coherent and unified than the controls imposed under the several conventions, which suffer from the defects that not all are ratified by a large number of states and, second, that there are significant variations in the states which are parties to the conventions. The 'package-deal' ethos of UNCLOS III requires that states must take both the 'good with the bad' – if, for example, they wish to benefit from the provisions of the regime on deep seabed mining, they must also accept more stringent standards on the protection of the marine environment. UNCLOS III also recognises, in art 237, that the provisions of Part XII are without prejudice to the obligations assumed by states under these pre-existing conventions; but that these obligations are to be carried out 'in a manner consistent with the general principles and objectives of this Convention'.

UNCLOS III will, however, make a significant difference in one particular area: that of enforcement. A major concern in the past has been that where enforcement of pollution prevention measures is left in the hands of the flag state, it is far too easy for these standards to be circumvented by the use of the so-called 'flags of convenience'. UNCLOS III envisages a limited shift away from flag state enforcement by making extended provision for enforcement by both coastal states (who will have considerable new powers within the exclusive economic zone) and by port states: see art 220. These latter, in particular, will now be able to exercise enforcement jurisdiction over ships in violation of applicable international rules to prevent marine pollution where the pollution is caused within their territorial sea or exclusive economic zone. Measures such as this will, it is hoped, significantly improve the potential for controlling and reducing marine pollution.

Of course, these developments will not in themselves ensure the necessary universal participation in the Convention. It is noteworthy that the vast majority of the states that had ratified the Convention before it entered into force in 1994 were developing states. However, as Anderson notes, 'there now exist much improved prospects for universal participation in the ... Convention ... 1994 could be a milestone towards the attainment of that goal': (1994) 43 ICLQ 886 at 893. Indeed, the UK announced in 1997 that it was to ratify the Convention. As and when such universal participation is achieved, the international legal regimes for deep seabed mining and the control of marine pollution will be significantly improved.

Chapter 14

The Use of Force by States

14.1 Introduction

14.2 Key points

14.3 Key cases and legislation

14.4 Questions and suggested solutions

14.1 Introduction

Due in part to the complex nature of the subject matter which they purport to regulate, the rules relating to the use of force are both controversial and unsettled. States are reluctant to allow judicial review of political decisions involving force which has resulted in a corresponding dearth of case law and judicial consideration. However, principles have been deduced from diplomatic statements and representations made by parties employing force and the reactions of the international community. The resulting principles and rules attempt to contain and limit conduct which is deemed unlawful by the international political consensus.

14.2 Key points

The doctrine of non-intervention

The legal equality and independence of sovereign states confers upon each state the right to conduct its internal affairs free from the interference of other states, subject only to the rules of international law. This is known as the doctrine of non-intervention and, as the International Court explicitly observed in *Nicaragua* v *United States (Merits)* (1986) ICJ Rep 14 at 106:

'The existence in the opinio juris of states of the practice of non-intervention is backed by established practice. It has moreover been presented as a corollary of the principle of the sovereign equality of states.'

States are obliged to refrain from actions which may be construed as 'intervention' in the sovereign affairs of other states. The classical definition of the term 'intervention' was elaborated in the following passage:

'Intervention is dictatorial interference by a state in the affairs of another state for the purpose of maintaining or altering the actual condition of things ... Intervention can take place in the external as well as the internal affairs of a state ... But it must be emphasised that intervention proper is always dictatorial interference, not interference pure and simple.' Oppenheim, L *International Law* (8th edition, 1955), Vol I, para 134.

Intervention has become synonymous with the use of force. This was clearly recognised by the International Court in the *Corfu Channel Case (Merits)* (1949) ICJ Rep 4. In reply to the contentions of the United Kingdom that minesweeping operations in Albanian waters had been carried out for the purposes of obtaining evidence for subsequent international litigation, the Court made the statement that:

'The Court can only regard the alleged right of intervention as the manifestation of a policy of force, such as has, in the past, given rise to most serious abuses and such as cannot, whatever be the present defects in international organisation, find a place in international law ...'

Attempts have been made to ascertain the content of the principle of non-intervention. General Assembly Resolution 2131 (XX) of December 14, 1960, the Declaration on the Inadmissibility of Intervention in the Domestic Affairs of States, declares the following duties to be a consequence of the principle of non-intervention.

a) No state has the right to intervene, directly or indirectly, for any reason whatever, in the internal or external affairs of any other state. Armed intervention and all other forms of interference or attempted threats against the personality of the state or against its political, economic and cultural element, are condemned.

b) No state may use or encourage the use of economic, political or any other type of measures to coerce another state in order to obtain from it the subordination of the exercise of its sovereign rights to secure from it advantages of any kind. Also, no state shall organise, assist, foment, finance, incite or tolerate subversive, terrorist or armed activities directed towards the violent overthrow of the regime of another state, or interfere in civil strife in another state.

These statements were reiterated in the General Assembly Declaration on the Principles of International Law Concerning Friendly Relations and Co-operation among States in Accordance with the Charter of the United Nations, GA Resolution 2625 (XXV), of 24 October 1970. A number of exceptions have been formulated to justify intervention, including the right of humanitarian intervention and the right of intervention to protect nationals. However, in the absence of a permissive rule of international law to the contrary, where a state employs armed force for the purposes of intervention, such action will be lawful only if permitted by the rules regulating the use of force, ie self-defence. The rules of non-intervention also regulate the rights of states to assist parties involved in civil conflicts and engagements.

In this respect, it is interesting to note that the military conflict in Afghanistan in October 2001 raised the issue of the scope of the right to exercise self-defence among other issues in international law. The subsequent sieges of Kabul and Konduz in November 2001 raised questions regarding the treatment of prisoners of war under the Geneva Conventions. The war initiated as a result of the events of 11 September 2001 against the United States has once again given rise to the debate concerning the treatment of prisoners of war captured by the United States and detained at the Guantanamo Bay camp.

Restrictions on the use of force prior to 1914

Only within the twentieth century have restrictions been placed on the use of force, and until 1945, these remained fragmented. Before 1918, the right to use force was considered a matter of sovereign prerogative and the waging of war was recognised as lawful under international law. As one commentator observed:

> 'International law has … no alternative but to accept war, independently of the justice of its origins, as a relation which the parties to it may set up if they choose, and to busy itself in regulating the effects of the relation.' Hall, WE *A Treatise on International Law* (1880), para 16.

Gradually customary rules were developed to circumscribe this absolute discretion. These customary rules included the following.

The laws of war

A substantial code of rules governed the actual conduct of hostilities on land and at sea. These originally developed from the customary practices of belligerents, but were ultimately codified in treaties. See the numerous Hague Conventions on the Laws of War of 1899 and 1907.

Reprisals

Reprisals are illegal military measures adopted in retaliation for previous illegal acts of another state. In the *Naulilaa Case* (1928) 2 RIAA 1012 a mixed arbitral determined that customary international law imposed three preconditions for legitimate reprisals:

a) the commission of a prior unlawful act;

b) unsatisfied demands for appropriate reparation; and

c) a degree of proportionality between the original act and the reprisal itself.

The use of force for the recovery of debts

The Hague Convention Respecting the Limitation of the Employment of Force for the Recovery of Contract Debts 1907, in art I stipulates:

> 'The Contracting Parties agree not to have recourse to armed force for the recovery of contractual debts claimed by the Government of one country by the Government of another country as being due to its nationals.'

However, the use of force was permitted if the debtor state refused or neglected to reply to an offer of arbitration, or after accepting the offer, rendered a compromis impossible, or, after the arbitration, failed to submit to the award.

The League of Nations and the Pact of Paris

Article 12 of the League Covenant provided:

'The Members of the League agree that if there should arise between them any dispute likely to lead to a rupture they will submit the matter either to arbitration or judicial settlement or to inquiry by the Council, and they agree in no case to resort to war until three months after the award by the arbitrators or the judicial decision or the report by the Council.'

This Covenant imposed two conditions on its members in relation to the right to wage war: members were obliged to seek a peaceful solution to potential confrontations; and, in order to avoid conflict in periods of high tension, a minimum three month period of respite was compelled. However, the Covenant did not outlaw resort to war ipso facto and did not regulate lesser manifestations of force.

If a Member resorted to war in disregard of its obligations under art 12, it was deemed to have committed an act of war against all the other members of the League which were obliged to implement measures to prohibit commercial, financial and national relations with the Member breaking this duty.

In 1928, the Pact of Paris, also known as the Kellogg-Briand Pact, was negotiated. This declares, in art 1:

'The High Contracting Parties solemnly declare in the names of their respective peoples that they condemn recourse to war for the solution of international controversies, and renounce it as an instrument of national policy in their relations with one another.'

This obligation was fortified by a subsequent undertaking on the part of signatories to settle international disputes by pacific means. Reservations were made on behalf of the majority of the parties to the effect that the provisions were inapplicable to measures for the purpose of self-defence.

The United Nations Charter

The following specific obligations are imposed on members of the United Nations.

a) Article 2(3): 'All Members shall settle their international disputes by peaceful means, in such a manner that international peace and security, and justice, are not endangered.'

b) Article 2(4): 'All Members shall refrain in their international relations from the threat or use of force against the territorial integrity or political independence of any state, or in any manner inconsistent with the purposes of the United Nations.'

The threat or use of force under art 2(4) is therefore unlawful when employed:

i) against the territorial integrity or political independence of any state; or

ii) in any manner inconsistent with the purposes of the United Nations which includes the maintenance of international peace and security, the prevention and removal of threats to the peace, and the suppression of acts of aggression or other breaches of the peace. The concept of aggression is expanded upon in the Definition of Aggression Resolution, GA Resolution 3314 (XXIX).

Article 2(4) also represents the customary rule of international law and is therefore applicable to all states, whether or not members of the United Nations: see *Nicaragua* v *United States (Merits)* (1986) ICJ Rep 14, paras 187–201. It effectively prohibits all measures of force except those permitted by the Charter. Only three exceptions have been established: self-defence, collective self-defence and measures authorised by a competent organ of the organisation.

A number of UN General Assembly Resolutions have interpreted the contents and implications of Article 2(4). General Assembly Resolution (XXV), the Declaration on the Principles of International Law Concerning Friendly Relations and Co-operation among States 1970, identifies the following duties.

a) Every state has a duty to refrain in its international relations from the threat or use of force against the territorial integrity or political independence of any state, or in any other manner inconsistent with the purposes of the United Nations. Such a threat or use of force constitutes a violation of international law and shall never be employed as a means of settling international disputes.

b) A war of aggression constitutes a crime against the peace for which there is responsibility under international law.

c) Every state has a duty to refrain from the threat or use of force to violate the existing international boundaries of another state or as a means of solving international disputes, including territorial disputes and problems concerning the frontiers of states.

d) States have a duty to refrain from acts of reprisals involving the use of force.

e) Every state has a duty to refrain from organising or encouraging the organisation of irregular forces or armed bands, including mercenaries, for incursion into the territory of another state.

f) Every state has the duty to refrain from organising, instigating, assisting or participating in acts of civil strife or terrorist acts in another state or acquiescing in organised activities within its territory directed towards the commission of such acts, when such acts involve a threat or use of force.

In *Nicaragua* v *United States (Merits)* the International Court stated:

'[The Court] considers that this opinio juris [in support of the customary incorporation of Article 2(4)] may be deduced from, inter alia, the attitude of the parties and of the states towards certain General Assembly Resolutions, and particularly Resolution 2625 (XXV) entitled "Declaration on Principles of International Law concerning Friendly Relations and Co-operation among States in Accordance with the Charter of the United Nations".'

The scope of art 2(4) clearly extends to uses of force which do not amount to war in the technical and legal sense of the term. However, it is unlikely that the provision relates to political or economic coercion, although this may be a violation of the duty of non-intervention.

The concept of aggression

Prevention of aggression is a stated purpose of the United Nations, and so aggression is prohibited by art 2(4) as being inconsistent with the purposes of the organisation. After a considerable period of discussion, in 1974 the General Assembly adopted the Resolution on the Definition of Aggression, GA Resolution 3314 (XXIX). Article 1 defines aggression as:

> 'The use of armed force by a state against the sovereignty, territorial integrity or political independence of another state, or in any other manner inconsistent with the Charter of the United Nations.'

First resort to armed force by a state in contravention of art 2(4) is deemed to be prima facie evidence of an act of aggression. The Security Council is empowered to determine whether or not an act constitutes aggression in the light of the relevant circumstances surrounding the action. A number of acts are identified as aggression, including:

a) the invasion or attack by the armed forces of a state against the territory of another state, or any military occupation, however temporary, resulting from such invasion or attack, or any annexation by the use of force of the territory of another state or part thereof;

b) bombardment by the armed forces of a state against the territory of another state or the use of any weapons by a state against the territory of another state;

c) an attack by the armed forces of a state on the land, sea or air force, marine and air fleets of another state; and

d) the sending by or on behalf of a state of armed bands, groups, irregulars or mercenaries, which carry out acts of armed force against another state of such gravity as to amount to acts defined as aggression.

This list is specifically declared to be non-exhaustive. Further, the Declaration states that 'no consideration of whatever nature, whether political, economic, military or otherwise, may serve as a justification for aggression'. A war of aggression is declared to be a crime against international peace and gives rise to international responsibility.

The right of self-defence √

The customary rule of international law on the right of self-defence was established in the *Caroline Case* (1837) 2 Moore Digest 412. In an exchange of diplomatic correspondence between the United States and the United Kingdom, it was stated that force may be used in self-defence only where it can be shown that there exists:

'A necessity of self-defence, instant, overwhelming, leaving no choice of means, and no moment for deliberation. (Also) it (must be shown) that the local authorities ... did nothing unreasonable or excessive; since the act, justified by the necessity of self-defence, must be limited by that necessity, and kept clearly within it ...'

This statement was reaffirmed by the International Military Tribunal at Nuremberg as representing the customary right of self-defence. Three criteria must therefore be established for the legitimate exercise of self-defence:

a) an actual or threatened infringement of the rights of the defendant state and an overwhelming need to take immediate action;

b) a failure on the part of the sovereign authorities to prevent the occurrence of an attack; and

c) a degree of proportionality or reasonableness between the original aggression and the actions taken in self-defence.

The United Nations Charter reaffirms the right of self-defence. Specifically, art 51 of the Charter provides:

'Nothing in the present Charter shall impair the inherent right of individual or collective self-defence if an armed attack occurs against a member of the United Nations, until the Security Council has taken measures necessary to maintain international peace and security. Measures taken by Members in the exercise of the right of self-defence shall be immediately reported to the Security Council and shall not in any way affect the authority and responsibility of the Security Council under the present Charter to take at any time such action it deems necessary in order to maintain or restore international peace and security.'

According to this article, the legitimate exercise of self-defence depends on the existence of 'an armed attack' against a Member of the organisation. Further, measures taken in self-defence are subject to review by the Security Council although such action does not depend on the prior permission of that organ.

Two theories have been adduced to describe the relationship between self-defence in customary international law and self-defence under the Charter provision.

a) Article 51 supplanted the customary law on the subject of self-defence. This would reduce the right of self-defence to the narrower interpretation under art 51, rather than preserve the more extensive customary right.

b) Article 51 does not affect the continued existence of the customary right of self-defence. Both regimes continue to exist in parallel.

This question is important in relation to the establishment of a right of anticipatory self-defence. Anticipatory self-defence is clearly prohibited by art 51 which expressly provides that self-defence is legitimate only 'if an armed attack occurs' against a Member of the United Nations. Preemptory action against a build-up of hostile forces on the border of a state would not qualify as action against an armed attack. However, if art 51 does not curtail the customary right of self-defence, it is open to argue that a right of anticipatory self-defence exists in custom and continues to be valid.

Collective self-defence ✓

The right of collective self-defence is expressly recognised to continue under art 51 of the Charter. This provision is the legal basis for mutual defence agreements such as the NATO Alliance and the Warsaw Pact. According to art 5 of the North Atlantic Treaty 1949 (34 UNTS 243) the parties:

> '... agree that an armed attack against one or more of them in Europe or North America shall be considered an attack against them all; and consequently agree that, if such an armed attack occurs, each of them, in exercise of the right of individual or collective self-defence recognised by Article 51 of the UN Charter, will assist the party so attacked (in order to) restore and maintain the security of the North Atlantic area.'

The Warsaw Pact contains comparable commitments. Measures taken in collective self-defence are equally susceptible to review by the Security Council. Further, such measures may only be taken until the Security Council has taken appropriate measures to secure international peace and security. An example of this is the Security Council Resolution 687 (1991) which provided for the establishment of a United Nations Special Commission (UNSCOM) to carry out site inspection tasks in Iraq.

Protection of nationals ✓

Prior to 1945, the protection of nationals abroad was construed as a legitimate exercise of the right of self-defence, recognised in both the writings of jurists and the practices of states. In the *Spanish Zones of Morocco Claim* (1925) 2 RIAA 615 Umpire Huber, as Rapporteur of the Commission, stated:

> 'It cannot be denied that at a certain point, the interests of a state in exercising protection over its nationals and their property can take precedence over territorial sovereignty, despite the absence of any conventional provisions. This right of intervention has been claimed by all states; only its limits are disputed.'

However, it is unclear whether this customary right continues to exist in the light of the restrictive interpretation of self-defence stipulated in art 51. Notwithstanding this uncertain legal situation, a number of states have justified the use of force for the protection of nationals, including the following.

a) The United States: this rationale was adduced to defend American action against the Dominican Republic in 1965, Cambodia in 1975, Iran in 1980, Grenada in 1983 and Panama in 1989.

b) Israel: in 1976 Israeli forces mounted a successful operation to rescue a number of citizens held by Arab terrorists in Entebbe, Uganda. This action was justified by reference to self-defence for the protection of nationals.

c) The United Kingdom: the protection of nationals was adduced to justify British action in Suez in 1956 and the Falklands in 1982.

d) More recently the residents in Gibraltar requested the United Kingdom government to intervene when the Spanish government declared that Gibraltar was officially Spanish.

Despite these illustrations, it remains unclear whether the international community as a whole is prepared to accept the legitimacy of such actions which clearly extend beyond the literal phrasing of art 51.

Humanitarian intervention ✓

The right to use force for humanitarian purposes was never clearly established in either state practice or doctrine. Such an exercise of force cannot be said to rest on self-defence and cannot be justified by reference to international considerations, particularly in the light of the existence of an international organisation with a mandate to protect against abuses of human rights.

In contemporary state practice, a number of situations have arisen in which states might have successfully claimed that their actions were based on humanitarian considerations, including:

a) the actions of India in 1971 to prevent widespread abuses of human rights by Pakistani forces in Bangladesh;

b) the intervention in 1978 by Vietnam in Cambodia to prevent the commission of atrocities by the Khmer Rouge.

However, in neither case was action claimed to be based on the exercise of a right of humanitarian intervention, but rather on the right of self-defence.

Humanitarian intervention is most justified to prevent the commission of genocide inside a state either by the government of that state or forces opposed to the government. In *Case Concerning the Application of the Convention on the Prevention and Punishment of the Crime of Genocide (Second Request for the Indication of Provisional Measures)* (1993) ICJ Rep 325, the International Court, while not ruling on the substance of the case, stated two fundamental propositions: (a) all states are under a duty to refrain from supporting forces within a state engaged in genocide; and (b) UN Security Council Resolutions condemning acts of genocide are prima facie evidence of the commission of such acts and may, in certain circumstances, justify intervention by forces acting on behalf of the international community.

See also *Case Concerning Armed Activities on the Territory of the Congo (Democratic Republic of Congo v Uganda) (Provisional Measures)* (2000) ICJ Rep 9 and *Case Concerning the Legality of the Use of Force (Provisional Measures) (Yugoslavia v Belgium, Canada, France, Germany, Netherlands, Portugal, Spain, UK and USA)* (1999) 38 ILM 950.

Self-determination and the use of force

General Assembly Resolution 2625 (XXV) of 1970, more commonly known as the Declaration on the Principles of International Law Concerning Friendly Relations and Co-operations among States, explicitly stipulates:

'By virtue of the principle of equal rights and self-determination of peoples enshrined in the Charter, all peoples have the right freely to determine, without external interference, their political status and to pursue their economic, social and cultural development, and every state has the duty to respect this right in accordance with the provisions of the Charter.'

The existence of this right creates a number of problems in relation to the regulation of the use of force. Can force be used in order to achieve the goal of self-determination? The declaration is unclear on this point, merely stating:

'Every state has the duty to refrain from any forcible action which deprives peoples ... of their right of self-determination and freedom and independence. In their actions against and resistance to such forcible action in pursuit of the right of self-determination, such peoples are entitled to seek and receive support in accordance with the purposes and principles of the Charter of the United Nations.'

It would therefore seem that the use of force by a people for the purposes of removing colonial dominion is not illegal. This is supported by the argument that art 2(4) prohibits force contrary to the purposes of the United Nations, but since self-determination is a stated purpose of the United Nations, force employed to achieve such a purpose is lawful. This is supported by art 7 of the Resolution on Aggression 1974 which stipulates that:

'Nothing in this Definition ... could in any way prejudice the right of self-determination, freedom and independence, as derived from the Charter, of peoples forcibly deprived of that right ...'

14.3 Key cases and legislation

- *Case Concerning Armed Activities on the Territory of the Congo (Democratic Republic of Congo v Uganda) (Provisional Measures)* (2000) ICJ Rep 9
  Considered the circumstances justifying intervention by international community

- *Case Concerning the Legality of the Use of Force (Provisional Measures) (Yugoslavia v Belgium, Canada, France, Germany, Netherlands, Portugal, Spain, UK and USA)* (1999) 38 ILM 950
  Considered intervention based on humanitarian law

- *Case Concerning the Application of the Convention on the Prevention and Punishment of the Crime of Genocide (Second Request for the Indication of Provisional Measures)* (1993) ICJ Rep 325
  A decision relating to the relationship between intervention and the crime of genocide

- *Case Concerning Oil Platforms (Islamic Republic of Iran v United States of America)* (2003) Judgment of 6 November (unreported)
  Considered the question of what amounts to unlawful force

- *Corfu Channel (Merits) Case* (1949) ICJ Rep 4
  Considered the use of force by states outside its own borders

- *Legality of the Threat or Use of Nuclear Weapons (Request for Advisory Opinion by the General Assembly of the United Nations)* (1996) 35 ILM 809
  Considered the legality of the use of nuclear weapons

- *Military and Paramilitary Activities in and against Nicaragua (Nicaragua v United States) (Merits)* (1986) ICJ Rep 14
  Considered the scope of collective self-defence

- Chemical Weapons Act 1986

- Covenant of the League of Nations 1919

- General Treaty for the Renunciation of War 1928

- North Atlantic Treay 1949

- United Nations Charter 1945

Note: these set out the regulatory framework within which obligations and compliances are set out.

14.4 Questions and suggested solutions

QUESTION ONE

In 1928, States A and B concluded an international Agreement in relation to their long-standing territorial dispute. The Agreement provides that the Parties agree to submit any disputes between them concerning its interpretation and application to the Permanent Court of International Justice (PCIJ) in accordance with the Court's Statute unless the Parties agree to settlement by some other peaceful means. There was also a supplementary Agreement between A and B concluded in 1930 to the effect that attempts should be made to use diplomatic means of negotiation to peacefully settle any disputes between the Parties before resort to judicial proceedings.

In 1995, A alleged that the armed forces of B encroached into its part of the previously disputed territory and asserted ownership. After some skirmishes between the two States, A reported the incident to the Security Council. The Council invited B, which is not a member of the United Nations, to participate in the discussions in the Council on the understanding that she accepted all obligations of United Nations members in a similar case. B accepted. The Council subsequently resolved that the two Governments should exercise restraint and immediately refer their dispute to the International Court of Justice (ICJ) for resolution in accordance with the Statute of the Court.

After attempts to further negotiate the matter between the two States failed, State A initiated proceedings against B before the ICJ, relying as a basis for the Court's jurisdiction, on the resolution of the Security Council and on art 25 of the UN Charter (which provides that members agree to accept and carry out the decisions of the Security Council). B argued that the Security Council's resolution was not relevant to the situation, that the unilateral application by A was unjustified under the Statute of the Court but, in any event, profoundly convinced of the justice of its case, she was prepared to appear before the Court.

With reference to the jurisdiction of the ICJ, formulate a legal opinion on the legal issues arising from the facts as they might affect the position of States A and B.

University of London LLB Examination
(for External Students) Public International Law June 2000 Q7

General Comment

It is certainly quite common for a question to appear on a paper in public international law directed to the question of the jurisdiction of the International Court of Justice (ICJ). The reason is that, because the ICJ does not possess compulsory jurisdiction, many cases are fought around the issue of whether the court is entitled to hear the matter. If it does not have jurisdiction then clearly the matter will not proceed to a hearing on the merits. Thus the ICJ's jurisprudence contains many cases where questions of jurisdiction are in issue. Moreover, since a government legal department often has unlimited resources, it may be prepared to advance a wide range of technical arguments designed to prevent jurisdiction arising. Thus questions of jurisdiction play a much greater role in public international law than they do in European law, where the European Court of Justice has compulsory jurisdiction. Some states are happy to prolong the jurisdictional arguments in the hope that they may reach a diplomatic solution and thus avoid a hearing on the merits. The difficulty of this question for the candidate is that there is quite a lot of material to read and analyse in a limited period of time.

Skeleton Solution

Jurisdiction of the International Court of Justice – the general principles pertaining to exercise of jurisdiction – the role of the United Nations – the effects of treaties and conventions.

Suggested Solution

We are asked in this matter to consider the jurisdiction of the International Court of Justice in the context of a long running territorial dispute; an action has been brought by State A against State B before the International Court of Justice. In particular, we are asked to consider the various legal issues arising between the parties. For the purposes of exposition it is sensible to take the issues in chronological order.

The 1928 Agreement

On its face this appears to be a bilateral treaty designed to resolve outstanding territorial issues between the parties. This provides for the submission of disputes on interpretation and application to the Permanent Court of International Justice (PCIJ) unless the parties agree to settlement by some other peaceful means. It is clear from the terms that the emphasis is upon submission to judicial determination in the absence of an agreement to settle by some other peaceful means.

The 1930 Agreement

This Agreement seems to be supplementary to the 1928 Agreement and in principle has to be read with it. As a matter of first impression, it seems that the 1930 Agreement pledges both States to try diplomatic negotiations first as a method of resolving the dispute. It is relevant to observe that diplomatic negotiation is but one method of peaceful settlement of disputes. It is certainly arguable that the 1928 Agreement and the 1930 Agreement are to be read and interpreted together, and the parties have in effect sought to regulate three matters: (a) whether a dispute arises between the parties, (b) to employ diplomatic negotiations as the first method of peaceful resolution, and (c) to submit the matter to resolution by the PCIJ unless they have agreed some other method of peaceful resolution.

The transition from the Permanent Court of International Justice (PCIJ) to the International Court of Justice (ICJ)

It is relevant to observe that art 37 of the Statute to the International Court of Justice 1945 provides that where a treaty includes a compromissory clause in favour of the PCIJ, that shall in respect of parties to the 1945 Statute be referred to the International Court of Justice. The difficulty here is that B is not a member of the United Nations and has not independently signed the Statute. I will return to this point below.

The 1995 incursion of forces by State B

In principle this conduct is a breach of the United Nations Charter and of art 2(4), and that, under art 2(6), the Security Council is entitled to act against non-members. State B appeared before the Security Council and agreed to accept the obligations of a United Nations member which prima facie includes the obligation to settle the matter peacefully under art 33 United Nations Charter 1945. Further, any member of the United Nations is ipso facto a party to the Statute of the International Court of Justice: art 93(1). The relevance of the incursion is that it is powerful evidence of a dispute between the two States.

The discussion within the Security Council

The Security Council are entitled to discuss the matter under the terms of Chapter VI and Chapter VII, and they have concluded that the dispute is in essence a legal dispute; in conformity with art 36(3) they have recommended that the matter be referred to the International Court of Justice. Given that the dispute concerns territorial boundaries, and their determination by treaty, this seems to be an eminently sensible conclusion. In normal circumstances the Security Council would order one or other party to withdraw to the status quo ante. Cases of boundary disputes often involve complex historical and legal research and are very suitable for judicial determination.

The commencement of proceedings by State A

State A has begun proceedings before the International Court of Justice, alleging that the Court has jurisdiction because the matter was subject to a recommendation by the Security Council under art 36(3) of the United Nations Charter, and on the further basis of art 25. These two claims of jurisdiction are misconceived and were rejected by the majority in the *Corfu Channel Case (Merits): UK v Albania* (1949) ICJ Rep 4, where it was held that neither represented an independent head of jurisdiction. This analysis has been accepted by the majority of textbook writers. The next question that arises is whether, having regard to the response of State B, the International Court of Justice has jurisdiction under any other head.

The jurisdiction of the International Court of Justice

It is arguable that the International Court of Justice has jurisdiction under one of two heads. First, the doctrine of forum prorogatum holds that a state may consent to the jurisdiction of the Court subsequent to the initiation of proceedings. This doctrine has been applied in the past (see *Corfu Channel Case (Preliminary Objections): UK v Albania* (1948) ICJ Rep 15; *Monetary Gold Case* (1954) ICJ Rep 19) and it will be relevant here, having regard to the subsequent conduct of State B. It does seem that State B has subsequently consented to the jurisdiction of the Court.

Second, there is the technical argument that the 1928 Agreement included a compromissory clause which became binding under art 37 of the Statute of the International Court of Justice 1945 when State B agreed to accept of the obligations of a member of the United Nations, which included the provisions of art 93 of the United Nations Charter which makes members ipso facto a party to the Statute of the International Court of Justice. For the purposes of the clause, there is clearly a dispute between the two States as to the interpretation and application of the Agreements regulating the long standing territorial dispute: see the *Ambatielos Case (Preliminary Objections)* (1952) ICJ Rep 28; *Aerial Incident of 27 July 1955 Case (Preliminary Objections)* (1959) ICJ Rep 127; *Barcelona Traction Case (Preliminary Objections)* (1964) ICJ Rep 6.

Conclusion

Our conclusion on this matter can be briefly stated. The International Court of Justice is likely to conclude that it possesses jurisdiction, but not on the grounds asserted by State A, and the case is likely to proceed to a hearing on the merits. Such a hearing will be directed to the true interpretation and proper application of the 1928 and 1930 Agreements. It may be that the proper interpretation of the Agreements will yield a solution to the long running territorial dispute. As it appears that the International Court of Justice may have jurisdiction on the merits, the Court and the parties may wish to consider whether any interim orders would be appropriate in respect of the precise position of the armed forces of State B.

QUESTION TWO

The population of the State of Despairia consists of two ethnic groups, the Wabenzi, who make up 60 per cent of the population and who control the government and the armed forces, and the Ba-Audi, who comprise the remaining 40 per cent. After an outbreak of unrest amongst the Ba-Audi minority, many Ba-Audi have been arrested and their villages burned by government troops. The situation has provoked a mass exodus of Ba-Audi refugees into the neighbouring state of Zenubia, causing there major economic problems and a breakdown of law and order.

Zenubia has approached the Security Council of the United Nations, asking for authority to intervene in Despairia in order to enforce the establishment of a protected zone for the Ba-Audi people. The government of Despairia has warned that any intervention within its territory would amount to a flagrant breach of fundamental principles of international law as incorporated in the United Nations Charter.

Advise Zenubia as to:

a) how the Security Council is likely to respond to Zenubia's request; and

b) whether, in the event of no action being taken by the Security Council, international law entitles Zenubia to intervene unilaterally?

University of London LLB Examination
(for External Students) Public International Law June 1996 Q5

General Comment

This problem requires an understanding of the power and functions of the Security Council with reference to intervention and the use of force in the affairs of another State. The candidate should be aware of customary international law and the provisions of the UN Charter in relation to State sovereignty and the use of force. In addition, an acquaintance with the doctrine of humanitarian intervention is necessary to answer part (b).

Skeleton Solution

a) State sovereignty; art 2(7) – power and functions of Security Council – Iraq and Somalia precedents – workings of Ch VII.

b) Article 2(4) – art 51 – humanitarian intervention – conclusion.

Suggested Solution

a) The presumption of international law is against interference in the domestic affairs of a State. International law on the relationship between States is based on the principle of sovereign equality between States. The origin of this principle may be found in the Peace Treaty of Westphalia 1648. The notion of sovereign equality means that all States have equal rights and duties. All States are entitled to exercise exclusive jurisdiction over their domestic affairs, and no one State may intervene in the domestic affairs of another.

The modern reiteration of this principle is found in the UN Charter, which recognises sovereign equality – the Security Council notwithstanding – and which states in art 2(7):

> 'Nothing contained in the present Charter shall authorise the UN to intervene in matters which are essentially within the domestic jurisdiction of any state.'

The Security Council may, however, effectively override these provisions if the consequences of the domestic affairs of a State threaten international peace and security. By art 24 the Security Council is given primary responsibility for the maintenance of international peace and security. The Council has first to determine any threat to international peace and then once that determination is made in accordance with art 39 the Council may act. What amounts to a threat to international peace and security of the world community is not defined in the UN Charter. It is for the Council to determine as each situation presents itself.

Zenubia could argue that there are precedents supporting UN action in the internal affairs of other States. The most relevant precedent is to be found in Security Council Resolution 688 which was passed in the aftermath of the Gulf War. The failure of the Kurdish revolt against the Iraqi regime resulted in a mass exodus of Iraqi Kurds (an ethnic minority) into the neighbouring States of Iran and, principally, Turkey. The actions of the Iraqi government were condemned by the UN and measures were instituted to protect the Kurdish minority in the north of the country. The mass exodus of refugees was deemed to have a destabilising effect on the region and was thus a matter of concern to the Security Council in its role of sentinel of international peace and security. The situation in Despairia is somewhat similar. The mass exodus of Ba-Audi refugees has caused considerable internal problems to Zenubia.

Zenubia will also find a precedent in UN actions in Somalia. Security Council Res 794 authorised a United States force to intervene in Somalia with the proviso that they report their actions to the Security Council. The purpose of the force was to restore order to the disintegrated state of Somalia and 'to speed food and medical supplies to the … victims of drought and civil war' (President Bush). The justification for this action was humanitarian as there was little evidence that the civil war in Somalia was having a significant effect in destabilising the region. Zenubia could, however, cite this precedent, as presumably one of the reasons it wishes to establish a protected zone for the Ba-Audi people is because of their harsh treatment by the government of Despairia. While the UN Security Council authorised action in Bosnia may provide a superficial precedent it should be pointed out that Bosnia, a recognised State, invited the UN and then the IFOR troops into its jurisdiction. Moreover Zenubia's possible reference to these precedents is only useful as a means of persuasion, because the Security Council is not bound by its own decisions. In addition, the Security Council is only as active or inaction as the Member States, and particularly the Permanent Members, wish it to be. Under art 27 decisions of the Council must be made by an affirmative vote of nine members including the votes of the Permanent Members. An abstention by a Permanent Member is not, however, treated as a veto.

Zenubia, it should be noted, has asked for authority to intervene in Despairia rather than asking for UN troops to intervene. Under Ch VII art 42 the UN is authorised to use force to maintain international peace and security and the UN is permitted to delegate its functions to Member States provided they are authorised by the UN. In the Korean War the Security Council passed a resolution recommending that Member States send forces to help South Korea. This was passed under the terms of art 39 and the result was a UN force under the command of the US President. Zenubia's forces could therefore 'wear the blue helmet' but be under the control of the Zenubian government. UN authority to act is the key to understanding the legal justification: without the UN authority to act the legal justification is much more limited (see below). A different situation arose in the Gulf War where by Res 678 the Security Council authorised Member States, co-operating with the government of Kuwait, to use all necessary means to restore international peace and security in the area. The Gulf War coalition was not composed of UN troops, rather they were UN-authorised troops. Similarly the no-fly zones over Iraq are UN-authorised but enforced by the United States, the United Kingdom and France. Zenubia is therefore perfectly entitled to ask for authority to intervene in Despairia but whether this is granted or not is a separate matter.

b) Zenubia's entitlement to act unilaterally is much more open to question. Article 2(4) of the Charter states:

> 'All members shall refrain ... from the use of force against ... the political independence of any State.'

Zenubia is also prohibited from infringing the territorial integrity of other States. This view is supported in customary international law and repeated in *Nicaragua* v *United States (Merits)* (1986) ICJ Rep 14.

How, then, may Zenubia make out a case for intervention?

Zenubia could argue that it is entitled to intervene on the grounds of self-defence. The mass exodus of Ba-Audi refugees has caused a severe disruption to its domestic situation. Under art 51 a State is entitled to use force for the purposes of self-defence. What amounts to self-defence is not defined in the article, perhaps deliberately so, and has been a cause of contention. In 1972 India intervened in the civil war raging in East Pakistan arguing that its territorial integrity and security was being threatened by the mass exodus of people from East Pakistan to West Bengal. Such a justification was not without controversy because the move resulted in the defect of the Pakistani army and the establishment of the State of Bangladesh.

If Zenubia were to plead self-defence then the action must be limited to the threat and have no ulterior purpose. The 'action taken must not be unreasonable or excessive': *Caroline Case* (1837) 29 BFSP 1137. The situation must also leave no other choice. This is not the case here because the Security Council has chosen not to act rather than being unable to act.

Brownlie (*Principles of Public International Law* (4th ed, 1990)) argues that a State may not empower itself to intervene, by force, unilaterally in the affairs of another State. The custodian of the international legal system is the UN and in particular the Security Council. The contrary view, supporting the right to self-defence if the UN fails to act, is supported by such legal writers as Bowett and Lillich.

One is told that the Ba-Audi do not control the government and the armed forces. They have also been treated harshly, having their villages burned and being subjected to what appears to be mass arrest. Such a situation may support the contention of Zenubia that it is entitled to intervene on humanitarian grounds.

Humanitarian intervention was a doctrine espoused particularly in the nineteenth century and which provided the legal justification of one State to forcibly intervene in the affairs of another. The origins of the rule may be found, inter alia, in the writings of Vattel and Grotius, who adhered to the view that if a ruler was abusing the rights of his subjects then intervention was justified. France, for instance, intervened in the nineteenth century to protect the rights of the Christian population in what is now Lebanon. Whether this is applicable today is open to question. As with the right of self-defence, the legal justification of a State to act unilaterally must be examined in the light of the functions of the Security Council. Even where the Security Council has taken actions which are akin to humanitarian intervention, as in Somalia, it has seen fit to put in a caveat. The preamble to Security Council Res 794 in relation to Somalia talks about the 'unique character of Somalia' as one of the justifications for allowing the UN and United States troops into the country for humanitarian purposes. This phrase was inserted to calm third-world fears about the resurrection of humanitarian intervention. While India's action in East Pakistan (see above) looked to have the character of humanitarian intervention, India was careful to argue self-defence. Rather than being entitled to intervene, Zenubia may find itself condemned by the Security Council.

QUESTION THREE

Within State P, tension has long existed between the two ethnic groups which make up its population – group X, the members of which constitute the majority of the population and hold the most important posts in the government and armed forces, and group Y, most of the members of which live in Y-land, a region located in the south of State P. Recently, persons belonging to group Y have perpetrated acts of terrorism against government offices in State P. In response, State P's armed forces have proclaimed a state of martial law in Y-land and have detained without trial a large number of persons belonging to group Y. Amnesty International has issued a report claiming that many of the persons so detained are being tortured. A number of persons belonging to group Y have also been found dead, having been killed by persons unknown.

State Q, the majority of whose population is composed of persons belonging to group Y, wishes to send its armed forces to Y-land in order to protect the members of group Y living there from State P's army.

Advise state Q: (i) whether the United Nations may authorise it to undertake such an operation; and (ii) whether it may lawfully undertake such an operation without any authorisation from the United Nations.

University of London LLB Examination
(for External Students) Public International Law June 1992 Q3

General Comment

A problem-type question requiring the application of the law to the facts presented. In essence, the examiner requires the answer to deal with two separate issues: the power of the United Nations to take appropriate measures; and the right of states to intervene for humanitarian purposes.

Skeleton Solution

i) Powers of the United Nations to intervene – arts 24 and 39 UN Charter and art 2(7) – previous examples, including the use of allied forces against Iraq.

ii) Article 2(4) of the UN Charter; self-defence exception – principle of non-intervention; *Nicaragua Case* – doctrine of humanitarian intervention.

Suggested Solution

i) Article 24 of the United Nations Charter confers upon the Security Council 'primary responsibility for the maintenance of international peace and security'. In order to discharge this responsibility, the Security Council is authorised to undertake enforcement action to counter threats to the peace, breaches of the peace or acts of aggression. These measures can be adopted under Chapter VII of the Charter.

The Security Council must therefore determine whether the actions of State P constitute a threat to the peace, a breach of the peace or an act of aggression under art 39 of the Charter. Due to the existence of the veto, determinations under art 39 have been rare and consequently there are few precedents available to assist to determine whether the actions of State P constitute any of these three offences.

Nevertheless, it is relatively certain that the activities of State P do not constitute acts of aggression. General Assembly Resolution 3314 (XXIX) on the Definition of

Aggression defines aggression as 'the use of armed force by a state against the sovereignty, territorial integrity or political independence of another state'. Since the facts presented in the question provide no indication that State P has acted against another sovereign state, it is unlikely that State P's conduct can be characterised as an act of aggression as specified in art 39.

What type of behaviour constitutes a breach of the peace is not defined and, judging by the past practice of the Security Council, is decided on an ad hoc basis. However, the fact that the actions of State P are confined within its own borders does not prevent its behaviour from being considered a breach of the peace. This is clear from art 2(7) of the Charter which prohibits the United Nations from intervening in matters which are 'essentially within the domestic jurisdiction of any state', but the terms of which are specifically inapplicable in the event of enforcement measures under Chapter VII of the Charter.

Further, in the past, the Security Council has been prepared to consider activities in a single state to be a threat to the peace. For example, Security Council Resolution 221 (1966) declared the unilateral declaration of independence by the white Rhodesian government to be a threat to the peace despite the fact that the declaration itself was an internal political instrument.

While the United Nations Charter envisaged the setting up of a military command under United Nations auspices to provide armed forces for enforcement and peacekeeping activities, this agency has never been established. This has resulted in the practice of the Security Council authorising individual states or, more often, coalitions of allied states, to undertake enforcement or peacekeeping activities on its behalf. Past history indicates that the Security Council is fully empowered to authorise states to undertake military operations to prevent the continuation of a breach of the peace.

Thus, in the Security Council Resolution of 25 June, 1950, permitting the use of force against North Korea, the Council authorised Members to furnish such assistance to the Republic of Korea as necessary to repel the attack and to restore international peace and security to the area. Similarly, Security Council Resolution 678 (1990) authorised UN members cooperating with the Government of Kuwait to use 'all necessary means' to restore international peace and security in the area. However, in both of these cases, individual states were authorised to cooperate with the government of the states affected rather than take measures specifically directed against particular states.

The one notable exception was the creation of the safe havens in the north and south of Iraq after the Iraqi invasion of Kuwait. In May 1991, the Security Council authorised the creation of demilitarised zones in both areas to prevent the commission of further abuses by Iraqi forces against the Kurds and Shiites. These zones were protected from air attack by authorising the United States and other allied forces to prevent Iraqi aircraft entering these zones.

Therefore, it is likely that the UN Security Council may legitimately authorise State Q to undertake a military operation within State P to protect the members of group Y living in the south of State P. However, any such operation would have to comply fully with the wording of the Security Council Resolution authorising such action and would therefore probably be confined to the protection of the population and could not involve the forcible overthrow of the government of State P.

ii) The issue of whether or not State Q could undertake such protective measures without the authorisation of the UN Security Council is a different matter and involves quite separate principles of international law.

Article 2(4) of the United Nations Charter quite clearly specifies that all states must refrain in their international relations from the 'threat or use of force against the territorial integrity or political independence of any state'. Naturally, any proposed intervention on the part of State Q, without the express authorisation of the Security Council, would contravene the terms of this principle.

At the same time, in the *Nicaragua* v *United States (Merits)* (1986) ICJ Rep 14 the International Court observed that coexisting with the principle prohibiting the use of force is the principle of non-intervention. It is implicit in this principle that no state has the right to intervene, directly or indirectly, for any reason whatever, in the internal or external affairs of any other state; see General Assembly Resolution 2131 (XX), the Declaration on the Inadmissibility of Intervention in the Domestic Affairs of States. Acts of intervention are therefore prima facie unlawful and the International Court has stated that so-called rights of intervention are 'the manifestation of a policy of force, such as has, in the past, given rise to most serious abuses and such as cannot, whatever be the present defects in international organisation, find a place in international law': *Corfu Channel Case (Merits)* (1949) ICJ Rep 4.

Yet, neither of these principles is absolute. Article 51 of the UN Charter, for example, provides an exception to the application of art 2(4) and allows Member States to act in self-defence in the event of an armed attack so long as such measures remain in proportion to the original offence. But from the facts presented, State Q clearly cannot rely on this right since there has been no armed attack by the forces of State P against its territory.

However, there is authority to support the view that art 51 has not supplanted the pre-existing right of self-defence applying prior to 1945 when the United Nations Charter came into existence. In other words, there may be a broader right in customary international law to adopt measures in self-defence other than the right stated in art 51.

The point here is that, prior to 1945, the protection of nationals abroad was construed as a legitimate exercise of the right of self-defence. As Umpire Huber commented in the *Spanish Zones of Morocco Claim* (1925) 2 RIAA 615:

'It cannot be denied that at a certain point, the interests of a state in exercising protection over its nationals and their property can take precedence over territorial sovereignty despite the absence of any conventional provision. This right of intervention has been claimed by all states; only its limits are disputed.'

One of the most recent instances of a state acting to protect its nationals was the United States action against Grenada in 1983. Among a host of other justifications raised by the United States government for the invasion was the right to intervene to protect nationals which was generally accepted by the international community.

In the event that states continue to possess the customary right to take measures in self-defence for the protection of their nationals abroad, it could then be argued that State Q has the right to adopt protective measures to prevent atrocities against kindred ethnic groups. Although the nexus between a state and its nationals is stronger than between a state and cognate ethnic groups, at least an argument can be made for allowing State Q to act in self-defence to protect members of group Y. However, it must be acknowledged that it is an inherent weakness of this argument that the members of group Y are not nationals of State Q. The *Case Concerning Oil Platforms (Islamic Republic of Iran v United States of America)* (2003) Judgment of 6 November (unreported) illustrates the considerations taken on board by the International Court of Justice in deciding whether the use of force by one state against another is lawful or unlawful.

As regards the doctrine of non-intervention, the right of humanitarian intervention has never been clearly established in either state practice or doctrine. In contemporary times, there have been two main instances of unilateral action by states based on humanitarian considerations. In 1971 the forces of India acted to prevent widespread abuses of human rights by Pakistani forces in Bangladesh. Similarly, in 1978, Vietnamese forces intervened in Cambodia to prevent the commission of atrocities by the Khmer Rouge. However, in both these cases, the intervening states based their actions not on the principle of humanitarian intervention but on the right of self-defence based on border incursions and hostilities.

State Q would therefore best be advised to engage in vigorous diplomatic protests to the authorities of State P pointing out how the actions of the government, and the wilful torture and murder of members of group Y, constitute violations of the accepted norms of international law. In the event that this proves unsuccessful, State Q should bring the matter before the UN Security Council for an emergency debate. While at this point State Q could offer its services for deployment in State P, the matter is one of international concern and therefore the responsibility of the Security Council. A failure of the Security Council to act will probably not justify State Q in unilaterally invading State P even for the purposes of preventing atrocities.

QUESTION FOUR

State S lies immediately to the south of State T. The southern region of State T is known as U-land. The overwhelming majority of the population of U-land consists of the Us, a people who are ethnically quite distinct from the rest of the population of State T. In 1987, a U Liberation Organisation (ULO) was set up among the Us of State T to campaign for the independence of U-land from State T. The Government of State T refused to accede to the ULO's demands. Consequently, in 1988, the ULO launched an armed struggle against the Government of State T to achieve the independence of U-land. The ULO initially scored some military successes. However, by 1991, the ULO's forces found themselves in extreme difficulties and, on 20 May 1991, the ULO called on State S to assist it in its struggle against the armed forces of State T's Government.

On 31 May 1991, the President of State S makes a speech on television denouncing the Government of State T for its refusal to accede to the ULO's demands for independence, declaring that the people of State S 'will not stand idly by and permit their brothers and sisters in U-land to be oppressed' and vowing that State T 'will soon learn in more practical terms of the uncontainable anger which the people of State S feel'. On 3 June, all reservists are called on to present themselves for military service in State S's army. On 5 June, 50,000 troops of State S's army take up positions within five miles of State S's border with State T. On 7 June, State S's air-force begin to fly up and down the border taking photographs of State T and listening to State T's army's radio traffic. On 9 June, 30,000 troops of State S's army and all of State S's airforce conduct a military exercise with live ammunition within 10 miles of the border. On 11 June, State S's troops are issued with extra ammunition, fuel, and provisions.

Late on 11 June 1991, State T's airforce enters State S's air-space and attacks State S's army and airforce. State T's airforce also attacks and destroys State S's navy and many of State S's port installations, power stations, bridges, railways, roads, civil and military airfields and government buildings.

On the morning of 12 June 1991, the President of State S calls on State V 'to help State S defend itself against the vicious attack launched on it by State T'.

Advise State V.

University of London LLB Examination
(for External Students) Public International Law June 1991 Q9

General Comment

This is a fairly complicated hypothetical factual question concerning the right of states to use armed force to intervene in the affairs of other states.

Skeleton Solution

The right of self-determination – the principles of self-defence and non-intervention – arts 2(4) and 51 – *Nicaragua Case*.

Suggested Solution

It appears that the population of U-land will not be able to take advantage of the principle of self-determination in order to cede from State T. Article 2 of the Declaration on the Granting of Independence to Colonial Territories and Peoples does affirm that 'all peoples have the right to self-determination' by virtue of which they are free to determine their own economic, social and cultural development. This right was subsequently confirmed in the 1970 Declaration on the Principles of International Law. However, while there is little doubt that the right of self-determination exists, there is considerable confusion as to its scope.

The concept of 'peoples' is generally considered to be confined to populations that are the subjects of colonial domination. This limitation is derived from the decision of the International Court of Justice in the *Western Sahara Case* (1975) ICJ Rep 12, where the Court stated that the principle 'must be considered in the context of the decolonisation process'.

However, from the facts presented, it is not apparent that the ULO represents the interests of the people of U-land, or that the incorporation of U-land into State T was the result of the acts of a colonial overlord. If the ULO had been able to rely upon the principle of self-determination, then it might have been able to invoke against State T the rule in the 1970 Declaration that:

> 'Every State has the duty to refrain from any forcible action which deprives peoples ... of their right to self-determination and freedom and independence.'

The territorial sovereignty of states is protected by two principles of international law: the prohibition on the use of force and the doctrine of non-intervention.

The prohibition on the use of force is embodied in Article 2(4) of the UN Charter which provides:

> 'All Members shall refrain in their international relations from the threat or use of force against the territorial integrity or political independence of any State.'

This is subject only to the right of self-defence contained in art 51 of the Charter and the authority of the UN Secretary to authorise the use of force to counter threats to the international peace and security of the world.

The doctrine of non-intervention obliges states to refrain from interfering in the internal affairs of states in which there is armed strife and was extensively considered in the *Military and Paramilitary Activities in and against Nicaragua (Merits) Case* (1986) ICJ Rep 14. In this decision, the International Court declared the principle to be a rule of customary international law that prevented states from using armed intervention or any other form of interference to coerce a state into granting advantages of any kind.

From the facts presented, it does not appear that State S has infringed either of these rules.

First, the doctrine of of non-intervention prohibits all states from organising, assisting, fomenting, financing, inciting or tolerating subversive, terrorist or armed activities directed towards the violent overthrow of another state, or interference in the civil strife of another country. Prior to June 1991, the government of State S appears to have observed this obligation despite the ethnic bonds between the people of U-land and those of State S.

The one possible exception is the speech by the President of State S denouncing State T for refusing to accept the demands of the ULO for independence and declaring the support of the people of State S. Nevertheless, this communication did not threaten the use of military force against State T, and, although being tantamount to propaganda, could not justify any acts of force other than proportional countermeasures, such as the jamming of broadcast transmissions into the territory of State T. Certainly, such an act alone could not justify the use of armed force in alleged self-defence.

But, State S subsequently mobilised its forces, positioned large numbers of troops close to the borders of State T, commenced reconnaissance activities against military and strategic installations in State S, and practised military manoeuvres close to the border. The question is whether these activities constitute measures of force which justify an armed response from State T in self-defence.

Article 51 of the UN Charter reserves the right of state defence to states against which an 'armed attack' has occurred. In the absence of an actual armed attack against the territorial integrity or political independence of a state, force cannot be justified in self-defence under art 51.

However, there is some support for the view that art 51 does not codify the customary right of self-defence that existed prior to the negotiation of the UN Charter and that the customary principle embodies the right of anticipatory self-defence. This was the argument used by the Israeli government to justify pre-emptive strikes against its Arab neighbours in the 1967 Arab-Israeli conflict. At least one authority is prepared to argue for the existence of this right because no state can be expected to wait until an armed attack has occurred if such an attack is imminent and significant evidence has been gathered to support the allegation: see D W Bowett, *Self-Defence in International Law* (1958), p188.

There is no evidence in the traveaux preparatoires or the language of the text of the Charter to support such a proposition and the doctrine has not been stated with sufficient precision to allow an objective determination of when such a pre-emptive strike may be justified.

But, if the principle of anticipatory self-defence can be upheld as a legal proposition, then it is likely that State T acted lawfully in attacking the armed forces of State S massed on the border. All the evidence suggests that State S was preparing to attack State T. Not only did State S mobilise its troops on the border, but it also issued them with sufficient ammunition and logistic support to allow them to attack State T. The International Court of Justice has decided that the use of force in self-defence can be declared as unlawful if there is sufficient evidence pointing to an alternate and peaceful settlement of the dispute.

It is true that the International Court did say, in the *Nicaragua Case*, that the conducting of military exercises in Honduras by the United States was an unfriendly act, but these activities did not justify the use of force in self-defence, rather the employment of countermeasures. The preparations of State S have exceeded those of mere exercises and now amount to a provocative preparation for an assault on the territory of State T.

In these circumstances, it appears that the State T was permitted to attack the armed forces of State S, but in fact, State T also attacked a number of targets which were not involved in the immediate offensive against State T. It is an accepted principle of international law that any use of force in self-defence must remain in proportion to the original offence and must be conducted within the rules of the laws of military conduct. It is questionable whether State T's actions remain within these confines.

Article 51 of the UN Charter not only authorises individual, but also collective self-defence. In other words, a state may go to the assistance of another if that state is the object of aggression. For example, the North Atlantic Treaty of 1949, art 5, states that the contracting parties agree that an attack against one or more of them shall be considered an attack against all of them. Collective self-defence not only exists under multilateral arrangements, but can be effected on a bilateral basis between two states.

It is also likely that there is no rule of international law prohibiting one state from rendering assistance to another, even without a prior agreement, if the state under attack has not been guilty of infringing any rules of international law.

Under international law, State V could render assistance to State S if there existed treaty obligations which rendered an attack on State S to be an attack on State V. If State V considered the activities of State T to amount to aggression, State V could also render assistance. Alternatively, State V could take the matter before the UN Security Council and seek multilateral collective action along the lines taken by the Council against Iraq in the latter part of 1990.

QUESTION FIVE

'The Falklands hostilities in 1982 illustrate yet again the fundamental importance of the principle of self-defence. The United Nations failed to provide machinery for the resolution of the underlying disputes concerning title to territory and self-determination and displayed for all to see the inadequacy of the system of collective security embodied in the Charter of the United Nations.'

Discuss and consider what improvements in United Nations machinery might be acceptable to Member States of the United Nations.

Written by the Author

General Comment

This question requires consideration of the role of the United Nations in prohibiting the unilateral use of force in the resolution of international disputes and how this is achieved.

Skeleton Solution

Brief description of the role of the UN – the role of the Security Council – art 51 and the right of self-defence – methods of resolution exercised by the UN – the efficacy of these methods or measures.

Suggested Solution

The whole object of the regime established under the Charter of the United Nations is to prohibit the unilateral use of force in the resolution of international disputes. To this end art 2(3) of the Charter provides that all members shall settle their international disputes by peaceful means, in such a manner that international peace and security, and justice, are not endangered. This provision is reinforced by art 2(4) which provides that all members shall refrain in their international relations from the threat or use of force against the territorial integrity or political independence of any state, or in any other manner inconsistent with the purposes of the United Nations.

However, the invasion of the Falkland Islands by Argentina illustrated that where a state does resort to armed force in the settlement of its international disputes, then the United Nations is powerless to stop it and ineffective in enforcing the provisions of the Charter. Following the Argentine failure to comply with Security Council Resolution 502 demanding inter alia an immediate withdrawal of Argentine forces from the Falklands, it was left to the United Kingdom to exercise its inherent right of self-defence preserved under art 51 of the Charter and seek to remove the invaders by force. Article 51 of the Charter allows a Member of the United Nations to exercise the right of self-defence if an armed attack occurs against it until the Security Council has taken the measures necessary to maintain international peace and security. The Falkland hostilities serve to illustrate that the Security Council is usually unable to take such measures.

Nevertheless machinery does exist under the Charter for enforcement action by the Security Council. Until recently, however, the power of the veto ensured that, in practice, the Security Council seldom acted. Under Chapter VII of the Charter which deals with enforcement action with respect to threats to the peace, breaches of the peace and acts of aggression the Security Council has two forms of enforcement action available to it. Under art 41, action not involving the use of armed forces and under art 42 action by air, sea and land forces. But in practice the power of veto meant that the measures envisaged in Charter VII were virtually useless. In any situation involving an East-West conflict of interest it was usually impossible for it to achieve the unanimity necessary for it to work. For example in Berlin, Palestine, Indio-China,

Hungary and Suez the Security Council never used its enforcement powers. Only on two occasions prior to 1990 had it done so, Korea and Southern Rhodesia. But even then the action by the Security Council over Korea was only possible because of the fortuitous absence of the Soviet representative who had been boycotting the Council.

It remains to be seen whether the new found cooperation of the five permanent members over the invasion of Kuwait will invest the Security Council with powers under Chapter VII of the Charter that will subsist beyond this dispute.

It was this use of the veto rendering the Security Council impotent that led the General Assembly in 1950 to pass the resolution on Uniting for Peace under which the General Assembly may act to maintain or restore international peace and security if the Security Council because of lack of unanimity of the permanent members cannot exercise its primary responsibility. This procedure has been used on several occasions and does serve to alleviate some of the problems caused by the veto.

The major problem therefore has been the power of the veto which has rendered the Security Council unable of acting when, as was usually the case, East-West conflicts of interest were involved. This in turn has given rise to another major problem, that of the lack of consistency on the part of the United Nations in condemning acts of aggression. Wherever a double standard exists whereby certain states use aggression and are condemned while others do so with impunity, then the provisions of the Charter will never have universal respect. There will always be one state which thinks it can get away with it or shelter behind the veto of its sponsor on the Security Council. Argentina, for example, in the Security Council debate on the Falklands, raised the example of Portuguese Goa, invaded by India in 1961. When Portugal raised the matter before the Security Council it refused to act, and today India remains in possession of this territory she seized by force. Therefore, even with the machinery to act, international politics and the self interest of states will in practice override the principles and purposes of the Charter. It is therefore doubtful that any improvements in the United Nations machinery would alter this state of affairs even assuming that such improvements would be acceptable to the states Members of the United Nations. It may be, however, that the end of the Cold War rivalries will mean that the existing machinery will have greater effect.

Chapter 15

The United Nations

15.1   Introduction

15.2   Key points

15.3   Key cases and legislation

15.4   Questions and suggested solutions

15.1 Introduction

The United Nations remains the most significant universal international organisation from the international legal perspective, despite its constitutional handicaps. The UN Charter, perhaps the most ambitious and ambiguous international agreement ever drafted, not only created an organisation to regulate international affairs, but also redefined the foundations of international law in the post-1945 era. Students should be acquainted not only with the various organs of the organisation, but also the history of its attempts to maintain international peace and harmony through law and order.

15.2 Key points

The purposes and principles of the United Nations

Article 1 of the UN Charter identifies the following as the purposes of the Organisation:

'(1) To maintain international peace and security, and to that end: to take effective collective measures for the prevention and removal of threats to the peace, and for the suppression of acts of aggression or other breaches of the peace, and to bring about by peaceful means, and in conformity with the principles of justice and international law, adjustment or settlement of international disputes or situations which might lead to a breach of the peace;
(2) To develop friendly relations among nations based on respect for the principle of equal rights and self-determination of peoples, and to take other appropriate measures to strengthen universal peace;
(3) To achieve international co-operation in solving international problems of an economic, social, cultural or humanitarian character, and in promoting and encouraging respect for human rights and for fundamental freedoms for all without distinction as to race, sex, language, or religion; and
(4) To be a centre for harmonising the actions of nations in the attainment of these common ends.'

The degree of generality with which these purposes have been drafted has allowed two different perceptions of the role of the Organisation to develop.

a) Western states perceive the primary purpose of the United Nations as preserving international peace and security.

b) Developing countries emphasise the social and economic purposes of the Organisation, ie self-determination.

The Charter specifies seven important principles on which the Organisation is founded.

a) Article 2(1): the Organisation is based on the sovereign equality of all its Members.

b) Article 2(2): all Members, in order to guarantee the rights and benefits resulting from membership, shall fulfil in good faith the obligations assumed by them in accordance with the present Charter.

c) Article 2(3): all Members shall settle their international disputes by peaceful means in such a manner that international peace and security, and justice, are not endangered.

d) Article 2(4): all Members shall refrain in their international relations from the threat or use of force against the territorial integrity or political independence of any state, or in any manner inconsistent with the purposes of the United Nations.

e) Article 2(5): all Members shall give the United Nations every assistance in any action it takes in accordance with the present Charter, and shall refrain from giving assistance to any state against which the United Nations is taking preventive or enforcement action.

f) The Organisation shall ensure that states which are not members of the United Nations act in accordance with these principles so far as may be necessary for the maintenance of peace and security.

g) Nothing contained in the present Charter shall authorise the United Nations to intervene in matters which are essentially within the domestic jurisdiction of any state or shall require the Member to submit such matters to settlement under the present Charter; but this principle shall not prejudice the application of enforcement measures under Chapter VII.

Membership of the Organisation

Membership of the United Nations is confined to states and is classified into two categories.

a) Original Membership: those states which signed and ratified the Charter at the negotiating conference in San Francisco or signed the 'United Nations' declaration by the anti-Axis wartime forces in 1942 are conferred with original membership.

b) Subsequent Membership: the conditions for subsequent membership are stated in art 4(2). In order to be eligible for subsequent membership, a candidate must be a 'peace-loving' state which accepts the obligations of the Charter and, in the judgment of the Organisation, is able and willing to carry out these obligations.

The admission of a state to membership is made through a decision of the General Assembly, based on a recommendation of the Security Council. In the *Conditions for Admission of a State to Membership of the United Nations Case* (1948) ICJ Rep 57 the International Court declared that existing Members, voting in the Security Council or the General Assembly, were not permitted to invent additional criteria for admission other than those of art 4(1). In particular, consent to admit new members could not be withheld in order to secure a political balance in the membership of the Organisation.

Under art 5, a Member against which preventative or enforcement action has been taken by the Security Council, may be suspended if the General Assembly, on the recommendation of the Council, decides accordingly. The exercise of that state's rights in the Organisation may be reinstated by the Security Council.

A Member which has persistently violated the principles of the Charter may be expelled from the Organisation under the procedure established by art 6. The General Assembly carries out the expulsion on the recommendation of the Security Council.

The organs of the United Nations

The United Nations has six principal organs:

a) the General Assembly;

b) the Security Council;

c) the Economic and Social Council (ECOSOC);

d) the Trusteeship Council;

e) the Secretariat; and

f) the International Court of Justice (ICJ).

In addition, a number of specialised agencies are considered part of the United Nations system, although no provision for such a relationship is contained in the Charter. These include: the International Labour Organisation (ILO); the International Civil Aviation Organisation (ICAO); the International Bank for Reconstruction and Development (IBRD); the International Development Association (IDA); the International Finance Corporation (IFC); the International Monetary Fund (IMF); the Food and Agricultural Organisation (FAO); the UN Educational, Scientific and Cultural Organisation (UNESCO); the World Health Organisation (WHO); the Universal Postal Union (UPU); the International Telecommunications Union (ITU); the World Meteorological Organisation (WMO); the Intergovernmental Maritime Consultative Organisation (IMCO); the World Intellectual Property Organisation (WIPO); the International Fund for Agricultural Development (FAD); the UN Industrial Development Organisation (UNIDO); and the General Agreement on Tariffs and Trade (GATT).

The General Assembly

The General Assembly consists of all the Members of the Organisation. It is essentially a deliberative organ which proceeds on the basis of recommendations rather than binding decisions. Recommendations have no legally binding effect on the Members unless made under a specific provision vesting such authority, as for example, in the approval of the budget which establishes the obligation of a Member to pay its contribution.

The General Assembly is conferred with the following powers.

a) To discuss any questions or any matters within the scope of the Charter or relating to the powers and functions of any organs provided for in the Charter, and, except as provided in art 12 (limitations in respect of Security Council consideration) to make recommendations to the Members or the Security Council in relation to such questions or matters: art 10.

b) To consider general principles of co-operation in the maintenance of international peace and security, including disarmament and may make recommendations on this subject: art 11(1).

c) To discuss and make recommendations on any particular issue relating to peace and security brought before it by a Member state, the Security Council, or a non-Member accepting in advance the obligations of pacific settlement: art 11(2).

d) To initiate studies and make recommendations for the purpose of:

i) promoting international co-operation in the political field and encouraging the codification and progressive development of international law; and

ii) promoting international co-operation in the economic, social, cultural, educational and health field, and assisting in the realisation of human rights and fundamental freedoms: art 13.

e) To make recommendations for the peaceful adjustment of any situation likely to impair the general welfare or friendly relations among nations.

The General Assembly has a considerable discretion in relation to formulating resolutions which embody such recommendations. The relationship between the purposes and functions of the General Assembly and recommendations made in the pursuit thereof was considered in the *Certain Expenses of the United Nations Case* (1962) ICJ Rep 151. This duty of the General Assembly was further seen to surface when the UN General Assembly requested the ICJ to 'urgently render an advisory opinion' on the legal consequences that may arise from the construction of the wall being built by Israel on the Occupied Palestinian Territory.

The General Assembly is given power to discuss matters pertaining to international peace and security. In the exercise of this function, in 1950, the General Assembly passed the Uniting for Peace Resolution, GA Resolution 377 (V). This instrument declares that, henceforth, the General Assembly:

'1 Resolves that if the Security Council, because of the lack of unanimity of the permanent Members, fails to exercise its primary responsibility for the maintenance of international peace and security in any case where there appears to be a threat to the peace, a breach of the peace, or act of aggression, the General Assembly shall consider the matter immediately with a view to making appropriate recommendations to members for collective measures, including in the case of a breach of the peace or act of aggression the use of armed force when necessary, to maintain or restore international peace and security ...

7 Invites each Member of the United Nations to survey its resources in order to determine the nature and scope of the assistance it may be in a position to render in support of any recommendations of the Security Council or of the General Assembly for the restoration of international peace and security.

8 Recommends to the state Members of the United Nations that each Member maintain within its national armed forces elements so trained, organised and equipped that they could promptly be made available ... for service as a United Nations unit or units, upon recommendation by the Security Council or the General Assembly ...'

This Resolution was adopted by 52 votes to five, with two abstentions. However, the recommendation is consensual, and not mandatory. Measures are recommended in order to harmonise international policy towards a threat to the peace. Even under this Resolution, the General Assembly could not compel a Member to adopt a certain course of action against its wishes. However, the Resolution has formed the basis for General Assembly peacekeeping actions in a number of cases.

In the *Certain Expenses Case* (above) the ICJ made the following comments on the legality of peacekeeping actions by the General Assembly:

'The responsibility conferred (by Article 24) is "primary", not exclusive. This primary responsibility is conferred upon the Security Council, as stated in Article 24, "in order to ensure prompt and effective action". It is only the Security Council which can require enforcement by coercive action against an aggressor.

The Charter makes it abundantly clear, however, that the General Assembly is also to be concerned with international peace and security ... While it is the Security Council which, exclusively, may order coercive action, the functions and powers conferred by the Charter on the General Assembly are not confined to discussion, consideration, the initiation of studies and the making of recommendations; they are not merely hortatory. Article 18 deals with "decisions" of the General Assembly "on important questions" ... Moreover, these powers of decision of the General Assembly under Articles 5 and 6 are specifically related to preventative or enforcement measures ... The Court considers that the kind of action referred to in Article 11, paragraph 2, is coercive or enforcement action.'

The Court therefore held that, in exercise of its secondary responsibility for the maintenance of international peace and security, the General Assembly was acting constitutionally in organising peacekeeping measures.

The Security Council

According to art 23, which was amended in 1965, the Security Council is to be composed of fifteen members, which are classified into:

a) Permanent Members: there are five such members, including the United States, the Soviet Union, the United Kingdom, France and China.

b) Non-permanent Members: these are selected by the General Assembly for a period of two years, with due regard being given in the election processes to the contribution of the candidate to the maintenance of international peace and also geographical distribution. A formula for geographical allocation was adopted in General Assembly Resolution 1991 (XVIII)A.

Voting in the Council is regulated by art 27 which states:

'(1) Each Member of the Security Council shall have one vote.
(2) Decisions of the Security Council on procedural matters shall be made by an affirmative vote of nine Members.
(3) Decisions of the Security Council on all other matters shall be made by an affirmative vote of nine Members including the concurring votes of the permanent Members; provided that, in decisions under Chapter VI, and under paragraph 3 of Article 52, a party to a dispute shall abstain from voting.'

The requirement of the concurring votes of the permanent Members creates a veto power in favour of these parties. This power has effectively destroyed the potency of the Security Council. Only one concession has been made in this respect. Where a permanent Member abstains, as opposed to casting a negative vote, this has been interpreted as concurrence. In the *Namibia Case* (1971) ICJ Rep 16 the International Court refused to declare unconstitutional an abstention by a permanent Member as a bar to the adoption of a resolution.

The functions and powers of the Security Council are enumerated in arts 24–26 of the Charter. The Council has as a 'primary function' responsibility for the maintenance of international peace and security. Where the Council acts intra vires, the Members of the United Nations are bound by its actions and, under art 25, they 'agree to accept and carry out the decisions of the Security Council in accordance with the Charter'. The Council's primary function, to maintain international peace, is exercised in two dimensions.

Pacific settlement of disputes

Chapter VI lists the ways in which the Security Council may facilitate the settlement of international disputes.

Enforcement action

The enforcement capacity of the Security Council operates through two provisions: art 41, regulating measures not involving force; and art 42, regulating measures involving force. However, before deciding on enforcement action, the Council is obliged to determine the existence of 'any threat to the peace, breach of the peace, or act of aggression', in accordance with art 39.

Action under art 41 has been taken five times – with regard to Rhodesia, following the Unilateral Declaration of Independence of 1965, South Africa in 1977, Iraq in 1990, Libya in 1992 and Serbia in the same year.

On the other hand, art 42 has been infrequently employed by the Security Council. In the two most notable cases of intervention under United Nations auspices – against Iraq and in Somalia – this provision was not involved in either case. Thus, against Iraq, the resolution authorising the use of 'all appropriate measures', in Security Council Resolution 678 (1990), was not passed on the basis of art 42 and hence the force deployed was considered an 'allied force' as opposed to a UN force.

Events in recent years relating to terrorism have increased the efficiency and speed of the Security Council. For example, the terrorist bombings of 7 August 1998 in Kenya and Tanzania were condemned via a Resolution on the 13 August 1998. The Afganistan situation was considered in December 1998. In October 1999 the Security Council passed a resolution imposing sanctions on the Taliban and required states to cooperate against terrorism, and this resolution was subsequently reviewed in December 2000. The events leading up to the attack on the World Trade Centre in New York on 11 September 2001 were condemned almost immediately by the UN Security Council (12 September 2001) via Resolution 1368. Subsequently, a more comprehensive resolution on the subject of terrorism was passed on 28 September 2001. As a result, Resolution 1442 has been extensively reviewed by the United Nations Security Council.

Economic and Social Council

The Economic and Social Council (ECOSOC) consists of 54 Members elected under art 61 for a period of three years. Matters of international economic and social concern are delegated the concern of ECOSOC. Article 55 details the matters with which ECOSOC has become concerned, including the promotion of:

'(1) higher standards of living, full employment, and conditions of economic and social progress and development;
(2) solutions of international economic, social, health, and related problems; and international cultural and educational co-operation; and
(3) universal respect for, and observance of, human rights and fundamental freedoms for all without distinction as to race, sex, language, or religion.'

ECOSOC has drafted conventions, carried out studies, recommended courses of action, called conferences, and assisted other organisations in their functions. In addition, this organ co-ordinates the work of the specialised agencies. It has a complex organisational structure and maintains relations with regional and universal governmental and non-governmental organisations.

The Trusteeship Council

Under the League of Nations, a number of German and Turkish colonies were detached from their colonial masters and placed into the Mandate system. These colonies were classified into categories A, B and C, according to the stage of development attained. Each colony was placed into the trust of an overseeing state which guaranteed to supervise the development of the mandate territory. Reports had to be sent to the League of Nations Council.

The Trusteeship Council of the United Nations has assumed the continuation of this function. The Trusteeship Council is composed of those Members administering trust territories, the Members of the Security Council and any other Members of the United Nations elected to serve on the Trusteeship Council: art 86.

For practical purposes, this organ of the United Nations is defunct. All trust territories administered under the system have either been granted independence or absorbed into an existing state. The last trust territory was the Pacific Islands, administered as a strategic area by the United States. However, in 1987, the Reagan administration announced these territories were to be withdrawn by the United States on a unilateral basis. This effectively terminated the functions of the Council.

The Secretariat

In accordance with art 97 of the Charter, the Secretariat is to comprise a Secretary-General and other such staff as the Organisation may require. At present, the Secretariat numbers around 20,000 personnel, recruited on the basis of geographical distribution, and in practice forms an international civil service. The Secretary-General and his staff are obliged to act impartially, and without national allegiance. They may not seek or receive instructions from any government or authority external to the Organisation and cannot engage in any action which might undermine their position as officials responsible only to the Organisation. The Secretary-General is assisted by Under Secretaries-General and Directors of departments and offices.

Article 97 also regulates the appointment of the Secretary-General, who is to be appointed by the General Assembly on the recommendation of the Security Council. The term of office is five years, although re-appointment is possible. The Secretary-General is the head of the United Nations administration, but also is entitled to exercise 'such other functions as are entrusted to him by these organs'. In addition, art 99 empowers the Secretary-General to bring to the attention of the Security Council any matter which in his opinion may threaten the maintenance of international peace and security.

Recent times has witnessed the 'sensitive' rule of the Secretary-General. An example of this is when the Secretary-General flew to Baghdad in February 1998 to conduct negotiations with the Iraqi government in relation to the implementation of the resolutions concerning inspection of weapons facilities. The present Secretary-General, Kofi Annan, was re-elected to serve a second term of five years in June 2001. Mr Annan has been very successful in promoting international cooperation and administrative reform and was thus one of the recipients to the Norwegian Nobel Peace Prize in 2001.

15.3 Key cases and legislation

- *Certain Expenses of the United Nations Case* (1962) ICJ Rep 151
  Advisory opinion on the legality of General Assembly participation in peace-keeping functions

- *Conditions for Admission of a State to Membership of the United Nations Case* (1948) ICJ Rep 57
  Advisory opinion on the criteria for admission to the United Nations

- *Namibia Case* (1971) ICJ Rep 16
  Dicta relating to the effect of abstention in the voting of the permanent Members of the Security Council

- Covenant of the League of Nations 1919

- United Nations Charter 1945

Note: these set up the structure and operative hierarchy and organisation of the UN.

15.4 Questions and suggested solutions

QUESTION ONE

'The Charter of the United Nations was drafted at a time when the only threats to international peace and security were perceived to be through the actions of states. The legal machinery of the Charter, and of Chapter VII in particular, requires reform, as it is ill-adapted to deal with the situations with which the United Nations has had to deal since the end of the Cold War.'

Discuss.

University of London LLB Examination
(for External Students) Public International Law June 1999 Q6

General Comment

This is a question that is directed to the experience of the United Nations after the end of the Cold War. It is a matter of common knowledge that the Security Council is no longer subject to the exercise of the veto. The candidate who seeks to answer this question will need to know something about actual interventions in Somalia, Yugoslavia, Rwanda, Sierra Leone, Haiti and Kosovo. The evidence indicates that the Security Council has adequate legal powers to rule on particular situations; the difficulty arises when the Security Council seeks to enforce those resolutions. Lacking its own military arm, the United Nations requires member states to contribute military forces. Many states are happy to contribute forces to peacekeeping operations, but they are reluctant to allow professionally trained armies to involve themselves in peace making. A candidate who was aware of the memoirs of Secretary General Boutros Boutros Ghali would know that the difficulty in recent years has not been in the ability to pass resolutions, but the capacity to enforce them.

Skeleton Solution

Introduction – the situation in 1945 – the control of state conduct – the difficulties experienced by the Security Council in the Cold War period – the rise and intensity of internal conflicts – the provisions of Chapter VII – problems with resources – changing nature of peacekeeping – conclusion.

Suggested Solution

We are asked in this question to consider a quotation that comprises two sentences. It is sensible to examine each assertion in turn.

The first sentence reads: 'The Charter of the United Nations was drafted at a time when the only threats to international peace and security were perceived to be through the action of states'. In broad terms this first assertion is correct. One of the objects of the draftsmen of the United Nations Charter 1945 was to enable member states to avoid conflict and to promote the peaceful resolution of disputes. These general objectives were set out in the preamble and are stated more specifically in art 33 of the United Nations Charter. However, the draftsmen of the United Nations Charter were looking back to the events of World War I and World War II and were conscious that these conflicts had been caused by the aggression of individual states. The specific desire to restrict such aggression was set out in art 2 of the Charter.

However, the world of 1945 was a different one from that of today: the colonial empires remained in place and the number of states was much more limited. Indeed the post War world within the United Nations can be divided into three distinct periods, namely: (a) the period of decolonisation up until 1965, (b) the period of the Cold War which lasted until 1985, and (c) the post Cold War world. The draftsmen of 1945 were pre-occupied by the experience of the League of Nations and the defiance of the Council of the League by Japan, Germany and Italy. It was to strengthen the system of collective security that the Charter was drafted in the manner it was. In 1945 the main threat to peace was considered to be not innumerable internal conflicts, but the expansionary designs of the Soviet Union in Eastern Europe. To this end the draftsmen prohibited the acquisition of territory by force and they hoped that, by promoting decolonisation, self-determination and economic co-operation, they would be able to introduce peaceful and evolutionary change. Indeed the draftsmen of the Charter hoped that United Nations agencies would be able to raise the general standard of living in poorer countries.

As the quotation indicates, the draftsmen saw the main threat to peace as coming from states controlled by governments with aggressive ideologies, such as Fascism or Communism. To an extent the Charter has been successful in preventing state A seizing by force the territory of state B, and where that has taken place, as with the Falkland Islands in 1982 or Kuwait in 1990, the seizure has been reversed. However, the problem that developed after 1945 was partly caused by rapid decolonisation; many of the new states were poor, politically unstable and, in the case of Africa, the boundaries paid little regard to ethnic and tribal divisions. Problems began to emerge with secessionist movements, liberation struggles and regional conflict. During the Cold War the Security Council was often unable to act effectively because of the existence of the veto power and the irresponsible conduct of the Soviet Union in fueling regional conflicts. In general, after 1945 Europe and North America remained at peace and economic prosperity raised living standards to unprecedented levels; in other parts of the world regional conflict, ethnic tension, corrupt government and poverty often lead to internal conflicts. In many decolonised states social elites had underestimated the difficulties and challenges posed by independence, and one party rule often lead to civil war. Potentially prosperous states, such as Nigeria, found their economy damaged by political turmoil. Thus the quotation in its first sentence is correct to observe that the threats perceived in 1945 were very different to those that grew up after 1945.

The second part of the quotation reads: 'The legal machinery of the Charter, and of Chapter VII in particular, requires reform, as it is ill-equipped to deal with the situations with which the United Nations has had to deal since the end of the Cold War'. It must be open to doubt whether this part of the quotation is accurate. It is a matter of record that Chapter VI and Chapter VII did not work as well as they might because of the exercise of the veto power during the Cold War. Indeed one of the problems prior to 1989 was that states (such as the Soviet Union) when they were not frustrating the work of the Security Council, were busy breaking international law as in Hungary in 1956, Czechoslovakia in 1968, and Afghanistan in 1979. It is arguable that the Cold War began to come to an end with the arrival in power of Mr Gorbachev in 1985, and since that date the Soviet Union, and later Russia, have tended to work within the framework of the United Nations Charter.

In broad terms, the problems that can arise in international society may be categorised as: (a) conflict between states, (b) internal conflict/civil war, (c) decolonisation struggles, and (d) terrorist activity. All the evidence since 1989 is that these various problems have complex causes and it is doubtful whether much is to be achieved by seeking to redraft the United Nations Charter. Indeed one of the successes of the United Nations Charter is that it has managed to restrain aggression between states. The seizure of the Falkland Islands in 1982 was condemned, and the invasion of Kuwait was reversed; it is generally agreed that the conflict between states is not likely to be a problem when those states are governed under democratic constitutions.

An examination of Chapter VII indicates the wide powers available to the Security Council. Article 39 permits the Security Council to determine a threat to peace, while art 40 allows provisional measures to be taken. In respect of substantive action adequate powers are available in arts 41 and 42. In this context it is noteworthy that some of the provisions of the United Nations Charter, far from needing re-drafting, have simply not been implemented; the most obvious being art 43 providing in effect for a United Nations corps. As the memoirs of Secretary General Boutros Boutros Ghali indicate, the difficulties are more complex. In some situations it might be argued that the Security Council did not act fast enough to restrain a humanitarian catastrophe; this argument might apply to Rwanda in 1994. Second, the United Nations has laboured under the difficulties caused when member states fail to meet their contributions. Third, in many cases the Security Council might pass resolutions, but member states have proved reluctant to enforce those resolutions: to some extent this was the problem in the former Yugoslavia.

It is important to say a little about the subject of internal conflict. Internal conflicts often have a complex history, sometimes linked to a colonial past; ethnic and cultural differences often cause the conflict to be conducted by irregular guerilla forces rather than professional armies. Often it has proved difficult – as in Sierra Leone or Yugoslavia – to prevent the various parties obtaining access to arms. Often an internal conflict is accompanied by a humanitarian crisis (as with the Kurds in Iraq or the Albanian population in Kosovo) which itself has raised the separate question as to whether there is a right of humanitarian intervention.

While internal conflicts pose their own particular problems, it is important to note the attitude of some Western powers. The United Nations has no specific forces of its own and relies upon the goodwill of member states. Most Western societies are democracies with expensively trained (non conscript) armies: politicians cannot commit such military forces without being answerable to an electorate. As experience in Somalia (in 1992–1993) indicates, Western democracies are only prepared to supply military forces for specific objectives and not open-ended commitments. Since 1989 the expression 'mission creep', and the desire to avoid it, is a phenomenon in the conduct of international relations. Moreover, since Western democracies seek to avoid casualties, there has been a tendency to employ air power if at all possible (see the Gulf War, Kosovo and Yugoslavia). A review of these particular conflicts indicates that the problem has been one of practical concerns; there is no suggestion that adequate powers do not exist (see Haiti in 1993).

The next matter concerns intervention. Throughout the history of the United Nations there has tended to be a distinction between 'peacekeeping' – ie where a United Nations force guarantees a peace already negotiated – and other forms, such as 'mixed peacekeeping' or 'peace making'. After the end of the Cold War there has been a tendency to assume that the United Nations might play a role in situations where the peace was far from secure (ie Somalia in 1992–1993, Rwanda in 1994 and Yugoslavia in 1991–1996). Experience indicates that problems arise not because the Security Council lacks legal powers under the United Nations Charter, but because member states are unwilling to contribute forces in internal conflicts unless there is a clear humanitarian objective.

The second part of the quotation seems misconceived. Experience since 1989 indicates that while problems have arisen, these problems have not been due to a lack of legal powers: they have been more the result of inadequate resources and unclear mandates together with a failure to preserve the distinction between 'peacekeeping' and 'peace making'. Further, one has to be very careful about generalising about internal conflicts; the problems in Sierra Leone in 1996 were very different to those in Haiti in 1993. The evidence for this is corroborated by the conduct of the United Nations itself in reviewing the entire question of peacekeeping; at the millennium summit in September 2000 it was accepted that difficulties had arisen in respect of inadequate resources.

A further problem arises in that any intervention under Chapter VII is very expensive, and complex internal conflicts cannot be the subject of action unless help is forthcoming from the United States. In Kosovo, Haiti, Yugoslavia and Somalia the active help of the United States was required. In most situations the problem has been the need to obtain resources; it is true that in the *Lockerbie Case (Libya v United Kingdom) (Provisional Measures)* (1992) ICJ Rep 3 the question arose as to the meaning of the expression 'threat to peace', but in most situations of internal conflict it has been accepted that such a threat existed. It is also true that the action in Kosovo, although subject of some Security Council resolutions, was in fact undertaken as an exercise in international humanitarian intervention.

Any review of the evidence since 1989 indicates that the Security Council has not hesitated to use its legal powers in respect of internal conflicts that threaten regional stability; however, the experiences in Sierra Leone, Somalia, Rwanda and Yugoslavia indicate that the real difficulty arises in persuading states to contribute military resources. Our conclusion must be that the quotation is only partly correct.

QUESTION TWO

In which circumstances may a State invoke the right to self-defence under Article 51 of the United Nations Charter?

> University of London LLB Examination
> (for External Students) Public International Law June 1997 Q5

General Comment

From the time of Grotius one of the central concerns of international law has been to identify and formulate rules as to when a State is justified in resorting to force. Today that discussion begins with consideration of the provisions of the UN Charter. In this question the candidate will be concerned with: (a) the relationship between art 51 and the other provisions of the UN Charter; and (b) the different schools of thought as to the correct interpretation of art 51. The nature and scope of art 51 tends to be discussed at times of international crisis. A good answer will include some reference to how the Security Council has responded when individual States make wide-ranging claims under art 51. This is a very fair question, and the only problem for the well prepared student is that there is so much material on the topic that it is difficult to reduce it into a short essay.

Skeleton Solution

Introduction: the UN Charter, art 2(4) – practical questions under art 51 – the different schools of thought as to the correct interpretation of art 51 – the practical consequence of this division of opinion – the relationship between art 51 and customary international law – conclusion.

Suggested Solution

We are asked in this problem to discuss the circumstances in which an individual State may invoke the right to self-defence afforded by art 51 of the UN Charter.

It is quite clear that the provisions of art 51 have to be read alongside the other operative provisions of the UN Charter. It is common ground that art 2(4) places a prohibition on the use of force by States. The consensus of scholarly opinion is that the UN Charter only provided four exceptions to the general prohibition on the use of force contained in art 2(4). The relevant exceptions are: force employed in self-defence under art 51; force authorised by the UN Security Council under arts 39–51; force undertaken by the five major powers before the Security Council was functional as provided by art 106; and force undertaken against enemy States in World War II as provided by arts 53 and 107.

It is accepted that the only relevant exceptions today are (a) and (b) above. Thus, art 51 represents a most significant exception to the general prohibition in the UN Charter on the use of force.

While there has been limited discussion as to the meaning of art 2(4) there has been considerable debate as to the correct interpretation of art 51. It is clear that art 51 gives rise to the following problems, namely: (a) what is meant by 'armed attack'?; (b) what is meant by an 'inherent right'?; (c) is an armed attack the only circumstance giving rise to a right of self-defence?; and (d) how is collective self-defence to be organised? These problems of interpretation have given rise to two broad schools of thought as to the correct interpretation of art 51.

a) The first school of thought holds that art 51 of the UN Charter restricts any right of self-defence existing under customary international law and can only be relied upon once an armed attack has taken place. Writers who broadly take this view would include Jessup, Henkin and Brownlie. This school of thought is sometimes referred to as the 'restrictionist' approach.

b) The second school of thought holds that art 51 was not intended to curtail rights arising in customary international law. This school of thought holds that the word 'inherent' indicates that customary rights were not to be infringed and is sometimes alluded to as the 'counter restrictionist' approach. Writers broadly within this school would include Bowett, McDougal and Stone. Such writers base their opinion not only on the words of the text but also the travaux preparatoires of the UN Charter.

This division of opinion as to the meaning of art 51 is of considerable practical importance because it is only those who hold the 'counter restrictionist' view who would be prepared to acknowledge that a right of anticipatory self-defence exists in international law. The problem with anticipatory self-defence is that it depends on a judgment made by the individual State as to whether or not it is about to be attacked. The precise limits of art 51 have tended to be discussed in the United Nations at times of diplomatic tension. Since 1945 it is possible to point to three significant occasions when differing views have been advanced as to the meaning of art 51. Three major debates took place within the Security Council – during the Cuban missile crisis of October 1962, during the Middle East War of June 1967 and after the bombing of the Osarik reactor near Baghdad in October 1981. More recently, debates have taken place since the events of 11 September 2001 and the attacks on the United States and British embassies in the African continent as well as in the Middle East.

Although the case of *Nicaragua* v *United States (Merits)* (1986) ICJ 14 at 94 does include some observations that would seem to support the counter restrictionist approach, it is important to consider also opinions expressed in Security Council debates. An examination of recent debates on art 51 indicates quite clearly that Member States are most anxious to ensure that there is no resort to indiscriminate acts of anticipatory self-defence particularly where this may inflame regional tensions.

It is quite clear from recent debates on the employment of art 51 that the article must be interpreted within the UN Charter taken as a whole. It is then argued that since the UN Charter contains a general prohibition on the use of force art 51 as providing an exception must be interpreted narrowly.

Some have endeavoured to achieve the same objective by arguing that art 51 should be interpreted in the light of prior customary international law. It is argued that Daniel Webster's letter in the *Caroline Case* (1837) 29 BFSP 1137–1138 represents an accurate statement of the law. In broad terms Webster argued that the necessity for self-defence must be instant and overwhelming, and the response must be proportionate. The attraction of this approach is that it is in line with the earliest writers on international law, such as Francisco Suarez (1548–1617) and Francisco Vittoria (1480–1546), who stressed the need for proportionality in State conduct. The problem, however, remains in the modern world that an all-out attack by State A on State B may so damage State B as to destroy its capacity to defend itself at all.

Applying the above considerations to the present problem it can be seen that any State that employs force bears the onus probandi that the use of force did not violate the UN Charter. At a risk of over simplification such a use of force will be justified under art 51 if: (a) if an armed attack has taken place and the response is proportionate; (b) if an armed attack is imminent and the measures taken are both necessary and proportionate; and (c) if the armed attack is not imminent, but foreseeable, then any steps taken must be carefully weighed and should be no more than is absolutely necessary to rebut the threat and should be proportionate to the foreseeable danger.

QUESTION THREE

To what extent did the drafters of the United Nations Charter learn from the mistakes of the League of Nations Covenant and to what extent may the shortcomings of contemporary international organisation be attributed to constitutional deficiencies?

Written by the Author

General Comment

An essay question requiring a rather descriptive analysis of the development affecting the United Nations.

Skeleton Solution

Constitutional deficiencies of the Covenant and the counterpart provisions of the UN Charter – political considerations and factors in the operation of both organisations – the source of the present shortcomings in international organisation.

Suggested Solution

In many respects the United Nations bears a considerable similarity to the League of Nations, although the two organisations are by no means identical in either constitution or function. The League of Nations was established by the Treaty of Versailles which settled the geo-political framework in Europe at the end of the First World War. The objective of the League was 'to promote international co-operation and to achieve international peace and security'. To this end, a system of collective international security was envisaged, based on a number of principles including: disarmament (art 8); pacific settlement of disputes and limitations on resort to war (art 11–15); a collective guarantee of the independence of each Member (art 10); and sanctions for failure to abide by the obligations established under the Covenant: arts 16 and 17. However, from the outset, this programme was destined to fail for a number of reasons which can be attributed both to the constitution of the League and the political climate surrounding its operation.

The League had only three principal organs: the Council, the Assembly and the Secretariat. The Council was an organ of limited membership and had as a mandate the supervision of international peace and the implementation of sanctions against states resorting to war. The Assembly was the plenary organ and each Member was entitled to a seat and a vote, decisions being made on the basis of a simple majority. The Assembly operated thorough six committees, and made recommendations on a number of deliberative subjects. The Secretariat was an international civil service designed to lubricate the functions of the Organisation.

The primary failure of the League was that it only postponed the right of Members to wage war until the fulfilment of a number of criteria established in art 12. It was true that this was subsequently fortified by the undertakings in the Pact of Paris 1928 which prohibited war as a means of pursuing international policy objectives. However, this regime suffered from two fundamental defects. Firstly, in terms of technical legal construction, not all manifestations of force amounted to a relationship of war. Lesser uses of force, such as intervention and reprisals, were not prohibited by the Covenant. Further, as states began to enact domestic legislation which prohibited assistance to one or other parties engaged in a state of war – the obligation of neutrality – declarations of war became conspicuously scarce in order to prevent such mandatory restrains being placed on the supply of war materials. Consequently, the Japanese invasion of Manchuria in 1931, the Italian invasion of Ethiopia in 1936 and the Russian invasion of Finland in 1938 were all achieved without recognition of an official state of war.

This constitutional defect was exacerbated by the fact that neither the Covenant, nor the Pact of Paris, defined or restricted the use of force in self-defence. Broad discretion on the use of force in self-defence was therefore given to Members. In the absence of enquiry by the League into hostilities, a plea of self-defence was often accepted as sufficient to prevent the initiation of collective measures. Only in the case of the Italian aggression against Ethiopia were sanctions levelled against an aggressor, and in this case these were limited to an economic boycott with no prospect of success. The tendency away from recognising a state of war crippled the collective enforcement mechanisms established under the Covenant. In the absence of such a determination, the Council was rendered impotent. Although the system of sanctions and enforcement measures under the League remained decentralised, it was constitutionally necessary for the League Council to make a determination of aggression before sanctions could legitimately be invoked. As a result of this technicality, and a lack of political desire on the part of the Members themselves, no effective military force was ever levelled by the Council against aggression.

Other constitutional defects also contributed to this situation. The League Covenant allowed a state to terminate its membership of the Organisation and, thereby, to renounce the obligations of the Covenant. A number of states, including Germany and Japan, left the League through constitutional processes, and were thereby left free to pursue their aggressive policies in the knowledge that the League of Nations could not call them to account in the Council. In addition, decisions in the League Council were based on the unanimity rule and this crippled the Council as an effective organ. The move towards the Assembly in order to discuss matters of genuine international concern was a clear vindication of the advantages of majority voting.

Political factors also assisted in the demise of the League. From the outset, the League was considered as an integral part of the post-war settlement in Europe. Germany was not an original Member and, throughout the history of the League, it regarded the Organisation as stigmatised by the taint of defeat. Even after Germany's accession to the Organisation in 1922, its participation was perceived as ill-advised, and Germany was one of the first Members to withdraw from the Organisation.

In addition, the United States, despite the enthusiastic contribution of US President Wilson in the drafting of the Covenant, refused to join the League. As a consequence, the Organisation was often construed as a Euro-centric structure, maintaining the traditions and values of colonial Europe. It certainly did not function as a truly universal international organisation from the perspective of membership.

In the final evaluation, the constitutional defects of the League could have been easily remedied. However, the political will to do so was not present. In the absence of a universal political consensus to achieve certain goals, nothing can be achieved. The considerable and noteworthy successes of the League in the fields of economics, finance, public health, mandates, transport, communications and social policy, paled in comparative significance and the League was recorded in history as failing to prevent the Second World War.

The drafters of the UN Charter did have the records of the first experiment in universal organisational theory to learn from, but only chose to learn selective lessons. It is clear that, in the political climate after the Second World War, nations still did not seek to resurrect a universal organisation which would supplant their sovereign authority to regulate foreign policy. As a result, the United Nations was also subject to the adverse effects of political considerations in the drafting of its constitutions.

The former enemy states of the 'Allied Powers' were automatically represented in the United Nations. Further, the Charter was conceived in such a manner as to be completely separate from the post-war settlement in Europe and the Far East. Thus, the Charter has not been tainted by characterisation of an unequal treaty. However, representation on the Security Council has been confined to the Allied Powers, and this has remained unchanged despite the self-evident changes in the balance of global economic and military power.

The United States was a co-sponsor and founding member of the United Nations. Its participation, along with that of the Latin American States, and India, ensured that the Organisation would have a universal character. The Euro-centric stigma of the League of Nations was therefore abandoned.

In an attempt to create a more effective international organisation, the United Nations was endowed with six principal organs. The Security Council is given primary responsibility for the maintenance of international peace and security. For this purpose, a collective and centralised security system was devised under the Charter. This was designed to circumvent the problems involved in the decentralised system of sanctions envisaged under the League Covenant. Further, the use of force, not only war, was absolutely prohibited as opposed to the conditional prohibitions established under the League. In theory this should have led to a more effective organisation. However, in practice the architects of the Charter failed to recognise, or did not wish to acknowledge, that political conflicts and differences between the permanent Members of the Security Council would effectively emasculate the Organisation. By requiring unanimity among the permanent Members, the prospects of collective action to enforce security were substantially diminished. This was a lesson that was not learned from the experience of the League. The unanimity rule in the Council resulted in a movement of power towards the League Assembly which was not hampered by rule of unanimity. This development has been mirrored in the United Nations, and is illustrated in the Uniting for Peace Resolution 1950.

A number of constitutional lessons were learned however, and the Charter does not provide for the withdrawal of Members from the Organisation. Members may withdraw from the United Nations, but the criteria for such action remain ill-defined in the Charter. Further, a separate organ, the Economic and Social Council (ECOSOC), was established in recognition of the success of the League in social and economic matters. In addition, the International Court of Justice was constituted as a principal organ of the United Nations.

However, in the final evaluation, it is the political wills of states which ultimately determine the success or failure of an international organisation. This is the primary lesson to be learned from the history of the League, and one that perhaps is not acknowledged in the Charter, certainly not in the constitution of the Security Council.

Revision Aids

Designed for the undergraduate, the 101 Questions & Answers series and the Suggested Solutions series are for all those who have a positive commitment to passing their law examinations. Each series covers a different examinable topic and comprises a selection of answers to examination questions and, in the case of the 101 Questions and Answers, interrograms. The majority of questions represent examination 'bankers' and are supported by full-length essay solutions. These titles will undoubtedly assist you with your research and further your understanding of the subject in question.

101 Questions & Answers Series

Only £7.95 Published December 2003

Constitutional Law
ISBN: 1 85836 522 8

Criminal Law
ISBN: 1 85836 432 9

Land Law
ISBN: 1 85836 515 5

Law of Contract
ISBN: 1 85836 517 1

Law of Tort
ISBN: 1 85836 516 3

Suggested Solutions to Past Examination Questions 2001–2002 Series

Only £6.95 Published December 2003

Company Law
ISBN: 1 85836 519 8

Employment Law
ISBN: 1 85836 520 1

European Union Law
ISBN: 1 85836 524 4

Evidence
ISBN: 1 85836 521 X

Family Law
ISBN: 1 85836 525 2

For further information or to place an order, please contact:

Mail Order
Old Bailey Press at Holborn College
Woolwich Road
Charlton
London
SE7 8LN

Telephone: 020 8317 6039
Fax: 020 8317 6004
Website: www.oldbaileypress.co.uk
E-Mail: mailorder@oldbaileypress.co.uk

Company Law

2001–2002 LLB Examination Questions
and Suggested Solutions

University of London
External Examinations

Solutions by Susan Barber

Old Bailey Press

The Old Bailey Press Integrated Student Law Library is tailor-made to help you at every stage of your studies, from the preliminaries of each subject through to the final examination. The series of Textbooks, Revision WorkBooks, 150 Leading Cases and Cracknell's Statutes are interrelated to provide you with a comprehensive set of study materials.

You can buy Old Bailey Press books from your University Bookshop, your local Bookshop, directly using this form, or you can order a free catalogue of our titles from the address shown overleaf.

The following subjects each have a Textbook, 150 Leading Cases, Revision WorkBook and Cracknell's Statutes unless otherwise stated.

Administrative Law
Commercial Law
Company Law
Conflict of Laws
Constitutional Law
Conveyancing (Textbook and 150 Leading Cases)
Criminal Law
Criminology (Textbook and Sourcebook)
Employment Law (Textbook and Cracknell's Statutes)
English and European Legal Systems
Equity and Trusts
Evidence
Family Law
Jurisprudence: The Philosophy of Law (Textbook, Sourcebook and
    Revision WorkBook)
Land: The Law of Real Property
Law of International Trade
Law of the European Union
Legal Skills and System
    (Textbook)
Obligations: Contract Law
Obligations: The Law of Tort
Public International Law
Revenue Law (Textbook,
    Revision WorkBook and
    Cracknell's Statutes)
Succession (Textbook, Revision
    WorkBook and Cracknell's
    Statutes)

Mail order prices:	
Textbook	£15.95
150 Leading Cases	£12.95
Revision WorkBook	£10.95
Cracknell's Statutes	£11.95
Suggested Solutions 1999–2000	£6.95
Suggested Solutions 2000–2001	£6.95
Suggested Solutions 2001–2002	£6.95
101 Questions and Answers	£7.95
Law Update 2004	£10.95

Please note details and prices are subject to alteration.

To complete your order, please fill in the form below:

Module	Books required	Quantity	Price	Cost
		Postage		
		TOTAL		

For the UK and Europe, add £4.95 for the first book ordered, then add £1.00 for each subsequent book ordered for postage and packing.
For the rest of the world, add 50% for airmail.

ORDERING

By telephone to Mail Order at 020 8317 6039, with your credit card to hand.

By fax to 020 8317 6004 (giving your credit card details).

Website: www.oldbaileypress.co.uk
E-Mail: mailorder@oldbaileypress.co.uk

By post to: Mail Order, Old Bailey Press at Holborn College, Woolwich Road, Charlton, London, SE7 8LN.

When ordering by post, please enclose full payment by cheque or banker's draft, or complete the credit card details below. You may also order a free catalogue of our complete range of titles from this address.

We aim to despatch your books within 3 working days of receiving your order. All parts of the form must be completed.

Name

Address

E-Mail
Postcode   Telephone

Total value of order, including postage: £

I enclose a cheque/banker's draft for the above sum, or

charge my ☐ Access/Mastercard ☐ Visa ☐ American Express

Cardholder: ....

Card number

☐☐☐☐ ☐☐☐☐ ☐☐☐☐ ☐☐☐☐

Expiry date ☐☐☐☐

Signature: ....Date: ....